Short-Stories of
KATHERINE MANSFIELD
Development of Technique

SHORT-STORIES OF KATHERINE MANSFIELD DEVELOPMENT OF TECHNIQUE

A.S. ANAND MURTY

ANAMIKA PUBLISHERS & DISTRIBUTORS (P) LTD.
4697/3, 21A, Ansari Road, Daryaganj
New Delhi 110002
Phone: 2328 1655

First Published 2007

ISBN 81-7975-148-1

PRINTED IN INDIA

Published by Anamika Publishers & Distributors (P) Ltd., 4697/3, 21A, Ansari Road, Daryaganj, New Delhi 110002. Typeset by VGA, VP-216A, Pitampura, Delhi 110088 and Printed at Nagri Printers, Delhi.

In contritely remorseful

memory of

my saintly father

Contents

Preface

The implication of the topic restricts the scope of the present study.

'Short-Stories of Katherine Mansfield: Development of Technique' implies evolution of technique as an integral creative whole in the finished narrative pieces composed by the author. The term 'technique' is used here in a comprehensive sense: it applies not only to Miss Mansfield's particular treatment of the material which had to be unified but also to the medium of the specific literary form which she had chosen to work in.

It seemed imperative to have a comprehensive view of 'technique': assessment of the developing technique in Miss Mansfield's short-stories demanded consideration of consummation of the technique hitherto judged only as her particular treatment of material.

Consummation of technique presupposes functional involvement of the effectually concomitant attributes peculiar to the medium the artist has chosen to work in. Concomitance of these attributes is also instrumental in specifying the theme or the meaning. The means towards definition of the theme are thus inclusive of these attributes. The choice of the means of realizing the artistic intention and the choice of the specific medium that will consummate this realization are simultaneous. Choice of a specific genre is a spiritual necessity. The eventually embodied genre is not a mechanistic imposition or a cast-iron matrix. It is not a preference, either, involving critical exercise of discriminatory will. It is always an inevitable literary phenomenon. The 'short-story' as a distinct species of modern prose-fiction has a technique of its own. What evidences peculiarity of this technique is the unavoidable concomitance of some unalterable attributes; the attributes resolve into one single distinctive feature; the literary composition that is a 'short-story' reads like a piece of narrative presenting an aesthetic rendering of a crisis or a turning-point in a life in intent imaginative concentration. (It is, perhaps complete indifference to the value of these attributes that accounts for substitution of the loose word 'story' or 'tale' for the precise term 'short-story'. As a compound word, 'short-story' is two words hyphenated into a terminological amalgam, designating a specific literary genre.)

Simultaneous speculation on probability of the functional involvement of the attributes peculiar to the genre was, therefore, necessary to judgement of consummation of the technique transparently recognizable as Miss Mansfield's particular treatment of material. Consideration of the functional significance of the attributes involved examinations of their relationship to the vital aspects of Miss Mansfield's art of rendering: that is, it seemed imperative to see whether the requisite sense of a crisis or a turning-point was involved in the meaning or the theme which Miss Mansfield had sought to convey through her particular treatment; whether intent concentration demanded by the intensity of the captured moment or singleness of the crisis harmoniously governed, artistically unified and essentially pervaded the technical means employed, whether rendering of the crisis in concentration was compact enough to make the selected material seem vibrant with a sense of drama that is climactic from the start; whether the requisite narrative element was retained for transmission of the sense of progression which deepens or intensifies the characteristically incomplete meaning; whether within the purview of the concentrated imaginative vision even fragility of an evanescent emotion was made to seem instinct with a lyrical beauty; etc. In a word, it had to be judged whether the short-story under consideration was a 'precipitate'.

Guided as they are by their unquestioning conviction that exactly the same critical procedure is in order for realistic fiction as for a poem, the critics of Miss Mansfield's short-stories have been obstinately blind to the probability that the technical means creatively invented and the concomitant attributes subconsciously exploited can advantageously reciprocate in a work. It seems that their critical studies of Miss Mansfield's short-stories would in all probability be the same even if the short-stories had been composed as novels, sketches, memoirs, or scenarios. What accounts for the critics' inability to see the wood for the trees is their exclusive concentration on the author's particular treatment of material as the whole of her technique. They have found Miss Mansfield's technique developing in a narrative piece also when there is serious lack of balance. They forget that the narrative piece within which the means of meaning—realization evolve and coalesce is not a short-story but a sketch or a reportage. They do not seem to have seen the simple fact that all beauty in a formless or loose composition is irrelevant as a pocket in a shroud. Their explications of Miss Mansfield's short-stories are no doubt profoundly intelligent, but they seem to have remained undesirably narrow. They have not tackled consummation of technique as the most vital issue. So re-assessment of the essentials of technique in Miss Mansfield's short-stories seemed imperatively necessary.

Now, revaluation of technique evolving as an integral creative whole demanded re-consideration of each of the selected short-stories as an aesthetic whole. Naturally there was concentration on this vitally urgent problem, and this restricted the scope of the study.

Since the problem of the study was to ascertain and place in focus the pattern of each selected short-story as a complete aesthetic whole, I was obliged to confine my choice to the essential and the typical; the short-stories I selected seemed typical enough to represent the significant phase in the development of Miss Mansfield's technique: the other short-stories by the author did not seem to stand for anything specially distinctive in the evolution; even when they did seem to feature something remarkable in their own way they had to be kept out because the remarkable feature was found sufficiently exemplified in the short-stories already chosen.

The selected short-stories have been viewed in the chronological order of their composition. (I have allowed myself to be guided by the dates of their publication only when I have found it difficult to determine the precise dates of their original draft.) Throughout the study I have kept to chronology, but in one instance the chronology has been telescoped for convenience: *Ideal Family* and *Marriage a' la Mode*, although composed later than *The Fly*, seemed to manifest characteristics resembling the features of short-stories forming an earlier phase: the two short-stories have been discussed accordingly. This does not impair the rationale of the chronological basis as setbacks or reversions have been peculiar to all evolution.

The nature and scope of my present study preclude any attempt to consider the manifestations of the author's genius outside her short-stories. I have been obliged to refrain from discussion of even her significant fictional works (like Aloe, the earlier form of her first song of innocence, Prelude, or like By Moonlight, Spring in a dream, etc.). Avoidance of their discussion seemed proper; the full text of any of them was either out of print or inaccessible. There are some 'unfinished' narrative pieces included in the complete collection of her short-stories. There are, again, stories which Miss Mansfield seems to have dashed off in her Journal and in some of her Letters: they are also unfinished as short-stories. The restriction imposed by the precise implication of the title of my present study has necessitated exclusion of all such raw or 'half-baked' material.

The restricted implication of the proposed topic required insistence on revaluation of Miss Mansfield's technique as an integral creative complex or of her work as an aesthetic whole. The critical procedure that such revaluation involved seemed to afford little scope for the customary bio-data excursions or consideration of the facts of the author's history. None of such facts helped to explain to what extent the narrative piece under consideration was successful as a short-story; how the technique even as Miss Mansfield's particular treatment of material was harmoniously consummate; whether the work was aesthetic enough to re-echo the truth 'on the side of life' as a truer truth, a poetic truth, a beautiful truth. I have, therefore, touched on the facts of the author's history only when her life and her art have revealed themselves as a transparent continuum. All critical faith in biographical determinants or manifestations is but faith in heredity and transmission of traits in the domain of aesthetic creation.

What Miss Mansfield's short-stories imperatively demand is a purely aesthetic approach. One who seeks their specified meaning must steer one's boat cautiously between the Scylla of comparative criticism which harbours dangers of partial evaluation and the Charybdis of biographical criticism which involves risks of unintegrated digression.

The main body of the discussion consists of six chapters (with chapters 4 and 5 divided, respectively, into two and three sections) and there are Notes appended to each chapter or to each section. The last chapter (i.e. chapter 6) presents the conclusion.

The appended Notes contain such matter as references to scholarly studies which would provide supporting data; documentation consisting of further examples from the text of the short-story under consideration; and disagreements with particular critics, especially if they involve lengthy comments. Mid-analysis refutations of critic's statements would have occasioned distractingly intermittent copious digressions; I have, therefore, relegated all refutations to the appended sections distinctly entitled **Notes to chapter**.

Each of the first three chapters or each of the sections into which chapters 4 and 5 are divided consists of three parts discernibly separated: in the first, there are introductory remarks; in the second, there is concentration on detailed analysis of Miss Mansfield's short-stories; in the third, there is enunciation of the conclusion deduced from the analysis. The introductory and concluding portions are comparatively short: neither covers more than three pages. The reasons underlying this deliberate curtailment may be summarised thus: we have had enough of generalisation; delving into the text is more rewarding than skirting the text; the black words on the white page can tell us anything and everything that we need to know.

It is through analysis of these 'words on the page' that I have tried to tackle the vital problem of the indispensably simultaneous appraisal of author's philosophy of life. Thus the study aims also at assessing the evolution of her poetic philosophy that the development of her technique as an integral creative complex naturally involved.

Chapter 1 names the two important discoveries made in course of this study: lyricalness as the essential characteristic of Miss Mansfield's creative vision; and intensity of 'will to live' as a philosophy of life distilled from her personal experience of a life-in-death and purged as an objective poetic truth. The very first narrative composition that she fashioned affords sufficient illustration. An attempt is made in this chapter to present a formal explication of the composition. The explication is meant to illuminate all this dark assertion. The discoveries are simultaneously corroborated by the first evidence of the author's lifelong conscientious endeavour to achieve expedient reciprocity between her vision and the 'truth'. My analysis of Miss Mansfield's short-story is also an attempt to substantiate a significant fact that her personal sense of truth was assisted by a 'gift' which consisted in her innate capacity for an infallible recognition of a subject-matter intrinsically oriented to the specific form of the short-story. The subject which Miss Mansfield's personal sense of truth discovered as a short-story-oriented theme was at this early stage, perhaps, a moment of intense 'will to live', to be, to have the feel of individual existence in freedom, imaginary or real. I think it is necessary here to interpret the features of this 'moment of being' as I have understood them. To live means to give existence to the possible: every moment one literally makes oneself by choosing from the future (which is the 'realm of possible': Dr. S. Radhakrishnan). When one makes oneself one lives creatively. To live creatively is to triumph over the force of non-being. Every act of creative freedom evinces actualisation of Being. A free choice is deliverance from bondage; it is not connected with the past. One exists only when one has freedom and this freedom is true and real only when one is oneself. It was, perhaps, this subject that Miss Mansfield kept drawing upon as an inexhaustible source of her short-story-oriented themes. I have tried to show how evolution of Miss Mansfield's technique as an integral complex involved gradual revelation of dimensions inherent in the subject.

In Chapter 2, while examining Miss Mansfield's next short-story, I have endeavoured to cope with the mooted question: how far is it true to say that the short-story is an original work and not a plagiarized version of a masterpiece of her 'guru' Chekhov? The comparative study has revealed some significant features of this transitional phase: Miss Mansfield was still too young to achieve Chekhov's art; but her re-composition of the Russian masterpiece did enable her to recognize her affinity with Chekhov. The subject-matter provided by Chekhov's masterpiece was only a variation on the theme which her personal sense of truth had recently discovered—a hopelessly tragic moment of intense 'will to live'.

The next phase in the development of technique is viewed in Chapter 3. The phase has revealed itself as a natural stage of trial-and-error process; it has been interpreted accordingly. I have tried to substantiate this interpretation with examples which reveal surprising fluctuations: tendency to revert to superficialities persists even after achievement of what induces an impression of 'depth of perception'. I have found that the range of the subject-matter was still limited to the tragic dimensions of the moment of choice from the realm of the future.

Chapter 4 with its three sections depicts three significant phases of Miss Mansfield's tentative yet zealous experimentation with different aspects of the technique.

The first section of Chapter 4 is an assessment of the subsequent phase of 'blissful peace' during which Miss Mansfield experimented with 'the expanded scale'. I have assigned the reason for her choice of the scale to an aesthetic realization now growing upon her; she had come to realize the need for comprehension of a whole range of shades and nuances and in-between emotions involved in the evaluation of a complete psychological situation. I have discovered that in spite of her choice of the scale she did not lack insight into the intricate amazing richness of the ordinary. My attempt to appreciate her genius for the poetry behind the commonplace has facilitated my search for the poetic philosophy of life pervading the phase under consideration. I have found that the range of the subject-matter even during this period of blissful phase was only intensively exploited and not extensively explored, at least in the first two of the three representative pieces. But it still seemed restricted to the dimensions of the moment of choice from the realm of the future as a means of palpable experience of one's individual existence in freedom. But the third piece seemed to me to have registered Miss Mansfield's precocious vision of truth as beauty, a vision which was to reveal itself later as the culmination of all her insights into the subtle truth, 'the moment of being'.

The second section of Chapter 4 deals with a momentous crisis in Miss Mansfield's career. Here through analysis of three representative narrative pieces I have tried to show how her aesthetic concentration on the crisis in her life proved expedient: her concentration not only helped to intensify her creative potentialities; it also facilitated subjection of the gift of imaginative empathy to the capacity for self-abeyance. My analysis of the third narrative piece is an attempt to show how the technique achieved through her protracted yet dreamy concentration on the crisis in her life was at once dramatic and impressionistic, complex and delicate and thus transparent enough to reveal deeper poetic dimensions of the subject-matter: choice from the realm of the future was now simultaneously individual and collective: the moment of nascency of new life in a family was rich in the poetry of the incomplete meaning of 'possibilities'.

In the third section of Chapter 4 an attempt has been made to assess the importance of Miss Mansfield's experimentation with Point of View. I have tried to show how this experimentation was for her a means of sharpening the capacity for personal detachment necessary to achievement of dramatic quality in the narrative style. Analyses of narrative pieces have revealed to me a phase characterized by temporary suspension of the exploration of other possible dimensions inherent in the subject-matter and exclusive exploitation of a single technical aspect of the art.

The whole of the next Chapter 5 which comprises two sections, is devoted to detailed analyses of the short-stories which seemed to me to have registered Miss Mansfield's mounting success as an artist in words. I have endeavoured to show how these short-stories exemplify Miss Mansfield's impressive achievement of the consummate comprehensive technique which reveals itself as an effectual means of 'discovery'—not only of the subject-matter but also of an objective standard of values.

The first section of this Chapter 5 explores the phase which evidences Miss Mansfield's achievement of the most essential aesthetic quality of the short-story: the 'dramatic effect'. Here I have explained how her creative capacity was further intensified by another psychological crisis in her life: the crisis this time was her obsession with the idea of her imminent death. Short-stories of this particular phase seemed to me to have registered the consequential intensification of her insight into the subject-matter. Modified by the pessimistic philosophy of life pervading the period of this crisis, the subject-matter was now the moment of intense actualization of being just before extinction of life, in a physical or spiritual sense. The short-stories expressive of this poetic philosophy have been viewed as a collective evidence of the fact that Miss Mansfield's imaginative vision of life was not yet calm enough to evince comprehension of the grim metaphysical reality of physical or spiritual death as part of Reality or Truth that is Beauty.

In the complementary section of this penultimate chapter (i.e. v, ii) I have analysed the four famous short-stories which represent the last creative phase in the development of Miss Mansfield's mind and art. Through detailed textual analysis of these masterpieces I have endeavoured to show how technique was now 'content' fully 'achieved': Miss Mansfield's aesthetic rendering of the 'content' now evidenced her discreet competence to make her subjective selection of materials reflect an objective standard of values. The theme she had exploited during the antecedent phase now revealed its deeper dimensions: the moment now depicted was that of nearness to the palpable manifestations of the impalpable Reality that is timelessly instinct with serene beauty. Technique was now an adequately potent means of realising a literary matter which is comparatively independent of the controversial and unstable orders.

Before I conclude my Preface I should like to make a belated confession. A fault in the technicality of the presentation of Notes and References appended to each chapter shames me into sheepish apology. I have not been able to give the page numbers of a few sources. The print of some of the numbers recorded in the original typewritten copy of my thesis has grown illegibly faint. I own up to acting in gross violation of a prescribed rule. I cannot recollect that I have ever felt a severer pang of shame than on thinking of what may justly be put down to vexatious impropriety.

A.S. ANAND MURTY

Acknowledgement

It is my pleasant duty to thank the Registrar and through him the Hon'ble Vice-Chancellor of Patna University for the permission they were kind enough to give me to have this thesis published.

To my distinguished teacher and supervisor Dr. D.P. Singh (then Professor of English, North-Eastern Hill University, Shillong) under whose guidance this study was completed. I owe an amount of debt cannot quite express. The task would have remained unfulfilled but for his useful practical suggestions which always reflected his sympathetic understanding of my problems.

I express my profound reverence to my learned and stimulating teacher, Prof. Jagdish Pandey (Head of the English Department, H.D. Jain College, Arrah), the perennial source of inspiration to me in my career as a student of literature. I am indebted to him for his affectionately solicitous interest in my work and for his warm good faith which exercised itself in palpable, practical ways.

My grateful thanks are due to my illustrious teacher, Dr. H.P. Upadhyaya (then Associate Professor of English, Surrey University, England) who consented to expound his own views which helped to enlighten and enrich my understanding of the mind and art of Miss Mansfield.

I must also thank my honourable friends Dr. Rajiv Verma (Research Scholar, University of London, now Professor of English, Seth Karorimal College, New Delhi) and Dr. Mahendra Kishore Verma (Professor of Linguistics, University of York, England), for having procured xeroxed copies of relevant critiques published in inaccessible English Journals.

My thanks are also due to my younger brother Dr. B.S.M. Murty (then in the Department of English, R. D. and DJ College, Monghyr) for having helped me in several ways. He not only procured a considerable amount of relevant material but also offered to be on the alert to see that the technicalities were not bungled.

I should be ungrateful if I did not register my indebtedness to my son Sitaram Sharan whose practical help has facilitated publication of this thesis.

Lastly, I should like to thank the staff of the British Council Library, Patna, the Sinha Library—especially the Scholarly Librarian, Dr. Ram Shobhit Singh, the National Library, Calcutta, and the American Studies Research Centre, Hyderabad, for their gracious courtesies over a long period.

A.S. ANAND MURTY

1. The Individual Talent

Invariably manifest as a peep-hole view of the flux of life, Miss Mansfield's creative vision is essentially lyrical. This is what individualizes her talent.

Her very first narrative composition, *Tiredness of Rosabel*, is a representative product of this lyrical gift.

The moment dramatized in intense concentration is that of a tragic psychological crisis: it is the moment of an experience characterized by intensity of 'will to live'; the experience culminates only in a piteously vague emotional complex; and all this inner drama occurs as a happening in obscurity. The aesthetic vision of the moment seems to have been that of a tragically static situation.

The intensity of the character's 'will to live' has its various manifestations.

It is manifest as the restlessness of her longing for escape: she earnestly craves for escape from the routine monotony of her existence into what she infallibly believes to be 'life' ("... That was life, thought Rosabel"). She feels helplessly tied in hopeless bondage to a humdrum existence. Her existence in the present is lifeless and sterile: her experience of monotony has been hopelessly enervating; it has stagnated the very flux of her life; it has reduced her existence to a state of non-being. Now she wishes to 'be', to 'live' a real life, to have the feel of true existence. What endures as monotony of existence in the present is persistence of the past She can have the experience of true and real existence if she can escape from this monotony. Her existence can be real if she is free to choose from the future. This freedom of choice from the future will mean liberation from the bondage of the past that warps the present: the moment of this free choice is not continuous with the past. She seeks freedom from the bondage of the past-dominated present. The reason is simple: to be free is to exist: one exists only when one has freedom. The future as the realm of the possible is the only realm of true and real freedom, and where there is true and real freedom, there is true and real existence. It is the future, alone which as the realm of the possible can promise fresh thrills. It is in this realm that she can have the feel of a true and real existence.

Restlessness of her longing for escape to the realm of freedom as the realm of true and real existence is so inordinate: she indulges in her dream of this realm as a recollection of an actual experience already derived in the past; at the climactic moment, this dream of the future indulged in as a recollection of a past experience seems to the character to have become a palpable living reality in the present. This impulse to let her innermost self drift into the animating life-stream of existence is intrinsically characteristic of intense 'will to live': the drift is a desperate means of having the feel of 'life'.

The intensity of the character's 'will to live' is indicated also by the urgency of her instinctive need as an isotate: what she is naturally in need of is happy and whole togetherness. Painfully aware of 'the enamel coming off the basin' in her own dark "dull room" she naturally imagines a married life as a life perfected by smug affluence and imperturbable insouciance. Her concept of wholeness as a value in married life is defined by her imagination of a temperamental affinity between her partner and herself: "She would lean over ..., talking with that charming gaiety which Harry so appreciated. Afterwards a matinee, something that gripped them both, and then tea at the 'cottage' ". The character's urge for whole togetherness is so passionate: she imagines she has already been familiar and intimate with her partner. Her imagination of emotional affinity with a husband grows so passionate that it envisages moments of not only "joyous intimacy" but also fusion of their individual identities: "Afterwards a matinee, something that gripped then both, and then tea at the 'cottage' ": the impression of this fusion seems to have been conveyed by the elliptical wording of the mental pictures: distinctness of their individual identity is blurréd through omission of verbs ("Afterwards a matinee" ... "and then tea at the 'cottage'") and fusion of the pronouns in the accusative case ("them"): the impression of this fusion is clinched by the sense of finality of whole togetherness implicit in the pronominal adverb, "both". The character's mental picture of her wedding is so vivid; it is complete with topographical details: "They were married shortly afterwards at St. George's, Hanover Square, and motored down to Harry's old ancestral home for the honeymoon; the peasants in the village curtseyed to them as they passed". This vividness also is due perhaps to the character's intensified instinctive urge for whole complementary togetherness in her life—a life which is barren of all possibilities of consummation of her individual selfhood as a woman.

Intensity of 'will to live' is obliquely evident also as the character's acute consciousness of her isolation from the crowd of people she meets daily. A crowd is a static mass; it only submerges and obscures one's individual identity. Thus it precludes an individual, who is lost in the crowd, from experiencing the freedom even of recognition of his distinct individuality or identity. To stand out of the crowd is to be oneself. The very consciousness on the part of the character of the crowd as a static mass implies her subconscious awareness of her isolation as a distinct individual: this subconscious awareness of her isolation from the crowd evinces her unconscious recognition of her distinctly individual entity. Here we have perhaps the faintest manifestation of the character's 'will to live'. But this makes us see one thing: the whole of the character's being is poised for escape into 'life'. Experience of one's existence as a part of the static mass that "humanity" is, is "sickening", 'tiring', enervating: the character's "tiredness" is perhaps due also to her depressing awareness of her life as a part of the static mass, a life that is still without an experience of a fresh thrill. But the very awareness is perhaps the evidence of the nascency of a new being. Again, the character not only stands out of the crowd; she also seems indulgently attentive to the flux of life in the world without: she is not 'staring' fatuously, blindly, vacantly.

All these manifestations of the character's 'will to live' culminate only in a vague expression concealing a pathetic emotional complex. This whole experience inclusive of its culmination is made to seem a tragic happening in obscurity: "So she slept and dreamed, and smiled in her sleep, and once threw out her arm to feel for something which was not there, dreaming still". This moment of culmination is a vague temporal complex. The sudden shift of viewpoint here helps to accentuate the tragic fact about the character's experience: the experience evolving in obscurity culminates only in a vague emotional complex; the abrupt shift of viewpoint is necessitated by the author's sense of appropriateness: perhaps an objective point of view alone could preserve the requisite tragic sense of obscurity at this climactic moment: the character's pathetic experience which has already been tragic because of its evolution in obscure privacy seems all the more tragic for its culmination in an obscure emotional complex. This obscurity of the emotional complex is preserved through objective registration of the character's facial expressions and her one single convulsive gesture. The emotional complex is formed by the character's indulgence in a dream of the future as a recollection of a past experience and also as a feeling of the thrill of an actual experience in the present. The facial expressions and the gesture are too abstract and vague to give us an inkling of the time to which the inner drama may be assigned: all the three 'levels of time' seem to have been fused into a vague temporal complex. The very moment in a dream is a moment isolated from Time. The character 'once throws out her arm to feel something which is not there'. Perhaps she is blithely free to re-live the past in her dream. But was there ever any such past for her to re-live? And doesn't the present also seem unreal? Or is it that she is dreaming of a physical thrill in the future? But does she not also seem to "feel something" in the present? Why is there that "vague tremor on her mouth"? Is it an index of her impulse in the dream to kiss or be kissed? But doesn't she seem to be enjoying a kiss, recalling a kiss, and also imagining a kiss, all at the same time? Or is she is 'mouthing' words as she has seen the girl on the bus doing? If she is, in which tense is she speaking in her dream? Or is it that she is rehearsing a speech for a future rendezvous? But doesn't she seem to be only thinking aloud in the present, of some possibility in the future as a reality already past?—Vagueness of the emotional complex is rendered perplexingly inconclusive by the vagueness of the temporal complex.

The inner drama has been evolving in obscure privacy. The single impression that lingers is that of a tragedy in obscurity. All of this inner drama seems to be what we may call just a flicker of being mocked by dark obscurity. This flicker of being remains unnoticed in the apathetic world of 'staring faces' and self-centred selves: the eyes in the 'staring faces' of the "people on the opposite seat" are too vacant to take notice of the flicker presumably reflected in her eyes: the eyes have already begun drinking in the beauty of 'Life' with its picturesque diversity: this diversity has introduced a fresh novelty into her routine life. The girl reading the "cheap-edition novel" 'does not look up' when the character 'stumbles and lurches against her on her way out'. Harry with his impishly insolent demeanour is carelessly apathetic: his admiration of her 'prettiness' is not indulgent and sympathetic: he remains blind to the flicker glowing as her restless passion for whole togetherness. Her mirrored reflection too, remains restricted to her own vision. On all these occasions of her contact with the "people" in her world on the fateful day of the crisis, the manifestations of her 'will to live' remain unperceived, unnoticed, unheeded.

It is the tenseness of this inner drama evolving as a gradually intensifying emotional experience and culminating in a vague emotional complex that seems to have called for a rendering in intent concentration: perhaps only a concentrated creative vision could help to register the gradual intensification of the character's experience on the day of the crisis.

The concentrated creative vision envisages the natural process in which this inner drama evolves. The drama evolves as a gradually intensifying experience of the crisis; it is climaxed by a vague emotional complex. So the process of the evolution which the creative vision is consistently focused upon is that of gradual interiorization of the character's consciousness. Thus first we have an introspective analysis of impressions and experiences in the present. All this changes into indulgence in a dream as a vivid imaginative recollection of an actual experience in the past. This gradual interiorization of consciousness gravitates towards an obscurely private emotional experience in sleep.

Thus a neatly patterned narrative design is forged. The design helps to register the intensification of the character's emotional experience of the crisis. It reflects the process of gradual interiorization of the character's consciousness: it naturally involves a sense of overlapping 'levels of time'; the temporal levels understandably coalesce at the climactic moment as a vague temporal complex.

The concentrated creative vision simultaneously forges another concomitant pattern which helps to accentuate the 'caustic pathos' intrinsic in the story element: the pattern that emerges from the narrative design is a pattern of contrasts.

The one is the ironical contrast between the character's biological urge for food and her indulgence in the dream of a 'butler'. The character's hunger for food in 'real' life is pitifully manifest in this image of a 'butler' that occurs later in her dreamful reverie.

The other is the contrast between the inordinate 'tiredness' that she experiences in her 'real' humdrum life and the sybaritic exhaustion that she imagines as a reality already experienced. The character's ignorance of the ironical contrast helps to intensify the pathos.

There is also a parallelism marking the narrative design. It is formed by the similarity between the girl reading the novel on the bus and the central character herself. The girl engrossed in the novel is heedless of the 'lurch' as she reads on; the protagonist slumbering in her sweet dreams 'sits up' in bed and feels "the cold fingers of dawn ... over her uncovered hand", too; but she remains "half-asleep". She too keeps 'smiling' as she dreams on: the "nervous tremor round her mouth" is presumably due to her own silent 'mouthing' of 'words'. The parallelism stresses the dramatic irony of the character's unawareness of the abstractedly dreamy girl on the bus as an externalized image of her own self that will keep 'smiling' and dreaming even after the feeling of "the cold fingers of dawn". Reference to this significantly dramatic chance encounter naturally merits conspicuity in the typographical design of the verbal build-up.

One more example of parallelism is presented by the correspondence between the image of the fictitious character in the novel and the image, which the 'real' character assumes for herself in her dream of a ball dance. Exactness of correspondence serves to bring out the pathetic irony implicit in the character's assumption of an image that is already fictitious and unreal.

The creative vision thus helps to maximize the effect of the minimum that it is focused upon.

The thought-process that is registered is exclusive of the character's recollection of the whole range of her experiences in the past, which have driven her to realization of sickening monotony as a grim reality negating the very spirit of life; the short-story captures the moment of culmination of the experiences: the episode meant to evince this culmination is illuminating enough to reveal the nature of the experiences in the past; one afternoon's return from the shop is typical enough to evidence the manifestations of the character's intensifying 'will to live'. The opening section is given to depicting a consciousness that is fully wakeful and also soberly sensitive to the continuity of exterior events or to the contrast between her own state and the immediate physical surroundings: even here we have only suggestions of the character's unconscious yet intensified impulse to 'live'.

Refinement or dissolution of complexity accrues from the unobtrusive employment of a concentric design; this design helps to convey the irony of psychic interiorization only gravitating towards an obscurely private emotional complex. Refinement of complexity characterizing the story element is due to the suggestive nature of several other compositional elements—contrast between the character's own impulses or feelings; similarity between the character herself and her counterpart on the bus; correspondence between the image that is already fictitious and the image that is assumed; subtle variation of tense in depiction of the dreamful reverie quietly registering fluctuations between past participle and simple past tense;[1] temporal ambiguity of a dream seen as a reality already experienced in the past; references to the image of 'a button that came off this morning'; and registration of a convulsive gesture expressing only a vague emotional complex.

Her contemporaries had already accepted 'disintegration of the continuity of exterior events'[2] as something natural to more realistic registration of interiorized life. But she was found it inadequate as a means to the specific end her present narrative composition was meant to achieve: she went a step further and dissolved the time strata: (she makes the character imagine the future as a real past in the present and proceeds to register the tragic culmination of this whole self-deceptive thought-process in what suggests only an obscurely vague temporal complex.)

Increase in dramatic effect is perhaps naturally consequent upon refinement of complexity. It sensitizes and concentrates the reader's critical awareness of the subtleties of the bare dramatization of the 'tired' girl's consciousness. It enables him thus to 'understand more than the protagonist'.[3]

Miss Mansfield's short-story is the outcome of 'a personal sense of truth'[4]: the form of her short-story is lyrical; it is characteristic of a vision which is essentially subjective. The tragedy of the 'tired' girl is the tragedy of an individual that remains tensely poised—for escape from life-denying monotony of the present into life-giving diversion which the future alone can promise; for freedom as the only means of 'being'; for choice from the realm of the possible.

The personal sense of truth that Miss Mansfield's short-story illustrates is born of her highly cultivated, exquisite sensibility which sees 'a world in a grain of sand and a heaven in a flower'. It is this sensibility which accounts for the present or persistent lyrical vision of the truth ('will to live') as she found it in Nietzsche, the one philosopher she had, presumably, been in emotional accord with before she wrote *Tiredness of Rosabel*.

Miss Mansfield's criticism of life is non-moral: she makes her subjective selection of materials 'reflect an objective standard of values'.[5]

We shall see how this personal sense of truth born of her calm reliance upon a highly cultivated, exquisitely refined sensibility persists throughout her literary career.

Miss Mansfield seems to have carved out her own path with her pen.

But this 'individual talent' was not yet integrated. *Tiredness of Rosabel* is no doubt an anacheronistic marvel in the realm of Miss Mansfield's own fictional writings. What interferes with our sense of wonder at this marvel is our simultaneous awareness of the nascent author's natural failure to have perceived either her weakness or her potency as a story-teller: she could not see the illogicality of a sudden shift in the protagonist's point of view; nor could she recognize the potentiality of the narrative technique unconsciously achieved: the protagonist's knowledge of the source from which the girl customer procured her hat only strains the reader's credulity; the narrative build-up the author has unconsciously composed is expressive enough to obviate recourse to explicit explanatory statements as interspersed expository sentences, or parenthetical insertions, or 'sympathetic summation'.

However, the individual talent as a specific natural endowment or 'gift' that ... produced '*Tiredness of Rosabel*'[6] was compounded of almost all the intrinsic potentialities of a good short-story writer. She was endowed with the perceptive faculty of imaginative sympathy, though it was not yet controlled by the requisitely concomitant capability of 'personal detachment'.[7] She could have the lyrical vision of a truth implicit in the subtle transition that even fragility of an evanescent emotion involves; this capacity for a lyrical vision is an essential attribute of the creative process which concentrates on the culminant moment or only on indeterminate middle that is in between the beginning and the end. She had an intuitive grasp of correspondence between the nature and scope of the story element and the verbal range and mode of the specific fictional genre; that is, she did not lack the understanding of the fundamental principle on which the aesthetics of the short-story is based; she was gifted with a genius for an objective, aesthetic rendering of a selected typical moment in intent concentration; this concentrated creative vision involves the choice nor only of an expedient point of view from which the moment is to be rendered but also of a correspondingly adjusted time scheme that helps to sharpen the focus of narration.

This specific natural endowment of 'gift that ... produced *Tiredness of Rosabel*'[8] helped its author also to discover a truth abundantly rich for her as the source of a story element: the truth discovered here was 'will to live' which is manifest only as a tragic choice from the realm of the possible: many of her later short-stories would be variations on this theme.

The 'gift that ... produced *Tiredness of Rosabel*' was inclusive of the author's precocious understanding of one basic factor: the ways and means of expression which the theme for a short-story calls for must help to achieve maximization of the effect of the minimum. Miss Mansfield was endowed with the faculty of the aesthetic realization that devices help to complete the intended meaning. Fusion of the 'levels of time', concentric design of characterization, pattern of contrasts, externalization of the character's emotion, ambiguity of the ending: these are some of the devices which the 'gift' forged in what it 'produced'. In this first characteristic short-story of hers they helped to discover or consummate the meaning. In her subsequent short-stories she would re-employ many of these devices; there would be more and more fruitful exploration of their creative potentialities; as techniques they would be as much complex as the compound of the possible dimensions intrinsic in the subject-matter.

But she had found the 'form' by 'a fluke' the achievement was only precocious. The subsequent short-stories make us feel that the 'form' had yet to be recognized: the occasional lapses are at times incredible; the trial and error process betrays lack of sureness of grasp; she kept making intermittently unsuccessful attempts at 'personal detachment'.

NOTES AND REFERENCES

1. "'What is it exactly that I want, Harry?' she *had* said ... The girl glanced at Rosabel laughingly", *Collected Stories of Katherine Mansfield*, p. 526.
2. Quoted by Saralyn Daly, *Katherine Mansfield*, p. 113 (from *Mimesis* by Erich Auerback).
3. Saralyn Daly, *op. cit.*, p. 113.
4. David Daiches, *Novel and the Modern World*, p. 193.
5. Saralyn Daly, *op. cit.*, p. 113.
6. Antony Alpers, *Katherine Mansfield*, p. 108.
7. William Walsh, *A Manifold Voice*, p. 162.
8. *Ibid.*, 132.

2. The Guru and the Disciple

The reason for Miss Mansfield's choice of the masterpiece by Chekhov (*Sleepy*) as a model for her own short-story, *Child who-was-Tired*, was at once psychological and aesthetic. The psychological reason was her emotional affinity with the character portrayed; the aesthetic one was, perhaps, her impulse to undertake imaginative exploration of further dimensions supplied by the story element symbolically dramatizing her own traumatic experiences of longing for relief of suffering or for escape to freedom:[1] the impulse indicated her earnestness to recover 'the gift that had produced *Tiredness of Rosabel*';[2] she sought this recovery through re-composition of what she intuitively believed was a real short-story: the story element in Chekhov's short-story seemed to fit in with her vague concept of the peculiar subject that the short-story as a specific genre readily accommodates.

Attraction for the short-story by Chekhov was magnetic: with the character her affinity was emotional; with the creator of the character, it was aesthetic.

Her composition, *Child who-was-Tired*, was also naturally subsequent to her previous exploration of the theme of the tragic futility of intense 'will to live'; for here too she explored a situation similar in this specific sense to the one she had already intuitively conceived and created in her previous short-story, *Tiredness of Rosabel* . The central characters of both these short-stories are 'tired' and it is their 'tiredness' which defines their individual situations. The means of escape they seek is ironically pathetic: inevitability of their reversion to the state of 'tiredness' is certain; either situation is a deadlock.

But Miss Mansfield's exploration of the tragically static situation which her 'gift' had discovered in the short-story by Chekhov was an indefensible failure: she had failed to conceive an emotional complex tense enough to match the degree of intensity intrinsic in the tragic emotional experience adequately embodied in the original short-story by Chekhov.

Loss of intensity in her plagiarized version is due to clumsy exploitation of devices, effects and touches, either borrowed or original.

(A) DEVICES: I/BORROWED

(a) Recurrence of the road image in dreams

In Miss Mansfield's short-story we find a pattern formed through recurrence of the road image. It is obviously meant to reveal the innermost longing of the child. But this image pattern raises questions, which baffle the reader and interfere with his aesthetic appreciation of the intensity of the character's 'will'. What is the reason for this curious emotion? Is the child really so 'tired' as to sigh for what lies beyond all that exists as accepted reality? Is this persistent, day-appearing dream antenatal, resurrected as the innermost longing of the innocent soul ("Once upon a time she was walking along a white road", etc.)? Is she irresistibly, uncontrollably sleepy if she can ponder and deduce a hypothesis ("If I walked far enough up this road," etc.)? How can her smothering of the baby ensure her escape to the strange region of her dreams? Chekhov's Varka sees the image only in her drowsy naps. Her "passionate longing for sleep" is so intense that even in her dreams of the road she finds her own situation projected: images of "people with valets on their backs and trudging along" seem to be multiplied projections of the character herself who, burdened with "the screaming baby" only 'somnambulates' wearily through her darkened world: "the people with their valets and their shadows fall on the ground in the liquid mud". Varka is dying for any place to sleep in, howsoever horrid and miserable it may be; she yearns for any place in this hell of a habitation, any place where she can grab off a bit of shut-eye ("flop on to the floor regardless of everything, and to sleep"); her innermost self seems to experience vicarious satisfaction in its vision of the people that "fall sound asleep, and sleep sweetly" on the "broad high-road covered with liquid mud": the vision is the manifestation of her deep unconscious "passionate longing for sleep".

There is a poignant contrast too: there are people who "fall sound asleep, and sleep sweetly" even on "a road covered with liquid mud"; and there is Varka who cannot doze even surreptitiously, although she lives in a habitation unquestionably more sheltered and homelike than the place that is not only odd but also despicable. This faint inkling of contrast is another dimension of the depiction of the tragic experience already intensified by a glaring contrast that the actual world around the "sleepy" girl presents: it is the world in which "the master and the apprentice Afanasy are snoring"; it is the world in which "that soothing music of the night" has perhaps lulled all to sleep (with its few faint sounds—the snore, the creak, the murmur, the chirrup-evoking the atmosphere of a world blind with sleep); it is the world in which "at last", when "the visitors have gone", and "the lights are put out", "the master and mistress" can "go to bed".

The road image in Miss Mansfield's short-story has its origin in a vision that does not seem to be convincingly inherent in the emotional complex which is meant to seem intensifying as murderous frenzy. The pattern of parallelisms formed by the recurrence of the same dream in reveries or in catnaps connects the tragic essence of the story element with sources outside the range of the child's recorded experience.[3]

In Chekhov's short-story the road image has its source in the character's traumatic experience: after her father's death she had to trudge along a "high-road covered with liquid mud ... her mother Pelageya ... walking beside her, hurrying her on", both "hastening together to the town to find situations", begging of the people all the way up. But the character is too sleepy to remember where the road led. The sense of what that road led to is conceivably implicit: it helps to deepen the tragic effect: the road led to this "stuffy" hovel of a shoe-maker, with its "smell of cabbage soup, and of the inside of a boot shop"; she was separated from her mother somewhere in the course of her journey along this road and then Varka was left alone, all by herself, in a family where even a mother was a monster. This fall from a frying pan into a fire defines the tragedy inherent in the whole situation.

Recurrence of the image in Varka's drowsy dreams helps to intensify also the tragic sense of link with the past: the present of Varka's situation is still continuous with the past, and this precludes the possibility of freedom which is the *sine qua non* for actualization of existence ("prevents her from living", or "does not let her live"). The road image is imperceptibly operative in Chekhov's aesthetic rendering of this essential aspect of Varka's tragic experience.

(b) Rhythmical pattern of parallelisms

The rhythmical pattern conspicuously marking the structural design of the verbal build-up only works against the desirable consummation of implications as a convincingly coherent meaning.[4] Perhaps there is nothing within the range of the child's recorded experience which may help the reader to recognize the motive that induced a desire so fantastic ("a little road that led to nowhere, and where nobody walked at all"). Of course, recurrence of the same wistful dream even after the climax does help to convey the sense of interminability of her longing in the present. But this longing is so unreasonable, so fantastic that the pattern leads the reader from nowhere to nothing.

Recourse to the design of a rhythmical pattern of parallelisms in Chekhov's *Sleepy* is necessitated by his keener aesthetic vision of continuity of the past which as the grim reality of the present defines the very essence of his character's tragic experience. Whereas Miss Mansfield's road image leads us from nowhere to nothing, Chekhov's stimulates our creative imagination making us realize that Varka has moved only from one dark world to another and that thus the present is still continuous with the past.

The sense of the tragic continuity of the past is conveyed through a pattern effected by registration of what seems to be a life-long correspondence between the kindred natures of the past and the present: the past in "a dark stuffy hut" without a candle and the present in another "stuffy" dwelling without a glimmer of hope: the past with the father who was "not among the living" and the present with the girl herself who does not know what "prevents her from living"; the past ringing with father's "Boo-boo-boo-boo" and the present humming with the girl's own murmuring at the baby's cradle:" 'Hush-a-bye, my baby wee'"; the past without a moment of sleep on the road where "she would be down with enjoyment but" where "her mother Pelageya walking beside her kept hurrying her on" and the present with its "minutes when she longs to flop on to the floor regardless of everything, and to sleep"; the past in which "somewhere there/was/a baby crying, and Varka/heard/someone singing with her own voice" and the present in which there is again a baby 'screaming' with Varka really singing in her own voice the same song. The parallelisms registering correspondence between the past and present situations help to bring out the tragic truth about the experience the short-story is meant to embody: the present is continuous with the past, not liberated from it: possibility of the feel of freedom from the past—as an experience of the beginning of a new real existence—is darkened. A sense of tragic stasis in which continuity of the present with the past precludes all possibility of experience of liberation as the experience of existence itself, is conveyed.[5] Sustained use of the present tense serves to naturalize the effect. Chekhov's use of the present tense for the narration of even the past recollected experiences helps to communicate the sense of this tragic continuity. The elliptical opening ("Night") aptly images forth the whole darkly static 'atmosphere'.

(c) Externalization of emotional experience

The effect of externalization in Miss Mansfield's short-story is spoiled every time by the subsequent elaboration of the element of contrast which the images involved in the process present. We find ironically contrasted pictures: there is the child dragging her wagon; there is a man who is also driving his wagon, but he is whistling; again, we see the child with her burden, and we also see girls with their bundles on their shoulders, but the girls are laughing together as jolly companions. The element of relief that this ironical contrast involves shows relaxation of intensity. Of the fact that the subsequent image ('the sun pushing by a heavy fold of grey cloud and spreading a warm yellow light over everything') may also be taken to have been meant to reflect the child's awaking consciousness, Miss Mansfield seems to have been innocently unaware. She ought to have been wary of introducing any such image into her narrative framework originally meant to achieve a cumulative effect of inordinate sleepiness. The bracing effect of the sunny interlude seems incongruously subordinated to the desired total effect. The phantasmagoria that naturally begins to float in her drowsy consciousness as the day draws in provides another example. The callous Man and the Frau that seem "to swell to an immense size" have already become the projected images of terror in the child's consciousness; the cradled baby who suddenly has "two heads, and then no head" at all is the grotesque image in the child's unconscious of a double burden ("another coming"). All externalization goes awry: the child's unconscious attitude or intention is partially revealed; the force that has prevented her from "living" has been identified; the tragic effect of the situation in which the child has to kill the baby is mitigated; the centralized emotional impact of the child's last act is weakened.

The purpose of externalization is defeated also when the rendering of the projected images is unnecessarily inclusive of interpretation: "As she walked up and down her great big shadow on the wall like a grown-up person with a grown up baby. Whatever would it look like when she carried two babies so!", or "The Frau seemed to be as big as a giantess, and there was a certain heaviness in all her movements that was terrifying to anyone so small".

Miss Mansfield does not seem to have mastered as yet the whole art of tell-tale externalization of a character's emotional experience, that is, symbolic externalization as subordinated to the total impressionistic effect of the narrative composition.

All externalization of Varka's experience contributes to the one single impressionistic effect of inordinate sleepiness. Intermittent recurrence of images ("a green patch on the ceiling from the ikon-lamp", "the shadows from the trousers and the baby clothes") registers the emotional tension between her innocent will to "live" through sleep even for a while and her awareness of all that vaguely looms as a "force" opposed to this 'will'. This helps to accentuate the effect of tense sleepiness. Occasional fusion of the images intensifies this effect too: "the cricket churra in the stove; the green patch on the ceiling and the shadows from the trousers and the baby clothes force themselves on Varka's half-opened eyes again, wink at her and cloud her mind". Even at the single brief moment when this tension seems relieved, Varka is "fearfully sleepy".

There is no ironical contrast involving an element of relief. "The green patch, the shadows, and the cricket seem to laugh and wonder too", but they only "seem" to; the hallucination only mocks her, for "she has failed to grasp such a simple thing before"—to "understand the force which prevents her from living". The objects are symbolic. The "green patch" seems to laugh and wonder because Varka has not seen the simple means of realizing her being in sleep; the shadows, because she has been unreasonably resigned to what could be easily eliminated; and the cricket, because she has foolishly denied herself the opportunity to be lulled to sleep by "the soft music of the night". We can see how all these images contribute to one single effect as they all seem to externalize her own mockery of her failure to have grasped such a simple thing before. There is no sunny interlude in her life: her consciousness only seems to be awaking even when she can realize "it will soon be morning": "there is nothing to force itself on her eyes and cloud her brain. But she is as sleepy as before, fearfully sleepy". "The air outside turning blue", the "morning" unfolding slowly, do reflect a consciousness awaking to the temporal and spatial reality, but the character's vision is sleepy-eyed. The effect is achieved through registration of a vacant, bored vision of a change in the changeless reality of her routinized life. Even the windows getting dark or revealing the colour of "the air outside" seem to be a projected image of Varka's sleepy or waking consciousness.

There is no such externalization of Varka's emotional experience as may reveal her unconscious attitude to the baby's parents or the baby himself. Unconsciouly she has been only innocently curious to know what it is that "prevents her from living"; the force is not identified earlier as it is in Miss Mansfield's short-story: it cannot be: Varka is confoundedly sleepy. The baby in the cradle or in his mother's arms is just the baby in the cradle or in his mother's arms. He is not revealed as an anathema that he is as a two-headed or headless freak of nature.

In Chekhov's short-story it is not the woman but the golosh that "grow, swells, fills up the room". The child's vision of the Frau "swelling to an immense size" betrays her unconscious attitude to the woman; Varka's vision of the golosh that "grows, swells, fills up the whole room" reveals only her intense "passionate longing for sleep": she "thinks how nice it would be to put her head into a big deep golosh and have a little nap in it": her sleepiness is all the more pitiful for her effort "to look at things so that they may not grow big and move before her eyes": she has to "strain" her eyes to make herself believe that she is not sleepy. She is not wakeful enough to identify herself with the objects around her: the child is made to imagine that the oven is "cold, like herself, and sleeping—dreaming of a little white road", etc. Varka is not made to think that "the green patch, the shadows, the cricket ... laugh and wonder" like herself.

Externalization of emotion in Chekhov's short-story is restrained. There is no straining after effect; there are no melodramatic touches.

(A) DEVICES: II/ORIGINAL

(a) Choice of specific tense for the narrative

The specific tense Miss Mansfield has chosen to tell almost the same story is the usual past tense. Miss Mansfield's perception of stasis characterizing the situation dramatized in her guru's crisp masterpiece is infallible. She has sought to achieve this effect of stasis in her own way. She has chosen to render the same static situation in a different tense, of course in the indisputable belief that the conventional tense for a story about such a situation also is equally expedient—that a situation as a reality of the past can also be made to seem static. Unchangeable permanence of the tragic situation is a sense intrinsic in the very story element which the guru and the disciple individually explore: what would have happened to Varka is as much easily conceivable as what would have happened to the nameless character created out of her: it is the sense of interminability of the piteously routinized life which completes the tragic meaning that the story element embodies: baby or no baby, the subjection of the poor innocent soul to the ruthless cruelties in the family seems interminable and absolute.

Thus the story element in its totality suggests a tragically static situation. Miss Mansfield has sought to achieve the effect perhaps also by taking a shorter time-span for the narrative. There is scrupulous "elimination of ... flashbacks"[6]: the only exception appears in recurrence of a dream that is deliberately made to seem antenatal; the past is referred to only in a casual conversation within earshot ("she's the free-born one—daughter of the waitress at the railway station", etc.). Miss Mansfield has aimed for the Aristotelian unity of time too. The living present-ness of the situation is vividly dramatized as a reality of the past. The 'dramatic effect' is achieved. But the pace is leisurely. The compositional elements which slacken the pace are easily perceptible: consistency of point of view is at times sacrificed when Miss Mansfield fails to resist the temptation to employ even abruptly different angles of vision of the child's tragedy; the element of contrast is bungled; the girl's tragedy is seen even from the baby's point of view; there is diffusion of interest which renders the treatment of the situation melodramatic; elaboration of the borrowed story element for a more tragic effect results only in a succession of sunny interludes in the dark drama of pain. The pace is melodramatically leisurely in the dramatization of the strangulation scene. Slackening of pace is symptomatic of loss in concentration. Miss Mansfield does not seem to have developed as yet the critical sense of correlation between time-span and pace in an aesthetic rendering of a crisis in intense concentration.

The time-span in Chekhov's *Sleepy* is not so short, and there is no elimination of flashback, either. Still the short-story has a good grip on the reader. The human element, the "passionate longing for sleep" as a manifestation of will to "live", is explored in intense concentration; the exploration is consummated in a momentous discovery of the essential tragic truth about the situation Varka is condemned to: this tragic truth is—continuity of the present with the past, which "prevents her from living". (Perhaps she has never known sleep since she left the "dark stuffy hut": out on the road her mother kept hurrying her on, regardless of her "passionate longing for sleep", which still persists: in the shoemaker's house too where her search for a job finally landed her, she has been denied even a moment of repose in sleep).

The same technical aspects—viewpoint, contrast, concentration, which are so clumsily handled in Miss Mansfield's short-story that the pace there is markedly slackened—seem primarily subordinated to one single aesthetic purpose: imaginative exploration of the tragic essence of Varka's experience of will to "live" as manifest in what seems to be her "passionate longing for sleep". The point of view remains consistently restricted to the central character's sleepy consciousness; the element of contrast does involve irony but this irony too is functional as a means of intensifying the grim pathos meant to mantle Varka's world. Concentration is too intense to accommodate registration of even brief spells of relief in the character's tragic experience in a "dark stuffy" world. The ending is swift: even a glimpse of the actual act of strangulation is obscured with a montage impression of gestures expressive of impish exultation over success in identification of "the foe who will not let her live". Comparative shortness of time-span is a misleading criterion.[7]

(b) Designation of individual characters

The abstract designation of the central character in Miss Mansfield's short-story raises some basic questions: how is "lack of reality in the major part of the child's day and expectations ... enhanced by the abstract designation"[8] of this central character herself? Is her anonymity meant to function as a means of universalizing or obscuring her private tragic experience (as the suffering of the soul condemned to hopeless isolation from the living world all around)? Isn't the 'rhythmical alternation of focused reality and unfocussed hallucination"[9] devised to create only the impressionistic effect of the central character's fitful drowsiness? How has the creative process involved here necessitated simultaneous recourse to abstract designation of the central character herself? How is generic designation of the parents themselves justified when the Child's consciousness registers their images also as 'solidly perceived'[10] images from 'focused reality'? Isn't the Child's consciousness as much wakeful in its infallible recognition of their distinct individuality as it is in its emotional awareness of the distinct identities of the impish children with their indistinct individuality? Are these 'solidly perceived' children meant to seem more real?

In Chekhov's *Sleepy* it is 'unfocussed hallucination' that is predominant; focused reality' is not 'rhythmically alternate'; rather it is subordinated to what seems to be a preconceived impressionistic effect of 'unfocussed hallucination': the effect is achieved through the build-up of a montage of audio-visual images; we have only objective reality without subjective colouring, all the images swimming in a sort of blurred mist in spite of the sharpness and distinctness of their outlines or features: of anything around her Varka is only sleepily conscious: she knows only that which induces or shatters her sleep, and keeps unconsciously looking for that which prevents her from sleeping. Even when she seems awaking or awake, she is only drowsily conscious: her eyes open, she sees what is there before her; even her dawning awareness of reality around her is just objective perception, infallible yet dull. When "there is nothing to force itself on her eyes and cloud her brain—she is sleepy as before, fearfully sleepy! 'Fully awake while running' to the shed for firewood", all that she can think of is the way in which sleepiness is easier to overcome. While "with a broad smile on her face and wide unblinking eyes, she walks up and down the room", it is a 'hallucination' that seems to have taken 'possession' of her: all her gestures seem somnambulistic. Generic designation of the master and the mistress of the household as "the master" and "the woman" is understandable in Chekhov's short-story in view of the oppressiveness of his central character's overwhelming somnolence. We can see that her somnolence admits of no consciousness wakeful or calm enough to encompass identification of the baby's parents with their distinctly individual names.

Varka's own father and mother are not so prosaically designated as the Man and the Frau and the child are, although they are characters temporally too remote from the grimmer reality of the situation in the present. The simple reason for the specific, distinctive designations of Varka's parents is perhaps the deep emotional attachment which she has been denied since her irrevocably final separation from them: the names are too dear now to be forgotten; they are the only real names in her memory of names.

(B) I EFFECTS: BORROWED

(a) Impression of Sleepiness

Miss Mansfield strives for the same effect of miserable sleepiness that she has noticed in the short-story by Chekhov. While aiming for a more tragic effect in what she means to be read as a new short-story with a new meaning, she has elaborated the picture of the situation to reveal some other possible dimensions of the tragic experience, and this elaboration only robs the total effect of its sustained intensity. This elaboration accounts for incongruity of brief spells of wakefulness in what is intended to seem an overwhelming drowsy state. There are moments when the Child's consciousness is fully wakeful. The Child seems aware also of something inside herself; this awareness is knowledge based on the evidence of her senses: "Again the smarting lump in her throat, the stupid tears that fell and kept on failing", etc. She has already experienced such a paroxysm of weeping ("she shook back her head, a great lump ached in her throat and then the tears ran down her face on to the vegetables"): she is wakeful enough to recall a recent experience ("Again"). She can dwell on the baby "cutting his teeth". She speaks "in a voice of immense authority, pulling of the bedclothes and giving the boys sundry pokes and digs". She impersonates the Frau, and this impersonation presupposes her escape from or negation of her sleepy self. She watches the whole drama that the impish children enact. She herself approaches the Frau to request that she should tell her what chores remain to be performed ("what must I do now?" She asked): the inkling of a respite from the drudging, exhausting toil, when she herself can be ready to accept or ask for more of what has been shattering her sleepiness, does not harmonize well with the intended meaning of sleepiness, so uncontrollable as to drive the girl to murderous frenzy. The child's consciousness is fully wakeful also because she does not have to strain her faculty of remembering as she recalls past experiences. Even the one single moment when she has to strain this faculty ("who had told her that story?" etc.) is a moment when her mind's registering of sensation and perception involves simultaneous functioning of her different sense organs: her awareness is sensitized: "A wind had sprung up ... blowing like little green hairs". Again, self-consciousness, which absorbs her for a moment when she turns up her sleeves, "frowning at her arms, as if to scold them for being so thin, so much like stunted twigs", unmistakably evinces wakeful consciousness. Her perception of natural phenomena is vivid: her mind cannot only register a perception; it can also conceive association ("away in the meadow she saw the grass blowing like little green hairs"): perception passes into apperception when she finds the sun has "pushed by a heavy fold of grey cloud and spread a warm yellow light over everything". The child is fully conscious also of "her comfortable sense of her maternal duties in good working order for the day". She identifies herself with "the oven" ("Perhaps it was cold, like herself, and sleepy ... perhaps it had been dreaming of a little white road"): this empathy too is characteristic of conscious perceptual experience. The child is fully awake when "the one in her arms" seems to her to "understand the contemptuous loathing of her tired glance". She is conscious of reciprocity of perceptions, her own perception as well as that of the baby. Her consciousness is never dim; it has become full awareness. Awareness, we know, implies a keener response or greater alertness that encompasses rational judgement or objective evaluation. Even when she thinks of "the nearness of bedtime" she shakes "all over with excited joy". She can laugh and clasp her hands too.

Chekhov's critical sense of singleness of the crisis calling for a rendering only in intense imaginative concentration accounts for his non-indulgence in unnecessarily exploratory elaboration: his artistic vision of the rich complex of emotional dimensions inherent in the intensity of the single experience is simultaneous consciousness of the intrinsic potentiality of the genre chosen-maximization of the effect of minimum; this concentrated creative vision obviates the need of elaboration for inclusion of other possible piteous aspects of the situation. Chekhov concentrates on the character's throbbing experience of irresistibly overwhelming sleepiness. All that his character "longs" is "to flop on to the floor regardless of everything, and to sleep". The Child has been fully awake before she 'she has sprung to her feet, poured/the man's/coffee'; she has "frowned at her arms, as if to scold them for being so thin", etc. But Varka "lays her head on the edge of the cradle, and rocks her whole body to overcome her sleepiness, yet her eyes are glued together, and her head is heavy". Miss mansfield has borrowed this touch of a gesture only to show how her character has to endure physical 'tiredness': while "rocking him" the Child has to rock her own body; but she does not seem to be rocking "her body to overcome her sleepiness"—that sleepiness which is meant to climax as a murderous delirium. She rocks her body to rock the baby to sleep, but she herself is awake. Varka rocks her whole body to keep herself awake. The latter's experience is the more painful. What the borrowed touch of this gesture is meant to suggest is consistent only with the limited implication of the title Miss Mansfield has chosen for her new composition. We are made to see, how with her eyes open Varka is blind with sleep; we have the feeling that her eyelids are distended but heavy. We can visualize her goggling eyes fringed with sleep: "She shakes her head, opens her eyes wide and tries to look at things so that they may not grow big and move before her eyes". She opens her eyes "with an immense effort" but as the story unfolds we find she does not have to make such an effort again. Varka remains struggling with her sleep. She seems to have sand in her eyes. Chekhov refrains from direct explicit statement; he dramatizes the "effort".

Again, in Chekhov's short-story we notice unconscious gestures characteristic of overpowering sleepiness: "Her head droops over the table, the potatoes dance before her eyes, the knife tumbles out of her hand". Her visual or auditory perception at the moment is peculiar to her sleepy consciousness: "the potatoes dance before her eyes" ... her fat angry mistress is talking so loud that it makes a ringing in Varka's ears. The similes evoke the reader's own experience of sleepiness: "Varka presses her temples that feel as though they were made of wood", etc. Her forehead, characteristically again, knocks against the birch tree she has been dreaming of; she is still too sleepy to realize that the birch tree is nothing but the cradle. The preconceived impressionistic effect of sleepiness is achieved obliquely. Unlike the Child's, Varka's perceptions are drowsy and dull. Even the degrees to which her consciousness is perceptual seem to be distinctly marked.

(i) Her perceptions are usually dull; they are infallible yet dim: her perception "of the lamp ... burning before the ikon ... baby ... clothes and a pair of ... trousers, etc." is utterly objective; it is too drowsy to be subjective. Here she is not looking: she simply sees because her eyes are open. "The little green lamp burning before the ikon" does not reveal its meaning as "the oven" in Miss Mansfield's short-story does: it is not burning, "like herself": we know that Varka is burning with an intense passion for the innocent fulfilment of a simple biological need. The "string stretched from one end of the room to the other" is not perceived as the road on which the child drags the little wagon ("If I walked far enough up this road", etc.) nor do the "baby-clothes and a pair of big black trousers hanging" on it come flapping in her face, and dance and jig, bulge out and twist as the "hangings" in Miss Mansfield's short-story do; they only "throw long shadows on the stove, on the cradle, and on Varka"; they all seem to be swimming as phantasmagoria so natural to drowsy consciousness. The "pair of big black trousers" is not even reminiscent of the wearer's sinister identity. Images that impinge upon Varka's consciousness at the moment are first visual ("A little green lamp ... a pair of big black trousers") and then olfactory ("a smell of cabbage soup ... of the inside of a boot shop"). All her perceptions are infallible, yet they are all objective, dull and dim. Even in the scene where she is suddenly conscious of the presence of her mistress, the mind's registering of perceptions is starkly objective. She has just been roused from her sleep; recognition of reality in the present is slow: first she is conscious of the sudden disappearance of the images conjured up in her dream: then she is conscious of the presence of "only her mistress": gradually she comes to see why the woman has come and where she stands nursing and soothing the baby. "While Varka stands looking at her and waiting till she has done" her mind seems only passively registering impressions. Fear of "the stout broad-shouldered woman" has dispelled all sleepiness, her look is vacant, but this vacant look registers only willing suspension of sleepiness.

(ii) The perceptions are often duller when her consciousness is drowsier. When the mistress tells her to "leave the baby" and give him to her, her "voice" seems only "familiar": next time when it repeats the order ("Give me the baby"), to

Varka it is only "the same voice": she is too sleepy to distinguish it, recognize it, ascribe it; even when she hears it for the second time, there is a dull perception of its obvious feature only: 'harshness', 'anger'. The talking voice of the mistress is only the sound of a voice; it is all reverberation ("it makes a ringing in Varka's ears"). Although the voice is "loud", it is only a sound jarring into Varka's sleepy consciousness. Her mind is registering simply a sensation. The sensation is not perception as yet. Varka is too sleepy to exercise her faculty of interpretation: she is not aware of what the woman has been talking about.

(iii) Her drowsier consciousness too is at times overwhelmed by her irresistibly overpowering sleepiness: at such moments her perception recedes into mere sensation. When "seeing the windows getting dark" she smiles, her smile is unconscious. Her consciousness at this moment is so confoundedly sleepy that she cannot attribute the intensity of her present feeling to her pleasing vision of a welcome occasion indicated by "the windows getting dark"—it is much too sleepy even to feel curious about the reason "why" she "smiles". The Child on a similar occasion shakes "all over with excited joy"; she is well aware of the reason of her impulsive, emotional response: "when she thought of the nearness of bedtime she shook all over with excited joy". The Child is not only alertly wakeful: she is also impulsively responsive. Varka's sleepiness is so overwhelming that the link between what induces the "smile" and the "smile" itself is vaguely obscured: the child's wakeful consciousness registers it crudely. Chekhov achieves obliquely what Miss Mansfield states explicitly.

(b) Intermittent disturbance of sleepiness

The pattern formed through dramatization of intermittent peremptory orders is also bodily borrowed. This borrowed pattern is a major compositional element. Because of padding in this pattern the dramatization of what keeps disturbing the character's sleepiness seems to have become sentimentally melodramatic. Let us take for example a segment of the pattern meant to register the sleep-shattering intermittence of peremptory orders: "'Salad, Salad': cries the Frau's voice from the house". The segment is typical in the sense that the pattern is formed by the recurrence of orders given mostly by this Frau alone: the man's orders are heard only on two occasions, once when he has "got to be off", and again, when he means he will thank her to "keep that baby quiet".

In Chekhov's short-story the pattern emerges as a neat rhythmical sequence artistic enough to reflect the coldly impersonal nature of what precludes fulfilment of the simple biological need: there is a rhythmical alternation of orders from the shoemaker and the woman, and the specific pattern thus formed, significantly, terminates in a quick succession of unidentified orders. The rhythmical alternation of commands helps to accentuate the more tragic effect of what we may call bilateral buffetings intermittently condemning her to the inescapably permanent static situation. Equal emphasis on the order of each of the two tormentors saves the orders from appearing lop-sided. Termination of the pattern in a rapid succession of unidentified orders reinforces the sense of their impersonal nature: the effect achieved is also that of a booming sinister echo: this booming echo of the orders thundered in quick succession is perhaps meant to linger as a permanent curse upon her sleepiness.

Miss Mansfield has bodily borrowed this swift succession of unidentified orders too, but the centralized impact of it is weakened by the immediate subsequence of distinctly identified orders, that is, by the unnecessary persistence of the pattern even beyond the climactic point in the narrative. Padding in the pattern in Miss Mansfield's short-story results from her choice of a volley of orders every time. The volley discharged by the taskmistress exacts simultaneity of domestic chores and thus keeps the poor soul transfixed in the same situation. But this way of defining the stasis in Child's life loses its artistic effectiveness because the transfixing volley seems monotonously repetitive within the restricted scope of the literary form chosen.

(B) II TOUCHES: ORIGINAL

Miss Mansfield seeks to achieve a more pathetic effect in her own re-characterization of the hapless Russian girl. But she has tried to improve upon what, perhaps, cannot be improved upon. She employs touches to deepen the tragic dimensions of a character to unfold other possible piteous aspects of a situation that only disintegrate a composite effect. She seems to have striven for a more pathetic effect: in her characterization of the Child she has made one of her main characters refer to her as a simpleton, a "half silly" Child. But the Child seems both silly and sane. Thus the Child is not so tragic as she is pathetic. Chekhov's Varka is sensible, normal, realistic: only she is miserably sleepy. It is only in her dreams that she sees fantastic images: she saw things as they were in the past when she lived in "a dark stuffy hut" where Pelageya had to look for "the broken pot with the matches"; where she could only hear her father, Yefin Stepanov, "moaning and rolling on the floor from pain"; where the doctor could not "be seen in the darkness"; where mother had to rush out to get "a bit of candle". She is the more tragic because she has seen things as they have been, and because she sees them as they are.

The Child is made to suffer from violent cruelties at the hands of the task-mistress: she is beaten unpitifully, several times on the day. She is tortured physically and mentally, and the torture is coldly, harshly callous. Chekhov's Varka is beaten only once in "lashing" succession and the mere appearance of the task-mistress or the shoemaker is enough to strike terror into her heart. Miss Mansfield's treatment of this aspect of the Child's tragedy is exaggerated: it is characterized by maudlin sentimentality. Chekhov's treatment of this same aspect is stiffly, austerely restrained; it is in a low key.

Miss Mansfield adds another original touch: the Child is loaded with an additional burden ("there is another coming"). This makes the reader concede a surmise that the woman may continue to beget children even after she has given birth to the one she is pregnant with. This original touch is no doubt an expedient one, but Miss Mansfield's failure to resist the temptation of indulgence in elaboration of this original touch proves detrimental to the intended effect of her re-characterization of the Russian girl. Chekhov's single baby is enough. The narrative scope of the crisis calls for intense concentration on one single situation with one single baby as the "force" that "prevents" the girl from "living". Chekhov achieves with one baby what Miss Mansfield fails to achieve with the one baby and the "coming" baby.

The model on which Miss Mansfield patterned her narrative composition was a paragon of the genre: it was the intrinsic integrity of the original as a real modern short short-story that facilitated the composition of her own narrative piece within limits defined by the distinctive elements of the specific form.

But the composition was an obvious plagiarism, and so whatever success she seems to have achieved in recovering the 'gift' was by no means creditable.

Of course, her impulse to resort to plagiarism even after an achievement which had come unaided may be put down to her diffidence about conceiving an original plot. But it may also be construed as her eagerness to perform an exercise by way of mastering the technique she had achieved earlier only by a fluke.

Even as a plagiarism the composition of her own narrative piece was not without its positive gains. It enabled her to learn various ways and means of intensifying pathos inherent in a tragically static situation. This is evident from her introduction of some original touches and effects. It also afforded her an opportunity to learn to dramatize a culminant moment that is tense from the start, and thus helped her to study the Chekhovian art of 'dramatic effect' which accrues from intense concentration on the indeterminate middle. The most substantial gain was her realization of aesthetic affinity with Chekhov as an author writing as she herself longed to write.

But her acquaintance with Chekhov's technique of story-telling was only superficial; it was not yet comprehendingly and judiciously critical: she still lacked understanding of the way the effect of minimum had been maximized in Chekhov's short-story. The very sense of tenseness meant to characterize the situation in the Child's life was dissipated by diffusion of interest. The critical sense of adjustment between the scope of the theme and the range of imaginative concentration was not yet fully developed. The result was inevitable: dramatization of the static situation in her own short-story degenerated into tear-jerking maudlin melodrama; her re-employment of the devices and the effects used by Chekhov only exaggerated the pathos; even with her introduction of some original touches and effects she failed to create an equally tense 'atmosphere' on the page. She was thus still only a young learner of 'the art of story-telling'. Her immaturity was largely due to her lack of capacity for 'personal detachment' which controls imaginative empathy.

Miss Mansfield had yet to achieve her guru's sober and rigorous austerity as a short-story writer.

NOTES AND REFERENCES

1. "The child is 'indubitably Katherine Mansfield in the summer of 1909—the

Katherine wearied with pain and crying in vain for rest. The peasant household is ... merely a symbol of her experience of life'."—Ronald Sutherland, "Katherine Mansfield: Plagiarist, Disciple, or Ardent Admirer?", Critique, Spring—Summer, 1962.

2. Antony Alpers, *Katherine Mansfield*, p. 108.
3. Cf. "The Child, illegitimate and a kind of indentured servant, conjures up a vision of an empty 'little white road with tall black trees on either side', symbols of the release and protection which she desires, and for which Katherine Mansfield herself was yearning". Ronald Sutherland, *op. cit.*, p. 67.
4. Cf. "The Child, in contrast to Varka, has subconscious desires for freedom and protection, symbolized by the illusional 'little white road'. In her mind, killing the baby was a positive action to realize her desires, to reach the dream road." *Ibid.*, p. 68.
5. Cf. "Miss Mansfield's story, like almost all her stories, focuses on one particular time, Chekhov's story explores the forces which have created the situation of the tale as is the case with almost all of his psychological studies". *Ibid.*
6. Saralyn Daly, *Katherine Mansfield,* p. 127 n. 11.
7. Cf. "There are differences.... The most important ... is one which shows the increasing tendency of the more modern writer toward concentration of time, scene, and interest. The Russian story begins earlier on the night before the crisis. The interval is occupied by the Child's half-waking dreams of her early life, by means of which Chekhov gives us rather a complete picture of her past. In the story of Katherine Mansfield we are kept more strictly to the present scene, the Child's past being suggested only by a few words of the mistress which she overhears".—Elisabeth Schneider, "Katherine Mansfield and Chekhov", Modern Language Notes, June, 1935, p. 396.
8. Saralyn Daly, *op. cit.*, p. 29.
9. *Ibid.*
10. *Ibid.*

3. Recognition of Form

The very first venture, *Germans at Meat* (a piece immediately subsequent to the plagiarism), seems to have registered Miss Mansfield's dawning realization that henceforth she would have to 'work' on her own. Perhaps the plagiarism proved to be a challenge to her capacity for original creation. Quite naturally during the present phase of composition of short-stories solely as contributions to three little magazines she seems to have endeavoured to recognize the real modern form of the shorter prose fiction. The endeavour started as a search for the story element, the essential stuff the short-story is made of: her exquisite sensibility was wont to perceive it as a lyrical truth illusively inherent in the most superficial aspects of life. This search for the story element persisted throughout this phase. *Germans at Meat* shows that she was not yet critically familiar with the precise nature of the content that finds its consummation only in the form of the short-story: absence of story element in or vacuous pointlessness of this original piece was quite characteristic of the initial stage of the search.

In this short piece perhaps she has mistaken the very occasion of the encounter with the German pensioners for the moment of a revelation. This shows that she has only found the form: she has come to see that it is a moment of some revelation that is central to the subject-matter of a short-story as a specific literary genre. That she has not yet 'recognized' the form is evident from the way she has dramatized the occasion of the encounter: what she means to be exposed is very crudely dramatized through prejudicial registration of the pensioners' speeches and gestures. The name of one of the German characters, "Herr Rat", seems to have been 'chosen with delight';[1] and the character is made to ask obviously preposterous questions ("what do you warm the teapot for?... One does not eat the teapot, I suppose?"). All this indicates the attitude of the short-story writer: her sole purpose seems to have been satirical caricature of the German people: she makes them voice such utterances as reveal not only their haughty jingoism but also their "misinformed chauvinism': their palaver gives them out to be a people[2] who live only to eat and eat only to produce kids after kids. The writer wants us to see that informality of their luncheon-room gossip at times borders on outrageous indecency and offensive obscenity; the concomitant gestures that she records also seem to have been spitefully selected, that is, with a view to making the people seem a race of unsanitarily nasty table manners ("picking her teeth with a hair-pin as she spoke", "he wiped his neck and face with his dinner napkin and carefully cleaned his ears").

If this caricature had been objectively presented, the author would have succeeded in providing her narrator with 'a subtle victory'.[3] But the narrator's intermittent comments persistently neutralize the potentiality of the typical details as self-revealing features of German demeanour; the very moral standard by which the art functions becomes explicit owing to inclusion of these occasional comments. The whole narrative structure creaks because of surprising *non sequiturs* occasioned by the narrator's tendency to make only spiteful selection of vulgar details.

Miss Mansfield is still innocently ignorant of the absolute indispensability of the elements that combine to specify a written composition as a short-story: a sense of a turning-point, a sense of progression, a concentrated vision, a functional point of view, and an objective treatment.

In her next narrative composition, *Baron*, Miss Mansfield seems to have succeeded to some extent in recognizing the form. Even this success is due to her use of a joke as a story. A joke has a plot, a story element, a beginning, a middle, and an end; the pattern is anecdotal; the narrative has a point, and all that is there tends towards this point: all the technical ingredients of the composition are functional; the point is made and the joke-teller stops short. The very efficacy of the point depends upon objectivity of treatment. The narration naturally begins *in medias res*. Thus there is dramatization of the comic element in intent concentration. Composition of *Germans at Meat* as a pointless narrative has failed to help the author to recognize the form; but the writing of *Baron* as a joke has been a help to a great extent. The moment of revelation is dramatized in concentration. The revelation is made to the narrator herself: there is a sense of change implicit in the participant-narrator's private discovery of the reality behind appearance. The participant-narrator is inextricably involved in the drama. *Baron* thus shows that Miss Mansfield has begun to recognize the form. But this recognition of the form is still vague: dramatization of the story element is not suspenseful: the reality behind appearance has already been revealed to the participant-narrator ("I noticed the Baron took three lumps of sugar, putting two in his cup and wrapping up the third in a corner of his pocket handkerchief"): her mid-story comments also substantiate this impression ("Myself, I felt disappointed that there was not a salute of twenty-five guns"). The final revelation is made inartistically: the Baron himself is made to 'volunteer' the 'information'. The point is made, but the narrator is allowed to go on.

The companion piece, *Sister of Baroness*, does, however, evince a definite improvement. The two pieces are really parallel in 'both theme and amateurish technique'.[4] The Germans' romantic folly of trusting to first impressions is exposed in both the short-stories, and in spite of the difference between the ways in which their folly is exposed, the theme emergent from the verbal build-up designed for either of the two satirical pieces remains the same: the sentimental folly of romantic glorification. In the earlier short-story (*Baron*), it is 'only the narrator that learns of the clay feet'; in the later (*Sister of the Baroness*), 'all are disabused'.[5] But neither method helps to specify the theme.

Perhaps the only reason why the method of exposure in the later short-story is more successful is discernible in its effect as a process of dramatic revelation: in the earlier short-story it is the Baron himself who is made to reveal the fact ("But he himself volunteered some information"): a revealing gesture performed by the Baron himself or an informative utterance voiced by one of the pensioners would have been a more effective means of exposing the 'clay feet'.

But "Sic transit gloria German mundi" is as 'schoolgirlish'[6] as "tableau grandissimo" is in the other short-story. With this 'anti-climactic summary statement'[7] the narrator only goes further and fares worse: the intended impact of the ironic ending which this 'anti-climactic summary statement' follows has already been neutralized by 'excessive comment and exaggeration'[8] in the earlier short-story and by extravagant 'caricature' and 'over-asserted ... contempt for German aristocracy and romanticism'[9] in the companion piece.

Modelled on the Chekhovian joke pattern these surprise-ending short-stories are no doubt good-humouredly amusing. But the way 'excessive comments and exaggeration ... dissipate what could have been clever intimations'[10] makes one feel they are careless and clumsy performances of an amateurish magician in words who lets the cat out of the bag again and again. The story element in either of the companion pieces has the potentiality of a real comedy. But the clumsy treatment spoils the comic stuff. The over-all impression is that of a story-teller who is still learning the art of story-telling.

Registration of 'a minute development of awareness'[11] on the part of the narrator in the subsequent narrative composition entitled *Luft Bad* does evince the development of the author's critical awareness of what really governs the form of a short-story; but the way she handles the sequence of tense in her registration of what is meant to be the recollection of a past experience is a bungle glaring enough to show that her conception of this governing factor is not yet clear to her. The intended effect of the ending is neutralized by the impression that the tense of the opening sentence creates: the reader may quite reasonably accept the opening statement too as the articulation of the narrator's final realization.

The turning point as the pivotal point of the short-story seems vaguely conceived or disconcertingly rendered. Even the later recognition of "the umbrellas" as "the saving grace of Luft Bad" involves a realization that is much too casual to have emotional depth; the result is, the story element seems insignificantly trivial.

Perhaps the only redeeming feature of the narrative composition is the unbroken consistency of the narrator's point of view. But consistency of a first-person narrator's point of view is rarely creditable.

Potentiality of a substantial story element which the critical reader unmistakably discovers in the complex 'psychology' of the character in the subsequent short-story, *At Lehmann*, is choked by the clumsiness of the technique. The ending as it stands on the page yields a psychological truth which illustrates only a moral 'protest' against what haunted the author throughout her life as a traumatic experience:

> In the silence the thin wailing of a baby.
> 'Achk' shrieked Sabina, rushing from the room.

An ending dramatizing an unreconciled emotional complex compounded of the character's horror of childbirth, her contempt for overwhelming maleness, and her sensual passion for the young man, would have been better: the ending that has been made to climax this story about the character's sexual awakening is not enriched by a sense of unresolved tension. The ending would have been richly suggestive if the hanging participle in the last sentence had been cast, for example, in this way: 'Achk' shrieked Sabina, wincing secretly, or in words to that effect. The resultant ambiguity would have helped to attain the richer effect of an unresolved emotional conflict as it would also have admitted of a sense of feminine masochistic pleasure: the reader impelled to disentangle this subtle ambiguity would have relished the wholesome aesthetic pleasure of a discovery of cross-cancelling implications. In the version we have ventured to offer, the character seems wincing not only at her horrifying complex perception of the sound from the "ugly-ugly room upstairs"; we imagine her wincing masochistically too in the massive muscle-corded mashing arms of the he-man. Obscured with this ambiguity, the complex image of the character, appropriately defined by her own inconclusively vague stutter, "I-I-", would have retained its intricate nature.

The character conceived is complex enough. She is an innocently pubescent girl: she is still so ignorant of the process of conception and birth that she believes Hans when he explains that his "filthy nails" were stained from birth because his mother had always got 'so inky doing the account. But her 'psychology' as a character is complex. This complexity of her 'psychology' is at once naturalized and enriched by the conflicting features of her experience of sexual awakening. She longs to ask questions, yet, being ashamed of her ignorance, keeps silent, trying to puzzle it out for herself ("But what has the man got to do with it?"); she also experiences "a curious thrill deep in her body" and "blushes looking across the empty tables" when the young man asks her what she is smiling at (she 'knows perfectly well' what he is hiding from her when he shows her "a coloured sketch of a naked girl"). Again, she dreads "getting varicose veins like Anna" and detests the Frau's room upstairs as an "ugly room" and is determined she "wouldn't be the Frau for one hundred marks.... To look like that", but, "half dreaming", she also imagines herself heaving up in her chair as she has seen the Frau doing upstairs. She is a sympathetically resentful virgin too: the Frau sighs out a broken utterance, "'I' m nothing. I don't matter'", and the protagonist's hand shakes while wiping the rim of the glass: she hates to hear Herr Lehmann shout for "two small beers" when his wife is in a bad way; at the same time, she is a clandestinely amorous damsel who loves to remember the young man's instructions to see that her hair does not " 'lose all its curves' "; she wishes "there was a great big looking-glass in this room". She is only self-deceptively jocular when she describes this young man in her life, "tapping her head" (" 'Got such a funny man. I think he's a little gone here' ").

The emotional fluctuations quickened, especially towards the climactic moment of the narrative, illuminate the whole complex image of the character. But the potentiality of such a rich story element intrinsic in the complexity of the character's 'psychology' is not imaginatively explored. Even the residue of it is spoiled by some lapses. There is lack of intent concentration. The impression is substantiated by shifts of point of view and influx of much irrelevance. Miss Mansfield has resorted to symbolization of passionate amour through the image of the "fire". She has also delayed the denouement for the sake of suspense. Such aspects of the composition do evince concentration of the imaginative vision. But the over-all impression is that of lack of control.

The story element inherent in the complex 'psychology' of the next character that Miss Mansfield created in her narrative piece, *Frau Brechenmacher Attends a Wedding*, has potentialities rich enough to yield a poignant short-story. Still the narrative composition as it stands finished seems so ruggedly controlled that all potentialities are dissipated.

The conclusion that the character is made to generalize from her experiences ("Always the same.... all over the world the same") only weakens the intended pathetic effect of the short-story. The viewpoint character is made to appropriate the omniscient narrator's complementary summation. The earlier dramatization of the obscurely private individual experience[12] is suggestive enough to yield the truth-vision that the character's summation explicitly states.

The crisis which Miss Mansfield has sought to render aesthetically is perhaps the character's sad realization of her own pathetic predicament as a wife; the character has remained enslaved in hopeless "stupid" bondage to a grossly wilful husband, a type of the notoriously inconsiderate aggressive sexual partner in married life. The character's realization involves only a rediscovery of what she has already discovered, and it is perhaps this rediscovery that evinces the minute development of awareness on the part of the character.

What substantiates this evidence of 'minute development' and also deepens the pathos inherent in the static situation is the brief spell of a wistful dream: the character only dreams of freedom from the present bondage when she desiderates her pre-marriage innocent girlhood unravished by the inconsiderately wilful sexual aggressiveness of the male.

The first section of the short-story, which dramatizes the character's preparation for the wedding party, shows failure of the artist to resist the temptation to present the expository situation material as an aid to understanding of the background. This failure to subdue a temptation is understandably natural to the young writer trying her hand at writing short-stories. A developed critical sense of a proper and expediently mutual correlation between the scope of the theme and the range of concentration is not to be expected of a literary tyro just lured into print.

Shifts of viewpoint and irrelevance of much of dialogue even in the scene central to the drama also account for the dissipation of potentialities intrinsic in the story element.

This short-story too misfires as a 'protest' because it fails as a work of art: the emotion of indignation is not recollected in tranquillity.

Frau Fisher, even as a humorous or satirical character-sketch, seems to have nothing to reveal as a comic truth about human nature. No change is perceptible either in the character that is portrayed or in the narrator that portrays. The reader finds no crisis involved in the situation dramatized. Perhaps the only meaning that the reader is able to extricate from the whole verbal build-up is the 'impossibility of German-English rapport'; this impossibility is stressed by the blatant vulgarity of the German people, which a racially phlegmatic Briton finds outlandishly quizzical. But this meaning does not seem to involve the sense of a crisis. The story element itself is nil: when this primary unifying element is absent from what is meant to be read as a short-story, the 'technical unity'[13] that seems to have been 'effected' is either artificial or superficial. How 'technical unity' of the whole narrative piece is 'effected' simply 'by the word squeeze' in the last sentence, the critical reader fails to understand; he naturally broods over the question after what he has reason to believe has been a dull experience of reading: he has found an irrelevantly discursive character portrayal much too desultory to have unity: it is only in the last section of the narrative that the reader finds evidence of the "consistent failure" of the 'squeezing' promised by Frau Fisher':[14] but even this last section seems to him to be only pointlessly self-consistent, apart from seeming oddly incongruous with the preceding sections which he has already discovered to be erratically rambling.

Even the innovation exemplified by registration of the interruption (caused by excerpts from "Miracles of Lourdes") is grossly inexpedient: Flaubert was probably the first to make this innovation in *Madame Bovary*:[15] in the hands of the father of modern fiction, it revolutionized the method of fictional presentation of meaningful contrast; in the hands of the learner of the art of fiction it remains just a bungle: it only attracts; it serves no purpose.

The author seems to be acquiring, however, the skill of narration in intense concentration-intent enough to enfold temporal succession summarily ("Followed a description in the hall") imaginative enough to register the expressive concomitant gestures ("'I like empty beds', I protested sleepily, thumping the pillow"), and also persistent enough to preserve consistency of a single point of view.

.But the art of implication has yet to be mastered: effectiveness of satire attained through objective registration of the Frau's obviously risque observations is weakened by the narrator's own unnecessarily explanatory comments.

Still, Miss Manfield's 'gift' for recognition of a culminant moment as the real subject suited to the form of the short-story produced another marvel, *Birthday*. The technique of the 'modern' short-story was achieved again, and this time too only by a fluke. We can see how tenseness of the moment captured is effectively registered through intense imaginative concentration and how the style of the narrative is charged with involved meaningfulness in the process.

The dark image of the character is illuminated in the flash produced by what seems to be a cyclical fluctuation of emotions too swift to be distinguishably discernible. The image stands poetically enriched by the irony that lies in the moment when 'death and birth are rolled together':[16] probably, the death here is not simply the dreaded one; it is also the death of the stubborn self-centred 'monster' in the husband that the character has been—a substantial businessman anxiously and ambitiously yearning for an heir; and the birth here is not only the birth of a boy; it is also the birth of a new Mr. Binzer, chastened and sobered by the ordeal he has endured. At the same time, the death seems to be the death of the apprehensive, solicitous, loving husband, and the birth, the birth of the insensitively selfish hard-boiled businessman who has commercialized his relation with his wife; the "birthday" of a new master Binzer is the birthday of a new Mr. Binzer.

The image of this new Mr. Binzer is meant to linger in the reader's memory as a shimmering image of a confoundedly complex character. What he 'wants to shout out before the doctor speaks' ("my beloved wife has passed away") is significantly, a calculatedly inarticulate cry of the dismally apprehensive, poignantly unhopeful husband. The silent cry is a mute prayer. His piteous attempt to prepare himself for the shock which he fatalistically feels to be imminent ("before the doctor spoke") betokens only the ineffable tenderness deep in his heart. The effect is reinforced by the starkly denotative yet emotionally charged implications of the two opening words intoning his startled yet heartfelt ejaculation: the possessive adjective "my" evanescently flashes his image as a love-selfish husband with his passionately possessive passion for his petite partner; the adjectival noun, "beloved", as a term of endearment spontaneously though inarticulately intoned for the first and last time during the intense experience of the crisis, unmistakably echoes the deep-souled feeling of tenderness and amour towards his wife.

But this nervously apprehensive husband is also "exultant" when he learns his wife has not only survived the ordeal but also "hooked a boy"; he seems "exultant" because the baby "she's hooked this time" is "a son who is going to be partner in the firm", a son sanguinely expected after the two girls, as the lineal heir he has been "working up the business for". The "glow" that spreads all over him seems to radiate from the "stubborn self-centredness"; it is perhaps this egotism which makes him accentuate the pronoun for himself ("me") as he feels relieved of his own "suffering"—of his own agony to which he has hitherto been subjected by his wife's terrifying "wails" or her accusations cumulatively reflected in her secret, cruel smile.

What he again concerns himself with is the thought of his own "suffering". It has been occasioned by his own guilt complex which has driven him to self-deception, made him roast in mockery and fly into a rage, and generated unendurable nervous tension: he has endeavoured in vain to play-act a 'man without temperament' selfishly aware again of his own "suffering" or even 'exultantly' conscious of relaxation of the strain he feels he has been subjected to. The 'stubborn self-centred' monster in him is still articulate: the husband who has always concerned himself about his own health, his own comforts, his own tastes, his own dreams, and his own stature, asserts himself again.

'His wife's suffering has presented itself as a form of cruelty to him'.[17] His awareness of her concern for his health has only intensified his susceptibility to this cruelty; it has, secretly and cruelly, made him feel mortified at his lust for an "heir"; this lust has only been fomenting his restlessness since his marriage to this thin slip of a petite wife who has 'all along' been "delicate", it has blinded him to the frailty of her constitution and driven him to frenzy of experiment with it merely as a means to an end, or by way of a gamble for a big gain: he has produced only girls; but all along he has been dreaming of a son ("a man needed a son"). Her cruelty to him seems to have mocked his own cruelty to her; her cruelty has reduced his own cruelty to a mockery of cruelty. This 'inversion of cruelty' involves 'collision or conflation of categories of experience', occasioned as it is by the protagonist's 'stubborn human self-centredness'. Perception of this 'collision or conflation' is heightened by the simultaneous vision of the irony intrinsic in the ambiguity of the moment when death and birth are rolled into one.

The character has awakened on this fateful morning to an intense emotional crisis in his life. Aesthetically rendered in concentration, this crisis reveals him as a piteously complex character at once tenderly 'human' and 'stubbornly self-centred'. What exacts intent concentration as the only requisite means of exploring the nature of the experience adequately is perhaps the severe tension between this tender humanness and stubborn self-centredness.

This tension is transmitted in all its immediacy through an aesthetic rendering which is ingeniously objective: it covers a whole gamut of the manifestations of the character's emotional complex. We note the reflections of his moods in the setting, his morbid susceptibility to impressions of sights and sounds, his subconscious or unconscious gestures, his wordless, vague expressions of feeling, his voiced articulate utterances.

But this rendering is never inclusive of the registration of what the character in his self-deception keeps from acknowledging; the character does experience an excruciating agony of guilt, but he fails to moderate stubbornness of his self-centredness: he never acknowledges his own cruelty to his wife: this cruelty has been lecherous and reckless, complacent and ignorant.

Even his calculatedly inaudible inarticulate utterances seem to originate from an emotional flux only eddying within a range interiorised by 'stubborn self-centredness'. "We can see that the character tends to shy away from sincere confession. But the specific character the artist has conceived is meant to reveal himself through self-deception and not through confession. Characterization of the protagonist as a self-deceiving character is the essential part of the technique that is used here as a means of discovering the specific psychological truth-vision.

The narrative is made to register only the effect of the cause, the culmination of the experiences, the wrought-up mood in the present; there is no narrator to present the situation material; and the story element, created as it is by the character's self-deceptively interiorized consciousness itself, admits of no lapses in consistency of point of view. But Miss Mansfield is not yet mature enough to sustain the tension that wearies the character she has conceived.

The wrought-up mood of the character at this tense moment of a crisis in his life is a confounded emotional complex. Since its manifestations are perceptible only as the effect of some cause and never as expressions of the character's conscience, we feel we can predicate upon assumptions only. As we share his vision of the immediate physical world around him, watch his gestures and expressions, or hear his voiced or unvoiced articulation, we feel he is inordinately uneasy. The emotional complex manifests itself through his subjective vision of the wind which seems to him to be shouting in mockery: the wind only blares out the doctor's mocking words: 'said she knew you were worrying' ... 'managed to peck a bit, I see, oh?'. The wind shakes the window sashes: the remark jars into his self-consciousness. He is perturbed deeply; he is touched to the quick; what is admittedly vulnerable stands exposed: his secret attitude to his wife has been perceived, recognized, defined: while his wife is solicitous, he himself can insouciantly concern himself with his own breakfast ('managed to peck'). When later the wind suddenly stops howling, he stands frozen with a cold fear, dazed at the thought of the disaster that Anna's death during delivery would mean; and here also we are aware of the emergence of the selfishly insensitive monster in him: if she dies, the child, his heir, may die, too; moreover, he will be losing the very means to the end he has been "working up the business for".

The four contributions that followed registered only a lapse in the development of Miss Mansfield's mind and art: they were *Modern Soul*, *Journey to Bruges*, *Truthful Adventure*, and *Advanced Lady*. They all turned out to be sketches; Miss Mansfield passed them off as short-stories. She again seems, expecially in the last three of them, to be looking for a definite story element. Again the search is understandably desperate and inevitably fruitless. The reader approves of a definite improvement in the first sketch: it is perceptible in the comparative restraint, which the author shows in her rendering of the comic situation. But the reader is baffled by the absence of any quality that may remind him of what she has achieved earlier, although only by a fluke.

But her 'gift' for exploitation of a culminant moment could still produce a story with a sense of drama that is climactic from the start and in a style that is charged with involved meaningfulness.The short-story produced was *Swing of Pendulum* with a theme that seems to be only a variation on the truth-vision already explored: intense 'will to live'.

The concluding passage of the short-story registers the last "swing of feeling ... back from the aggressive attentions of the stranger to Casimir";[18] this last 'swing of feeling' is only a tragic termination of the crisis which all her choice from the realm of the possible has been; the crisis has been a tense emotional situation characterized by tragic intensity of 'will to live' life as a sunlit life of whole togetherness and individual freedom. Thus the moment of 'choice' which has been manifest as a situation created through the character's intense will to live life in whole togetherness, is charged with tenseness. The tenseness of the moment of 'choice' as the moment of the crisis is due to the complexity of 'psychology' natural to the cyclic process of emotional fluctuations. The process reaches only an ironical climax as it terminates cyclically. The last passage captures this climax.

What decides Viola to return to Casimir is a confident hope ("we are bound to win") but this hope is blighted by uncertainty. The lover she counts upon is only 'apparently faithful'; he is as miserably 'poverty-stricken' as she herself is; the message he has sent reveals only a state of uncertainty and depression; her own resolve to return to her lover exemplifies only her piteous transfixation in a state of uncertainty: she only 'sees herself running towards him'; even her decisive voice is not without a faint wistful tone; the tone sounds doubtful, faltering, feeble: 'Do you love me still?'. Uncertainty persists also because the landlady's next conclusively decisive knock at the door is inescapably imminent ('It's cash—or out you go before twelve o'clock tomorrow').

The experience she has had with the 'sensual stranger' just now has of course been a "horrible" one; but what is there to guarantee that her experiences in a future with an 'apparently faithful' and equally 'poverty-stricken' lover are not going to be as much or even much more "horrible"? Does the lover fit in with her conception of a partner? Even if she feels sure they are "bound to win", will the "savage" female's craving for an indulgent life of "passion and adventure", a carefree life of sweet doing-nothing, a blithe life of congenial togetherness and also individual freedom, be wholly appeased? Uncertainty clouds what she only impulsively feels will be a sunlit life. This note of tragic optimism on which Viola's story ends reverberates in the reader's mind as a whole definition of all her choice from the realm of the future; the character throughout the short-story seems arrested, transfixed, and also pulsating with the intensity of 'will to live' manifest as 'swing of feeling'. The image defined by swings of feeling paralleling other swings on the deeper psychic levels, the subconscious and the unconscious, is reflected in the dimensions created by the parallelism. Here it may help to imagine the total design as a concentric one: the outermost vague circumference with its all-inclusive range may seem to represent uncertainty; the fringe of the concentric circle may be said to have been formed by the cyclical fluctuations; the inner circles may have been described by the swings on the deeper subconscious level ('Really, there's a fount of happiness in me, that is drying up, little by little, in this hateful existence. I'll be dead if this goes on-'); the centre, then, may be said to represent the unconscious where, because of intensification of concentration, a 'swing of feeling' is perceptible only in simultaneity of contrary feelings (will to live and will to die; irrepressible hate and suppressed passion; longing for togetherness and inclination to maintain the freedom of individual selfhood, etc.). These contrary feelings are simultaneously manifest especially at moments when she is "pretending" ("pretending not to see"), or when she does not "step outside" to "judge".

The tense moment of choice from the realm of the future is dramatized as her poise for immersion in Life. She stands poised, thrilled to the depths of her being by her experience of resuscitating approximation to Life ("people like that did one good—one felt 'made over' at the sight of them"). The Life she dreams of is a life in which one feels "made over—a life in which one has the experience of becoming a new self: it will be a life of freedom not only from her old self through resuscitating contact with a partner capable of 'living' his existence as an individual; it will be a life of freedom also of her own self in spite of her togetherness with such a partner; her dream of such a blithe life of congenial togetherness and also individual freedom defines the 'slant' of the poise dramatizing the tense moment of her choice from the realm of the future. Her longing for the experience of freedom of her individual self as the experience of true existence is manifest in her constantly intense self-consciousness or occasional self-assertion. The moment when she feels "made over" is that of a "fascinating interlude" in the general drama of pain that her life has been. Her experience of the tenseness of the moment is pleasant: tenseness of the moment is due to her poise for the thrill of an "adventure" into the realm of the possible and to her simultaneous inclination to desiderate the chance of "choice" missed ("'If I had that time over again ...' Was it possible that the strange man was still there?"). Intensity of her will to live is pitifully manifest in this experience.

It is a complex of such tense moments of choice from the realm of the posssible—all accumulated as a dramatic poignant moment of crisis in the character's life—that is rendered aesthetically in concentration. Restriction of the point of view to the psyche of the character involved in the crisis of choice is the natural immediate result of this intense concentration which tenseness of the moment of the crisis has called for. So occasional breaks in consistency of the point of view adversely affect the intensity of the experience embodied ("'what's she frowning for?' he asked. 'Is she worried about anything?'"). The total impressionistic effect of Viola's otherwise successful characterization is weakened by these lapses. Miss Mansfield does not seem to have mastered as yet the art of conveying the tragic essence of a viewpoint character without resorting to the other character's point of view as a means of revelation. However, even this single narrative viewpoint that is restricted to the psyche of the central character is comprehensive enough to accommodate a dense and varied narrative texture as required by the complexity of the character's emotional experience at the tense moment of choice.

The interior monologue is punctuated with recurrence of

transitions from indirect speech to direct speech. Thus it proves to be an expedient means of registering the 'swing of feeling' from one psychic level to another, from the subconscious to the conscious. The verbal design serves to reflect the continual process of intermittent exteriorization of self; the complex psychic process is quite natural to the tense moment of choice from the realm of the possible, the moment of intensity of will to live, to experience the thrill of being through recognition of assertion of individual selfhood: "At that moment, when he was not touching her, she quite enjoyed herself. She thrilled at her own angry voice". Feelings obscurely stirred up on the secret level of the unconscious are realistically and artistically concealed: sensitive and imaginative registration of tell-tale gestures and utterances provides an index of conflation of contrary feelings stirred up on both the psychic levels at the same time ("She burst out laughing, 'Oh, how dreadful I must look—one moment! She ran back to the wash-stand.... The door was still open.... She began to close the door slowly."). This helps to achieve the recurrent effects of tenseness that characterizes those moments of 'choice' which involve a secret tension between conscious and unconscious impulses.

The total texture of the narrative is enriched by that part of it which is all sensitive registration of the character's revealing utterances and gestures; this part of the narrative texture registers the darkly secret tension between the character's conscious and unconscious impulses. The point of view restricted—in the creative process of imaginative concentration—to the psyche of the tensely poised, sensitive character naturally covers a subjective vision or sensitized awareness of the surroundings: the objects in her surroundings reflect her unconscious recognition of her predicament; they are all coloured by her sentiment ("a jar of hyacinths ... exuding a sickly perfume from its plump petals; ... even rich buds unfolding ...").

The accumulated meaning emergent from this complex texture of the narrative is complemented by the ironical implication involved in the way the narrative is made to begin and end. What as a matter of fact helps to bring out the essential meaning is the ironical contrast in which the ending stands to the beginning: the last 'swing of feeling back to Casimir' is thus only an ironically tragic termination of the crisis of 'choice': all this crisis terminates in a state of uncertainty; this state of uncertainty is the only reality; all else is 'unreal'.

The story element that Miss Mansfield dramatizes, appropriately without a point-of-view character, in *Blaze* (a short-story included later in her collection IN A GERMAN PENSION) is spoiled because the concept of the meaning does not seem to be clear.

The concluding passage of the short-story leaves the reader deluged with multiplying questions. If 'the hint of the author's meaning rests in the ironies implicit in the somewhat deceived husband's final appraisal'[19] ('What a woman you are'), doesn't the husband seem to be only pitifully comic with his fatuous ignorance of a "blaze" that has flared up in his married life? Is he meant to be simply a poor innocent fool who doesn't know that his wife has 'lighted her bonfire' in his house? Wouldn't the reader's enjoyment of 'the ironies implicit in the final appraisal' have been a richer aesthetic experience if the man had been presented, say, as a husband moving about in society declaring his conviction that his wonderful woman loved him so much? Why does he 'wish Max would look Elsa up and tell her he won't be in till late' when he knows "she's not at all well"? Is he sexually frigid in his conjugal relation with his wife? Does he derive vicarious satisfaction in making his friend his proxy? Why can't he tear his gaze away from the sight of his friend "plunging through the heavy snow"__ the friend who "almost appears to be running through the heavy snow towards the town"? Doesn't he seem somewhat surprised at his wonderful woman's "boredom" even when he knows the man sent by him "has been here"? Does this husband seem also to take "pride" in the splendid animal health of his athletic wife naturally capable of wanton coquetry? What is that makes him burst out in that half-articulated rapturous exclamation ("what a woman you are")? If the husband simply glories in his wife's animal nature, doesn't he seem to be a pervert neurotic? Why does he seem to have preferred to be "nurse" to his dog Bobo who has "hurt her head" and is "not at all well"? Or is he a character who has assumed an attitude of self-dramatization? Is he innocent, or is he ironical, when he replies that "she hurt her head coming down the slide with Max"? Does he mean that Max has been recklessly heading for a disaster in his life when he warns him, "'you'll break your neck if you go careering down the slide that way'"? Or is it that he is really unconscious of the possible meaning of his words ("take some hot grog when you get in", etc.)? Again, which of the two characters, Victor and Max, is meant to be the central figure? What does Max mean by "us" when he asks Elsa "what's going to happen to us now?"? Does he mean only Victor and himself, or does he mean all the three, caught as they are all in the disastrous "bonfire" lighted by a woman of unpredictable nature, a woman who with all her plainness of an unblushing "confession" has also revealed her true nature to him as only an endless liar ("'you are always lying'")? And isn't this the reader's impression too? Doesn't he find her "lying" to her husband too when she tells him she "sent him home to change his clothes"?

If the structural composition of the narrative is designed with a view to stressing the irony of the husband's simple or even self-loved ignorance of the "bonfire" fed by Elsa's recklessly insouciant "just-let-things-occur" philosophy of life, what justification is there for the disproportionately lengthy dramatization of the scene in the savage woman's room? The purely objective omniscient point of view as the only point of view possible here has been judiciously chosen; how is it that there is a sudden shift to Elsa's point of view though even for a brief moment ("Someone came stamping up the stairs, paused at the door of her sitting-room, and knocked").

Rendering of the situation in imaginative concentration has naturally charged the details of the setting ("an immense tiger-skin under the piano—just the head protruding-sleepily savage") and the concomitant gestures of the characters ("Max half turned his back and stretched his feet out to the oven"; "The woman went over to the piano—stood there—striking one note", etc.) with effective expressiveness. But the ill-conceived story element, the structural disproportion, and irrelevant digression preclude integrated wholeness of the verbal build-up.

The Woman at Store, her contribution to a new 'little magazine', *Rhythm*, seems to have provided what was required by the editors—"an art that strikes deeper... drawing its inspiration from aversion", an art which "shall be real in its pity and its brutality".[20] Murry hailed it as "by far the best story that had been sent to Rhythm".[21] But one can see how the intrinsic beauty of the story element is marred by conscious contrivance.

Creation of the child character ("the kid") as the agent of revelation is only a cunning, artificial, convenient device: it shows through the design. What is revealed to the narrator is "the savage spirit of the country" embodied in a woman consumed by an emotional complex understandably manifest as wildly impulsive demeanour. The woman as revealed to the men from civilization is a natural product of the 'traditionless country' devoid of values established in the civilized world. She is a pathetically tragic character, forlornly lonesome yet recalcitrantly self-assertive, flightily impulsive and also shamelessly wanton, sadly forgetful as well as uncomfortably dazed. She embodies 'the savage spirit of the country'. Perhaps her full image is reflected in 'the trees that are still a moment, then quiver lightly and again are still'.

Of course the poetry of this embodiment is enriched by the sense of continuity of 'the savage spirit' as manifest in the child's inheritance of her mother's rash self-assertiveness and tart temper. But the poetry loses its beauty because of the crude artificiality of a convenient means of revealing the secret. With a view to facilitating the process of revelation, the child has been conceived as one who can draw; she is made not only to insist on the revelation but also to sleep in the room for the narrator, and even after their long enervating ride the two drunkards are made to keep awake so that the momentous discovery through her drawing may seem to have been unobtrusively brought forth.

Miss Mansfield's 'gift' produced another masterpiece, *How Pearl Button was Kidnapped*. Although it was produced again only by a fluke, it was probably the first technically flawless short-story that Miss Mansfield composed. 'Content' was 'achieved' probably for the first time.

The last scene depicts the tense climactic moment when the innocent child stands transfixed 'between two worlds': the "beautiful, lovely, lovely" Nature-oriented world "on the sand" where she has been one with Nature and her offsprings, wholesomely infused with her life spirit ("she got hot and wet"), and the mechanistic world far back on "the land" with its "House of Boxes" and "offices" and "nasty things"; the world where 'waves with white tops come leaping over the blue' and the world where all "live in a row"; the world where fruit juice "running all down her front ... doesn't matter" and the world where she is "taught" how "to sit in dusty places"; the world where it has been "quite silent except for the sea outside and the laughs of women" and the world where there are "like men in blue coats ... running with shouts and whistling". The image of the child precariously teetering here 'between two worlds' is a means of defining the tragic essence of the experience embodied. This image as a means of the definition is expediently complementary: the image pictured in the opening scene ("Pearl Button swung on the little gate in front of the House of Boxes") is also meant to represent a state of transition only in a different emotional context: the child seems poised for escape from "the House of Boxes" into the realm of freedom, the world of real life, the paradise of Innocence. The context contributes a suggestion: there is a friendly invitation from Nature herself; Nature beckons pearl as a company of "little" playful children would ("a sunshiny day with little winds playing hide-and seek in it"). The happy effect of the context is significantly neutralized by the grim sense of 'sudden' dissociation that the climactic scene is designed to convey ("Pearl slipped down on the sand and looked towards the land" ... "a crowd of little blue men to carry her back to the House of Boxes"); the grim sense is conveyed by the detail showing the child's separation from the woman she has just been "hugging" and "kissing", 'her little thin arms flung round the woman's neck'; the effect is accentuated by the abruptness of dramatic transition in the narrative sequence. Typographical isolation of the paragraph registering the climactic moment helps to heighten the effect. The tragic intensity of the character's emotional experience is not without immediacy. Her intense consciousness of the "blue colour" is an index of her dread of all that is sinister and evil about "the House of Boxes". Breathless repetition of paraphrased references to the bogies from "the House of Boxes" ("Little men in blue coats—little blue men ...—a crowd of little blue men ...") is naturalized by the staccato rhythm of the unvoiced thought. We seem to hear the very throb of the little pounding heart.—The ironical contrast that glares in this parallelism defines the irony involved in the crisis that the short-story is meant to render: the child escapes from a life of bondage only to return to the life of bondage.

Rendering of the specific crisis in concentration naturally involves consistently strict restriction of the point of view to the sensitiveness of the extremely innocent child: Pearl is characteristically susceptible to the charms of a "beautiful, lovely, lovely" Eden of Innocence as a microcosm hallowed by its close approximation to the world of Nature. Restriction of the point of view to the limited yet sensitive and curious awareness natural on the part of the extremely innocent child is necessitated, as a matter of fact, by what seems to have been intended to be an essential part of the total meaning—the intensity of the child's unconscious experience of freedom as an experience of existence. Freshness and purity of her sensations and perceptions makes us aware of the process of her liberation from the bondage of the static present: the child experiences the freedom that she has never experienced in "the House of Boxes"; she comes to know what she has never known: every time she comes to see and hear and touch what she has never experienced she seems liberated from some bondage. Her experience of this liberation is her experience of real existence. Experience of liberation as experience of existence itself seems intense only because sensations and perceptions are presented as fresh and pure experiences, and the sensations and perceptions seem fresh and pure only because the point-of-view character has been portrayed as an extremely innocent child.

The child is "kidnapped" to her own world—a world where she can be herself, liberated from the bondage of that static present which is continuous with the past; a world in which every moment is alive with the thrill of an exciting adventure into the realm of the new and the unfamiliar; a world peopled with angels of inviolable innocence living in constant and close contact with Nature that is eternal Innocence incarnate.

The world is a Heaven of freedom; it is a paradise of naturalness and integrity of being which accrues from freedom; it is a Home of Innocence where all experience is innocent as a complex of fresh and pure sensations and perceptions. The inhabitants of this inviolably sacrosanct isolated Eden of Innocence, Freedom, or real existence are naturally healthy and happy, friendly and helpful, kind and loving. What they speak sounds "funny", and the place they live in looks "funny", too; but they are not unfriendly strangers; the sea also looks sinister, but very soon its 'warmth' is palpable: in the child's supped hand it 'stops being blue' and menacingly sinister; it looks accessibly and intimately familiar, pleasantly homely and congenially companionable. Images of the inhabitants as animals seem to have been meant to represent them as "placid and self-contained" creatures that "do not lie awake in the night and weep for their sins".[22] The world is a dreamland. Its inhabitants are appropriately anonymous.

Realistic portrayal of the protagonist as a perfectly innocent child helps to naturalize the total effect of this parable of Innocence.[23]

That this parable of Innocence was only a precocious achievement is proved by the unmistakably perceptible inherence of technical flaws in the build-up of the subsequent contributions, *New Dresses* and *Little Girl*, both of which exemplify only underdone melodrama. The very meaning of the first short-story is devoid of the requisite sense of a crisis. The 'multi-personal point of view' which may be said to have been employed with a view to obscuring the pathos proves futile because there is no story element. The time scheme unnecessarily covers two or three days: dramatization of the situation could have been restricted to a single typical episode. The clumsy handling of the technique exposes the immaturity of the author's mind and art. This immaturity of Miss Mansfield's creative talent is perceptible also in the way she composes the ending of the other short-story, *Little Girl*. Let us re-arrange the syntactical units that compose the concluding portion of the short-story:

> She stirred suddenly, and sighed, and snuggled closer.
> 'What's the matter?' asked father. 'Another dream?' ...
> The dark did not matter. She lay still.

The passage is just an example of the way the original syntactical build-up could have been improved upon: repetition of an earlier phrase with its adverb inflected in the comparative degree (snuggled closer), omission of the little girl's words ("'oh, ... my head's on your heart. I can hear it going. What a big heart you've got, father dear.'"), and transposition of the two earlier narrative statements with a few dots preceding them ("... The dark did not matter. She lay still.") might have economically and obliquely evoked the desired effect of 'a change in feeling in the view-point charcter'.[24] The explicit articulation of the girl's 'feeling' employed as the revealing conclusion bungles what is already only skin-deep as a child's 'psychology': the story of the the "Little Girl" seems to be nothing more than the story of a child that melts into pity or love when one who has been hard on it softens into tenderness towards it. When the change in the father has already been revealed to the child ("carefully tucked up the child ... 'rub your feet against my legs and get them warmed'"), when the child has just soliloquised in pity for her father ("Poor father'. Not so big after all—and with no one to look after him"), this explicit appreciative articulation ("What a big heart you've got, father dear.") seems unnecessary. Even if this padding had been expunged from the verbal build-up and the ending recast the way we have ventured to suggest, the emotional content would have remained as shallow and superficial and slight as it is in its present dramatization. While we appreciate—though not without reservations of course—the extent of success achieved in consistent maintenance of the point of view and a realistic portrayal of the child's mind and heart, we fail to see how the form of the short-story is 'compact':[25] the focus of narration though appropriately chosen is not concentrated and sharpened by an appropriate time scheme; instead of being restricted to one single day typical enough to illustrate the whole psychological crisis the story is spread over several days: addition of characters cruel to the child only makes the short-story descend at times to sentimental melodrama; earlier revelations of the later realization only neutralize the intended centralized emotional effect of the ending; the reader is denied the pleasure of reading between the lines. The short-story as an ill-digested autobiographical narrative piece will go down only as the author's maudlin sentimental tribute to her father.

The reader's impression of Miss Mansfield's immaturity as a story teller is confirmed also by his discovery of her spasmodic tendency to 'revert to superficialities' without showing any influence of her own previous achievements. The next contribution, *Sunday Lunch*, may be referred to as an instance.

Even *Ole Underwood*, with all its potentialities of a substantial story element, is equally indicative of the author's immaturity. The concluding passage simply confounds the reader: it only raises intricate questions. Who can this man be—the man that lies "sleeping on a bunk"? the reader's attempt to disentangle the disturbing 'ambiguity' only vexes him, for he finds himself deluged with multiplying questions. Is the man sleeping on the bunk the man whom Ole 'killed long ago'?[26] Or is it that Ole sees only the image of the man he killed and not the man himself? But how can he be a man?[27] Did Ole kill a man? Or was it a woman that he killed? If it was a woman, did he kill her when she had already been killed? Even if the man here on the bunk is the image of the "man he killed long ago", is the story of *Ole Underwood* meant to be a story about his inordinate, insatiable, incessant thirst for revenge? If this is the psychological revelation meant to be made, does one also feel impelled to penetrate to the depth of this 'psychology'? Again, if the man on the bunk is 'a vision of Ole himself long ago',[28] does the narrator mean Ole is going to kill himself vicariously? Is this killer then going to ease his prickly conscience? But how is this desire for vicarious self-destruction consistent with "the old, old lust" that makes him set his teeth and mutter, "'I will, I will, I will'"? Or is he going to imagine himself as a man being killed because he is humiliatingly outcast everywhere? If this desire for indirect self-destruction is his motive for attacking the hallucinatory image of a man, does there seem to be much depth in the emotional complex? Still again, if the man on the bunk is 'an innocent stranger whom the madman is about to kill',[29] is the short-story meant to be a story simply about a "madman"? If it is simply about a "madman", is not one denied the opportunity of delving into the complexity of human nature that is richer within limits of normalcy? Is there any possibility of a moral struggle or a tragic flaw in the character of a 'lunatic' who only 'sees more devils than vast hell can hold'? But is Ole mad really? Does he not experience 'a moment of tenderness for a stray cat which recalls his faithless but beloved wife'?[30] Is he not susceptible to the sensuous impression of the "big girl with red hair" who 'throws back her head', of 'her great breasts which lift, shaking to her laughter'? Doesn't he 'shoot out an old claw and crush up the red pinks' as he hears his life-story interpreted?

What purpose, then, is served by this 'deliberate ambiguity' which seems to have 'fittingly completed the portrait within the viewpoint of the crazy man'?[31] and how is the portrait 'completed'? Why has it to be vague? The 'deliberate ambiguity' only complicates the questions that the story of the man raises. The reader wonders whether the author has a clear conception of the character. Consistency of point of view, which desirably remains unbroken and adjusted to the Aristotelian unity of time, would have helped to intensify the emotional effect of the crisis dramatized. But the very conception of the crisis is confounded.

The conflicting multiplying questions preclude the reader from appreciating the relevance of the images and colours. When the very meaning of the short-story is confused, 'the violently interrelated images' and 'the bright colours of the post-Impressionists'[32] are as useless as pockets in a shroud.

Miss Mansfield's creative talent was not yet sturdy enough to be successful in harmonizing plot, character and meaning; it was still too immature to achieve the simple art of unfolding even an anecdotal story. Immaturity of the talent in this respect is exposed by the weakness of the climax that we find delayed in her next contribution, *Pension Seguin* (Epilogue I). What weakens the intended comic effect of this rendering of the narrator's experience of disillusion is, in a word, looseness of the narrative structure: the climax of the short-story is not the only point in the narrative structure where the narrator's 'belief in appearances' is exposed: the reader finds the belief exposed even earlier: the moment of the climax is thus only that of a rediscovery of what the narrator has already discovered. Again, 'fluctuation of attitude'[33] is really so 'uncontrolled' that the narrative seems to evolve only through 'surprising *non sequiturs*': the narrator, one feels, is simply delaying the climax. The experiences of disillusion continue to accumulate, and the narrator fails to resist the temptation to record every shocking exposure. This sustained postponement of the intended climax would have been understandable if the climax had been unexpectedly different. The narrative piece is inclusive of even such statements as indirectly reveal the theme while the drama or the story element itself is potent enough to suggest it. (The reference here is to the statements made by the narrator-protagonist herself by way of philosophical defence of her 'belief in appearances'!)[34] Concentration here is not intense enough to exclude unnecessary reproduction of inane dialogue.

In *Violet*, Miss Mansfield presents a pointless story. The experience that the protagonist's old friend recounts is much too sentimental. The variation on the theme—dissipation of 'belief in appearances'—yields nothing new. The structure of the narrative composition is hopelessly loose. Even if it is 'split',[35] we shall be looking in vain for a substantial story element in either part of it.

But the very next short-story, *Bains Turcs*, evinces the quality of 'depth of perception' that Miss Mansfield has achieved in some of her earlier short-stories. The shattering impact of the momentous discovery that the concluding passage of the short-story registers reverberates through the reader's mind as tantalizingly speculative questions: Why does Mackintosh Cap stare after the two women? Why is her face like that of "a hungry child before a forbidden table"? Does this "ugly, wretched little German" secretly long to be as full-blooded and vivacious and buoyant as the two "stout" blonde women? Has she deceived herself when she has called the two blonde women "great big at pigs" or "nothing but a couple of street women"? Can she really 'get her husband to write to the management'? Or is it that her ugly pallid features have alienated her from her husband? Has she really "never been so insulted in her life"? Does she seem to be only flattering a false sense of self-esteem when she shrugs aside the social status of the two blondes by refusing to accept them as "respectable women", by calumniating them as "horrible, low creatures"? Is there any agonizing secret, which has embittered and terminated her married life? Why does she asseverate that she "cannot see what men see in such women"? Has she been denied "a husband and children and a home to look after"? Has she really had children, or is she only vicariously satisfying her natural motherly instinct which her ugly features have thwarted? Is the towel the only thing she has been "refused"? What else is it that she has been denied, "forbidden"? Is it full swing enjoyment of life itself that is manifest in the uninhibited "behaviour" of the women laughing and shaking to their laughter and eating and laughing again, of the two "stout" blondes bursting with youthful vigour and bubbling over with gaiety? Why do the lusty blondes seem contrasted against the "hideous" women who look "like beef steaks in chemises", against the "skinny" ones 'reading books and sweating at the moustache', against the inhibited ones "discussing whether or not they ought to tell their non-existent babies how babies come"? And is this "wretched" German lady 'named, for the nonce, Mackintosh Cap' because this helps to obscure or deepen the pathos presumably intrinsic in the 'complexity of human motive'?[36]

The speculations may be wild, but it is perhaps in these speculations that the wholeness of communication is consummated: the affectation concealing inscrutable complexity is obliquely conveyed by a detail of the setting: "It had terra-cota painted walls with a fringe of peacocks, and a glass roof through which one could see the sky, pale and unreal as a photographer's background screen". The attitude of affectation, which the woman has been made to assume and which her unconscious concomitant gestures are meant to indicate, is further dramatized by her vociferously accusatory allusion to false air characterizing demeanour of others. Her own false mannerism is made to seem obscurely pathetic perhaps also through suggestion of its implicit similarity to the false exterior either commonly perceptible in everyday life or universally characteristic of professions in which make-believe is just a routine matter. The narrator is, appropriately, withdrawn, and 'natural unity' of the narrative composition consists entirely of 'observations'. But towards the ending, the narrator unnecessarily summarizes what has already been dramatized or referred to. This intrusive comment tells upon objectivity of the vision that is requisite for the portrayal of concealed complexity. It is perhaps for this requisite objectivity that 'mockery of inmates is voiced in the amused conversation of the two women';

mockery through conversation of the characters themselves helps to distance the subject-matter from the narrator. But the narrator's lapse into a summarizing aside slackens the intensity of creative concentration. The first-person narrator might also be considered *de trop*: the story could have been told with equal effectiveness even if this character had been expunged from the narrative. What the short-story required was, perhaps, objective dramatization of the episode: the character's haughty demeanour seems to have been meant to be all make-believe. However, the short-story is not without a poignant story element.

Millie, the last of her contributions to 'little magazines' during the present phase, emerged as a natural culmination of a decade-long process of trial and error in tireless striving for achievement of the real 'form' defined by its distinctive quality of the dramatic effect. She seems to have not only recovered the 'gift' but also 'gone beyond'. After *How Pearl Button was Kidnapped* this is another short-story which exemplifies Miss Mansfield's precocious achievement of the technique that helps to discover the subject matter peculiar to the 'form' of the short-story.

The opening word of the concluding passage of the short-story ("And") vibrates with a complex sense of continuity: the sudden feeling of "a strange mad joy" that 'smothers everything else' involves an emotional complex as the culmination of a tense agonizing experience dominated by a deeply motherly sense of "justice". Millie is 'laughing and shrieking and dancing in the dust, jugging the lantern' because Harrison is responsible for leaving Mrs. Williamson "all alone with all those kids"; even her "kid", her "English Johnny", must be killed: he has orphaned "those kids". The character as an image emergent from the specific verbal complex is motherly love writ large. The emotional complex that this motherly love is involves a simple yet serene sense of justice never divorced from tenderness and warmth peculiar to a mother's heart. This sense of justice encompasses a sense of wonder at what seems illogical in the system of values, either human or providential (*human:* "'I don't care wot 'e's done, or wot 'e 'asn't done"... "I don't care anything about justice an' all the rot they 've bin spoutin' tonight"; *providential:* "Funny! she couldn't think of Mr. Williamson being dead! He was such a one for a joke. Always having a lark.") The sense of justice is manifest not only as intolerance of vacant frivolity even at the sight of "blood all over the barn" ("he picked a cigarette up out of the blood and smoked it. My word! he must have been half dotty"): it is manifest also as magnanimous acceptance of the same "half dotty" Willie Cox ("Not a bad young fellow"), although he is "a bit too free and easy for her taste". Millie feels tenderness towards not only Mr. Williamson, Mrs. Williamson and her orphaned "kids" but also Harrison who has killed Mr. Williamson and left Mrs. Williamson a disconsolate widow "all alone with her kids"—and not only Harrison, the killer, but also Willie Cox, who is out to kill this killer. She feels goodwill towards all: all are her own "kids", as it were. "Bloodlust" to which she seems to have 'reverted'[37] is not simply a violent, vindictive passion; it is an intensified emotional complex consuming the total self of a childless woman who cannot but feel solicitude for all "kids ... left alone". Millie is a mother with a capital M. Her logic is the logic of the heart. It is this logic of the heart, this essentially motherly sense of justice, that dominates the tense emotional experience the short-story is meant to dramatize.

What really defines the character is her imperturbably serene motherly sense of justice; it is individually yet quite psychologically characteristic of her childless womanhood. The tender impulses are an obvious manifestation of this motherly sense of justice; the savage ones also are expressions of the same emotionally moral sense. The alternate fluctuations of the two impulses within the same range of the sense of what we may call 'high morality' reveal a personality that is always whole and never split. Her "mad joy" is "strange" because it is an intensified emotional complex in which the fluctuation of the two impulses is dizzyingly cyclic: she works herself up only about "those kids ... left ... all alone": she never ceases to be the mother that she is. The dramatic moment marks a crisis in Millie's life and brings out into strong relief a vivid image of her total self.

Tenseness of the moment naturally demands a rendering of the whole drama in intense concentration which, in its turn, necessitates choice of a device potent enough to evoke a perfect image of the childless woman's total self as the image of a mother. The device is the 'combination of impersonal narration and interior monologue'[38]: impersonal narration apart from helping to record the character's gestures (suggestive enough to point to the essential nature of her personality), serves to capture the reflections of the character in the setting; interior monologue while unlocking her secret inner self registers those transient fluctuations of savage and tender impulses which illuminate the full image of the character, and also voices utterances recognizable only as those of her total self.

IMPERSONAL NARRATION

The posture the character is made to assume at the opening of the drama helps to characterize her personality. She feels solicitude for "that young man"("My word! when they caught that young man!"); she has also softened into tenderness towards Willie Cox who is "a bit too free and easy for her taste" but who has offered to be a help in tracking down the "young man" responsible for the dark future of "all those kids". Arrested by her equally intensified kindly impulses, Millie only 'nods her head a little and makes a grimace'. This transfixed image of the character's real self significantly appears in the very opening scene to reflect the whole truth about her.

Her casual gesture, ("put her handkerchief over her head and shaded her eyes with her hand") in the 'atmosphere' of the world on the page is consistent with the image of "the little pool of shade that lay around the house": the woman is an oasis in the comfortless desert, "the little pool of shade" itself, as it were; the shade over the eyes temporarily softens the hard 'glare' of light from the sun "burning like a mirror" and frames a more comfortable view of the hot chase in the dazzling distance: Millie has a cool-headed, calm motherly view of the victim and the victimizer. She has already been in the "pool of shade"; she cups her hand over her eyes for another shade: her vision is cooler; it is the serene mother in the barren woman that is looking out.

The seemingly spasmodic gesture ("She rushed into the road—she laughed and shrieked and danced in the dust, jigging the lantern") too is an index of the same wholeness of her being as a mother whose sense of "justice" demands that the murder of Mr. Williamson be avenged, that Mrs. Williamson's bereavement be compensated for, that their kids' appalling loss be counterbalanced. Significantly, also towards the ending of the short-story, we find her arrested by her simultaneously manifest violent and warm impulses: she rushes into the road and bursts forth in a revelling, howling dance, but she does not move farther: transfixation of the total image helps to 'round off' the narrative about a woman whose motherly sense of justice grows more and more intense within the same range of 'high morality'. At the beginning 'she doesn't wave back, she only nods her head a little and makes a grimace'; here towards the ending 'she rushes into the road—she laughs and shrieks and dances, jigging the lantern': it is the same mother that has worked herself up into a passion.

The image reflected in "the fly-specked mirror" naturally remains unrecognized by the simple woman whose conscious self doesn't "know" what her unconscious self is "going to do", the woman who doesn't "know what was the matter with herself that afternoon", the woman who does not know she is a mother; she feels "she could have a good cry", but she can discern no reason for her wish ("just for nothing"). It is the innermost self, the mother in the childless woman that longs to "have a good cry": "a dreadful thing" has happened: Mr. Williamson has been "murdered", "And Mrs. Williamson left all alone with all those kids". The simple childless woman does not recognize the mother that is her real self: "stare" is natural to the character.

The character is defined also by other scenic details.

The photograph reflects the essential features of her own nature: the details of the background that pop into her view correspond to the features as their symbols: the fern tree, the mountain, the waterfall, the snow—they are all objects conventionally invested with symbolic expression; some of the conventional interpretations of their supposed characteristics are relevant to the emotional context of Millie's characterization. The fern tree is symbolic of sincerity; the waterfall, of the flow of life; the mountain, of exalted loftiness; and the snow, of absolute purity. Thus the fern tree objectifies the integrity of the woman's moral character. She is what she is; she is intolerant of "too much side"; her sense of justice is imperturbably calm and serene: even while she experiences a strange mad joy she does not cease to be a solicitous mother. The waterfall points to the elemental mother in her. She is on the side of positive values of life: she cannot "think of any one shooting Mr. Williamson"; she cannot "think of Mr. Williamson being dead"; she has never seen anyone even "in a dead faint before"; she cannot brook denial of life to anybody; she would denounce any situation in life which produces a victimizer and a victim. The mountain seems to be the externalized image of her sense of 'high morality'. She has a sense of justice that overrides all other considerations and this sense of justice is wholesomely motherly: it is as fixed as a mountain in the distance. The snow seems to have been meant to symbolize her quiet purity. She is genuinely pure with her intolerance of all assumption and pretension ("too much side"). With the integrity of her character that admits of no duplicity or hypocrisy; she is chastely pure as a childless woman who has even "forgotten her wedding day"; she is singularly pure in that 'traditionless country' where nobody seems as simple as she is—not even Mr. Williamson whose murder itself is a proof of his having been directly or indirectly involved in some explosive situation: his killer too has been wounded ("one of the trousers was stuck to his leg with a patch of dark blood").

"The little pool of shade" that the young boy has sought seems to be symbolic of the motherly spirit which dwells in the house, presiding over the locality which is exposed to the sun that is as much pitiless as the country is 'traditionless': Millie's emotional concept of justice, her simple logic of the heart, her equal love for both the victim and the victimizer, may be viewed as a clear stream of cool reason that has not lost its way into the dreary desert sands of traditionlessness. The simple scenic detail contributes to this preconceived effect of Millie's characterization.

Millie's awareness of similarity ("white as her apron") is characteristic of the motherly character: she is a kindly woman with a rough exterior: she is a savage mother, but she is not without the milk of human kindness. The colour ("white") heightens the sense of the unprejudiced, pure and simple relation between the woman as a mother and the boy as her "English Johnny". The elemental nature of the mother is manifest in the tenderly loving care with which she notes "the dust and sweat": the impersonal narrator's repetition of "and" ("wiped his face and his hair and his throat, with fingers that trembled") makes us note the loving tender care Millie is devoting to the boy. The 'gleam' on "his face" reflects the timeless universal light of love in the mother's heart.

The woman's real self speaks "savagely" even while solicitously rationalizing its motherly sense of justice. The image of this real self is defined also by a symbolic dramatization. This dramatization underlines not only the polarity of interest in what the two waking members of the family have been "listening" for but also the fusion of the two tensely alert beings on the elemental, animal level ("Millie lay on her back, her eyes wide open, listening".... "The dog stopped, but she knew it was listening"). The typographically isolated paragraph is poetically 'rounded off'.

The hard 'glare' of the background ("the glaring yard") is relieved by the dramatic situation objectifying the characters' emotional intercrossing. The drama of this intercrossing involves a change in the human situation while the background against which it is enacted remains exactly the same: "She ... dashed ... across the glaring yard" ... "he followed her across the glaring yard". Reciprocal reliance even in the tense explosive situation evinces inviolability of 'high morality' as a value. The scenic complex images forth the moral beauty of the paradox that the woman's character presents. Even the gun is snatched up "from the kitchen corner", a place which of all places in a house is most intimately associated with a woman who feeds and thus mothers the family.

INTERIOR MONOLOGUE

There is sudden emotional transition from piteous apprehension ("My word! when they caught that young man!") to righteous indignation ("Well, you couldn't be sorry for a young fellow like that"). This transition illuminates the full image of the character as an embodiment of motherly sense of justice: even by "a young fellow like that" she means only that type of young boy who has "left Mrs. Williamson all alone with her kids". It is with this understanding that she reiterates her husband's argument ("if he wasn't strung up where would they all be?"). Later when she is face to face with the "young fellow" himself, there is only shift of sympathy; the range of moral sense remains the same.

The discrepancy between what 'she means to say' and what 'she says instead' to the "face", which seems to her to be "dreadful, frightened", helps to define the author's full concept of the character: what she "means to say' ("'Any minute. They're on their way now'") is the voice of her inner self, the self that shares the universal moral faith in all righteous retribution; what "she says instead" also emanates from the depths of the same self, of the same sense of justice that is consistent with this faith. The assuring voice ("'Not till arf-past ten'") that lulls the boy into comparative security is, as a matter of fact, the echo of the same inner voice: one who is responsible for the kids' bereavement is himself a kid and a mother does not know one kid from another. The "dreadful, frightened" face seems to be an index not of the mind of the boy but of the mind, the heart, the total self of the woman herself who reads the face. The woman is 'speaking very slowly'; her tone is determined, unemotional, emphatic; yet it is not menacing: the woman only identifies her

"English Johnny". She does not snatch up her gun here: she doesn't even know she has one. Again, even what she seems to be speaking in cold anger ("'I must have been blind in me two eyes not to have known you from the first'") is the expression of the same total self, for her speech is ambiguous enough to mean also that she has ceased to see him with her naked eyes ("blind in me two eyes"): she has already begun to see him in the innermost recesses of her heart—— as "nothing but a sick kid" ("known you from the first").

There are several moments in her interior monologue when she names herself fully: "What are you going to do, Millie Evans?.... 'Go on' see what it is, Millie Evans'". The pattern formed by the recurrence of her full name in her own interior monologues helps to illustrate occasional manifestation of her unconscious awareness of her total self.

Some of Miss Mansfield short-stories do evince 'depth of perception'. What baffles the reader who studies the short-stories in IN A GERMAN PENSION in their chronological order is their author's erratic tendency to revert to superficialities even after she has achieved the quality of 'depth of perception'. But what accounts for this curious tendency is, perhaps, the uncontrollably impulsive earnestness of her endeavour to explore the possibility of dimensions inherent in the most superficial aspects of everyday life. The reader is perplexed also by her failure to have retained or maintained the previous technical achievements in her subsequent narrative pieces. What this failure exposes is only her ignorance of her own capacity or potentiality.

What the creative process of her recognition of form actually demanded was her critical awareness and exact realization of her own creative potentialities as a short-story writer. Her eagerness to develop this awareness and achieve this realization was evidenced by what subsequently evolved as systematically self-instructive experimentation with modes and aspects of the art of shorter prose fiction.

NOTES AND REFERENCES

1. Saralyn Daly, *Katherine Mansfield*, p. 30.
2. *Ibid.*
3. *Ibid.*
4. *Ibid.*, p. 34.

5. *Ibid.*
6. *Ibid.*, p. 35.
7. *Ibid.*
8. *Ibid.*, p. 30.
9. *Ibid.*, p. 35.
10. *Ibid.*, p. 30.
11. *Ibid.*, p. 31.
12. The dramatization of the experience is distinctly conspicuous in the emotional design: "She forgot her five babies and her man and felt almost like a girl again. The music sounded sad and sweet.... While the music went on she was afraid to look anybody in the face, and she smiled with a little nervous tremor round the mouth.... She imagined that all these people were laughing at her, more people than there were in the room even all laughing at her because they were so much stronger than she was".—*Collected Stories of Katherine Mansfield*, p. 724
13. Cf. "The technical unity of the sketch is effected by the word squeeze", Saralyn Daly, *op. cit.*, p. 36.
14. *Ibid.*
15. The reference here is to the scene where Emma and Rodolphe grow more intimate (Madame Bovary, chap. VIII): cross-montage of dialogues here facilitates expressive sharpening of the idea: two lines of speech are interlaced: the speech of the orator in the square below, and the conversation of the future lovers. The climax is reached through a continuation of this cross-cutting and the word-plays.
16. William Walsh Edmund, *A Manifold Voice*, p. 175.
17. *Ibid.*
18. Saralyn Daly, *op. cit.*, p. 38.
19. *Ibid.*, p. 39.
20. Quoted by Saralyn Daly from *Rhythm, Ibid.*, p. 41.
21. *Ibid.*
22. A phrase from Walt Whitman's poem "Animals", The New Pocket Anthology of American verse, p. 555.
23. Cf. The 'wish-fulfilment account ... rejects the ordinary conventional life from which *Rhythm*, despite its slogan of realism, recoils'. Saralyn Daly, *op. cit.*, p. 44.
24. Cf. 'Miss Mansfield's story develops a change in feeling in its viewpoint character'. *Ibid.*, p. 46.
25. Cf. 'Except for two small lapses in her interior monologue ... the diction consistently maintains the child's viewpoint and the structure is formally compact' *Ibid.*, p. 46.
26. Cf. 'The man on the bunk with his head on a red pillow ... may be the man he killed long ago, a vision of himself long ago, or an innocent stranger whom the madman is about to kill'. *Ibid.*, p. 47.
27. Saralyn Daly seems to have overlooked what is unmistakably explicit in the text: " 'When he was a young follow, thirty years ago, a man 'ere done in' is woman, and 'e foun' out an' killed 'er', *Collected Stories*, p. 575.
28. Saralyn Daly, *op. cit.*, p. 47.
29. *Ibid.*

30. *Ibid.*
31. Cf. 'deliberate ambiguity fittingly completes the portrait within the viewpoint of the crazy man'. *Ibid.*
32. Cf. '[Ole Underwood] is violent in content and intensely visual in the bright colours of the post-Impressionists and Fauvists'. *Ibid.*
33. *Ibid.*, p. 48
34. *Ibid.*
35. Cf. 'I've nursed the Epilogue to no purpose. Every time I pick it up and hear 'you'll keep it to six'. I can't cut it. To my knowledge there aren't any superfluous words. I mean every line of it'. Letters. pp. 5-7.
    Cf. Saralyn Daly's comment: 'Perhaps the story could not have been cut by one half page, but it could have been split in two' Saralyn Daly, *op. cit.*, p. 49
36. Cf. 'In this closing Miss Mansfield has finally reached her top pitch in achieving the objectives of *Rhythm:* a brutal analysis of the woman's motive for her calumniations, inextricably blended with a sudden flash of insight and consequent pity'. *Ibid.*, p. 50.
37. Cf. 'Millie ... the ... childless and hard-hearted wife who becomes momentarily human when a youth who has shot a man takes refuge from his pursuers in her wood stack—again is a creature stunted by her circumstances; she softens into motherly pity for the exhausted boy when she is alone with him, but reverts to blood-lust as soon as the hunt is on again'—Antony Alpers, *Katherine Mansfield*, p. 192.
38. Sylvia Berkman, *Katherine Mansfield: A Critical Study*, p. 49.

4. Experiment
(i) The Long Short-Story

Miss Mansfield had not yet mastered the form when the opportunity afforded by freedom from subordination to 'limited ... space' and 'editorial policy'[1] beckoned her to a new dimension of fictional mode—the form of the long short-story. This new dimension represented straight narration of occurrences without reversal of their original temporal order, complete with copiously established situation material at the start, and a pre-conceived denouement as a natural culmination of a development thoroughly traced.

Perhaps the reason for this transition to a spell of quiet experimentation with the traditional form of the long short-story was as much aesthetic as it was environmental: hitherto precluded from experimentation by 'the taste and probably the environments of *New Age and Rhythm*' and also by the lack of a 'ready publisher',[2] Miss Mansfield was now free to 'begin to find her way back to and to go beyond the achievement of *Tiredness of Rosabel*'.[3] Of course, 'for the moment she was not writing for any magazine', and was 'limited neither by the demands of space nor editorial policy'.[4] But she was unmistakably speculating on further dimensions of the form of the shorter prose-fiction when she produced a few short-stories 'more than twice as long as her usual ones, and far more carefully wrought'.[5]

But Miss Mansfield's genius was essentially that of a short-story writer. She had delved into exploitation of the culminant moment in some of her earlier short-stories: we find them all unmistakably characterized by effect of instantaneity and intensity of effect. The exploitation of the moment now changed into imaginative exploration of the whole range of a character's emotional experiences in a developing situation. The attempt at an understanding of the way emotional experiences intensify within the range of the situation was necessary to achievement of capacity for discovery of their whole gamut within the restricted scope of a culminant moment. She was perhaps only trying to analyse what in her later attempts at 'dramatic effect' she would subdue, or obscure, or leave only inferentially implicit; or, she was relaxing the intensity of 'concentration' only to 'recover the gift that had produced *Tiredness of Rosablel*'[6] still inspiring her as an example of her unconscious achievement of the art that occasions the 'dramatic effect'. Thus even while experimenting with the expanded scale she was perhaps only exploring other ways of imaginative concentration, which invariably has to be intense enough to give rise to simultaneous impression of 'depth of perception'[7] and relevant gratuitousness. The experimentation was just an unconscious preparation for mastery of the technique of the 'dramatic effect' which by virtue of its intensity and quality of immediacy is potent enough to create the simultaneous impression. The technique was to be a means of not only discovering the nuances of an intensely complex truth-vision but also getting into 'that real living simple truthful full life'.[8]

Her composition of the first long short-story, *Something Childish but very Natural*, enabled her to see how a 'design of ironic echoes'[9] meant to reverberate throughout the narrative could be made to seem unobtrusively patterned: it also capacitated her to ascertain the extent to which the elaboration of the design necessitated by the rhythmic pattern of 'ironic echoes' could force expansion of the scale. The effect of sustained reverberation of the 'ironic echoes' is achieved. But it is weakened towards the end by a detail meant to indicate the point of pathetic termination.

The ending of the short-story is not 'unsatisfactorily vague'[10] but disconcertingly unsatisfactory: what spoils the reader's aesthetic enjoyment of the 'pathetic irony' of nascent love nipped in the bud is the injudicious use of the bare word' "telegram"; the word only tends to weaken, nay, destroy the desired effect of final disappointment: failure to restrain the tendency to dash off the revealing word shows the author's immaturity as a story-teller striving for the mastery of the art of implication. The very word "telegram" with its familiar ring of omen seems to betray the secret of the way the narrative is going to end. The word is deplorably inept.

Perhaps substitution or shift of the vaguely suggestive phrase, "just a folded paper", would have been congruous with the preconceived impressionistic effect of what the verbal build-up up to this point seems to have established: the intended effect is perhaps that of a psychic flux into paralysing vertigo induced by conflation of the character's experiences in the realms of dream and reality. This effect of vertiginous experiences is traceable here to the transitions from an illusion of the approaching child as "a moth" to the recognition of her real human appearance ("No, it wasn't a moth. It was a little girl in a pinafore") back to a vision even of the "telegram" as a "funny present". The effect is attributable also to sensitive registration of the character's evanescent yet complex mood—the mood of detached amusement which finds its expression through a fantastic image and his simultaneous apprehension that all his present blissful experience of confident expectancy will have only a tragic termination. We find this effect reinforced by the absolute absence of even an inkling of the nature of the message telegraphed: this utter absence of any clue to the precise wording of the message is understandably due to the wordless dumbness of the character confounded by his dark realization of the negative reality that a dream is as the only reality. The reader feels tempted to ask: what was the message? Was it simply 'Sorry, Not coming', or was it a conclusive 'Forget me'? What accentuates the effect of vertiginous experiences in realms of dream and reality is the curious narrative statement: "He laughed gently in the dream", which induces the impression that this whole climactic moment is that of dizzy trance: even the vision of 'shadows spinning a web of darkness' over the character's total awareness at the moment seems to be characteristic of a dream, although the way the narrator's account of the climactic moment is worded creates a simultaneous impression of the character's full wakefulness. The contrary impressions are simultaneously evoked. The desired effect is achieved.

Reference to Henry's transfixation ("But Henry did not move") at this climactic moment takes on a metaphorical significance and becomes a telling finishing touch: the final revelation of the tragic truth about the crisis in Henry's life is delicately subtle: "But" in "But Henry did not move" seems to point to transfixation that has already set in: Henry has remained psychically transfixed since his latest impassioned expression of a restless longing for choice from the realm of the possible ("The thing is . . . how I am going to wait until evening"). The paralysing vertigo in which all his psychic flux culminates is perhaps meant to signify the sad termination of his 'youthful belief'[11] in a dream as the reality. Henry's is a tell-tale posture.

The tragic transfixation of the whole of his being at this culminant moment contributes a parallel. The narrative has already registered an earlier moment of his transfixation when Edna has parted company with Henry for the first time. The moment is dramatized significantly at the central point of the structural design, that is, just at the first intense moment of the experience of choice from the realm of the possible: 'the train stops' with Henry transfixed but poised at the precise point of the tense moment when the realm of the possible begins ("She said breathlessly, 'I come down from London every evening' ... 'you-you-you do-really?'"). The character's microcosm here (the train) has just emerged from the 'dark tunnel' of alienating void; it has glided into "a sprinkle of lights and houses"—into the realm of possibilities of a happy and whole togetherness; and then it has come to a standstill. The effect of the character's psycho-physical transfixation seems to have been heightened by this coincidence. ("shall we or shall we not shake hands? Raced through his brain. One hand was on the door handle, the other held the little bag."). The swift process of this psycho-physical transfixation that evolves between the moment when the train seems to be "stopping" and the moment when it 'stops' is sensitively registered.

Vibrant with ironic echoes the parallelism is significantly conspicuous in the design of the narrative structure: the ending of the first section is made to correspond to that of the last section: both the structural points register the character's psycho-physical transfixation and reveal the tragic truth about the crisis in his life at a moment of choice from the realm of the possible. Again, the ending of the opening section dramatizes the process of transfixation at a moment of wakeful consciousness: Henry simply stares as Edna leaves "without a word or glance"; that of the last section rhythmically repeats disclosure of the same process at a moment of drowsy awareness: the character does not know for certain whether he is in the realm of a dream or in that of reality or whether he is in both the realms at the same time.

Gradually and irresistibly drawn into the eddying vortex of the vertiginously revolving realms of dream and reality, the character sinks deeper and deeper into the dark abysmal depths till he is lost in a realm where a dream is the reality and the reality is all dream.

Structurally the narrative design stands divided into seven sections. Broadly, in the first four sections we have the dramatized registration of the point-of-view character's experiences in a state of wakeful consciousness; but in the first two we are also aware of what may be defined or conceived as a gossamer veil draped over concrete reality. After a long process of emotional intercrossing, there is intimate revelation of kindred natures and longing for fleshly thrill culminating in a tranquil passion ("'will it make you love me less?' 'oh no', he said. 'Nothing could—nothing on earth could'"). In the next three sections the texture of the narrative grows denser to capture the character's concurrent experiences in the realms of dream and reality. This transition from a state of wakeful awareness to that of alternately drowsy and waking consciousness reveals the romantic dreamer's gradual, unconscious withdrawal from the real world without into the unreal world within, which his 'youthful belief' creates as a microcosm unquestionably real. Of this accelerative attraction towards a dream as a reality or a reality as beautiful as a dream—a characteristic feature of 'youthful' love as "something childish but very natural"—the character is ironically unaware. The irony intrinsic in his unawareness of the irresistibility of attraction is conveyed by his intermittent awakening to the dreaded reality of a dream as only a dream. The texture within the latter part of the structure is expediently characterized by a neat rhythmical pattern formed by the intermittence of the character's awakening to the dreaded reality. This pattern helps to reveal the source of the 'ironic echoes': the source may be defined as the paradox of the character's love for and dread of a dreamlike state.

Termination of this pattern in a climax suggesting conflation of dream and reality accentuates the tragic irony of the character's unawareness of the real nature of his state: is there only a lurking suspicion manifest as an ominous dream? Or is it his awakening to the hard reality of temporary or permanent separation from his girl?

This whole 'design of ironic echoes' is conspicuously punctuated with terminal points stressing the irony of the girl's immutable separateness: each section ends on a note reverberating as an ironic echo of the harmony growing between the two lovers as each other's alter ego: with all his dream of or 'faith' in their whole togetherness as "two children" in the inviolably sacrosanct seclusion of an Eden of idyllic love, Henry remains estranged from Edna, a girl he has discovered to be his second self.

Equally conspicuous and diametrically contrary is a concurrent rhythmical pattern registering the point-of-view character's growing 'youthful belief"; it runs a whole gamut of secret feelings: indecision, misgivings, invocation, certitude, and finally potential "faith" ('I feel just like God'), which, the reader comes to see, is not without a 'pathetic irony'. This concurrent pattern evolves through the opening of the first section, the second section, and the last section, that is, through all the significant points of the narrative structure where the point-of-view character seems "all, all alone": we find him left all by himself, naturally groping in uncertainty, assailed by dim misty misgivings, oscillating between diffidence and certitude. The impression of this contrarily concurrent pattern registering the protagonist's growing 'belief' seems to run counter to that of the pattern which is meant to reveal immutable separateness despite all harmony and affinity. The broader criss-cross pattern that emerges thus reflects the rich complexity that characterizes the irony intrinsic in the total situation.

This complex 'design of ironic echoes' thus helps to discover the characteristic dimensions of the character's story which as only a story of his unconscious dramatization of a romantic lyric is intrisically ironical: the character's unawareness of the fact that he only lives the poem after he has memorized it is in itself a 'pathetic irony'.

The 'design of irohic echoes' is thus meant to define the tragic irony inherent in the character's experience of a 'youthful' choice from the realm of the possible; it finds its consummation in the contrast that Edna's characterization presents despite all its suggestions of kindred nature: Edna is a character meant to function as a foil to the protagonist with his headlong passion and 'youthful belief': her own romantic temperament is mollified by her practical sober philosophy of life; her inheritance of "wild blood" is sublimated as faith in platonic love; her final willingness to let Henry "hold" and "kiss" her is contrasted with something in her nature that occasions suspicion or warrants apprehension. "Weeping and laughing for the same reason" she remains arrested, transfixed, static, shut up in some "square", as it were, tantalizingly "half-hidden", embarrassingly shy, modestly but mysteriously withdrawn: even after she has overcome her shyness, she keeps Henry floundering in uncertainty about herself.

It is perhaps this complexity characterizing the irony inherent in the total situation which accounts for the spacious planning and the leisurely slow-winding movement of this ode on nascent love.

Conception of the theme implicit in the next narrative piece, *Indiscreet journey*, presupposes serenity of an ecstatic vision. But the technical essence of the narrative composition is that of a reportage and not that of a short-story. The 'world' conjured up on the page is not without immediacy; but this 'world' is too static to involve a sense of drama occasioned by a crisis. The form tends towards the static, but the content is static too. Miss Mansfield was not yet mature enough to convey the sense of a crisis even though a structural 'form' designed as that of a sketch. Only after much exploration of what may be called 'the static situation' as the dominant story element would she be able to compose a sketch with a subtle yet definite story element. We can compare the first draft of the narrative piece, recorded as a journal entry, with its revised and enlarged version handed down as a short-story, and see how there is only a change of style and there is no sense of crisis or transition involved.

Thus the revised version evinces 'change' only in Miss Mansfield's creative process which has achieved 'a more concentrated vividness'.[12] For there are questions that embarrass the critical reader who finds the second version passed off as a short-story: Is there a story that involves a change? Is there any crisis in the narrator's life? Is there any evidence of a new awareness on the part of the narrator? The reader is at once baffled and delighted. He is baffled by the author's insouciance with regard to, and by her critics' tendency to shy away from, the basic technical questions: he is delighted at the 'concentrated vividness' which seems to him to have been 'achieved' with a view to capturing the dimensions of the truth-vision conceived. This ambivalence precludes a pure aesthetic pleasure.

The second version of the raw transcript of reality as registered in the JOURNAL delights the reader only as an artistically vivid record of a subjective vision of reality which Life is as Truth that is Beauty.

The image of "the sunny air ... all broken up and trembling with" the "noise" seems to define the whole atmosphere of the world the verbal complex is meant to conjure up. The ambiguity of phrasing ("sunny air"—where both the words have more that one meaning), the conflation of audio-visual impressions ("air broken up and trembling with—noise"), the suggestion of a living cacophony as a rich symphony ("air", or melody, of cheerfulness agreeably synchronized with the "noise")—all fused into a rich complex seem to lend a shimmering quality to the image. This shimmering quality of the image reflects the Beauty that Life as Truth is—the Beauty that is at once impalpable and sensuous, riotous and harmonized, evanescent and perpetual. The sun-warm atmosphere is scintillating with insouciant hilarity of the people; they all seem to be in closer approximation to the source of all life, the sun (presumably 'shining through the windows' in the revised version, too); the men stripped of their "blue and red coats" and "short swords and belts" and thus mingled with the civilians sit basking in "the sunny air". Primarily the image with this specific implication seems to reflect the diffused suggestion—throughout the narrative—of the lifelong intimate nearness of man to both Nature and his fellow-beings. The symphony of cheerful, 'chirruping' and "loud impatient voices", and the sensuous sounds of the eggs in the pan ("ssssh"), the clattering plates and the pop-popping corks, echoes what in the war-silenced world is agreeably audible as 'sweet music (of human speech); it also suggests the instinctive human craving to 'eat, drink, and be merry'. The ongoing gay rhythm of Life audibly manifest here as the symphony of voices and sounds harmonizes all contrariety and endows the everyday world of man with a charm that is fadeless. this everyday humming world of man is a microcosm inviolably sacrosanct as an eternal Shangri-La: no war can ever dash into this ongoing rhythm, no war can outrage its beauty, no war can rob it of its poetry. The narrator with her synthetic, aesthetic vision seems indulgently attentive to the ceaseless flow of this rhythm that is occasionally audible in the Shangri-La on this side of the horizon: a crash is followed by a soundless pause; hilarity alternates with a mute cry; a broil is succeeded by a bellylalugh; apathy is concurrent with sympathy; and the rhythm flows on.

Contrary yet concordant manifestations of human nature also seem part of this ongoing rhythm: that "scrang of a woman in a black shawl" with all her rough exterior is condescendingly genial: "still scolding and muttering she took four glasses from the cupboard and a big bottle". This ongoing rhythm of the poetry of Life is not without the beauty of its lyrical moments when incomprehensibly deep yet touchingly and consummately eloquent poignant stories seem enacted, poetically in the obscure privacy of an individual's own microcosm.[13] The essential goodness of human nature as a positive feature of Life, the lyrical dimensions of fleeting moments in the ceaseless flux of Life, are abiding beauties ensconced, so to say, in the sanctuary of this Shangri-La (!) which no war can outrage. The beauty of this symphony with a capital 'S' is defined also by the reciprocity of human relationships which establish positiveness of human solidarity as an inviolable value. Stripped of their short swords and belts, with their 'blue and red coats hanging upon the walls', the soldiers are their normal social selves again, rubbing shoulders with the civilians as they sit "eating". The war-drawn line of demarcation between the soldiers and the civilians is obliterated: even those on duty are essentially human; their humanity is not denatured. All military regulations stand nonchalantly and mockingly defied. Humanity seems to be spilling over barriers: human relationship transcends all national boundary ("Ma tante Julie et mon oncle Paul ... more real, more solid than any relations I had ever known"). Sensitive registration of spontaneously used English and French phrases in conversations and use of a simile or two picturing people both primitive and civilized ("the tall black trees ... grouped together like negroes conversing", "like any English lady in any French novel"), reinforce the desired impression of a cosmopolitan outlook on the part of the narrator. There are emotional links minimizing all distance that alienates, establishing the more "solid relations", making the "unfamiliar" "familiar". They are manifest in deeply emotional inter-crossings, helpfully friendly demeanour, instinctive sexual attraction. They are perceptible in affectionate gestures and terms of endearment, in cordial greetings and heart-breathed farewells, in sympathetic utterances and impulsive generosity. It is these links that preserve human solidarity.

The shimmering quality of the ambiguous image ("the sunny air") as a vague complex of subtle suggestions thus helps to define this complex iridiscent beauty in the everyday world of man: the microcosm seems much too remote from the world destroyable by war; it is perhaps too remote to seem to have its human figures distinctively named and its topography sharply outlined or substantially identified ("a Nameless Official", "said a bayonet", "Buffard— no, Boiffard", "said the sea_gull", "you must change at x.y.z.", etc.). The narrative element of the narrator's unfamiliarity with the topographical particulars of the strange, forbidden territory is significant ("What is the name of the station where I have to change? Perhaps I shall never know", etc.); it is at once an element of realism and a means of appropriate objectification of what in the narrator's moral-aesthetic philosophy of Life is an eternal Shangri-La. What seems to be natural in the circumstance has been used as a means to an end.

The other expedient means of defining the sublime beauty of this poetically conceived microcosm are: use of 'religious imagery'[14] drawn from the Holy Bible and assignment of the happenings to Time as an eternal Now; use of 'religious imagery' and assignment of the events to Time as Eternity also seem to have been necessitated by the sense of sublimity inherent in the specific truth-vision: the whole of this microcosm has been envisioned as a reality that is hallowed—a reality with the capital initial; 'religious imagery' is a naturally concomitant compositional element when the time of the happening seems to the narrator to be a manifestation or an aspect of the sacred Great Time itself. Time manifest in its perpetual presentness is a living entity: the present is continuous with the past: it is alive with "sweet memories" that never fade; the present itself is substantial enough to enable one to "take the last breath of day"; the present is also the moment of choice from the realm of the possible: it is pregnant with possibilities: the train of Time rushes past "tall, blind houses to let"; there are dreams of a "drift along... rivers", of marriage across the seas, of a taste of "excellent—excellent whiskey". No war can come by this spirit of Life that is eternally ensconced in the sanctuary of Time itself.

The passage which affords a peep-hole view of the microcosm reveals the fundamental characteristic of Time as an eternal Now, Manifest as it is in what the narrator cannot but describe in the present tense ("a woman leans", "I can see a kitchen, and the cook in a white coat breaking eggs", "The blue and red coats of the men who are eating hang upon the walls. Their short swords and belts are piled upon chairs."): the narrator seems to be breathlessly aware of the perpetual beauty that a scene in the everyday world is. Sudden transition in the sequence of tense has perhaps been necessitated by the sense of the narrator's sensitive awareness of the abiding beauty intrinsic in the changeless changefulness of Life: the temporal flux is at a standstill revealing its true nature as the eternal Now. The vision is tranced. It is only the "noise" that jolts the narrator out of this trance. (But even this "noise" is aesthetically apprehended as the burst of a symphony of cacophonous voices and sounds. For throughout the narrative the aesthete in the narrator seems emotionally sensitive to this pattern in the ongoing rhythm as it alternates between soundless silence and a splintering crash, the hush of the starry night and the hssh-hssh of an engine.) The sudden transition in the sequence of tense involves the sense of the narrator's submission to an evanescent mood of intense attentiveness to what as the perpetual beauty of everyday world reveals itself vividly only in absolute, sacrosanct isolation from the profane, passing time.

This perpetual beauty of everyday world revealing itself only in the eternal instant is inclusive of the deathless charm of love between a man and a woman. The clock between the two pictures, which depict respectively the nascency of love and the consummation of it ("premiere Recontre", "Troimphe d' Amour"), is significantly represented as a blank faced clock: pointing to all time at the same time, the clock has its own time equated with the Great Time; this attribute of the specific clock, which is manifested twice but substantiated on neither occasion, helps to contribute a sense of everlastingness to what the pictures depict. The total meaning emergent from the image complex seems to relate to a primordial beauty in the world of man manifest as an interminable pattern in the universal pulsating rhythm of human relationship: the microcosm of 'a maid with her wight' remains an inviolably isolated sacrosanct beauty even 'in the time of breaking of nations': it is a perennial beauty—a beauty which, like nature, is in nearest approximation to the inviolably sacred Great Time. The clock ticking "to a soothing lilt, c'est c,a , c'est c,a "supports this truth. The lilt re-echoes the universal throbbing rhythm which keeps incessantly alternating between nascency of love and consummation of it.

It is in this sacred Great Time as an absolutely unrelated reality that the narrator's microcosm seems to evolve. Quite naturally the narrator moves through this microcosm without a watch ("I hadn't a watch") and the clock time varies as a subjective reality ("'Look at that clock ...' ... 'It 's fast'" ...). There is also a moment when the narrator experiences a feeling of the true nature of Time as the eternal instant: "And years passed. Perhaps the war is long since over".— This feeling in the presentness of the future as a past is a feeling of all time at the same time, of the Great Time which really is an all-at-once rather than a one-thing—after-another, of Eternity which both unfolds and enfolds all succession.

The adventuring narrator stands entranced at a Door of perception.

But what she experiences only justifies her calm conviction that the ongoing rhythm of Life is an abiding value mocking all war as an outlandishly ludicrous absurdity.[15] It is this moral preoccupation that characterizes the narrator's aesthetic interest. Moreover, the narrator's deepening realization of the profound truth-vision is made neither to seem a culmination nor to reach a climax. Thus a new awareness on the part of the narrator is out of the question. The meaning emergent from the verbal complex, therefore, is not the one that is produced when character and action cohere: the verbal complex does not involve 'a coherent relating of action, character and meaning'.[16]

Little Governess, the result of Miss Mansfield's third experiment with the form of the long short-story, successfully covers a whole range of an innocent adventurer's 'fluctuating feelings of security and fear'[17] culminating in a shocking experience. The style despite expansion of scale is suggestive enough to elevate the narrative piece to the dignity of an allegory of Innocence caught in the coils of Experience. But the story element that filters in through the design of the narrative seems only flatly and inanely stereotyped. There are other lapses which dissipate the potentiality of the story even as an allegory. As a stepping stone to achievement of the art of the 'dramatic effect' the composition of this short-story seems to have proved inexpedient.

The little governess is an adventurer who has chosen to travel all by herself—"unprotected"—and who 'gives herself up to the excitement of being really abroad'. Quite naturally, she 'yields to the warm rocking' of the ship and, later, 'leans against the dark rushing ... to be carried away and away' in an effortless drift. With a sensibility that seems dreamily exquisite and innocently poetic she enjoys her journey as an adventure into the realm of the unfamiliar beauty of the familiar. Her sensibility is attuned to Nature that is always what it is with an inviolably isolated life of its own; she is sensitive to the ongoing rhythm of Life itself which, she exquisitely feels, is much more thrilling in a strange place: she is the image of an innocent soul blithely adventuring into an unfamiliar, strange world for sheer thrill of its exploration. The full image of the girl specified as an innocent inquisitive adventurer is strikingly etched for a moment when she is shown 'rubbing a place' on the window panes.

Dimensions of this thematically central concept of innocence that the girl is meant to embody as a character seem to have been imaginatively explored. "She moved forward with the sleepy flock, all knowing where to go to and what to do except her": this temporary lapse into what obviously is blissful ignorance of the destination or the aim of the excursion is naturally characteristic of the innocence of this girl. Alienated through her ignorance of the destination or the aim, the girl stands out as a thorough stranger in a strange country: this alienation enforces the sense of her thoroughness as a stranger in a strange place; it also contributes the sense of intense actualisation of her being at this moment of an eager quest for thrill through adventure into the realm of the unfamiliar and the unknown: standing out of the crowd the girl seems to be having an experience of her individual existence in absolute freedom. The image of the "flock" helps to make her innocence seem lamb-like, pure, and virtuous. The "flock of sheep" that pops into her vision as her train rushes past the world beside the track is perhaps the projected image of this intrinsic innocence. It is this intrinsic innocence that seems to have made her think of the passengers' crowd as a "flock". Her fancied image of a baby in a perambulator is, then, indicative of her unconscious awareness of herself as a "baby" just born into a world absolutely new to it. It is perhaps this unconscious awareness of her innocence as an adventurer that makes her call herself a "baby" with a "grandpa" to 'look after' her.

The sense of ignorant credulity as another intrinsic dimension of this central concept of innocence is exemplified by the girl's inability to see through the motives of the people who do not show their true colours; she commits the folly of trusting to first impressions uncorrected by careful observation; she fails to recognize or even suspect the irony implicit in the old man's statements concealing his wanton thoughts "The man with the black cap" whom the girl takes for "a guard or a station master" is revealed to her as a "robber". This minor episode foreshadows the major event that precipitates the crisis the short-story is focussed on: the old man taken for a "grandpa" turns out to be a 'gay deceiver': like the "robber", "the man with the black cap", he "pounces upon" the "unprotected" girl. The smile of the woman who has "smiled at her in the glass" also seems to have been the 'secret smile'[18] of some all-knowing being: this being is perhaps mocking at her consciousness of her own beauty on the ship ("doing her hair in the Ladies Cabin") or on the train; the smile is also a sneer at her folly of ignorant credulity or indiscreet gullibility. The character's folly of believing in first impressions, especially when she is travelling alone, "unprotected", in an unvisited, unrevealed, unknown world of people, is characteristic of her innocence. The mirrored reflections of a "smile" and a "frightened" face seem to be oblique allusions to the girl's ignorance of the secret or possible meaning of the smile, and of the cause of her subconscious fear. These allusions naturalize and accentuate the effect of the absoluteness of the girl's innocence as an adventurous traveller in a strange country simultaneously conceived as a "dark" hell of patent duplicity and loose morals. The "dark landing-stage" is the natural starting-point of the innocent girl's journey into such a country. Her train too only takes her deeper and deeper into this "dark" world: the people here are all so "muffled" that it is almost impossible to recognize the sheep and the goats; they not simply disappear into the "dark" but live in "dark" flats with their bed-rooms and corridors all "dark"; even the policeman as the custodian of law and order is only a "doll".

With a style so richly suggestive the narrative composition would have become an allegory of innocence caught in the coils of the evil ways of the world. But some serious lapses in the composition preclude the consummation of the story's potentiality as an allegory: there is lack of control; uncertainty of intention is finally manifest in shift of 'point of view': the 'point of view' not only leaves the reader 'wondering whether the short-story is focussed on the evil aggressiveness of the porter or the ironic advantage of taking good advice';[19] it also shifts so illogically that it is difficult to see the justification for recourse to combination of direct and indirect narration ("But if Germany was new to her he hoped she would find something interesting there too. 'I am sure I shall'"). Incredibility of an episode tells upon the realistic effect: the girl is "careless 'in not discovering that her promenade will make her late for her appointment.[20]

The immediate advantage that accrued from the choice of the mode, the long short-story, was practical: the choice enabled her to exploit shades of emotional meaning, gradations and nuances of a given situation, the half feelings and in-between emotions of characters involved in the drama.

Experimentation with this mode also facilitated her task of achieving a form which might help to accentuate the subject unobtrusively: such accentuation was possible perhaps through choice of the expanded scale: immaturity of the young romantic lovers is impressed upon us through stylistic devices which dissolve the alternate impressions of dream and reality (*Something Childish but very Natural*): a thin veil of poetic beauty is draped over the familiar reality in the world of man 'in Time of Breaking of Nations' (*Indiscreet Journey*): 'the girl's fluctuating feelings of security and fear' are inconspicuously blended with her intense longing for thrills of adventure in an unvisited country (*Little Governess*).

The experimentation also helped Miss Mansfield to perfect the technique of admixture of interior monologue and dramatic action. This technique, which she had already employed in her previous rendering of tense moments—perhaps most satisfactorily in *Millie*—was perfected during this particular phase: it was now 'flexible and spontaneous' enough: it could represent gradual concentric interiorization of features of consciousness, through a 'design of ironical echoes' defining the irony intrinsic in the experience of 'youthful belief' (*Something Childish but very Natural*); it could depict a dramatized consciousness registering impressions coloured by the narrator's non-moral preoccupation with the inviolability of Life as Truth that is Beauty (*Indiscreet Journey*); it could register fluctuations of the 'feelings of security and fear' meant to enforce the desired effect of a state of uncertainty in course of the adventure of innocence into the dark world of Experience (*Little Governess*).

The advantages derived from the exhaustive exploitation of the new mode would help Miss Mansfield to enrich and naturalize the 'dramatic effect' in her later short-stories.

The technique of Miss Mansfield's short-stories during this particular phase did show 'encouraging signs of progress'. Conceptionally and structurally the three long short-stories do create 'a concentratedness of mood and have singlemindedness of purpose;[23] only the effect seems cumulative and not instantaneous. But there is overrunning of the frame because the beginning is unnecessarily so thoroughly developed: the beginning at least in *Indiscreet Journey* and *Little Governess* is reminiscent of the way a short-story by Maupassant starts and this is absolutely uncharacteristic of Miss Mansfield. The short-story technique as a whole was not yet potent and creative enough to seem to have helped to yield a truth-vision instinct with substantial poetry and specified by the distinctively intrinsic features of the genre chosen. In *Something Childish but very Natural*, for example, the technique is potent enough, but the theme falls short in respect of substantiality.

Disproportional reciprocity between the individual potentialities of the form and the content still persisted.

NOTES AND REFERENCES

1. Saralyn Daly, *Katherine Mansfield*, p. 25.
2. *Ibid.*
3. *Ibid.*

4. *Ibid.*, p. 51.
5. *Ibid.*
6. Antony Alpers, *Katherine Mansfield*, p. 108.
7. Daly Saralyn, *op. cit.*, p. 37.
8. Quoted by Saralyn Daly, *op. cit.*, p. 112.
9. Saralyn Daly, *op. cit.*, p. 55.
10. Antony Alpers, *op. cit.*, p. 198.
11. "The phrase 'the lament for youthful belief', *Letters* I, pp 604-5/describes *Something Childish but very Natural.*"—Saralyn Daly, *op. cit.*, p. 87.
12. Sylvia Berkman, *Katherine Mansfield: A Critical Study*, p. 79
13. For example, "In her fat hands, adorned with a wedding and two mourning rings, she held a letter. Slowly, slowly she sipped a sentence, and then looked up and out of the window, her lips trembling a little ... she smiled and folded the letter. 'It is from my son—the first we have had since October. I am taking it to my daughter-in-law'. *Collected Stories of Katherine Mansfield*, pp. 629-630.
    "In his white face his eyes showed, pink as a rabbit's.... The water ran down his face, off his chin on to the table. He rubbed the place with his coat-sleeve, and then, as though forgetful, went on rubbing, ... staring in front of him", etc.—*Ibid.*, pp. 639-40.
14. For example, "She is like st. Anne". Etc.—*Ibid.*, p. 628.
    "He locked as though he had escaped from some holy picture, and was entreating the soldiers' pardon for being there at all...." *Ibid.*, p. 632.
    "The faces lifted, listening. 'How beautiful they are! 'I thought 'They are like a family party having supper in the New Testament'" *Ibid.*, p. 643.
15. The view is inspired by Saralyn Daly's enlightening comment: "It is the beauty of [the] people which in every case challenges the reality of war and renders its concerns absurdly impossible."—Saralyn Daly. *op. cit.*, p. 56.
16. Cleanth Brooks, *Understanding Fiction*, p. 27.
17. Saralyn Daly, *op. cit.*, p. 59.
18. One of the 'images' which 'obsessed Katherine and were rooted deep in her psychological history'—Celeste Turner Wright: "Katherine Mansfield and 'the Secret Smile': Literature and Psychology V (1955) p. 44. *Comment* Mr. Wright has traced the image through Miss Mansfield's writings, revealing 'the workings of the creative mind'; but he does not seem to have felt the necessity of examining this 'detail' in relationship to the entire aesthetic framework of the composition in which it occurs.
19. Saralyn Daly, *op. cit.*, pp. 59-60.
20. *Ibid.*, p. 59.
21. John Cournos, "Introduction", *A World of Great Stories*, p. 4.

4. Experiment
(ii) 'Elegy in Prose'

Miss Mansfield's dissatisfaction with 'the plots of ... stories'[1] she had turned out so far was occasioned by a momentous crisis in her life which was intense enough to overwhelm her with a profound sense of 'a debt of love'.[2] The crisis jolted her into realization that the condition required for achievement of the real 'form' was deliberate restriction of her creative vision to the range of her personal world of 'people' and happenings. What sublimated her realization as an attitude at once aesthetic and spiritual was a calm vision of 'the life of life'[3] as a serene beauty.

But exploitation of her talent within the range of individual experiences could prove expedient only if her 'remembrance' was subjected to 'discipline'. 'Discipline of remembrance' would sharpen her capacity to nurture the 'gift of empathy'[4] more imaginatively and to inculcate the 'attitude of detachment'[5] exalted by a 'vision of love'[6]: her sympathetic imagination would give her a subtly perceptive insight into the psychological or lyrical meanings of the moments recollected; it would invest her practice of re-creation of the 'actualities' with 'sureness of touch';[7] 'personal detachment'[8] would simultaneously enable her to allow freedom to the subject; her re-creation of the 'actualities' would seem agreeably characterized by 'a remarkable absence of manipulation'.[9]

Success in poetic re-creation of the 'actualities', however, would depend on the extent to which the 'creative action of memory working in the familiar setting'[10] was assisted by fruitful reciprocity between the two attributes of her creative process, namely, the 'gift of empathy' and 'attitude of detachment'. The 'gift of empathy' controlled by the 'attitude of detachment' would preclude disproportion between the scope of the pregnant moment captured and the range of intent concentration exercised; the 'attitude of detachment' enlightened by the 'gift of empathy' would, in its turn, allow free play to the subject and suffuse its casual nature with a substantial poetic meaning.

For nostalgia, as the first two episodic pieces unmistakably show, was also 'the occasion for indulgence'.[11]

The calculatedly inaudible chuckle of the participant-narrator in *Apple Tree* is piteous and affectionate; but it is also exultant and gloating: the stern father is made to cut a sorry figure. Re-creation of the father-image seems to have fed Miss Mansfield's ancient grudge. However, the image this time is created with more restraint than the one pictured earlier as a tribute to her father (*Little Girl*). The attitude to the 'people' of her personal world was now compassionate and sympathetic: 'it was developing into a vision of Love and Innocence'.[12]

Re-creation of the tensely emotional experience in her first 'elegy in prose',[13] *Wind Blows*, involves no emotional discipline. The intensity of the cognate moods of rebellion and grief is too emotional to seem to have been aesthetically recollected in tranquillity; the story element is too subjective to seem independent of the autobiographical element. The tragedy swallows up the creative spirit of the artist: the spirit does not seem to have risen in triumph above the tragedy. But Miss Mansfield still rationalized the fallacy that her re-creation of emotional experience was an aesthetic performance:[14] but her tear-drops were not pearls as yet. The first attempt at composition of an 'elegy in prose' naturally falls short of our acceptance of it as an aesthetic performance: the elegy does become what it is meant to be a short-story; but it is deliriously lyrical.

Of course the word "But" in the penultimate sentence of the concluding paragraph ("But the ship is gone, now") is there to turn the sketch into a short-story: the "sister" awakens from what has been a fragile yet vivid dream of a future when they will be recalling this "windy day", and finds herself again in the same state in which "everything is ugly" and life is "hideous" and "revolting" and "dreadful"—back in the same world in which even "solitude" is "tragic" and all music is drowned in "the wind—the wind".

The moment of this second awakening to the same sordid reality, then, is perhaps the moment of the crisis which the narrative composition is meant to dramatize. It seems tragic because it is a moment of awakening from a dream in sleepy wakefulness: the character awakens this time from a dream or vision of a "dark" realm where all temporal, spatial and existential demarcation is a vague blur: the future is a palpable reality with all its immediacy of presentness and the present seems relegated to the limbo of the past ("Do you remember? ... That day—how many years ago?"); the place where "they", who "can't see those two any more", stand at the moment is indistinguishable: are they "on board leaning over the rail arm in arm"? Or are they still on the "little island" bidding "goodbye" to "those two"? And where, again, are "those two" who "can't be seen any more"? On the island or on board the steamer? There is conflation of their individual identities too: "they seem indentical with "those two": which pair is bidding goodbye to which? Which is which? "The dark" stretching "a wing over the tumbling water" enfolds them all. The realm is adequately defined by the dots: "she cuts through the waves, making for the open gate between the pointed rocks that lead to...." The vision is transcedent: the realm is darkly obscure; the ship bound for it remains unaffected by the wind ("the wind does not stop her"); it is hallowed by a "Light" ("it's the light that makes her look so awfully beautiful and mysterious"): it is an image of death ("A big black steamer ... with lights everywhere"). Awakening from this blissful dream of an occasion for the final "goodbye" to the "little island" where "life" is "hideous ...—revolting, simply revolting" parallels the 'sudden' awakening from sleep "in her room": the realm of the dark depths of sleep and the realm definable only by dots are mysteriously indentical; the awakening, too, either from the earlier real sleep or from the later sleepy wakefulness is awakening to the same grim reality of the character's 'emotional turmoil' externalized as "the wind". This parallelism helps to accentuate the effect of the tragic stasis that characterizes her life. She is meant to seem condemned to a static situation. The effect is reinforced in two ways: the one is direct; the other is oblique: the tense used for narration is consistently 'present'; dramatization of all that happens after her first awakening is so ingeniously presented that it admits of an illusion of 'action': probably even at the moment of her second awakening the character is where she has been, only squirming and tossing in bed. The elegy thus seems to be a short-story.

What spoils the reader's aesthetic enjoyment of this 'elegy in prose' is his failure to find satisfactory answers to several questions that it seems to raise.—Isn't the emotional turmoil externalized in excess of the chain of events which the character seems to have experienced? Isn't the impetuosity of the wind itself in excess of what it is meant to externalize? How is the narrative piece an impassioned expression of the author's 'intense grief'[15] at an unforgettable domestic bereavement? Is the communication of this sincere experience aesthetically consummate? Or does the narrative piece as an aesthetic expression of the author's 'intense grief' find its consummation only in that wholeness of communication which calls for the reader's knowledge of the author's traumatic experience? If the piece is an expression of grief at the death of the author's brother, how is it that the image of the brother doesn't seem to haunt the author's counterpart from the first? The impression that the character's mood is 'rebellious'[16] is substantiated of course by what it is identified with or clinched by the specifically worded title. But why doesn't the character then wish to escape alone? Why does she dream of an escape along with her brother? Has he been as much 'rebellious' as she herself? How is the brother also the character's alter ego?

What justifies the reader's refusal to revise his impression of the author's immaturity as an artist in words is also the glaring conspicuity of an unnecessary insertion: "At the thought".

The incoherently and deliriously lyrical nature of this 'elegy in prose' precludes the consummation of the intended meaning as a poetic truth-vision: its central unifying symbol ("the wind") obviously exaggerates the emotional turmoil as an externalized image; its last-minute accommodation of a character who does not share the narrator's mood is surprisingly gratuitous; its impression of diffusion of interest and of lack of concentration dissipates even generous possibility of multiplicity of meaning; the artist's 'mood' seems to be much too private and subjective. Re-creation of the experience fails to substantialize and universalize the theme. The very attempt is abortive.

Miss Mansfield's nostalgia was 'a discipline of remembrance' only during her composition of that real 'long elegy in prose' *Prelude*. It was in this re-creation of a major past event in the life of a family as a whole that there was expedient concomitance of the two attributes of her individual creative process: 'an attitude of personal detachment' and 'a gift of empathy'. She could now write short-stories in which her 'feelings were strong but disinterested'.[17] Her sensibility was sobered now by 'a joyous and loving acceptance of life':[18] all ancient injuries had been forgiven: a new condition of being was achieved; her vision now was the vision of Innocence,

Imagination, Love. Now Miss Mansfield had power 'to see and feel the beauty of the truth'.[19]

Thus, in *Prelude*, Miss Mansfield's 'attitude of detachment', enlightened by her 'gift of empathy', discovers in the free and natural evolution of the nascant life in the new house a cumulative meaning of 'mystery, richness and goodness', which as an abiding value is the beauty of the 'life of life'; and, simultaneously, controlled by the 'attitude of detachment', her 'gift of empathy' concentrates only on the subtlety of the poetically incomplete sense of 'possibilities'[20] and forges a specific structural form which helps to explore dimensions of the moment of nascency of a new life in the new house.

The loose episodic structure is naturally characterized by what seems to be a concentric design of human characterizations: with a compendious image as a comprehensively suggestive symbol at the centre, the design mirrors a whole evolutional microcosm, a whole realm of being as revealed at the moment of nascency of a new life.[21]

Let us begin at the centre of the design where we have sensitive registration of a revealing correspondence between the central symbol, the aloe, and the central character, Linda. This centre of the design provides a peep-hole view of the central character's new life as a "prelude" to the rest of her life in the new house: it registers the 'crucial' moment when she makes her own choice from the realm of the possible. What it reveals is the 'deeply complex emotional life' of the woman as it is manifest 'at a crucial period in her development'.[22] The image of the character as she stands between the "dream" that seems so intensely and vitally real and "the house" which is simply mundanely and grossly real embodies the whole meaning inherent in the author's conception of her as the protagonist: the character is a tragic soul that is suffering dreary 'imprisonment' and is at the same time poised for an unreturning 'flight'.[23] What concentrates this whole meaning in the localized image of the character is the symbolical image of the aloe which functions as 'an effective objective correlative' for the woman with her 'tanged emotional life of love and hatred, sensitivity and cruelty, fertility and sterility'.[24]

The compendious symbolic complex formed by 'mingled images of imprisonment and flight, love and hatred'[25] is an index of the dark emotional complex which accounts for the tragic stasis characterizing even her new life in the new house. The "dream" itself and her subjective vision of the aloe which has induced the "dream" seem very "much more real" as they define and analyse for her the complex of attitudes she has been wistfully longing to repose in: they seem to correspond to what is truer in her life. They encourage and reinforce her disdainful yet resolutely complacent attitude to "the house where the children lay sleeping and Stanley and Beryl played cribbage"

"*Love and Hatred*": She particularly likes "the long sharp thorns": it is, presumably, these thorns which make her like the aloe itself "more than anything": it is because of these thorns that she feels sure she 'will remember the aloe long after she's forgotten all the other things'; she seems oddly enchanted by this singular, forbidding feature of the aloe. This oddity of her enchantment is an index of the emotional complex involving sharply contrary feelings of 'love and hatred'. If there is love for others in her heart, it is only for the two members of her family, her husband and her mother.

Her love for her husband is not unmingled with her emotional attitude of hatred; her love for her mother is pure but not potential enough to survive "the sight" of "the long sharp thorns that edged the aloe leaves"; "the sight" makes "her heart grow hard". Almost the full nature of her love for her husband is manifest in the decisive yet concessive utterance that she mutely mumbles immediately after this entrancing vision of the aloe has faded: "Nobody would dare to come near the ship or to follow after.... 'Not even my New found land dog ... that I am so fond of in the daytime'". The subsequent interior monologue is the recollection of her emotional experiences in tranquillity: she analyses his character quite dispassionately, recalling presumably her traumatic experiences of sexual intercourse when "she had longed to say the most coarse, hateful things"; she recognizes the ambivalence of her present attitude to him as the final distillation of her experiences. The interior monologue is registered as the distillation of her traumatic sexual experiences with a husband who has been an animal by night and "the soul of truth and decency" "in the day-time"; this distillation consists in her final recognition of her irreconcilably contrary attitudes of 'love and hatred': "her feelings of him" are all "sharp and defined, one as true as the other"—like the "cruel leaves and fleshy stem" of "the fat swelling plant" she has discovered in the garden ("for all her love and respect and admiration she hated him".... "It had never been so plain to her as it was at this moment. There were all her feelings for him, sharp and defined, one as true as the other" ... "she could have done her feelings up in little packets and given them to Stanley"): her love for him is manifest in her scarce gesture of seemingly passive submission ("she smiled and curled her fingers into the big red hand she held") or in her utterances inviting his protective embrace ("'yes, clasp me'"), although the precise nature of this love remains obscurely secret: the fingers are "curled", not submissively relaxed or invitingly extended, like "the curling leaves" of the aloe; the "curled ... fingers" also seem to be "hiding something". Even her utterance connotes something more than what it obviously means: it is a "voice from a well".

There is perhaps one single moment when the secret longing of this poetess of exquisite passions may be said to have been externalized: "Pat, Pat: She heard the servant calling. But Pat was evidently hard to find; the silly voice went baa-baaing through the garden". But even this externalization, if it is one, affords no clue to the precise nature of what she secretly longs for or of what now in her calm despair she cannot stand being "discovered" ("she felt as though the moon had risen—that she was being strangely discovered in a flood of cold light. She shivered".) "only she seemed to be listening with her wide open waterful eyes, waiting for someone to come who just did not come, watching for something to happen that just did not happen". Who is that "someone"? What is that "something"? The answer lies deep within the dark privacy of her interiorized consciousness.

Her hatred of her husband is not only for the "Businessman" in him whose only juicy talk—even in the privacy of their bedroom—is a gossipy tidbit or two about what he has "got dirt cheap"; it is also for the muscleman that he is with "rock" or "iron" in his amalgam. Quite naturally, she does not rest again until the final slam of the front door tells her that he is 'really gone'. It is perhaps this hatred for a tough, thick-skinned husband that accounts for her aversion to "all the old paraphernalia" in the new house, or for her lackadaisical attitude to the house itself.

Her love for her mother is manifest in her appreciation of mother's richness, in her recognition that 'order is the adjunct of her mother'[26] and, in her awareness that "there was something comforting in the sight of her that she felt she could never do without". When 'she stops rocking and gets up' to go and "find mother", she stops being 'wavering and uncertain': she is out in search of one who 'represents value and definition' which she has found 'lacking in her own nature'.[27] Her mother represents for her a wholesome and experienced wisdom not passively but grittily resigned to reality: this realization, too, involved as it seems to be in the subjective vision of the way the plant stands ("High above them, as though becalmed in the air"), is natural to the moment when her mother herself is there with her: the poetess feels even her own view is their common view. She feels the aloe ship is coming towards them both and thinks her mother "too" shares in her feeling; she also agrees with her mother "those are buds", and puts her hand on her mother's arm and they walk down the steps, round the island, and on to the main drive that leads to the front gates' opening—by extended implication, on to the realm of freedom. When she sets off her "dream", which seems "much more real", against the commonplace senseless reality of her return to 'the house where the children lie sleeping and Stanley and Beryl play cribbage', she thinks of herself in association with her mother: "How much more real this dream was than that they should go back to the house", etc.

Her mother is perhaps the only member in the family for whom she seems to have real, intimate, deepening love; her love only for her mother seems unquestioned, unrelenting, undying. But despite all her intimacy and affinity with her mother in whom her 'ideal and hold on reality'[28] are combined, she forgets her when 'her heart grows hard' and dreams of her own escape; her longing for liberation becomes selfish; the escape sought is absolutely individual: "nobody would dare to come near the ship or to follow after".

Perhaps finally her romantic aspirations do become 'strong enough to submerge her appreciation of mother's richness;[29] the "dream" seems "much more real" than the "value and definition" themselves that her mother 'represents': it is perhaps her own secretly and firmly inculcated 'ideal' that finally supersedes the values her mother seems to represent or combine. One may venture to add that it is this sense of supersession that accounts for the absence of reference to her second visit to the kitchen which during her "first time" visit she has found saying " 'mother' all over". Her indulgence in "dream" is "much more real" than her return even to this kitchen in "the house" where she has found "everything ... in pairs."

"*Sensitivity and Cruelty*": What seems to correspond to the tangled emotional complex involving the character's "sensitivity" as a poetess of tender romantic passions and her 'cruelty' as a wife, a mother and a sister, is perhaps the combination in "the fat swelling plant" of the "fleshy stem:" and the "cruel leaves", of its lofty inviolate upper extremity 'becalmed in the air' and its deep-lying gnarled "roots" fiercely clutching the earth as "claws".

Her sensitivity as a poetess is manifest especially in her 'strange empathetic faculty of sharing in the secret life of things.[30] 'All the time nervously anxious to evade reality',[31] this poetess of romantic fancies is often intensely aware of the furtively secret flux of life in the world of things. The presentness in the world of things seems "much more real" than the moment of even her own choice from the realm of the possible: she feels the presentness of the 'free floating life of her own feelings'[32] is in nearest approximation to the timeless, darkly obscure flux of life in the microcosm of "the members of a secret society". The presentness of this inviolably secret flux of life is "much more real" to her even than the timelessly and intensely real presentness of life in the world of the children. What registers this comparatively greater intensity of her experience of a reality that seems "much more real" is a dramatic transition in the narrative sequence. This transition involves a sense of coincidental choice from the realm not only of the possible but also of the "much more real": Kezia, recalcitrating against Isabel's "government", snaps a vaguely evasive answer ("'oh, just away ...'") and obeys only her 'exciting impulse to discover', which makes her 'innocence' seem 'not merely negative but a living capacity for experience'.[33] Linda detaches her mind from the children's world outside ("she didn't hear them any more."): she seeks absolute interiorization of her consciousness in the solitude of her room which she wishes were dark enough to be conducive to her communion with the reality underlying the microcosm of "the members of the secret society". Kezia's adventure into the realm of the possible and Linda's adventure into the world of the "real" coincide. The eternal presentness of some secret life seems to her to be "much more real" at this 'crucial period in her development: she is resigned to a life of calm despair as a tragic culmination of all her experiences of thwarted secret longings; all vital reality of the present, all nascency of life in the new house, seems to her to consist simply in the "coming alive of things".

Linda experiences absolute freedom during her communion with "the secret life of things"; this intense experience of individual existence heightening her tactile responsiveness gives her a renewed sense of self-identity: she feels, naturally, that she is 'much more really' "alive" than she is in her life with the members of her family where she finds herself only confronted with an agonizingly unanswerable question: "why this mania of hers to keep alive at all"? Her dreamily sensory experiences of the thrill of communion with the secret life of "things coming alive" are climaxed by a feeling that is almost mystical: she is at one with "the minutes, tiniest particle"; she seems to be enjoying the thrill of levitation without being airy ("she did not feel her bed, she floated, held up in the air"); her "eyes" seem "to be listening": the sensory organs have exchanged their functions. The moment of choice is frozen, still, static: the next moment is not there; 'something to happen just does not happen'.

But the "things coming alive" in the unconscious realm of her psyche assume alarming proportions; they 'grow bigger and bigger' omening a hopeless future in which her choice from that realm of the possible will contend with the 'intensifying menace'[34] it will be an ironically promising future in which she will only have 'more of what she has, more of what she does not want',[35] that is, more and more of what only justifies the callous, apathetic, cynical attitude she has chosen to repose in. The realm of the future will have only "whole fleets of aloes to choose from".

"The aloe leaves", which seem "cruel" with their "long sharp thorns" and a "blind stem cutting into the air as if no wind could ever shake it", help to image forth her own cruelty not only as a wife but also as a mother. To her husband who is obsessed with 'terrors about sudden disasters',[36] piteously apprehensive as he has been of the sudden death of his "darling", she is unsympathetically and pitilessly cold-hearted: the welcome she offers to this nervously apprehensive husband is always cold, formal, perfunctory ("Hullo, are you home again?"). The husband's inquiry every time is equally troubled—it is always breathless, eager, sincere; but the wife's reply is always routine. When the husband brings her back "a bottle of oysters and a pineapple" and feels he has "brought her back all the harvest of the earth", the wife's reference to them is nonchalantly casual ("Let me put down these silly things"): she also behaves in a quaintly absurd manner ("'what have you got in your buttonhole—cherries?' she took them out and hung them over his ear".), which evinces only her inconsiderate insouciance. The husband has to tell her again he has brought them for her ("'They are for you'"), but her acknowledgement of the genuine offer is only suavely and reluctantly polite ("'you don't mind if I save them. They'd spoil my appetite for dinner.'").

"Fertility and sterility": The 'seldom-blooming' aloe tree seems to objectify still another equilibrious combination of two fundamental attributes of the character, 'fertility and sterility'.

The one attribute, 'fertility', is manifest perhaps only as her prolificity as a mother who has "had three great lumps of children already" and can still "go on having children". By extended implication, this 'fertility' as the attribute of the character seems inclusive of the positive qualities of her nature which suggest evolutional possibilities and which persist in spite of her indulgence in 'hatred' and 'cruelty'. The positive qualities are manifest in her love for her husband and her mother; in her capacity for dispassionately critical yet understandingly sympathetic view of her husband's character; in her secret longing for something of abiding value, something that her husband's money, the new house, the garden, the children, cannot give, something that is soul-satisfying and not merely fleshly; in her concentrated and fierce desire for experience of her individual existence in absolute freedom; and in her sensitive appreciation of "truth and decency", order and harmony, 'value and definition'.

The other attribute, 'sterility' is dramatized as psychic transfixation of the character. This transfixation is occasioned by (a) her attitude of resignation to a life of self-centred isolation in obscure privacy even in the lively atmosphere of a fresh nascent life for the family in the new house: (b) her tendency to be in communion with the secret flux of life in the timeless world of things; (c) her conflicting attitudes to her husband and to the other members of her family with whom she is united by ties of consanguinity; (d) her secret longing as a concentrated and fierce desire for what she cannot even vaguely define and which is articulate only as a voice that 'goes baa-baaing through the wilderness that the world in and around the house is.

The high sustained tension generated by the emotional conflict which her attitudes, her tendency, and her longing abstrusely involve seems to have been symbolically externalized as the antithetical feature characterizing the total image of the aloe tree; "High above them, as though becalmed in the air, and yet holding so fast to the earth it grew from, it might have had claws instead of roots".

(a) Her withdrawal into self-centred isolation is suggested by the immediate surroundings of the place she is found sitting in or dramatized by her own postures and gestures: this image of the character is pictured in miniature, as it were, by a statement that Beryl succinctly words in her letter to her friend Nan Pym: "My sister who is a mile away does not know a soul here"; her loneliness is emphasized by the scene where "in a long cane chair ... she lay before crackling fire". The members of her family present in the room are all individually engaged or "absorbed": Burnell and Beryl, "the only ones in this house with a real feeling for food", partaking of "fried chops" and "tea"; Isabel "combing the curls in a gentle absorbed fashion"; the mother probably lost in her own thoughts, "snug" and "placid" as she is by nature. The "crackling fire" unheeded by them seems to be the image of herself, languishing in deliberate isolation as she 'lies' there; "the room" stretching dark and bare to hollow windows" defines, as it were, the world itself that the isotate dwells in, the world that is obscure, bleak, hopeless.

Later we find her voice ringing only in "a shadowy quiet": Stanley and Beryl begin their "game of crib" not even caring whether she is left under the light of a lamp or outside the pool of it. "With the cold wet dew on her fingers" she seems tinglingly conscious of the exposure of her innerself to the world without. She also 'shivers' *to realize she is* "being strangely discovered in a flood of cold light". The postures she has habitually acquired bespeak a recluse: "prostrated" in the buggy after her departure from the old house, "rocking to and fro ... her arms above her head", reclining "in a long cane chair, with her feet on a hassock and a plaid over her knees ... before a crackling fire", she looks a picture of stolid, stoic, static passivity. The gestures—naturally scarce as she is granted exemption from all domestic chore—are noted at significant moments during 'the crucial period in her development' as a character constantly withdrawing herself into obscurity of reclusive privacy.

The image of the character languishing in obscurity not only pensively and dreamily but also wearily is conveyed (i) through registration of the answers she makes to inquiries, (ii) through omission of her answer to a major decisive question central to the story element, and (iii) through indirect suggestion of her habit of awaking first of all.

(i) When her husband wishes her to partake of the "tip-top meat" and turns to her, inquiring, "'you're sure you won't change your mind, Linda darling?'", her answer ("'The very thought of it is enough'") is expressive only of her self-enforced abstinence, of an attitude crystalized after her realization of the "mania of hers to keep alive at all" ("blind aloe unshaken by the wind"). Later, she begs to "save" the cherries her husband has brought not in his pocket but in his button-hole, and adds, "'They'd spoil my appetite for dinner'". With her listless attitude to all sustenance as a means of subsistence, she stands in sharp contrast to "the only ones in this house with a real feeling for food"; this contrast helps to indicate her intense awareness of the imminence of her death, of the futility or meaninglessness of subsisting on food and drink. The character languishes physically too. Again, when we hear her emphatically affirmative answer (to "'Not asleep, are you?'") it is clear to us that she has been in a vacant mood: her mute listening silence while he gushes over what he has "got dirt cheap" cannot be interpreted; and this impossibility of interpretation deepens the obscurity she dwells in now.

(ii) She interrupts her sister's statement the moment she finds it is going to explain her listless attitude to the new house ("'of course it does not matter to you because—'") and reminds her of "the buggy" and "Pat" ("'But there's the buggy', said Linda 'Pat can drive you into town whenever you like'"): here we have only the impression of her cynically stoic resignation to a life of self-centred isolation. The implication that this dramatic transition in the dialogue involves entangles the emotional complex that the character's 'psychology' is; it obscures the privacy of her self-enforced isolation. she cannot bring herself even to hear anybody else in the family defining the reason why "it does not matter" to her; the reason relates to her soberly fatalistic philosophy of life—to an attitude that she nourishes in what seems to be sworn secrecy. Earlier her daughter's sudden interruption has saved her from making an answer which she has been loth to express: "'Kezia is drinking tea out of Aunt Beryl's cup'". On both these occasions the major decisive question about her attitude to the new life in the new house is expediently darkened by interruption. The secret is meant to remain locked in the labyrinth of the character's heart.

(iii) Her habit of waking first of all in the family is revealed in the scene of the first day-break in the new house: we can see the implication that the private world she lives in is so distracting that she cannot sink into a night-long deep restful sleep.

(b) Psychic transfixation of the character manifesting the attribute of "sterility" is occasioned also by her tendency to choose not from the realm of the future but from that of the present itself: the realm of eternal presentness that she has discovered as an obscure haven for herself in her resignation to a life of self-centred isolation is the timeless or non-temporal realm of the secret life of things: here the past and the future as distinguished in the human world stand resolved into eternal presentness. (Linda exists not by choosing from the realm of the possible but by exploring the non-temporal dimensions of the very moment of the choice, the dimensions of the eternal presentness in the secret world of things. The liberation she seeks as a means of experiencing her existence is this absolute freedom in the world of things; here the present is not continuous with the past and no choice from the realm of the possible has to be made and still there is a secret ceaseless flux of life).

This tendency to hide in the secret haven of the microcosm of things also accounts for the stasis that seems to characterize the isotate's situation.

(c) The sense of 'sterility' is conveyed through (i) a rhythmical pattern of recurrent narrative statements expressing ambiguity in the omniscient narrator's point of view (which accentuates the irony inherent in the paradox of dichotomized conjugality), and (ii) externalization of what is an intensified emotional experience of "two" remotely isolated yet abstrusely involved worlds.

(i) Stanley and Linda are united by ties of marriage, but at every moment of their clandestine intimacy, the one married partner seems to be "apt to drift away" from the other, or 'they do not so much want to get ahead as to keep near enough to talk—to keep near perhaps that is all.' The irony inherent in this paradox of dichotomized conjugality is stressed by the occasional ambiguity in the omniscient narrator's viewpoint: "By God, he was a perfect fool to feel as happy as this!". The point of view, apart from seeming the narrator's own, appears to be a viewpoint which might as well be Stanley's as Linda's.

If it is Stanley's, it reveals his sudden shudder at the thought of her "delicate" health or her imminent death, and also his enthusiasm for the company of "the number of chaps at the club" ("as though this were intensely interesting"), his eagerness to do anything and everything for his "darling" ("as though he had brought back all the harvest of the earth", "as though he were going to leap at the moon for her").

If it is Linda's point of view, it shows how every time she seems cruelly ironical or inconsiderately insensitive to the fervency of his love for her.

The paradox of dichotomized conjugality is registered appropriately through intermittent repetetion of hypothetical narrative statements ambiguous enough to indicate coincidence of two contrary angles of vision: what is revealed is a premonitory symptom of sterility or utter impossibility of consummate psycho-physical communion in their life hereafter in the new house.

(ii) The one scene dramatizing the climactic moment of intensified emotional experiences is set in the room where Stanley and Beryl are enjoying a "game of crib" It is appropriately conjured up just before Linda 'stops rocking to and fro' and gets up to escape into the world of her values and ideals which she rediscovers to be "much more real" than the unendurable reality inside "the house where Stanley and Beryl play cribbage". The moment when Linda 'stops rocking to and fro' is perhaps the first and last high-tide moment in the 'crucial period in her development': we find her making a choice from the realm of the future, although the choice that she makes is again a choice from the realm of the present itself, the realm of the secret life of the aloe as a ship. The climactic penultimate moment when Linda is eavesdropping upon Stanley and Beryl's conversation of "those two" during their "game of crib" is dramatized as a tense moment: it is the moment of Linda's intensified emotional experience of the one major tragic fact in her life as a marriage partner. Intermittent recurrence of the word "two" throughout the rendering of the experience facilitates accentuation of the effect of conflation: we find two worlds on the scene: the world of the forlorn lovely wife, on the one hand, and the world of Stanley and Beryl as lovers, on the other; or, the world of the husband and wife, and the world of the second woman; or, also, the world of the husband, and that of his two 'mistresses'. Each pair of worlds flashes upon Linda's inward eye. The game gains momentum and Linda's experience, as she sits "rocking to and fro", is intensified as a vertigo at once subjective and objective: she is intensely aware of conflation of the pairs that the "two worlds" form. The experience culminates in the vision of the "two moths" as Stanley and Beryl, Stanley and Linda herself, or Linda herself and Beryl; all the pairs flash in a succession too quick to be perceptible: one of the three pairs must "fly away before it is too late", before the life of the pair is irremediably embittered, or before the life of one who does not form the pair is dismally isolated. Linda's subjective vertigo is symptomatic of her psychic transfixation; the experience is barren of a definite decision or conclusion: the situation in the isotate's life is absolutely sterile. The experience of conflation reaches a climax, and Linda jerks herself out of the rocking chair, her innermost longing for "flight and escape" unbearably intensified.

(d) 'Sterility' as the attribute of the character is revealed also

> by her failure to articulate her secret longing or her tendency to muffle in discreet silence even the initial syllable of articulation, if there is any; the failure or tendency is due to her own dark realization that even this residue of articulation is only a cry in the wilderness that she has been wearily and listlessly roaming as an inmate either of this new house or of the old house. What blankets her words is her fatalistic philosophy of life crystallized through her recognition of the irrevocability of the one tragic fact—it is touch-and-go with her as a heart patient. It is not only because of the cyclic fluctuations of these conflicting attributes that Linda seems 'imprisoned', arrested, transfixed; it is also because of the tension generated by the irresistibility of the attraction of the "much more real" world, her privately secret world which promises thrills of a refreshing experience of her existence as an individual being in absolute freedom.

Inclusion of equally intimate characterizations of the other two adults, Beryl and Stanley, is necessitated by the importance of their direct involvement in the tragically static situation that the 'crucial period' of Linda's development defines.

Beryl makes the choice from the realm of the possible, the future, and not like Linda, from that of the real, the present; but she too seems to stand 'arrested' at the very moment of her choice. At the moment of her choice from the realm of the future Beryl is fretfully impatient of what seems to her to be dull tedious delay in occurrence of the promising future; she is also apprehensive about the loss of her youthfulness ("'I' ll get to be a most awful frump in a year or two' ... 'when I'm mother's age', etc."); Although she dreams of the occasion when she will wear the new dress she has made out of "that white satin dress", she does not know when she will have the occasion. Always on tiptoe with excitement, this hothead finds mother's "deliberate way of doing things ... simply maddening" and puts it all down to "old age". She adores the new opportunities for fantasy but is appalled at being shut away to rot in the country: "'I must say the house and the garden are awfully nice—a million times better than that awful cubby-hole in town. But buried, my dear. Buried isn't the word'." Truly, "buried" isn't the word: with all her fatalistic attitude and impotent fury ("'one may as well rot here as anywhere else', she muttered savagely, digging the stiff brass safety-pins into the red serge curtains") and with all her stoic resignation to the irrevocable position of affairs and unemotional vacant moods of 'acceptance' ("'oh, well, at any rate it won't kill us', she said dryly, putting down her empty cup ..."), she feels that the possibility of voluntary excursion to the "town" is "a consolation"; at the same time she longs to stay back for a reason which she cannot consciously acknowledge but which she cannot even for a moment dismiss, either: the reason is probably her nascent love for Stanley that makes her "put her hand over his, pointing out something so that he should see how white her hand is beside his brown one".

She seems 'marked by ... arrest of development'[37] also because she loves Stanley and hates him at the same time. She not only takes care to look "charming" to Stanley, to dress herself attractively "for the benefit of Stanley", and attract his attention to what she feels "there's nobody to look at"; she also feels fleshly masochistic thrill in "exaggerating her woe because she know how he loved winning". Despite this secret love for him, she hates the businessman in him: this businessman is concerned about the "harm done" to "the tables and chairs ... left on the veranda"; he "thinks the frame might fetch something some day or other"; he has bought this house 'lock, stock and barrel', he "has been threatening to take a place in the country" where she is 'shut away to rot'. —He is not the young man of her dreams but one who is just one of the herd, walking about with his "men from the club ..., rather fattish," all "pulling up their trousers every minute". Her narcissistic visions are disgustingly dissipated by unwelcome interruptions; 'her romantic fantasies are 'punctured by bouts of frantic domestic activity'[38]; all impulse of enthusiasm for the experience of individual existence through self assertion or through liberation from the bondage of the present is consumed in 'grim moments of self-recognition'[39]: her total self thus remains arrested in a state of barren stagnation. Her subconscious realization of this sterility as the fundamental attribute of her own total self is registered by her "harsh laughter". Her perplexity at the experience of stasis at the very moment of choice from the realm of the possible is reflected in the picture of the "surprised-looking" flower she has painted. Beryl's characterization is a variation on the same theme.

'Arrest of development' as the fundamental feature of the other adult character, Stanley, is quietly dramatized again and again in the narrative; the first time when after his morning exercise he is donning his shirt; the second time when on his way back home from office he feels 'Pat has put brake on again'.

Dramatization of the character's unconscious experience of 'arrest' on both the occasions is appropriate to the 'mood' of the moments in the narrative.

At the first moment the character is already set "worlds away from Linda" who has been watching him "as if from the clouds"; her apathetic attitude to his "amazing vigour", to his animal health and strength, to what only evokes her traumatic experiences of 'things rushing at her' and "killing" her, is unmistakably postured: "She lay on the white tumbled bed and watched as if from the clouds". The one detail of the setting is eloquent enough: the bed is "tumbled" and "white": Linda, the first member of the family to wake up on this first morning in the new house, has perhaps been restlessly sleepy; the "white" colour seems to reflect the sensibility that is purged of all sensual passion. Stanley's "shirt" too is "white": perhaps the image complex evolves to sustain the impression of the purity or elegance of his wife's sensibility which the animal in him has been offending by "butting into" or 'rushing at' her poetic self. The impression of this clash of sensibilities as a symptom of 'arrest' is also onomatopoeically evoked through a sequence of terminal hard dentals, 'd' and 't'; significantly, most of the words here terminate in these hard dentals: this sequence seems to accentuate the sense of conclusive finality implicit in all this drama of clash of sensibilities.

At the second moment when Pat seems to him to have "put the brake on again", the character has almost a palpable experience of 'arrest' ("He could feel it in the pit of his stomach"). The emotional context of the moment is that of a sad realization on the part of the husband: even his profitable intimacy with his wife has been an emotional relation only in dichotomized conjugality ("Talking things over with Linda was a wonderful help even though they were apt to drift away from the point"). Dramatization of the character's unconscious physical experience of 'arrest' quietly coincides with his realization of dichotomy which has rendered his married life static. Registration of the character's realization of the dichotomy imperceptibly shades off into the dramatization of his actual though unconscious experience of the static situation the dichotomy has created ("Hang it all. They weren't getting along very fast".)

The sense of impasse that confronts the marriage partners is quietly dramatized also when the husband's major decisive question relating to the future of their new life in this new house is irrelevantly interrupted by Isabel's absurdly inane prattle: "'Think you are going to like it?' Stanley said. 'I don't want to tell you but I think I ought to, mother', said Isabel. 'Kezia is drinking tea out of Aunt Beryl's cup'" The question remains unanswered, and the section (III) terminates at this very point. The sense of a future blighted by uncertainty and rendered dubious by cumulative absurdities 'growing bigger and bigger' is conspicuously yet unobtrusively accentuated.

The sense of impasse that precludes possibilities of development is suggestively rendered again in the swift unfoldment of a homespum drama in the candlelit dining-room downstairs and in the dark bed-room upstairs on the first evening in the new house.

Stanley is 'thrilled with the possibilities'[40] also of procreation and subsequent proliferation ("'That's where my boy ought to sit'"). But the moment he 'tightens his arm round Linda's shoulder', he 'flinches' from what his tightened arm around the shoulders of a "delicate" bedfellow makes him feel would be sheer lecherous cruelty: 'Sudden terror about the possible disaster' chills all his feeling of happiness and he sobers down, "By God, he was a perfect fool to feel as happy as this.'". The moment he makes the choice from the realm of the possible, he is 'arrested' by his 'sudden terror'.

The impression of impasse is conveyed again through dramatization of the conflict between the characters' emotional attitudes to each other even in clandestine privacy of the dark room upstairs: Stanley is "so confoundedly happy" not simply because he is alone with his wife in the seclusion of the bedroom but also because all his dreams of happy mundane existence have come true: a new house, a big garden, a buggy complete with its driver, a host of gay children, a "charming" sister-in-law in addition to a "delicate" wife, and his own "firm, obedient body" which is without an ounce of fat. There are so many reasons that he cannot explain his feeling at the moment ("'I don't know what has come over me.'")

Linda with her thorough understanding of the businessman's character or nature intuitively discerns the emotional complex that her husband's effusion involves. She is, therefore, perhaps sarcastic when she puts the counter-question ("'Are you?'"). She does not seem to share in his happiness. The 'bustling, muscle-conscious' husband, the hard-boiled substantial businessman has never bothered his head about what her own happiness consists in. When he 'protests' ("'I don't know what has come over me'") by way of explaining why he has "put his arms round her . . . again" and not lighted the candles, she is conscious simply of utter blank darkness and heavy cold dew outside and a dog barking far away: shivering all over with the chilling fear of "being discovered"—with the fear of the vain exposure of her secret longing to the business-benumbed sensibilities of her husband, she seems to have stopped reaching out towards him. We feel she has withdrawn into the obscure privacy of her own isolated lonesome world, routinized as it is in the dull companionship of a hard-boiled unregenerate businessman.

Both Stanley and Linda as individual married partners stand arrested in the new house at a moment when a life of possibilities is nascent: Stanley with his stabbing realization of his folly of imagining the "empty chair . . . at the head of the table" as a seat for his lineal heir, and Linda with her own married life as only a vain quest for what may illuminate the dark meaning of her existence itself ("her ring tapping on the marble mantelpiece as she felt for the matches").

Stanley seems 'marked by arrest of development' not simply because he is 'bustling and muscle-conscious ... flinching and uncertain within'[41] but also because his married partner, his bed-fellow, his better-half is impassively frigid, mysteriously introverted, curiously self-centred.

Now this static world of adults 'arrested' by their uncertain conflict is significantly encompassed by microcosm of evolutional nature.

This all-encompassing microcosm is created by the two extremes of categories of experience, Kezia representing the one extreme, Grandma, the other: Kezia stands for Innocence which as 'a living capacity of experience' involves ceaseless experience, and Grandma represents 'experienced wisdom' that is all acceptance without a question and is thus nothing but gentle and lofty innocence. It is this secret affinity or correlation between 'the very young and the very old' which sustains all 'variety' that characterizes the confounded worldly experience, for 'within the family the ideal lies in the combined keeping of the very old and the very young'.[42] The sense of correlation between the two extremes of categories of experience involves the sense of an abiding 'value'. It is this value which gives meaning to the vague complex formed by the overlapping of intermediary categories of agonized experience in a static world of 'arrested' individuals, all suspended in a state of uncertainty naturally as 'unformed' identities.[43] The value is an ideal. The ideal lies in the 'combined keeping of the very young and the very old' as representations of an abiding value. It sustains the variety of temperaments and attitudes which manifest the intermediary categories of experience. The value and the attitudes cohere. The sense of this coherence is central to the meaning that the narrative composition seems to have been meant to embody. Coherence of 'value' and 'attitudes'[44] forms a complex of evolutional nature. It is attuned to "a mysterious rhythm" which is always a "prelude". This "prelude" is a manifestation of timeless Innocence—Innocence which, in the ultimate analysis, all Experience is.

The very young with their innocence as 'a living capacity for experience', their 'vitality unqualified by the bias of *a priori*', 'their open nature with its exciting impulse to discover', 'represent the intensity with which we live';[45] they only live and do not know that they live; they are very much alive; they feel the naked throb of life through their innocence.

The very old with all their 'experienced wisdom', their calm 'acceptance', their vision of the realm of the possible as the hallowed beauty of life, are passively resigned to the drift of life; they live and know that they live; but they also know that is all that they know and need to know; all their experienced wisdom remains imperfect as helpless innocence.

The adults, although suspended in a state of uncertainty with their development 'arrested' and individually or existentially lost in some blurred misty sphere—somewhere between the intensely living world of the very young and the serenely tranquil realm of the very old—seek actualization of their beings in liberation from bondage of the past and also the present; they are intensely alive. But all intensity characterizing the process of their self-actualization is the intensity of their desperate 'will to be'; they remain puzzled, uncertain, immature; with their imperfect knowledge of a definite and comforting answer to the 'whys', they are equally innocent; they only do not know that they are innocent.

The adults are meant to seem marked by 'a certain arrest of development' in contrast to 'the very young and the very old'. This reinforces the intended effect of a world of 'formless' identities that seem only to vary individually in their ambiguously vague relationship with the new house: we see a world of adults 'much less sure of themselves than the very young, much more puzzled about what they aspire to than the old grandma'.[46] The world is thus made to seem ultimately subordinated to the ideal domination of the all-encompassing microcosm meant to demonsterate the abiding nature of the value, Innocence.

Thus the whole microcosm as revealed appropriately at the moment of nascency of a new life in the new house is Innocence given a local habitation and a name.

Naturally, only the two characters representing the essentially correlated extremes of categories of experience have innocent visions of the aloe tree. Kezia, who represents 'the very young', sees the aloe as one of the things she has "never seen"; the grandmother representing the extreme of all categories of experiences that the other members of the family have had on the first two days in the new house, sees the aloe as something new and strange ("Are those buds, or is it only an effect of light?"). The aloe tree as a thing the like of which she has "never seen" ("whatever could it be? she had never seen anything like it before. She stood and stared") points to her own innocence; the image of the same tree seen by her as something familiar yet unfamiliar reflects her strange, lofty innocence which her "experienced wisdom" has ripened into.

What betokens some secret affinity between these two innocent viewers of the aloe tree as something unseen and unfamiliar is the one trait common to them both: it is their 'vitality ... unqualified by the bias of *a priori*'. Kezia as a child is curious, thrill-loving, imaginative; the grandmother as an old woman of experienced wisdom is unprejudiced, solicitous, benevolent.

All affinity between the two characters consists in the secret correspondence between their individual innocent selves. Manifestations of this secret affinity are discernible in their irresistibly magnetic physical and psychical attraction towards each other. The impression of this secret affinity is sustained by the sense of sterling integrity that distinguishes their individual selves; it is sharpened by the sense of their reciprocal psychic orientation as representatives of the children at once innocent and precocious and of the adults at once experienced and ignorant. The effect of their individual characterizations is heightened by their instinctive love for order and harmony and beauty.

The essential correlation between the two extremes of categories of experience is revealed significantly by the same symbol that reflects all the contrary attributes of the central character representing the other 'formless' identities in her own tensely static world: the symbolical significance of the aloe tree is central to the meaning of the short-story: it reflects the coherence of 'value' and 'attitudes', which as a fused complex defines the full ultimate concept of all Experience as Innocence. It was perhaps this concentrated aesthetic vision of the aloe that determined the choice of the earlier title (The Aloe). Substitution of the present title (Prelude) seems, therefore, to have been necessitated by Miss Mansfield's later comprehensive vision of the whole complex as a microcosm with evolutional possibilities. With this lyrical title the 'long elegy in special prose' reads like a Song of Innocence.

The only question that puzzles us as we look back on this peculiar piece of narrative is: how is *Prelude* a short-story? The one answer that seems possible here is hypothetical: if potentiality of a story element can be inherent even in a vague sense of possibilities of development that nascency of a new life in a family may reveal, *Prelude* is a short-story.[47] The beginning of the new life in the new house discloses 'possibilities of development and contrast' in the 'nest of relationships';[48] this beginning is a "prelude" to the faintly conceivable later developments of 'relationships' in the 'nest' that the Burnells are now huddled in. Rendering in intense concentration alone could be the technique for the discovery of evolutional possibilities in the tingling moment of a faintly stirring transition or turning point in the life of the family. What evinces concentration is the automatic formation of a concentric design as the narrative structure with a comprehensively expressive symbol at the centre. The requisite sense of progression is inherent in the evolutional nature of the microcosm.

Discovery— in the past—of an evolutional microcosm as a manifestation of Innocence (which all human experience is because of the eternal nascency of its state) would be pursued again in *At the Bay*: but the technique would be more intricate, the emergent truth-vision much more comprehensive. However, the credit for the success achieved in that later masterpiece would perhaps always be given to this first 'elegy in special prose' (*Prelude*). What Miss Mansfield unconsciously learnt in course of her composition of *Prelude* would help her later also while she would be producing her other masterpieces of 'dramatic effect' or 'achieved content'. The one major technical achievement that composition of *Prelude* facilitated was not only expedient exploitation of the multipersonal point of view but also desirable naturalization of the 'dramatic effect' which is the most essential feature of the genre chosen. The intensity of moment dramatized and the appropriate effect of instantaneity achieved would be made to seem, respectively, low and half-veiled: the intermediate intensity characterizing the 'indeterminate middle',[49] or the feverish tenseness of the culminant moment, would be registered in a low key; the effect of instantaneity would be as naturalistic as that of the quiescent flow of life. Thus the flux registered by the narrative style would seem intensely and poetically enlivened as a flow of life at once secretively calm and palpably seething. The moment dramatized would seem tense yet lyrical; 'the story would be told with a sense of mystery, radiance, an after-glow'.[50] And thus the real form of the short-story would be mastered.

Naturalization of the 'dramatic effect' in the later masterpieces would be achieved also through objective and inconclusive dramatization of the tense yet lyrical moments through dispassionately 'subjective selection of materials' meant 'to reflect an objective standard of values'.[51] The form achieved through 'abeyance of self' and 'vision of Innocence'[52] would admit of no 'sympathetic summation'[53] by the ominscient author. Her sensitive perception of even a grim reality would be a-morally aesthetic: 'the snail under the leaf'[54] would be seen as a poetic beauty, somber, serene, and soul-awakening.

Perhaps it was in this sense that Miss Mansfield recovered in *Prelude* 'the gift that had produced *Tiredness of Rosabel* and even went beyond it'.[55]

But the artist striving towards the achievement of the real form naturally awoke to the need of experimentation with the unquestionably indispensable and admittedly potent means of effectual dramatization: point of view. Perhaps she sincerely felt that before she achieved the requisite narrative quality enlivened by a dramatic quality, it was necessary for her to exploit the potentiality of what as focus of narration governs the total structural-textural build-up. That mastery of this means alone could now complement and perfect all that she had achieved up till now in course of her practice of the technique peculiar to the short-story was undoubtedly an honest realization.

NOTES AND REFERENCES

1. *Journal*, p. 93.
2. *Ibid.*, p. 93,
3. *Ibid.*, pp. 80-81.

4. William Walsh, *A Manifold Voice*, p. 162.
5. *Ibid.*
6. J.M. Murry, *Katherine Mansfield and other Literary Portraits*, p. 85.
7. William Walsh, *op. cit.*, p. 160.
8. *Ibid.*, p. 162.
9. *Ibid.*, p. 160.
10. *Ibid.*

Cf. 'Chekhov, of course, did not always write as leisurely as in *The Steppe*. But he did consistently use the external method of description, relying to a great extent on reference to known types and Katherine Mansfield the New Zealander could not refer to types.... She could not assume her reader's familiarity with any containing society or class. Chekhov not only could but had to do this, since it is in the nature of his medium that the short-story-writer must assume his reader's familiarity with something.... Katherine Mansfield had nothing of the sort ... she must needs assume her reader's familiarity with "her people" and her "undiscovered country"—and, having done so, hasten to establish it.—Antony Alpers, *Katherine Mansfield*, p. 217. *Comment*—The remarks which issue from Alper's comparative study of the openings of Chekhov's *The Steppe* and Miss Mansfield's *Prelude* do not illuminate the reason for the authors' individual assumption of their reader's 'familiarity" they also disconcert the critical reader: he does not find the use of 'the external method of description' consistent in *The Steppe*; he cannot see how Miss Mansfield has not assumed her reader's familiarity with 'something' even in short-stories which are not about "her people" and her "undiscovered country". Most probably the reason for the authors' individual assumption of their 'reader' familiarity' varied with the individual pro-conceived effects of their short-stories. *The Steppe* as a story told from an omniscient narrator's point of view is intended to achieve a specific effect: it is the effect of the closest approximation of the world of man to the world of Nature: the world of man with all his distinctive features and individual contradictions and sufferings, and the world of Nature with all its naked features and its own contradictions between beauty and ugliness, or tranquillity and inclemencies: 'Both Man and Nature want to be worthy of each other' says Vladimir Yermilov, 'each suffers from the contradiction between beauty and ugliness, from senseless primordial forces and cruelty' (*A.P. Chekhov: 1860-1960* p. 139). The nature of the pre-conceived effect demanded an epic vision inclusive of an empathetic view of the objects of Nature—a vision comprehensive enough to capture the secret link correlating men and nature lower on the biological scale ("The grass ... was asserting its passionate desire for life", etc.). Miss Mansfield in *Prelude* seems to have assumed her reader's familiarity with "her people" and her "undiscovered country". She aimed for the 'dramatic effect' of the original real-life episodes themselves in course of her aesthetic recreation of a whole specific complex of a past experience; she had discovered a poetic beauty in the "people" and the "country" and in her nostalgic re-creation of them she succeeded in re-capturing the whole microcosm: unforced realism helped her to retain the original integrity of the episodes as contingencies instinct with poetic beauty. Choice of her specific methods (of dropping 'the reader suddenly and surprisingly into the middle of a scene and situation', of 'introducing Pat as if by accident in the headless course of two sentences about the children, of moving 'from one character's mind to another's') was necessitated by her aesthetic urge to register the very throb of the poetry of life that pulsated through her memory. 'For Miss Mansfield', says Eleen Baldeshwiler, 'form ... animates detail as it orders and illuminates what memory retains from its judgement of experience'. ("Katherine Mansfield's Theory of Fiction", *Studies in Short Fiction*, Vol. VI, Summer 1970, p. 428). The story begins *in medias res* because the effect sought is that of instantaneity: Pat is introduced 'as if by accident' because, as Alpers himself has remarkably discovered, his characterization functions as 'counterpoint to an exposition of the mother's attitude to her children, and of their bewilderment in the great upheaval'; 'the author (narrator?) moves from one character's mind to another's, now to Linda's, now to Kezia's, now to her own (?), detached, observing' for a simple reason: employment of the multi-personal point of view subordinated to a 'detached, observing' omniscient narrator's aesthetic point of view helps to trick the reader into familiarity with a poetic truth that nascency of a new life in a family may be instinct with; use of this multi-personal point of view is necessitated by Miss Mansfield's exclusive concentration on the human drama in 'the nest of relationships' revealing the possibilities of development and contrast as a lyrical truth in human life. But the omniscient narrator's point of view in Chekhov's short-story occasionally restrict itself to the consciousness of the boy: it is meant to cover a whole microcosm of man and nature by way of impregnation of the boy's youthful spirit with the mystery and beauty and terrors of the Steppe.

11. William Walsh, *op. cit.*, p. 156.
12. J.M. Murry, *op. cit.*, pp. 84-85.
13. *Journal*, p. 94.
14. "As to *The Wind Blows*, I put that in because so many people had admired it ... and queer people spoke so strongly about it I felt I must put it in".—*Letters*. p. 307
15. Saralyn Daly, *Katherine Mansfield*, p. 61.
16. Sylvia Berkman, *Katherine Mansfield: A Critical Study*, p. 79.
17. William Walsh, *op. cit.*, p. 156.
18. J.M. Murry, *op. cit.*, p. 88.
19. *Ibid.*, p. 160.
20. William Walsh. *op. cit.*, p. 86.
21. Cf. 'As Joyce built *The Dead* on the structural unit of the epiphany ..., Miss Mansfield builds her longer stories on the unit of the single, highly economical, significant scene. In *Prelude* ... she first utilized this technique'.—Sylvia Berkman, *op. cit.*, p.

    Comment—What, as a matter of fact, distinguishes Miss Mansfield's *Prelude* from Joyce's *The Dead* is the structural design oriented to a specific effect—the effect of 'possibilities of development and contrast' inherent in a crucial moment of choice from the realm of the possible, the future. The over-all structural design is that of contrasted characterizations and the design seems concentric with its centre defined by a symbolical image ("aloe tree") which embodies the whole meaning implicit in the microcosm called into being. The structural organization of scenes or episodes in Joyce's *The Dead* is meant to dramatize the conflict of pride with love, of ego with humanity through registration of simultaneous operation of both extrinsic and intrinsic forces effecting gradual extinction or attrition of the protagonist's personality: the episodes take place not in isolation but within the framework of the party: this party with its gaiety, its music, its hospitality symbolizes the inner warmth with which life is enveloped; the "snow" as the central symbol signifies the cold exterior with which the protagonist is implacably sheathed: appearing first as a scenic detail it develops into a symbol of expanded consciousness, orienting the protagonist's individual psyche to the larger world of humanity which is inclusive of "all the living and the dead". Centralization of the narrative structure on a compendious symbolical image is perhaps the only similarity between the individual techniques of the two short-stories but this similarity is superficial. The structure and the symbol in either short-story are specified by the nature of the frozen moment of crisis captured: the structure of Miss Mansfield's short-story conjures up a microcosm in evolution: it is vibrant with a sense of 'possibilities', the central symbol of the "aloe tree" registers the vibration; the structure of Joyce's epic of the Dubliners' life in miniature dilutes the distinctiveness of egocentric psyche with the tangled encircling vastness of the microcosm.

22. Eileen Baldeshwiler, "The Lyric Short-Story: The Sketch of a History", *Studies in Short Fiction*, Vol. 6, No. 4, Summer 1969, p. 447.
23. *Ibid.*
24. *Ibid.*
25. *Ibid.*
26. Saralyn Daly, *op. cit.*, p. 69.
27. William Walsh, *op. cit.*, p. 157.
28. *Ibid.*
29. *Ibid.*
30. *Ibid.*, p. 159.
31. *Ibid.*, p. 157.
32. *Ibid.*, p. 159.
33. *Ibid.*, p. 161.
34. Saralyn Daly, *op. cit.*, p. 69.
35. *Ibid.*
36. William Walsh, *op. cit.*, p. 158.
37. *Ibid.*
38. *Ibid.*
39. *Ibid.*
40. *Ibid.*
41. *Ibid.*
42. *Ibid.*, p. 161.
43. *Ibid.*, p. 157.
44. *Ibid.*, p. 160.
45. *Ibid.*, p. 161.
46. *Ibid.*
47. "'What form is it?' ... it's so difficult to say. As far as I know, it's more or less my own invention".—*Letters*, p. 74.
48. William Walsh, *op. cit.*, p. 160.

49. John Cournes, "Introduction", *A World of Great Stories*, p. 12.
50. *Journal*, p. 94.
51. Saralyn Daly, *op. cit.*, pp. 112-13.
52. J.M. Murry, *op. cit.*, p. 84.
53. Saralyn Daly, *op. cit.*, p. 24.
54. J.M. Murry, *op. cit.*, p. 92.
("This vileness, this snail on the underside of the leaf—always there!" —*Letters* p. 230).
55. Saralyn Daly, *op. cit.*, p. 25.

4. Experiment
(iii) Point of View

What Miss Mansfield actually sought to achieve was that specific narrative quality which enlivened by a dramatic quality would help to capture the flux of 'truthful full life'[1] and present it 'with a sense of mystery, a radiance, and an afterglow'[2]. This was the end in view when she decided to embark on experimentation with Point of View. The creative process involved in her endeavour to achieve the purpose demanded capacity for recognition of the nature and range of the subject conceived; it called for detachment which controls the creative power of imaginative empathy. Persistent experimentation with the focus of narration alone could practically enable her to recognize its potentiality as an expedient means of revealing the essence of the character or of the situation: it could help her to inculcate 'the attitude of personal detachment'[3] already exalted by 'vision of Love and Innocence'.[4] Her deliberate choice of experimentation with bare dramatization as the most elemental form of objective portrayal was indicative of her growing realization that if she longed to achieve the requisite dramatic quality, she must recognize the true nature and distinctive potentiality of the elemental form. The stories she composed as plays and monologues after *Prelude* were all private literary exercises. These transitional experiments were trial performances practised by way of preparation for composition of short-stories with a markedly accentuated 'dramatic effect'. They were means to an end. But even as means the first two of these transitional experiments bore evidence of content creatively achieved.

The first, *Two Tuppenny Ones, Please*, reads like the monologue of a woman who seems only to make believe she is enjoying the fulfilment of a fond but hopeless longing. The 'dramatic effect' is intensified by the silence of the interlocutor who is made to seem excitedly credulous. Intensification of the 'effect' is accomplished in two other ways: pathos that underlies the situation stands at once obscured and mocked by the conductor's routine yet sarcastic inquiry about the fare; the monologue is effusive enough to make the reader feel it might also be all make-believe. The woman seems to be a re-created image of the Frau in *Bains Turcs*. Through bare dramatization of the situation Miss Mansfield has effected increase of dramatic quality, but she has expunged the element of narration from her composition. Her achievement of the dramatic effect that is heightened by the guessable responses of the interlocutor and intensified by the conductor's formal yet sarcastic inquiry shows that she was beginning to realize her private desire to present a story 'with a sense of mystery, a radiance, an afterglow'. (In *Bains Turcs* a similar effect might have been achieved but for the oddly obtrusive presence of the narrator within the narrative framework.) But what precludes consummation of the content as the content of a short-story is the absence of the requisite element of narration.

Late at Night, the second 'experiment in dramatic form' as a soliloquy, reflects gradual interiorization of the character's dramatized consciousness, registering ephemerally transient emotional fluctuations. This whole process culminates in an unreconciled complex of conflicting emotional decisions. The effect achieved is that of the tragic cry of a lonely soul tense with an impassioned will to effect the consummation of her inhibited womanhood. Mrs. Virginia has remained arrested in a state of uncertainty and stasis; all smouldering of her animal passion has been only wasting in obscurity. The dramatic effect derives its intensity from the very nature of the emotion registered. But in this experiment too the 'narrative quality' is subordinated to the 'dramatic'. If Miss Mansfield had re-worded the stage directions as narrative statements we would have been able to test her capacity for 'personal detachment'. The composition as it stands finished is, however, a shade superior to the preceding one.

Although both the pieces lack the indispensable requisite, the 'narrative quality', they seem to have been the means of rehearsing the effect of a monologue for a later short-story *Lady's Maid*. With a similar dramatic form but with a concentrated emotional impact that makes the uninterrupted speech linger in the reader's memory as a more poignantly pathetic lyrical cry of a lonely soul,[5] this monologue emerges as an exquisite masterpiece.

Black Cap aims at the rendering of a crisis which seems to have been over-estimated: the 'psychology' of the woman is only skin-deep: the theme is too trivial to merit an unusual technique compounded of dialogues shifting through five scenes and a structural design interspersed with the protagonist's soliloquies. A sudden shift of point of view[6] when the form is meant to seem objectively dramatic only detracts from the purpose. Perhaps except for the inclusion of a participation shot by way of externalization of the nature of the protagonist's passion, which is too reckless to admit of tolerance of any manifestation of senescence,[7] the composition seems to have noting so distinctive and remarkable as to arrest critical attention.

The borrowed black cap clamped on the husband's head exasperated the wife; the dramatic form designed so ingeniously seems to have been grafted upon the story element to intense exasperation of the critical reader. The reader's critical experience corresponds to the wife's emotional experience.

Still the composition has its importance in the sequence of experiments. Miss Mansfield seems to be trying here to read the mind of a wife shuttling between her husband and her lover. The wife is a type whom Miss Mansfield, after her mastery of the dramatic form, would use as a pathetic or tragic nonentity listlessly languishing in obscurity.

Pictures, which 'confusedly combines short-story and play techniques' (?)[8] yields nothing more substantial than what *Tiredness of Rosabel* and *Swing of Pendulum* have already offered. The pathetic sense of transfixation of the character in a state of uncertainty is conveyed again by the protagonist's tendency to imagine the future as a past. It is intensified by the ambiguity of the 'snigger' which is expressive at once of the protagonist's cynical mood and her moral sense of propriety; but this is only a variation. There is loss of dramatic effect too: this loss is due to repetitive registration of similar experiences of doors banged shut in the face: it is due also to crudeness of touches often obtrusively externalizing the emotional situation.[9] Intensity of 'dramatic effect' is weakened by mid-narrative emergence of melodramatic passages.[10] The only interesting features of the narrative composition are: the author's first use of montage impressions at the appropriate moment when the emotional experience seems to have reached its climax,[11] and diffusion of a few touches[12] which are subtly expressive of the pathos and irony underlying the situation.

The focus of narration loses in concentration: the author has failed to withstand the temptation to make the situation of the woman seem piteously pathetic; we find repetitive accentuation of the effect of frustration the woman has experienced everywhere; there is tendency to indulge in creation of some tear-jerking episodes; objectification of the character's psychological experience or of the situation itself is obviously crude. This failure to conquer the temptation to make a pathetic situation seem more pathetic even at the cost of loss of intensity would recur even in a later short-story, *Life of Ma Parker* (although that narrative piece would be one not only composed after many of her creditable achievements but also based on a ready-made material supplied by a short-story by Chekhov: *Lament*).

However, ambiguity of the ending—occasioned here by objective registration of the look reflecting the protagonist's ambivalent attitude at the climactic moment—would be more poetic in later short-stories (*Bliss, Man without Temperament, Daughters of the Late Colonel, Marriage a la mode, Garden Party*).

The composition of the subsequent short-story, *Mr. Reginald Peacock's Day*, has registered Miss Mansfield's realization of her failure in *Pictures* to have achieved the specific narrative quality she had failed, even after her increasing recognition of the extent to which the elemental form of objective presentation had helped her to capture the desired or desirable 'after-glow'. In her still earlier employment of the protagonist's point of view she had only intermittently been successful in making the focus of narration potent enough to communicate the essence of the character or of the situation involving the character. The reasons for her usual failure were—first, her tendency to self-intrusiveness for sympathetic summation[13] (*Tiredness of Rosabel*), which persisted as tutored generalization[14] (*Frau Brechenmacher Attends a Wedding*) or compassionate re-estimation[15] (*Little Girl*); secondly, her failure to resist the temptation to view the pathetic or tragic situation from angles extrinsic to the chosen point of view, which resulted not only in diffusion of the dramatic effect but also in relaxation of intensity (*Child who-was-Tired, At Lehmann, Frau Brechenmacher Attends a Wedding, Swing of Pendulum, Birthday, Little Governess*); thirdly, her inability to recollect the recent emotional experience in tranquillity, which led only to sentimentalization of the character conceived (*The Wind Blows*). She had succeeded in exploiting the protagonist's point of view as an effective means of preserving the essence of the character only in two or three of her early short-stories (*How Pearl Button was Kidnapped, Millie, Something Childish but very Natural*): the structural-textural build-up in these short-stories evinces sensitive registration of the gradual unfoldment of a process that illuminates characterization.

The narrative quality achieved in composition of Mr. Reginald Peacock's Day is distinguished by the continuity of dramatic effect; the continuity is preserved through choice of a point of view expedient enough to reveal the essence of the character or of the situation itself: the choice of the protagonist's point of view has helped to preserve the specificity of the character figuratively defined by the very name he is made to bear. Miss Mansfield seems to have recovered the capacity for imaginative exploitation of the protagonist's point of view as a potent means of illuminating characterization. The capacity is exemplified by her achievement of a verbal complex specified through mingling of the narrative and the dramatic quality. What occasions the mingling is the reciprocity between the creative functions of the chosen focus of narration and the intense imaginative concentration.

The aesthetic rendering of the crisis is consummated through appropriate choice of a point of view expedient enough to reveal the nature of the protagonists static pang. The point of view is almost consistently the protagonist's. Choice of his point of view is necessitated by the irony inherent in the 'excessive articulation' with its tragic dimensions: the articulation is not without its suggestions of the character's unconscious indulgence in self-dramatization and of his unawareness of contrasted elements in his own nature; his excessive articulation follows a discovery he has already made and ends in a hollow utterance at a tragic moment of a rediscovery of what he has already discovered; display of his conceit or "vanity" as a conspicuous aspect of his excessive articulation is tinged with the tragic irony of the absence of a "friend". The articulation, again, is not without its innermost questions which are barren of answers ("What was the matter with her? What the hell did she want?… why had he married her?… Tied and bound like this, how could he help the world to escape from life? … Must it ever be thus?") What the questions combine to intone or echo is a sense of perplexity intensified by an empty dream ("If only I felt that she was here to come back to") and a desperate rationalization ("When so many women in her place would have given their eyes … yes, he knew it … why not acknowledge it?").

Perhaps only the sufferer's point of view in a third-person narrative frame could help to discover the tragic irony as the essential element of the short-story.

If the story had been told from a first-person point of view in the past tense, the culminant nature of the experience dramatized would have revealed itself at several points in the narrative and spoiled the tragic effect of the static situation which is defined by only a rediscovery. The earlier revelations of the culmination of experience on the "day" would have weakened the centralized emotional impact of the ending. The effect of rediscovery could perhaps be achieved only through recourse to straight narration in chronological order, which facilitates registration of emotional development. An autobiographical recollection of the momentous emotional experience with the tragic climax which has left a scar may also give us the same story but it would not make the same short-story with the same meaning. That different story would begin after the protagonist's rediscovery of the tragic truth; his cordially courteous reply to his pupils would every time seem to betray his subconscious awareness of an ironical similarity between the lingering echo of "the only words he could get out" and the sound of his own voice in reply. An "I" as the narrator could not be made to indulge in "operative gestures" and to cut open an envelope as gracefully as if he had been on the stage. Absence of this comic element would have robbed the characterization of the very pathetic element inherent in the concept that the character is meant to embody. The emotional intensity characterizing the culminant moment of his experiences could be preserved and the dramatic quality intensifying the narrative quality could be achieved only when the climactic scene depicting the protagonist's last desperate effort to win the "enemy" was presented from a point of view which facilitates distancing of the drama. The first-person point of view would have failed to preserve the objectivity of the registration of a tell-tale gesture naturally characteristic of the tense climactic moment: Mr. Reginald simply hurls the one boot he has "pulled off" and strides across the floor with the other boot still laced up: he is hot for whole togetherness. Reginald's unawareness of the ironical contrarieties in his life on the "day" or of the contrasted elements in his own nature is a subdued element of his characterization. This subdued element heightens the tragic effect of his unconscious self-dramatization as a Philip drunk. Revelation to us of this essential aspect of Reginald's characterization was possible only because of the distancing achieved through choice of the specific point of view registering fresh experiences on the "day" in their natural chronological order.

Intensity of Reginald's awareness of the one undismissible contrariety in his life has culminated as quiet tenseness manifest as blissful ignorance of the contrasted elements in his own nature. He bursts into "a shout of triumph" ... "upon the word 'wedded'"; but he does not know how "the laughing mirror" in his song mocks the "Lohengrin" in him—how his romantic philosophy of life is all comedy, how his life has been all 'practice before a flass'. "Vanity, that bright bird, lifted its wings again, lifted them until he felt his breast would break", but he is convinced he is "not ... vain" ("Not that he was vain—he couldn't stand vain men—no"). He is unaware of the irony that his own words imply: "objectively you may not know that, but subjectively, it's the case": he has been dramatizing himself; he has been fancifully dreaming of a partner with "her bare scented arms round his neck" ... "covering him with her long perfumed hair". Objectively he may not know all that, but subjectively it's the case. He imagines his latest, most charming pupil putting "her bare scented arms round his neck", but he has perhaps never imagined such "enchanting scenes" with his wife. He adores his pupil's "white frock, her little blond head tilted, showing her milky throat", but never does he even seem aware of the physical features of his wife.

Only an airily vague image of his wife is inferentially implicit in what as the distillation of a past experience is now only metaphorically definable. She had caught him at a weak moment, and this first plunge into reality had bewildered and overwhelmed him for a time. Perhaps this first experience was that of sheer fleshly sexual thrill: "the weak moment" must have been the moment of his incapacity to resist the first attractive force of his partner. The total image is only presumably conceivable; the woman was, perhaps, alive with animal health and virile passion. It is perhaps this woman who, presumably of course, after her own past experience of a shock of recognition, lies "asleep", her passion rationally tamed by her stoic resignation to a life without even a remote possibility of the fulfilment of her own dream of a happy conjugal togetherness: the woman that lies "asleep" "squeezed over to her side of the bed" has withdrawn into a shell of solitude in her conjugal life; she now wants this shell to remain dark: she lies "asleep" in the interior of "a dark flat" in a room from which she has chosen to exclude all "light".

Mr. Reginald does feel convinced his wife like any other married woman is "insatiable"; but he does not know his word can be used in the depiction of his own nature: his thirst for more and more adoration and fame is unquenchable. His own unconscious indulgence in self-dramatization as a means of escape from the reality of life sharpens the irony of the impersonation that he teaches.

He advises one of his pupils to 'sing as if she were in love'; he also 'shows' how to do it; 'Let yourself go. Confess yourself. Make proud surrender,... There must be a kind of exultant defiance as well—'But he does not know he himself will have to let himself go ... confess himself' ("tell her everything") ... make proud surrender ("win her").

The phrase in the song, "'yes, I know you love me'", is finally "quite perfect"; but he seems unaware of the ironical contrast between perfection of musical phrase and imperfection of his life without whole togetherness.

When he finds Marion Morrow awfully miserable, he strikes up closest possible intimacy, 'you don't care to tell me what it is!' But he does not seem to have put any such question to his wife; if he has ever put such a question, he has put it to himself: "what was the matter with her? What the hell did she want?" Does he seem to have bothered his head about the moments when, we have reason to presume, his wife's eyes also might have "filled with tears"?

Sudden shift of point of view ("It was nothing in particular. She had those moods sometimes when life seemed almost unbearable") for the explanation of the girl's own inner response betrays the experimenter's failure to resist the temptation to make the implicit irony a shade clearer—the irony of a similar situation in the individual life of his partner. The irony would have been more effectively stressed if Miss Mansfield had only suggestively dramatized the girl's response: an eloquent look, a telling gesture, or an ambiguous speech would have served the purpose and the consistency of the chosen point of view would have remained unbroken.

However, the potentiality of the protagonist's point of view has been imaginatively exploited. The protagonist's excessive articulation serves to obscure the tragedy in the individual life of his pining married partner; his censure of his wife's attitude or demeanour prejudices the reader's mind; the reader can see what the protagonist thinks or feels, supposes or construes; but he is denied the knowledge of the truth about the partner; his attention is distracted from the tragedy that the partner mutely suffers. He hears the question the protagonist voices, but he is given no definite clue to what the wife's reserve conceals; he is kept in the dark even about her mien while he is almost made to share the protagonist's sensuous experience of "bare, scented arms" and "perfumed hair" and "milky throat". The protagonist's statements about the comforts he has insured, the latitude he has allowed, eliminate even the conceivability of the reason for discontent in his partner's individual life. His suspicion of his wife's motives render even the residue of her image ambiguous. The protagonist's music "would waft a hardened criminal to heaven"; why has this music failed to change "an enemy" into a friend? He is nonchalantly aware of his wife's presence in the house ("His wife came in"). She is a staid recluse (in the dark room of 'a dark flat' she 'lies asleep, squeezed over to her side of the bed'); she is stoically placid ("The noise woke up his wife with a terrible start. She sat up, pushing back her hair"): she is made to seem so cold—so cold that all charm in the protagonist's life flies away at the mere touch of her hand ("But of all those splendid things he had to say, not one could he utter").

This subordinated effect of another tragedy in darker obscurity serves to intensify the total effect of the protagonist's own tragic agony which is articulated in obscurity of the selfishly egocentric interiorization of his whole self: the deeper dimension of the darker obscurity encompasses the whole magnified dimension of Reginald's excessive articulation. Reginald comes to know for certain that he will never be able to break through her stoic reserve and so the whole situation in his real private life is tragically static—barren of all promise, of any possibility of whole togetherness for his own satisfaction. This subsidiary element of another tragedy in darker obscurity is also meant to stress the essential tragic fact: utter impossibility of reciprocity, temperamental or physical. Each of the partners is self-centred. Reginald's indifference to or unawareness of the reason of her stoic reserve is due to the constant interiorization of his whole self; he is solely interested in simply making her "interested ... in his triumphs and his artistic career": he never goes to the heart of the question: "what was the matter with her? What the hell did she want?" His wife's stony stoicism is consequent upon frustration of her animal passion now smothered in her resignation to a life without thrill of life.

Rendering of the crisis in intent concentration is facilitated by the choice of a single typical "day" from Reginald's darkly sunny life. The concentration in which the tense decisive moment is rendered is much too intense to accommodate dramatized flashbacks. There is only one flashback registered as a vivid recollection of a hauntingly recent experience of a clash between their individual standards of propriety. The clash is not dramatized in the natural chronological order of events on the "day", that is, immediately after the telephonic conversation between Reginald and Aenone Fell: it is "remembered suddenly" when his wife's posture ("His wife lay asleep, squeezed over to her side of the bed") seems to him to have defined only her inimical attitude. The recollection is naturally characteristic of the mood the posture has induced. The posture has "suddenly" created a tense moment when Philip sober and Philip drunk become one: "Must it ever be thus? ('his wife lying asleep, squeezed over to her side of the bed') he thought, the champagne still working". Reginald seems intensely aware of an unendurable aspect of the hard reality in his life: incorrigibility of the nature of his wife who is "off again" and again.

It is perhaps owing to the intensity of concentration on the tensely unfolding present of a typical "day" in Reginald's life that the event which could have been dramatized earlier at the point where we presume it must have occurred is only indirectly referred to in a flashback. Dramatization of an earlier event at a later point in a chronologically evolving narrative evinces Miss Mansfield's developing critical consciousness of the reversal of the temporal order that the rendering of a tense moment in concentration sometimes necessitates.

At the early stage in the chronological evolution of the drama on the "day" we find what we may call simply the distillation of Reginald's experiences in the past; there are no dramatized flashbacks; the past events are temporally too remote to retain the immediacy of recency; they have all dissolved into a vague impression; they have generated an emotional complex and faded into oblivion. Intense concentration on a decisively momentous "day" in Reginald's life leaves the past out of the focus of narration.

In course of the imaginative exploitation of the potentiality of the protagonist's point of view, the composition seems to have assumed a narrative structure telling enough to reflect the static nature of his hopelessly tragic agony. The opening and the ending respectively dramatize the protagonist's awakening and reawakening to the same hard reality: tragic permanence of the situation in his real, private life. The tragic sense of progression is conveyed by the sudden transition in the rhythmical pattern of the refrain ("so charmed!"). The song of his life is not "perfect. The life of the music teacher is all music without harmony.

Employment of the multi-personal point of view in *Feuille d' album* once again helped Miss Mansfield to maintain the narrative quality refined by a dramatic quality: she had to tell the story of the artist 'with a sense of mystery, a radiance, an afterglow': the very theme demanded concentration on an ambiguity vague enough to obscure what retains its poetic beauty only in its inviolably isolated privacy. She had exploited the potentiality of the multi-personal focus of narration in *Prelude* for sustained yet dreamy concentration on the poetically vague sense of 'possibility'.[16] In *Prelude* employment of the multi-personal point of view for incessant concentration on the amorphous concept of 'possibility' had naturally demanded the specific narrative quality which is intensified by a dramatic quality. *Blaze* and *New Dresses* were probably the only two short-stories in which Miss Mansfield had employed multi-personal point of view still earlier; but the specific narrative style that equal emphasis on the involved characterizations had called for had lost its potentiality of 'dramatic effect'. The reasons were: inclusion of a narrative statement conspicuously registering a focal shift, diffusion of interest or confusion of the intended meaning (*Blaze*); flat prolixity generated by persistent endeavour to obscure the pathos that palpitates only feebly; languid registration of events evolving through an unnecessarily protracted span of time (*New Dresses*). By the time Miss Mansfield came to compose *Feuille D' Album*, she had recognized the potentiality of the multi-personal point of view for sensitive registration of even an 'afterglow'.

The artist's experience of love for an image after his own heart is presented in perspective. The specific narrative structure is dictated by this perspective. The writer seeks to distance the tensely climactic 'happening' by obscuring it with cross-cancelling implications. Nascency of the artist's love is a remotely isolated reality in the world; the worldly vision is too superficial to evince recognition of the beauty of that lyrical nascent love which is at once evanescent and promising. The symbol of this nascent love is the egg that the artist offers. This symbol is central to the whole climactic situation.

The cross-cancelling implications which the concluding passage of the short-story obviously involves seem to indicate the obscurely enigmatic and curiously lyrical nature of the artist's nascent love for a partner after his own heart: the egg he hands can only incredibly be the one she may have dropped: if she had dropped the egg, it would have been broken; but he seems to asseverate it's the one she has dropped, although the reader has seen him going into and coming out of the dairy, and has reason to presume that the artist has bought another egg in the meantime. Even this new egg as a token of friendship—is not without contrary features: this 'shy offering of friendship' is at once 'fragile' and 'promising of life'.[17] The artist's facial expressions, too, seem to create conflicting impressions: he is "blushing more crimson than ever" and at the same time "looking at her severely" and speaking "almost angrily". Again, the possible response subsequent to this 'shy offering' is also of dubious nature: the girl would look into her basket and find her own purchase intact—she would then resent the offer; she would also accept the egg as an unmistakable token of friendship.

Dill Pickle exemplified Miss Mansfield's next experiment with point of view. The experiment this time was inspired by her discovery of the need for a bifocal point of view that operates effectually in objective dramatization of a situation involving two polarized characters with their individual points of view divergently concurrent. While employing this point of view in *Dill Pickle* Miss Mansfield did succeed in maintaining the desirable equilibrium between the narrative quality and the dramatic quality, but she failed to reveal the tragic essence of the story of the young couple because she could not adjust the bifocal point of view to the narrative structure. The dramatic quality which is maintained through objective registration of the concurrent evolution of the two individual points of view is not harmoniously adjusted to the narrative quality which goes beyond the point where the dramatic quality actually ends. Miss Mansfield's failure on this score is unmistakably symptomatic of her immaturity.

'Adaptation of the technique of semi-dramatic pieces ... Miss Mansfield was writing at the time'[18] does seem to have helped her in this subsequent experiment; it has facilitated registration of the tenseness of the static situation as the intricately complex culmination of the characters' accumulated experience of their conflicting temperaments, arrested inclination and 'immutable separateness'.[19] 'Closing with an omniscient point of view'[20] involves a focal shift that is startlingly abrupt. The image of the character whose story the short-story is meant to be would have been richer if there had been inclusion of the young man's concluding observation as an utterance within earshot of the protagonist: if both Vera and the young man had been made to leave together for a stroll and if the observation had been made to sound casual and Vera's response had not been registered, the latter's blank silence would have intensified the sense of uncertainty. Miss Mansfield seems concerned with telling us a story and not with letting the story tell itself: her tendency towards self-intrusiveness as an omniscient author still persists. What she conceals from her protagonist and reveals to the reader could have been made an integral part of the characterization of the protagonist: the characterization thus enriched would have helped to deepen the sense of stasis characterising the situation the short-story is meant to dramatize.

When she reverted to narration with a first-person point-of view character as the narrator in *Je ne parle pas Francais*, she was inspired by a practical and prudent purpose: perhaps she wanted to see how autobiographical recollection of emotional experiences could be made to seem a subjective rendering in imaginative concentration intense enough to evince accommodation of the subtle suggestions of the 'situation material'. But she failed as usual even in this ambitious attempt to exploit this specific potentiality of the first-person point-of-view. The potentialities of her early first-person point-of-view short-stories had invariably been choked because of several negative factors in the creative process involved in their composition: unnecessary inclusion of the uninvolved first-person narrator within the framework of the narrative composition (*Germans at Meat*, *Bains Turcs*); failure to suppress mid-story comments and expunge the compositional elements revealing the denouement earlier (*Baron*, *Sister of Baroness*, *Pension Seguin*); insouciance with regard to revision of what as a recollection of experience is inevitably coloured from the start by the narrator's prior awareness of the denouement of his story (*Luft Bad*). The ambitious experiment with the first-person narrator's point of view in *Je ne Parle pas Francais* evinces nothing that may impel us to consider revision of our impression. She always bungled this experiment; perhaps the only shining exception on the wretched record was *Lady's Maid*. However, she would succeed in exploiting the potentiality of this point of view imaginatively again only in her last employment of it in *Canary*: even *Poison*, the next attempt at exploitation of this angle of narration, would be as much a bungle as *Je ne parle pas Francais* is.

Even in the handling of the first-person autobiographical point of view in *Je ne parle pas Francais*, Miss Mansfield was not wary of falling into an error that strains the reader's credulity. The first question that the reader feels impelled to ask just after he has finished reading is simple yet compound: has the first-person narrator protagonist's expatiation a justification? The question involves two moot points: first, what was there so deeply moving in the implication of Mouse's phrase ("Je ne parle pas Francais") that precipitated such a distressing, moral crisis in the libertine's life and "overwhelmed" him so completely that he could not resist the impulse to expatiate upon the experience? Secondly, was the reason advanced by Dick for his inability to smell the rose of romance any longer with mouse, complex or grave enough to make him or even Mouse seem incomparably and infinitely "suffering"? The very psychological elements that are central to the emotional design of the short-story are exposed to the reader's incredulity.

The reader finishes reading the short-story only to find himself deluged with questions. Is the 'sense' of Mouse's hopelessness' really 'profound'?[21] Doesn't the explanation offered by her English friend sound childishly sentimental? Isn't it flimsy? Hasn't the author sentimentalised Mouse's predicament? How does Mouse seem 'helpless' when she herself has 'shrunk away' and her gesture has been recognized by the narrator as a "false move"? Is she 'helpless' simply because she 'cannot speak French' ("ne parle pas Francais") in France? Doesn't she manage to express her feelings even when she experiences this 'difficulty'? Is it this 'profound(?) sense of hopelessness' which finds its expression in the short-story? Is it because Mouse is the alter ego of the author herself and thus the author's own experience of 'a profound sense of hopelessness' has found its expression in the short-story? How does the similitude that 'the fate of Mouse'[22] bears to that of the author herself help us to understand the short-story which is also—if not predominantly—a story of a character restless in his own uncertain situation? If the sense finds its expression in the short-story solely through the characterization of Mouse as the author's fictional alter ego, Mouse becomes the central character; clearly, the short-story is then a story about a crisis in her life. But isn't the story also about a crisis in the narrator-protagonist's life? If the 'sense of hopelessness' finds its expression in the short-story, is it wrong to presume that the whole of the short-story is an expression of this 'sense'? How can the whole of the narrative piece be an expression of this one sense unless all the three characters seem condemned to a desperate predicament? How do all the three characters share a common fate in this sense? Or does the 'sense' find its expression in the sterility of the static situation? Is the sense of this sterility then even pathetic enough to move one's heart? Which of the two crises is rendered in singular concentration? Can the short-story as a specific genre aim at an aesthetic rendering of two or more equally momentous crises and still remain a short-story? If a 'double-plotted effect'[23] or 'a stereoscopic effect'[24] is the preconceived effect, are both the plots or pictures equally important? Or is it that the sub-plot (Mouse's story) is subordinated to the main plot (Duquette's story)? But if it is subordinated, how is it that every other element of the total composition seems to tend towards unfoldment of the sub-plot? If the 'form serves to engulf Mouse in the horror that is the narrator's character'[25] doesn't she seem to become more important than the narrator? And how is 'the narrator's character' a 'horror'? Isn't he penitent? Doesn't he seem to have sobered down? How is it that his expatiation towards its conclusion seems purged of all 'self-conscious literary idiom'?[26] Isn't he secretly fidgety? Where does he wish to "go"? When he was alone in a room with Mouse left all by herself, what was it that made him simply 'smoke the whole cigarette' why was it 'so quiet it might have been two o'clock in the morning'? Why didn't he seize the opportunity and practise the hedonistic philosophy of life that seems to have made his character a 'horror'? In what sense, then, does he represent 'the destructive elements of life'?[27] How does his characterization sharpen by contrast the genuine suffering of *Dick and Mouse* and help to 'convey the extremity of Mouse's betrayal?[28]

What makes the narrator-protagonist seem irrespressibly fidgety ("I must go. I must go. I reach down my coat and hat.") is perhaps his reproachful conscience impelling him to "go" to "the place again": his conscience seems to have been condemning him for his failure to have made "the final effort"; 'he has abandoned Mouse, but he does remember her'; she has 'made him break his rule': "there are dozens of tunes that evoke just her;" the present is haunted by dreams of a boy and a girl "going home together under an umbrella", stopping "on the door to press their wet cheeks together". He knows he still owes "that considerable amount for lunches and dinners", but it is, presumably, his sincere respectful appreciation of her 'difficulty' that makes him feel "it's vulgar to mention it in the same breath with the fact that he never saw Mouse again". It is, presumably again, because of intensity of his feeling of guilt and the naturally subsequent assumption of an attitude of self-mockery that he tends to indulge in self-dramatization: "I hear myself saying: 'But I've got the little girl for you, mon vieux. So little... so tiny'. 'I kiss the tips of my fingers and lay them upon my heart'", etc. The concluding portion of the written expatiation, which follows the verbatim reproduction of the fatal letter Dick has left behind, is an index of a Philip sober: we can see here that long before he wrote this penitent part of his confession, Duquette had already begun behaving and thinking as a changed man: the whole episode subsequent to Dick's final exit from the drama is there to substantiate this view. A 'regular' Lothario, Duquette had been living the fast life of a libertine before he got in touch with the "suffering" woman, but when he found this woman conclusively abandoned and lonely, he could not even bring himself to take undue advantage of the woman's predicament; rather he was intensely aware of the calm irony of his own unrecognized, unrequited love for Mouse ("'As one does'") and Mouse's secretly responsive love for him—the irony was accentuated by the "silence" and by what he still feels sure was her "false move". It was "his other self", his real self, that was conversing with the forsaken "suffering" woman. This self 'hated' the "one question" about "money": it was sensitive anough to realize that a "question" about her "plans" was "the most clumsy, the most idiotic": it was a self whose love was purged of all passion for fleshly sexual thrill ("at any rate spiritually speaking"); it was a self that was contritely remoreseful: Duquette felt he was like 'the base Indian' who 'threw the pearl away' ("—and now, I'd thrown her away. Oh, I could have kicked myself"); it was a self that was sincerely amorous and serenely integrated ("I wanted her back. I swear I was not acting then"). It is this sobered, remorseful self that seems in the present to be too fidgety to care about 'dining' ("'you haven't dined yet?'... 'No, not yet, madam'"). Perhaps Duquette's uneasiness has been so irrepressive that it has betrayed itself, too ("Madam knows me. 'you haven't dined yet?' She smiles"). His matter of fact answer to madam's inquiry is perhaps meant to suggest the momentous change in the very nature of his hunger as a "fox terrier": he has been 'preying' upon women and 'feasting upon their loneliness' but he has "not yet" fully relished this appetite for the joy of "an intensity of feeling so ... purely"; this is the one reason for which he has been coming back to this cafe, to "this seat in the corner", to this nook where he had "enjoyed" the "grand moment" of the sudden burst of the "swan song" upon his consciousness which was governed by his "rule ... never to regret and never to look back": this "swan song" had broken for ever all "spell" of creating fancy-titillating "bits about virgin", etc. Dick's song running through the short-story as the motif[29] provides a comment perhaps in this sense. What had been relegated to the limbo of his past history along with the girls' names and dirty jokes and the drawings of cups and bottles had suddenly emerged as 'a thing of beauty which is a joy for ever': the "stupid stale phrase" had "dissolved, melted" his former self: it had become "her swan song" for him. The "intensity of feeling so ... purely" had transcended the temporal limit of the one "moment" and had become eternalized for him. It had "overwhelmed" the whole of his being: it had thrilled him to the depths of his being and changed him from a beast of passion to a poet of passion. (It was perhaps in this sense that the author called this short-story "a tribute to love"). So, if corruption and depravity are not the only features of the character, if the narrator's character is not simply a 'horror', how is there an element of contrast? And if the suffering of Dick and Mouse is genuine, isn't Duquette's penitence or self-reproach genuine, too? Isn't his expatiation honestly candid? Doesn't it read like a 'confessional monologue'?

The reader is incredulous also of the simultaneity of two contrary impressions: the one, that of the persistent 'writing'—an impression sustained by occasional references to the actuality of the process ("all the while I wrote that last page", "I should have written all that", "what I've written", "what I am going to write", etc.); and the other, that of the narrator-protagonist's sudden bodily movement unmistakably indicative of his vacation of "the seat in the corner" ("I reach down my coat and hat"): the reader fails to understand how the narrator-protagonist is jerking himself out of the seat and scribbling the concluding words at the same time; even if he accepts the last isolated paragraph as the registration of his monologue' the juxtaposition of what is apparently being "written" and what is being registered as sensitized awareness seems to him to be violent, incongruous, sterile. The writer has not yet mastered the art of unforced realism.

Evolution of conflicting image-patterns inevitably natural to the erratically rambling expatiation in a clumsily 'self-conscious literary idiom' only precludes the harmonious consummation of implications; it disturbs and prevents a total impressionistic effect of the verbal build-up.

The impression that lingers in the reader's mind is that of a preposterously elaborate, distractedly delirious "tribute to love".[30]

Use in *Sun and Moon* of what we may call a compound point of view does help to mingle the narrative and the dramatic quality. But the concentrated vision unnecessarily covers characterizations of two characters who in the final analysis seem only identical. Experience of the crisis is restricted to the consciousness of Sun alone: Rendering of this crisis even in protracted concentration would have proved more expedient if the child's point of view had not been mingled with Moon's or with the omniscient narrator's. Inclusion of the two other points of view occasions loss in concentration and thus affects the intensity of 'dramatic effect'.

The meaning of the short-story is: an innocent child's experience of disillusionment consequent upon his perturbation at the wreck of beauty intrinsic in orderliness characterizing the dream world he likes to live in as a child. It would filter in unaltered, even though a design effected by the use of the boy's point of view alone. In *How Pearl Button was Kidnapped*, a short-story written much earlier about a child who is finally disillusioned in her experience of freedom as the experience of real existence, Miss Mansfield was sagaciously wary of diffusing the central point of view: her exploitation of the protagonist's point of view in that earlier short-story was also an imaginative exploration of its potentiality as an expedient means of capturing the essence of the character. Point of view in *Sun and Moon* is diffused from the start. The meaning emergent from the verbal complex remains the same even if the mingled point of view is demanded by the story element. The point of view here is just a convenient means; it has not yet been recognized as one that is expedient, indispensable and inevitable. Miss Mansfield's experiments with point of view were not extensive and exhaustive, but as means of self-instruction they did prove gainful. The one substantial advantage that accrued from her long experimentation with the focus of narration was development of her capacity for abeyance of self which she had already attained during her composition of *Prelude*. There was one more advantage: it was practical: the experiments helped her to recognize the potentiality of an austere style, and the quality of refinement, which she had already achieved through her composition of *Prelude*, an elegy 'in special prose',[31] was further intensified.

But Miss Mansfield had yet to see how abeyance of self could help her to cultivate the capacity to make even her 'subjective selection of materials reflect an objective standard of values'.[32] Exclusive concentration during this phase of experimentation with point of view was due perhaps to the low intensity of her emotional experiences: 'the gift of empathy'[33] had nothing substantial and profound to explore: there was no overwhelming obsession or pre-occupation. Naturally the themes conceived during this transitional phase fell short of substantiality. As a matter of fact the 'gift' that Miss Mansfield had recovered through composition of *Prelude* remained in abeyance in this specific sense till the last momentous crisis in her life. This last crisis was to be precipitated by her haunting obsession with the concept of death as a grim metaphysical reality.

The crisis, as we shall see very soon, would compel sustained aesthetic contemplation of the privately haunting image of 'the snail under the leaf';[34] the 'gift' would discover much for the cognate attitude of personal detachment to control and explore and enrich. The consequential organization of her speculative and poetical impulses would involve the whole of her being.

NOTES AND REFERENCES

1. Quoted by Saralyn Daly, *Katherine Mansfield*, p. 112.
2. *Journal*, p. 94.
3. William Walsh, *A Manifold Voice*, p. 162.
4. J.M. Murry, *Katherine Mansfield and Other L. Portraits*, pp. 84-85.
5. Cf. 'Elizabeth Bowen, in her story (*Pink May*), shows equal skill and subtlety in gradually drawing out the main character's story in this way.... Not all of the listener's interjections are in the form of questions: there is the occasional "Go on" and the sort of remark that prefaces a question—"I'd been going..."—the question itself (in this case, ... what was so-and-so doing at the time?') being anticipated and cut across by the very nervy woman telling the story'—E.W. Hildick, *Thirteen Types of Narrative*, pp. 75-76.
   Comments—The critical reader of the two short-stories, *Lady's Maid* and *Pink May*, doubts whether Miss Bowen 'shows equal skill and subtlety in gradually drawing out the main character's story'. In Miss Mansfield's short-story it is not only that 'the question that draw the story from the Maid are left unwritten', and that their gist is always obvious from the replies, which begin each time with three dots to indicate that there has been an interruption; even an interpolated casual phrase is charged with emotion; the narrator's emotion and her efforts to check it lend dignity and beauty to her allusion to the incident

of the broken engagement: "when I opened the door—believe me or not, madam,—that man was gone". 'It is not hard to believe that a man who has just had the door slammed in his face should have gone away.... But to Eileen who had crushed the strongest impulses of her own heart to slam that door, it seemed incredible that he whom she loved so much could have taken her words at their face-value and left her. She hated him to go and consequently believed against commonsense he would not go—and expected her interlocutor to be as amazed as she had been on finding her man had gone. There is a long tale of stifled emotion, of half-conscious longings and hopes in that short 'believe me or not" (I. Arnold & N. Diakonave, *Analytical Reading*, pp. 165-66. The critical reader of Miss Bowen's short-story fails to remember whether he has discerned such shadowy subtlety in the registration of the narrator's articulation ("He put me straight into a taxi and sent me—not took me—home ... I did see him several times after that. So his letter—his letter was a complete surprise" ...).

6. (*He jumps up and looks at himself in the glass anxiously, and fatuously, she decides*).—Collected Stories of Katherine Mansfield, p. 658.
7. For example, "The whole world shall be ours because of our love. Oh, be patient! I am coming as fast as I possibly can ... Ah, now it's downhill; now we really are going faster. (*An old man attempts* to *cross* the *road*)" *Ibid.*
8. Saralyn Daly, *op. cit.*, p. 65.
9. For example, "a pageant of Good Hot Dinners passed across the ceiling, each of them accompanied by a bottle of Nourishing stout ... a pageant of sensible substantial Breakfasts followed the Dinners across the ceiling". etc.—*Collected Stories*. p. 119.
   "the cashier ran across to look and put her arm round the waitress's neck." etc. *Ibid.*, p. 122.
   "There was a high, cold wind blowing; it tugged at her, slapped her face, jeered", etc. ... *Ibid.*, p. 127.
10. For example, "Look at the sparrows. Cheep. Cheep. How close they come. I expect somebody feeds them. No, I've nothing for you, you cheeky little things ..." *Ibid.*, p. 127.
11. For example, "'A nice little piece of evidence, *my lady* ... very well, Mrs. Pine. Cafe de Madrid. they have concerts there in the evenings ... 'why don't they begin?' The contralto has not arrived.... 'Excuse me, I happen to be a contralto; I have sung that music many times'.... It was almost dark in the cafe. Men, Palms, red plush seats, white marble tables, waiters in aprons, Miss Moss walked through them all. "—*Ibid.*, pp. 127-28.
12. For example, "'Give me back that letter ... "cried Miss Moss, who could not get out of bed because her nightdress was slit down the back". *Ibid.*, p. 121.
    "And young Mr. Clayton, playing the banjo on his walking—stick, sang". *Ibid.*, p. 124.
13. Saralyn Daly, *op. cit.*, p. 21.
    For example, "And because her heritage was that tragic optimism, which is all too often the only inheritance of youth, still half asleep, she smiled," etc.—*Collected Stories*, p. 530.
14. For example, "'Always the same, 'she said—' all over the world the same; but God in heaven—but *stupid*'"—*Ibid.*, p. 725.

15. For example, "A funny feeling came over her. Poor father! Not so big, after all—and with no one to look after him ... And every day he had to work and was too tired to be a Mr. Macdonald ... 'oh, ... my head's on your heart; I can hear it going. What a big heart you've got, father dear".—*Ibid.*, pp. 581-82.
16. William Walsh, *op. cit.*, p. 160.
17. Barbara Pannwitt, *The Art of Short Fiction*, p. 52.
18. Sylvia Berkman, *Katherine Mansfield: A Critical Study*, p. 179.
19. Saralyn Daly, *op. cit.*, p. 88.
20. *Ibid.*, p. 66.
21. J.M. Murry, *op. cit.*, p. 88.
22. Cf. "There is a moving personal symbolism in it which only I could understand. The fate of Mouse, caught in the toils of the world's evil, abandoned by her lover is Katherine's fate".—J.M. Murry, *Between Two Worlds*, quoted by Nariman Hormasji, *Katherine Mansfield: An Appraisal.*
23. Saralyn Daly, *op. cit.*, p. 66.
24. Antony Alpers, *Katherine Mansfield*, p. 243.
25. Saralyn Daly, *op. cit.*, p. 74.
26. Sylvia Berkman, *op. cit.*, p. 181.
27. *Ibid.*
28. *Ibid.*
29. Saralyn Daly, *op. cit.*, p. 76.
30. Quoted by Nariman Hormansji, *op. cit.*, (from *Between Two Worlds* by J.M. Murry).
    Cf. "I read it and wept for joy ... I did feel (I do) that this story is the real thing and that I did not once (as far as I know) shirk it".—*Letters*, p. 113.
31. *Journal*, p. 94.
32. Saralyn Daly, *op. cit.*, pp. 112-13.
33. William Walsh, *op. cit.*, p. 162.
34. J.M. Murry, *op. cit.*, p. 92.

5. Technique as Discovery
(i) Dramatic Effect

Miss Mansfield was in a fair way to achieve the quality peculiar to the technique of the short-story—the quality of 'dramatic effect'. Her talent had already been integrated during composition of *Prelude*. Her subsequent experimentation with the focus of narration developed and improved what she had already achieved: it increased her capacity for self-abeyance and helped her to recognize the potentiality of an austere style. She now possessed what was needed for achievement of the quality peculiar to the technique of the genre. She was about to resume exploitation of the gift that she had recovered through composition of *Prelude* when the last psychological crisis in her life, agonizing obsession with the concept of death as a grim metaphysical reality, awakened her to a profound truth: the truth was manifest as intense actualization of be-ing just before life ebbs away. The truth was intense enough to help her to conceive situations that would lend themselves to literary treatment most readily in the form of the short-story alone.

The creative concentration required for achievement of the 'dramatic effect' was intensified, perhaps, by her awakening to the poignant truth revealed in her own life—her intense 'will to live' in the face of imminent death. Her distressing obsession with the idea of death had started intensifying this 'will'. Intensification of this 'will' in her own life now helped her to register the realization of the profound truth-vision that flicker of be-ing seemed to exemplify. Since this universal timeless truth was felt on the pulse, the artist's 'gift of empathy'[1] could be exercised more easily, more imaginatively, more intensively. Naturally in the short-stories composed during this penultimate phase of her literary career there was fervid exploration of the grim manifestations of the spirit of death in life itself. The manifestations that her short-stories captured are exemplified not only by the way the dark negative force 'subtly intrudes upon and modifies the nature of the living in accordance with the blas of their being';[2] they are illustrated also by the psychic transfixation at the tense moment of intense actualization of the character's being. The short-stories record the Gorgonian effect of Death on life; the characters seem living and dead at the same time; 'the quick is deader than the dead';[3] all flux of life seems but an illusion of a flux. The 'dramatic effect' is vividly intensified.

Intensification of the dramatic 'effect' consists in faithful presentation of the 'life of life'[4] revealed as an unaccountably grim, a-moral objective reality. Naturalization of the 'effect' is achieved through preservation of the 'sense of mystery' that she found 'the life of life' warped in.

The result that accrued from this simultaneous process of intensification and naturalization of the 'dramatic effect' was refinement of the narrative quality as a dramatic quality: the artist's style of writing was now faithfully capturing 'real truthful life'[5] simultaneously picturing it 'with a sense of mystery'. 'The real truthful life' revealed only as a grim reality was utterly irresponsive to the artist's agonizing questions. Naturally the situation conceived was invariably inconclusive. It was too brief an episode to offer significant meaning. The moment now captured for rendering in concentration was unvaryingly dramatic and concentric. The rendering admitted of no scope for a beginning; the end was now outside the purview of the rendering; usually there was only an indeterminate middle. If there was a culminant moment there was nothing of what led up to it. The rendering now had to be true to 'the truthful life' revealed as a reality too contingent to admit of a complete meaning. The narrative quality was refined to the requisite extent: the artist could now register with restraint and delicate skill even the fragility of an evanescent emotion; she could now convey the emotion of a moment: now it was a moment caught on the wing and held while in a state of flutter.

Intensity of the 'dramatic effect' in the first short-story, *Bliss*, is primarily due to the intrinsic tenseness of the moment captured: what the author seeks to dramatize is a moment of simultaneous abandon and withdrawal, of intense actualization of be-ing characterized by a conflicting tendency to escape from the real self. The 'dramatic effect' of the rendering of the moment is also technically intensified: the narrative is composed in an exquisitely refined narrative style: this specific style is embiguous enough to reflect concurrence of conflicting impulses; it is also potent enough to yield the structural and textural means of defining the nature of the whole flux; the dramatic quality is indistinguishable from the narrative quality.

Let us begin with an analysis of the concluding passage of the short-story, which depicts the culminant tragic moment when the protagonist's total experience of emotional conflict terminates inconclusively.

The passage registers the blankly vacant mood of the protagonist. What has induced the mood is a shock that she has just suffered: her voice ("'Goodbye'") is, unmistakably, low-keyed, half-whispered, short-breathed. It sounds strained, dry, toneless; it does not seem to ring out like her earlier full-mouthed, impassioned, joyous 'cry' ("'Good-night, goodbye', she cried from the top step, feeling that this self of hers was taking leave of them for ever"); it does not sound like the cry of the earlier sunny moment when she has joyously found herself becoming her real self ("feeling that this self of hers was taking leave of them for ever"). "'Goodnight'" at this later moment, is dropped; "cried" has become a toneless "said". The jubilant voice has become, lifeless, vacuous, airy. It is now only a hollow echo of a voice dumbly heard: "'your lovely pear tree—pear tree-pear tree'". Even as a 'cry' the voice registers only a barren rhetorical question which seems to revolve itself in a dazed consciousness of the whole realm of the possible as an empty void: "'oh, what is going to happen now?'" The way the question is worded admits of no indication of any scope for exercise of the protagonist's individual will: the present progressive tense of 'go' with 'to' and an infinitive meant to indicate a future state is, significantly, patterned in such a way as to refer to external conditions or circumstances beyond the range of individual choice: Bertha does not cry 'what am I going to do now'? Shocked into despondent, inert, dead passivity, she stands dazed, her mind blank, her body insensate, her real self lost again: "Miss Fulton held her hand a moment longer": we have the sense of Bertha's agency this time: it is not Bertha taking Miss Fulton's arm; this time it is Miss Fulton holding Bertha's own hand: all that Bertha feels at the moment is that her hand is held by Miss Fulton; all that she seems conscious of is just a gross, contingent reality. Even the 'uneasiness' which she has experienced earlier 'before animal sexuality'[6] seems to have calmed: although Eddie's departure with Fulton reminds her of "the sight" of the two cats which only a short while ago gave her "a curious shiver", her perception seems only indifferently listless: "And then she was gone, with Eddie following, like the black cat following the grey cat"; the dull balancing of references to the two contrasted cats transmits the desired effect of the character's stoic listlessness. Her disillusion has extinguished all "blaze" of her sensual passion. She stands drained of 'life' ("Bertha simply ran over to the long windows"): the restricted specific implication of the adverb, "simply", helps to intensify the meaning of the phrasal verb, "ran over"; it fits in with the emotional context: the adverb denotes absence of complication or admixture: the impression of a mechanical (or desperate?) movement is unmistakable. The first word of the last sentence, "But" ("But the pear tree was as lovely as ever and as full of lower and as still"), generates the sense of an impasse; the last word, "still", completes it. The pear tree as "the symbol of her life" has no answer to her question: the sense of mockingly callous irresponsiveness intrinsic in the persistence of the curious paradox only intensifies the tragedy of the character's predicament; she has 'taken leave of' the 'arty set' 'for ever' after her sober recognition of her fancy paradise of modernity as only an illusion; she stands poised for realization of what 'all the feeling of bliss has been leading up to—for the palpable experience of the claim of life she has been foolishly denying herself, for the achievement of creative consummation of her 'self' as a real self, as a wife, as a mother. But she has found herself only teetering on the verge of an abysmal void of "now—?", the void of all her future as a barren realm ("'oh, what is going to happen now?'"); when finally she turns to 'her' pear tree, to what she has regarded as "the symbol of her life", she finds it barren of even an inkling of an answer to the question that confronts her "now".

The impasse that confronts the dazed character is tragic. It is this impasse that Bertha's frantically breathless quest for the answer to her mute problem is meant to lead up to. The short-story captures one of the tense moments in the life of this pitiful child of modernity. The moment is that of her feel of the periodical visitation of 'life'. Occurrence of such a moment is natural to a career in which her cultural sham has developed into an awe of a value which she dare not flout but which she has begun to realize as "absurd". Instinctively she longs to have a feel of her real self in freedom from bondage to a fad which denial of conjugal bliss has impelled her to cultivate—a feel of the intense actualization of her being in individual freedom of choice from the realm of the possible, a feel, in short, of the naked throb of life, the very quick of life, through submission to an impulse which is animal and meta-physical by virtue of its being beyond exercised will.

Tenseness of the captured moment is due to gradual increase of tension generated by what seems to be a constant battle between Nature and Culture, between a subliminal buoyancy and a sophisticated truancy. This tension is climaxed by the ironical triumph of nature over culture, a triumph in which nature seems only precariously perched on the verge of a dark void and culture stands conclusively exposed as only a fallacious proxy and a grotesque 'absurdity'.

It is perhaps the whole of this feverishly tense moment that is the moment of crisis rendered in intense imaginative concentration. What seems to have demanded concentration is the very nature of the experience that the short-story is meant to explore to the extent of its far-reaching, moral implications in the context of the art-fed life in the modern world—in the context of a life which is only an illusion of life, a pathetic irony, a shadowy pantomime[7]: the nature of the experience is revealed in the character's overwhelming bewilderment and her muffled articulation, and defined by the arrested possibilities in her life.

Thus the two features of the character, her overwhelming bewilderment and muffled articulation, also seem symptomatic of the arrest of possibilities. The first feature of the character, her overwhelming bewilderment, is obliquely suggested by a gesture natural to the mood of the moment or to her "usual" mood: ("No, that about the fiddle is not quite what I mean", she thought, "running up the steps" and feeling in her bag for the key etc).[8] The casual gesture is naturally captured in a 'close-up' framed by the imaginative fictional eye operating within the restricted range of the tense moment: it is eloquent enough to suggest the increasing intensity of the character's "feeling" ("running up the steps") and the naturally concomitant forgetfulness ("she'd forgotten it") or the accompanying vague uneasiness at her failure to define what she 'means', what the analogy of 'the fiddle' is too inapt to explain ("feeling in her bag for the key"). Her "usual" forgetfulness is natural to "moments like this when she wanted to run instead of walk", etc. At all such "moments" when there is a visitation of life descending on her like a divinity of instincts, when she experiences intense actualization of her being in freedom from bondage to self-sterilizing, imitative existence—Bertha's total self as an individual being, as a mother, as a wife, as a lesbian (?)[9], seems marked by a certain arrest of development: she seems psychically transfixed at the very moment of choice from the realm of the possible: 'she doesn't know what to do with this feeling'. The last words of the breathless sentence which forms the opening paragraph of the short-story, ("nothing—nothing, simply") register the climactic pitch of the character's ecstatic "feeling"; they echo ironically in the concluding words of this whole tensely emotional narrative piece: the concluding words suggest only negativity and stasis ("'oh, what is going to happen now?'", "and as still"), and the essential nature of the experience embodied within the aesthetic framework is defined: we feel we have what may be called a story of 'apathetic fallacy' or pathetic fallacy dramatized in obverse: we have here a living, willing and feeling being who has been denying the claim of life and assuming the vegetable calm of a pear tree despite the bloom of her youth. This apathetic fallacy is at the root of frustrated "bliss" in the paradise of modern bohemian culture.

The second feature of the character, her muffled articulation, which marks the next degree in the evolution of the character's self-expression in privacy, is manifest as her intermittent 'cry'. This cry of the pining mother in Bertha, the undivorced wife in Bertha, is the cry of a lonely soul, smothered in alienation. The 'cry' is not inaudible when she bids farewell to the 'arty set' from the top of the stairs, "taking leave of them for ever"; but even this loud ringing 'cry' of a rebel becomes a muffled lonely 'cry' of an isotate who is presumably going to live the life of a recluse in her own family ("oh, what is going to happen now?").

The sense of what has been called 'arrest of possibilities' is adequately conveyed by the ambiguity of overtones which at times characterizes Bertha's voiced and unvoiced utterances . One of the voiced utterances seems to be eloquent enough to convey this sense of arrest of possibilities or psychic transfixation: the tragic essence of the character is captured at a moment when she is intensely alive in her quest for "bliss" ("Bertha noticed that his socks were white, too—most charming.... 'But how dreadful' she cried). Ambiguity of overtones characterizing this voiced utterance seems to have been underscored by the objectivity of its registration. No choice modifier of the verb "cried" has been employed. The ambiguity has been underlined also by the typographical isolation of the objectively registered utterance from the brief paragraphs that precede and follow it: the utterance admits of two interpretations: Bertha is echoing Eddie as a sterilized imitative child of modernity; or, she is expressing her private feeling of disdain for all such extravagant histrionic (or is it that her ejaculation is muffled, hollow, blank?)

There are other similar moments when ambiguous overtones reveal the metaphor of a human half that the tension between Nature and culture seems to have made of Bertha: she began to laugh. "No, no. I'm getting hysterical". The character's "laugh" spills from "the cup of bliss". The impression is clinched simply through isolation of the short sentence registering the response awakened: the isolation is effected in two ways: typographically, through use of dots for blank and through paragraphic transition; and contextually, through a quick switch-over to registration of the voiced utterance censoring the subconscious. The blank for the sudden mysterious transition from the enchanted "mood" in which the total "effect" has been "most curious" and the floating phantasmagoria "so incredibly beautiful", becomes a narrative statement. The urge for the true joy of life which self-sterilizing doctrine of bohemian culture has been counteracting overwhelms her suddenly, and she begins to "laugh" at her own "mood" which she realizes as flippant, fantastic and freakish. But the very next moment, again mysteriously, she is impelled to choke back the swelling urge, and possibility of natural, liberated psychic evolution is arrested again: "No, no. I am getting hysterical". The simulated utterance is racially characteristic of bohemians who are only sentimentally disdainful of sentimentality: this time it is Bertha's indoctrinated self speaking: what she seems to mean is: "I'm not being elegant or artistic enough". This sudden withdrawal into the second-hand civilizational paradise is perhaps due to her lack of genius for active or passive receptivity and creative consummation: the withdrawal is symptomatic of self-deception that she has been practising by assembling art-things as a substitute for life in which she has found conjugal bliss lacking in intensity. However, even this "mood" is flittingly evanescent, "she seized her bag and coat and ran upstairs to the nursery" which is indelibly associated with her "little B." The word "And" too ("And she seized her bag and coat" etc.) has its ambiguous overtones: while indicating continuity of the fresh emotional context created by the chastened mood of escape from her sentimental self getting mawkishly maudlin, the conjunction also registers a sudden mysterious upsurge of the motherly solicitude for her baby, which is part of her free individual real self.

These swift emotional fluctuations registered through a style objective enough to admit of ambiguity help to transmit the desired effect of the character's psychic transfixation.

This psychically transfixed image of the character is fully reflected in the depths of the mirror. It is psychic transfixation as the essential feature of the character's image that the mirror reflects for the character herself to recognize fully. The character's intense awareness of her radiant charm and thus of secret satisfaction of her vanity ("smiling lips") is not without her subliminal recognition of frustrated "bliss" and utter impossibility of a full-swing soulful enjoyment of life ("trembling lips"); it is not without subconscious awareness of the mirror itself as only a "cold" civilizational reflector, only a bloodless substitute for a full-blooded husband or lover who can make her feel rivers of fire course through her "body". The tense tingling moment of poise for choice from the realm of the possible ("waiting for something ... divine to happen ..." etc.) captured in the two-dimensional, framed, "cold" reflector seems rather to image forth the essential tragic sense here of the arrest of all possibilities in the character's life. Even that which she interprets as a dreamy longing for "something divine" is a complicated emotional complex too vague to be precisely expressive of a definite direction in which she would like her sex life to evolve: possibilities conflict, and the character distinguished by this one psychological complex manifest as "all this feeling of bliss" leading up to what she cannot precisely define becomes a character marked by arrest of development: the very story element that Bertha's psychological complex produces, or more precisely, creates, seems to have become a richly complex vague 'objective correlative' for the tangled sex life of the character who has been denied the claim of life. The rich complexity characterizing this 'objective correlative' accrues from the one major aspect of the narrative: the style is abundantly rich in ambiguous overtones.[10] The "feeling of bliss" itself as a complicated emotional complex admits of several dimensions: what Bertha defines as "divine" may be that which all her "feeling of bliss" leads up to and which she fails to define; it may also be the psychophysical communion with one who 'means so much to her': Fulton seems to be both her rival and her self-projection as a hedonistic proxy, or her rival, her alter ego, her lesbian mate, all rolled into one. She seeks a full free fresh experience of life as a divinity of instinct: she calls civilization "idiotic" not only when she longs to "get in touch with "her married partner but also when she dreams of communion with Fulton. Ossified by the culture which de-normalizes individual selfhood or rationalizes such a hybrid philosophy of sex life as a sane philosophy sanctioned by nature, Bertha as a character seems to be a sphinx in the desert of modernity.

The concentrated creative vision naturally forges a narrative form composed of three internal patterns converging on identical climactic points.

Of the first two patterns the one emerges from recurrence of high-tide moments in the recorded experience when the character is naturally at a loss to decide what to do with the "feeling", "how to express it", etc.; the other is traceable in the intermittence of the character's impassioned "cry" in privacy—a cry wrung from the depths of blood, as it were.

The third pattern is created through evolution of the fundamental image ("the pear tree"). It unifies the total narrative structure: it registers the dramatic transitions in the character's mood as she stands psychically transfixed, almost consumed by the conflict between nature and culture, between assertion of 'life' as divinity of instinct and fascination for the ritual and romance of imitative existence on the evening. This third pattern is inclusive of the other two patterns.

This third encompassing pattern terminates in the paradoxical reference to the fundamental image of the pear tree.

The implications involved in the climactic point on which the first two patterns converge and in the terminal point of the whole narrative build-up designed to reflect the character's emotional fluctuations, assimilate readily: they transmit the sense of conclusive finality characterizing the sterile stagnation of all flux and becoming.

There are still two other patterns equally conspicuous in the narrative texture. They are discernible in the recurrence of the character's low "laugh" and her laconic comment ("Absurd"). Woven into the texture as inter-cutting patterns, they represent the concurrent emotional flux from the same source, the deep-souled "feeling of bliss"; this concurrent emotional flux contributes the sense of the character's dawning awareness of the risible 'absurdity' that all this ritual and romance of bohemian histrionics is.

The criss-cross design that emerges from these overlapping and inter crossing patterns terminating with a big question mark and an image involving cross-cancelling implications, helps to capture the shimmering yet frozen image of the character.

The quality of 'dramatic effect in *Man without Temperament* derives its intensity from intenseness of imaginative concentration on the wrought-up mood of the protagonist: there is exclusion of even an inkling of the clue to the traumatic shock he seems to have suffered. The very immediacy of the tingling moment compels speculation about the psychological background. The speculation proves to be a poetic experience. The quality of 'dramatic effect' finds its consummation: what is obscured by the 'dramatic effect' is poetically complementary.

Obscurity of the emotional complex that the character's attitude of stoic resignation seems to involve is deepened because of the objectivity of the narrator's point of view even as a shifting focus of narration.

The shifting point of view only obscures the root cause by leaving our expectations disappointed even at moments of what seem to us to be direct or indirect revelations of the cause:

(1) NARRATOR'S OWN VISION

1. (a) Narrator's vision as focused upon the reflections of the situation in the surroundings:
    - (i) The opening scene (the two topknots "sitting in the corner"; the American woman "against the glass wall"):

      The scene does not seem to have been viewed by "the man without temperament"; the fictional eye temporarily riveted upon the scene is an all-seeing eye, the narrator's eye. What substantiates the impression is not simply the conclusively revealing statement, "But he saw nothing", but also the echo of the American woman's personal mangled pronunciation ("knoo"): "the man without temperament" has been too self-centred, too self-concerned, too self-absorbed to bring himself to enter into the consciousness of anybody else, to echo the words or voice of any other being, to adopt the speech mannerisms of any other person. His disposition is so chilly, his personality so introvertive, that he cannot pet a poodle or be intimate with it.

The images reflect the aspects of the situation that has developed in the married life of the two sufferers: the wife herself who later in the short-story beseeches her husband to accept "just one" biscuit and lets her shawl 'drop off' while 'bending forward to hand him the biscuits', has been "rooting in" for the root cause of her husband's aversion to this exile with her ("'do you mind awfully being out here with me'"?); she has been looking for the missing emotional link between her husband and herself: she is pryingly curious to know whether her husband loves her still. The "coils of knitting slumbering like two snakes" seem to externalize the husband's horror of his sexual union with a thin slip of a diseased wife wrestling with a fatal disease.

The nameless horror of impossibility of sexual relation between the man and the woman may be said to have been imaged by "the shadow of a great creeping thing" which the American woman feels sure she is secure against ("On the other side of the verandah, after all"); quite naturally, she finds the "thing" outlandish ("she'd just go right away to her consul"). Klaymongso with "a pile of letters from home on top of him" may be an image of the husband himself who also seems equally unconcerned with the "letters from home": the husband slips them all into his pocket; his replies too are as ambiguous and vague as the poodle's 'sneeze'.

But the complex of images is only a vague index of the root cause of tenseness characterizing the moment of crisis.

There are two questions the short-story is meant to leave unanswered: what was the protagonist's traumatic experience which developed into his present attitude of stoic resignation? Is it simply the two-year exile or is it the permanent bondage itself he seeks escape from? The second question involves still another barren question: will the termination of the exile also be the termination of his suffering?

(ii) Scene: The husband's "finger on the bell" excites commotion in the hotel:

The narrator's concentrated vision this time is

focused upon what seems to be the externalization of one of the most intense emotional experiences of ennui in Robert's married life: the hurried commotion that the entire hotel is suddenly thrown into seems to be a projected image of the protagonist's inner commotion: all his half-defined feelings, his rhetorical questions, his inarticulate thoughts, seem to be clamouring at the same time. This is perhaps the only moment in the protagonist's experience of crisis when the subdued commotion is externalized. (There are other moments when this commotion within "the man without temperament" is manifest in his gestures and expressions and visions: the manifestations register the degree to which the commotion is violent or the feelings are intense. But the reason underlying the feelings running high is concealed. Even this externalization of the convulsive agitation within is a projection much too vague to give us even an inkling of the root cause of the tenseness, but the tenseness is almost palpably dramatized.

(b) Narrator's vision as focused upon what stands in contrast to the situation:

(i) Scene: The Honeymoon couple's return after fishing excursion: the scene is viewed by the narrator this time from the wife's angle (the husband is mentally or physically absent here): the wife has "turned her chair to look": she seems to be subconsciously aware of this beaming and glowing radiance of Life as a sharp contrast to what she feels has been only a mockery of life. The buoyant, gushing unjaded life of the youthful couple seems to mock her own sedentary life of uncertain convalescence. With her "thin bosom" and "thin hands", with her "small head" and slight figure, she seems to feel she is not fit to hold a candle to her counterpart who looks a picture of health. She finds her wistful bird-cage life stands bemocked by the vigorous, sportive, adventurous life of the Honeymoon couple bursting with health, excitement, happiness, and animated with the spirit of freedom which defines the true nature of life ("Their laughing voices charged with excitement beat against the glassed-in verandah like birds"); although only subconsciously, she also recognizes the "strange, saltish smell from the basket" as the ineffable ("strange"), lusciously fresh ("saltish") smell that a life of 'glad animal movement' seems to exude. The topknots, talking within earshot, speak of the couple's sound restful night sleep ("'you'll sleep well together'"): they seem to be speaking of a sleep the wife has been denied since the disease fastened itself upon her: she has not slept "well"; she has not slept "together": she has been only wakefully, uneasily sleepless: her sleep is disturbed either by a "hovering mosquito" or an agonizing question, "'do you mind awfully being out here with me?'" Even this element of contrast is no help: the tragic sense of a pulseless hopeless life is obliquely conveyed, but we are denied still another opportunity of tracing clues in the husband's individual reaction: the narrator's intent concentration on the wife's agonizing awareness of this contrast excludes all his gestures and utterances and facial expressions. We pass on but our curiosity is piqued: what must he be thinking? What is it that ails him? Will he stop turning his ring when he is back to the work he has been forced to give up for "two years"? If that is the only thing, why doesn't he do it here? If he is looking forward simply to the termination of the exile and longs to return to the only thing that he finds congenial, if this is all that is on his mind, if this is the root cause of all tenseness of the present moment, does there seem to be any emotional depth in the experience embodied? If there is no emotional depth, the short-story is simply a 'sketch' or pen-portrait or only a narrative essay on "the man without temperament", which it is not. The very intensity of the culminant moment presupposes gradual intensification of emotional experience consequent upon a trauma. The depth is there, but it is not simply emotional, it is poetic.

(b) Narrator's vision as focused upon details which help to obscure the central character:

(i) The protagonist's glance travelling "coolly, deliberately, over the round tables and basket-chairs scattered about the glassed-in verandah" is riveted soon upon "nothing". He stands "still", staring absent-mindedly into a void, as it were, his mind detached from the scene in the hall and presumably concentrated on the footfall of his wife coming downstairs. The blank void he stands staring into defines the fathomless void of his "temperament". The details of the scene in the hall registered at length through the narrator's imaginative perception of the 'atmosphere' of the protagonist's world then cluster in a consistent emotional context to eclipse the residue of the protagonist's appearance. The character's etherealization for the sake of the preconceived effect of obscurity as a means of defining the character "without temperament" is subtly effected.

(ii) The narrator's concentration on the utterances of the wife ("I must have told him about it sixty times at least, and still he doesn't bring it. Thank you.... That's very nice ... you won't have to go upstairs for a rug. Thank you, Robert.") keeps the image of the listener out of the frame: we are allowed only to hear her "thank" her husband, but we are denied even a vague glimpse either of the gesture for which she 'thanks' him or of the facial expression reflecting the nature of the listener's response: the listener is not shown nodding 'thanks'; he is not heard mumbling 'thanks' in return, either. The narrator does not take in the listener's response to the reproachful exclamation ("'Isn't it extraordinary?'") or to her statement of the one fact which has been intriguing and disquieting her, the negligent, flippant, resentful attitude of the people at the hotel ("'I must have told him about it sixty times etc.'")

(iii) The narrator's statement ("Back came Antonio with not only the hot water-with letters on a salver and three rolls of paper") sounds matter-of-fact, but it has not failed to register the emotional response of the character whose story the narrator has been presenting and who therefore is more likely to have been primarily affected by the arrival of the letters which mean only protraction of the listless ennui. The response registered through use of the dash and omission of the corollary ('but also') seems to be in the nature of a sudden shock. But the face reflecting the shock is out of the frame. The sense conveyed is not only that of absorption of the shock but also that of obscurity of the character's particular emotional experience at the moment.

(iv) Scene: The honeymoon couple's distracting appearance—The husband is mentally or physically absent here; either he is lost in his own distracting thoughts or he has already gone over "to the other end of the verandah"; he is blind even to the compelling distraction occasioned by the burst of Life. The sense of his listlessness is obliquely conveyed through obliteration of his image from the scene.

2. Narrator's vision concentrated as the protagonist's point of view:

   (a) For externalization of the protagonist's emotional complex:

      (i) Scene: The husband going upstairs for his wife's shawl.

      Breathlessness of the one long sentence developing into a whole paragraph is indicative of the 'swiftness' with which the husband rushes for the shawl that his wife has left in "their room" upstairs. This 'swiftness' betrays his pitiful, unconscious longing to shorten the protraction of bondage by as few minutes as possible: the suddenness and swiftness with which he turns into the hall gesture only his perfunctory, sooner-the-better attitude. The impression of 'swiftness' is conveyed by the tripping movement of the sentence evolving through sustained omission of prepositions and even of the possessive adjective ('its') as the sentence gains tempo-in the first part of the paragraph; it is communicated also through an abruptly emergent sequence of pronounced prepositions in a quick succession, climaxed by a faint fading echo of the syntactical rhythm of the first part.

      The emotional complex that the protagonist's nonchalant sense of dutifulness involves is obliquely reflected by the objects that pop into his vision as he rushes past them. "Notices of services at the English church" seem to point to his agonizing subconscious awareness of lack of time for mollifying distractions like "the services ... at the English church", away, from this outlandish world of mocking foreigners. "The unclaimed letters climbing the black lattice" seem to indicate that the protagonist has unconscious cognizance of the inarticulateness of his feelings that have only been accumulating and have never found their consummation in communication. The "huge 'presentation' clock that strikes the hours at the half-hours" is an ambiguous image rich in complexity of implications: it objectifies the protagonist's unconscious feeling of his life in a state of uncertainty as a static situation not only temporary but permanent. The one distinctive feature of the clock by which he recognizes it ("a clock that struck the hours at the half-hours") seems to define the major feature of his present existence; he has met his wife half-way; he is transfixed half-way between the present that is hopeless and the future that is uncertain. The distinctive feature of the clock ("struck the hours at the half hours") also corresponds to the essential aspect of his tragic experience: when a clock chimes the half-hour it gives only a vaguely half-articulate indication of time: if one hears only the half-hour chime and does not read the clock, one cannot know at which half-hour the clock has struck the hour. Again, this half hour chime is not represented as a sound heard: the writer does not say: 'the huge presentation clock struck the hour at the half-hour as he dashed past it', this vaguely half-articulate chime is referred to only as a feature of the clock: it is not allowed to be audibly manifest: muteness of what is distinguished by a feature suggesting only vague half-articulation corresponds to the secretiveness of the character who has been given speech only to disguise his thoughts; even the half-articulate utterances of the husband are obscurely inarticulate: dumbness of the clock at the moment seems to have been equated with the inarticulateness and uncommunicativeness of the protagonist's feeling. The "whistle" that remains unsounded in the opening scene defines this essential feature of the character. The painting of the "stout peasant children" mirrors in its depths the latent emotion of his longing for a life as carefree and natural as theirs. The protagonist's susceptibility to the features of the next image ("brown wooden bear") is an index of his subliminal recognition of his perfunctory dutifulness: he has been dead to all emotion of attachment as the insensate "wooden bear" has been unconcerned with or insensitive to all that is thrust into its "clasp": the "wooden bear" personates "the man without temperament". His sensitivity to the images of the "two palms" and the "two beggars" reveals his subconscious realization of the tragic fact that all possibilities in his life with a hopeless case on his mind are "crippled" and that their life together is going to remain as miserable as that of the "two beggars". His receptivity to the "piled-up wreckage of old tin boxes", etc. denotes his half-conscious awareness of the life-long accumulation of blighted hopes.

(ii) Scene: "the man" on the balcony overlooking the garden:

The chilly disposition of the character is not without its moment of intensely wrought-up moods. The moods reflect the darkly obscure depths of his agonized awareness of the static situation he finds himself condemned to; but such moods are furtive and evanescent, and it is the frigidity of his "temperament" that remains manifest as the whole truth about his personality. The emotional image of "a broken bird that tries to fly and sinks again and again struggles" occurs in a vision that is emotionally objective. Registration of the impressions in general is rather starkly unemotional: it is exemplified by the consistent use of colourless words and phrases in the rendering of the character's over-all audio-visual impression of the world beyond the "balcony". "The sky is the colour of jade": the wording sounds at once metaphorical and prosaic: the vision seems emotional and apathetic at the same time: the "man" is only seemingly "without temperament": the husband who is now simply a "man" is also a husband. The statement about the "stars" too seems to be matter-of-fact, but the very factual nature of the statement gives away the secret of the protagonist's sense of ennui and apathy. Our impression is strengthened by our simultaneous awareness of the onomatopoeic sound-effect achieved through choice of words with sounds having open-vowelled expansiveness "are ... great ... enormous ... white moon hangs over ... garden". Miss Mansfield does not say: 'The solitary moon drowsed between the trees like a great yellow moth', nor does she describe the moon as 'langurous', 'sleepless', 'listening', 'naked', 'desolate', or 'lingering': the one adjective ("enormous") is so factually and realistically descriptive that the sense of the viewer's apathy is automatically conveyed; the second adjective "white" is appropriate to the total emotional context. The moon only "hangs over the garden": is it a climbing moon? Or is it a setting moon? The ambiguity intrinsic in the vague statement about the pendulous "moon" obliquely images forth the character's tragic transfixation; he is in a state of suspended animation. The lights simply "shine across the garden path"; the husband simply exists, that is all. The lights do not need to be described as 'resting like a pale spotless shroud upon the path', or in words to that effect. "The sound of a piano" is described simply as something that 'is there' ("there is the sound of a piano"): there is no picturesque verb for either of the two nouns ("sound", "piano'"): the sound has not 'awakened': it is not a sound 'floating' from the salon; the "piano" has not been 'caressed'; it does not seem to have 'tinkled'. There are no colourful adjectives, either: the auditory image is not emotionally apprehended: the "sound" is not referred to as 'a tune'—a tune either 'plaintive' or 'half-remembered'. The sound of the piano is as plain or vague as the husband's own voice which throughout the short-story is simply the sound of a voice, empty and toneless and flat. The sound is as monosyllabic and dubious as the sound of his own voice ("Rot"). It is perhaps a kindred sound. Even the casual references to the woman as "the American woman" and the window as the "French window" tend to stress the irony of the husband's loneliness in a Hotel International. The American woman's question remains unanswered. The still silence in the garden seems to echo the silence of the stolid husband who is as much apathetic to the beauty of this "white" moon as he is to that of his wife with "her white hands ... her white cheeks ... her fair hair", all "silvered over". The husband sits still, transfixed, arrested—cabin'd, cribb'd and confin'd—reduced to a nonentity, a social "nobody", a "man".

The one image ("broken bird") that is obviously charged with emotion is one of the few fractions of the verbal complex that seems to have most sensitively registered the tragic anguish of the character. But the image remains poetically ambiguous: the reader feels impelled to ask—is it the husband's own image? Or is it his wife's? He finds the answer in the ambiguity itself which seems to him to be only one of the means of obscuring the tragic crisis in the protagonist's life; for what the total verbal complex seems to him to be aiming at is the portrayal of an obscurely tragic character much too static for a revealing development.[11]

(2) (b) For rendering of the protagonist's awareness of mockery and irony.

There is expressive dramatization of the protagonist's sensitized yet apathetic awareness of mockery that he is exposed to and feels roasted in, and of the irony that is distressingly implicit in his wife's innocent reference to "snow" and subtly manifest in the familiar appearance of this "snow" as a shroud enfolding the world of his lonely bedroom.

The experiences registered are both fresh and remembered. On the conscious level, the experiences are gained through sensitivity to the sounds and voices within earshot and to the objects that pop into the vision. On the subliminal level, there are lingering memories of the experiences of mockery and irony that he endured in the past.

This whole emotional complex leaks, though very slightly, from the outlet of his irrepressible questions which give away the secretiveness of his impulse to be avenged by mocking ironically: "Are you warm enough?" "are you sure?" The narrator seems to have imaginatively selected some culminant moments from the temporal range covered when tenseness of his emotional complex is manifestly at a flashpoint; but every time it is so objectively dramatized that it is only vaguely manifest, only sympathetically conceivable, only conjecturally definable; and even when it is so, it gives us no clue to the root cause. Subordinated to the pre-conceived effect of the 'hard-boiled' characterization of a man seemingly "without temperament", these occasional manifestations of emotional tenseness are, appropriately, either very quietly dramatized or only vaguely objectified. The narrator's vision of all such moments seems objectively yet imaginatively concentrated as the protagonist's point of view. This omniscient narrator is never allowed to betray the writer aiming at the specific effect of obscurity as the tragic feature of the experience.

(2) (c) For registration of the protagonist's manifest self-expression:

The narrator notes the successive degrees of the protagonist's self-expression.

The initial degree of the protagonist's self-expression, his occasional silence, reveals only that aspect of his personality which the plain essay-topic-like title of the short-story has already indicated: he remains unflustered even by mockery: he seems deafly impassive, utterly impervious, hopelessly unexcitable. This placid feature as an essential aspect of the character is revealed to us in the very opening scene; "he might have been going to whistle-but he did not whistle". Even this vague feature is blurred when the character with his dumb silence is etherealized. The next degree of the protagonist's self-expression is marked by his facial expressions. Here, too, the protagonist's "smile" and "frown" are as much vague as his "vacant look" and "stares". We have seen how a facial expression goes unregistered: the shock absorbed is indicated by a dash; the character is etherealized. The third degree of the character's self-expression is perceptible in his gestures and postures. The gestures express only his listless dutifulness and cold reserve, and on occasions reveal also the flash-points at which emotional intensity is unmistakably manifest. Of the only two postures recorded by the narrator the one is concomitant with a recollection which answers the one 'why' but which supplies no answer to the other 'why': why does the "man" dread the exile for "two years"? the other is pointed out in the registration of the recollection itself and this posture too leaves our interpretation of it at a dead end. The last degree of the "man"'s self-expression is exemplified by his audible articulate utterances.[12] Some of them are already vague: some of the others are only quibbles: the rest register only the tenseness of his diligence in the present. But none of the utterances gives us even an inkling of the definite reason for this tenseness.

The residue of the unobjectified yields no clue to the secret reason for the protagonist's chilly disposition. Characterization of an obscurely tragic character is thus effectually accomplished.

(2) (d) For transmission of intensity—through recourse to transition in the sequence of tense:

As the narrative progresses towards climax the sequence of tense undergoes a sudden yet smooth transition from the past participle to the historic present.[13] This transition is occasioned perhaps by the sense of the protagonist's stoic attitude of despondent and fatalistic, wearied and passive resignation to a routinized, groove-like life.

Intensity of 'dramatic effect' is weakened in the next short-story *Miss Brill*, by the interpretative nature of the protagonist's registration of impressions: concentration demanded by the singleness of crisis is not intense enough to assist refinement of the narrative quality. Communication of the element of pathos inherent in the conceived situation is crudely direct.

This is evident from the way Miss Mansfield has chosen to stop short: "But when she put the lid on the thought she heard something crying".

A comparison with an improvised substitute may help to substantiate this charge. 'A faint click was heard as the lid was put on'—we may venture to propose a monosylliablized substitute a la Mansfield-'and she sat there in her dark room, staring at nothing', etc. What Miss Brill feels at the moment deep in her heart would not have been inconceivable even if this different wording had been chosen: the first part of this substitute with its passive voice ("A faint click was heard ... the lid was put on") would have conveyed the image of Miss Brill as a lifeless automaton listlessly clamping the lid; the 'faint click' as a sound 'heard' would have helped to intensify the pathetic effect; it would have been indicative of the vacant mood induced by the shock; it would have suggested a faint mocking echo of that "something" which she has recognized as 'a something that makes one want to sing': it would have been in contrast with "the little chain of bright drops" which she has listened for and whose repetition has chimed in with the rhythmic beat throbbing presumably in the whole of her being in response to "the band": the 'click' as a sound heard and not listened for would also have transmitted the sense of accepted futility and unmistakable finality. Repetition of reference to 'her dark room'—already described as "a cupboard"—would have helped to accentuate the essentially relevant sense of the obscurely tragic privacy of her own lonely self as it remains oddly isolated from the pageant of Life. The terminating word, "nothing" would have been a fittingly conclusive definition of the meaning of the woman's situation: the sense of negative finality would have helped to sharpen the sting of the irony that all delusion motivating her self-dramatization is from the first exposed to: the fallacy that occasions her self-dramatization is inherent in her sanguine 'will to live' through participation in the pageant of Life.[14]

The concluding narrative statement as it originally stands written may make the reader feel 'she weeps and yet is too valiant to acknowledge it'.[15] But if the reader had been made simply to see that she only sat there in her dark room, staring at nothing, he would have enjoyed the richer aesthetic experience of imaginative penetration into 'the lonely reaches of the inarticulate'.[16] The sense of the lonely spinster's conclusive recognition of her true kinship with the fur-piece[17] would have been obliquely conveyed if—in the way we have ventured to suggest—both of them, the spinster and the fur-piece, had been fused at this climactic point into one image, statically cribbed or boxed up as they both are meant to seem in this darkly obscure seclusion of their respective 'boxes'.

The concluding narrative statement is typical. The character reads a meaning into most of the objects that pop into her vision and into most of the sounds that fall within earshot. When her interpretation of the sights and sounds in the public park is only conjecturally subjective, the record of her audio-visual impressions remains within the agreeably acceptable limits of realistic art: but the moment her subjective interpretation becomes a musing bordering on mystical philosophizing ("It was like a play. It was exactly like a play", etc.), the narrative account stifles the very art of shorter prose-fiction. The sense of the spinster's involvement in the "play" as one of the dramatic personae is automatically conveyed by the way she acts from the first and the way she defines what impinges upon her consciousness: 'she aspires to act as she costumes herself with the fur-piece in preparation for the entrance into the park';[18] she thinks of a "'special seat'", "the painted sky", "the drugged dog", "the hero and the heroine", etc. The cumulative effect of these allusions to what she feels to be "exactly like a play" is distinctive enough. There is no need of explicatory philosophizing.

However, Miss Mansfield's sensitiveness to the poetic beauty indwelling in the flux of life is artistic. The ceaseless ongoing rhythm of Life echoes as the orchestral music with its expected rhythmic beats: it is manifest in the occasional drift of leaves, the continual enactment of little stories, the changing hues of the sky; and all these manifestations continue even if they remain unheard, unmarked, unheeded. As a dramatic picture of this beauty the short-story seems to from a significant link between the earlier reportage, *Indiscreet Journey*, and the later sketch-like short-story *At the Bay*.

The quality of 'dramatic effect' achieved in the next short-story

Stranger, is exemplified by what transmits the intensity of the protagonist's emotional experience in all its immediacy: the record of the experience is sensitive registration of the intensified process of actualization of his be-ing just before his 'life' ebbs away. The 'dramatic effect' derives its intensity from the intrinsic irony of a life that stands defined by a death: the 'effect' is heightened through the consequential formation of a concentric design of characterizations. Characterization of the obscurely tragic character, the young stranger, is central to the emotional design of the short-story. The emotional design is made up of characterizations of three tragic characters involved in an obscure tragedy, at once individual and common. The design stresses the characterization of Hammond; it subordinates that of Janey as a means to this end; the young stranger's characterization achieved through second-hand reporting is set into the background. Hammond stands in the foreground; Janey is "half-hidden from the eye'; the young stranger is inscrutably remote. Hammond is seen most clearly: the narrative itself is the evolution of his impressions and moods; we know all that he sees and hears and thinks and feels. Janey is viewed objectively: the viewer is the character whose impressions and moods evolve as the narrative; through Hammond's vision, we see what she does and hear what she speaks; but, naturally like Hammond, we do not know what she thinks and feels when she smiles or looks into the fire: even with "her veil thrown back" she wears a Mona Lisa smile. The young stranger is not seen; he is only talked about: his name is not known; it could not be known what he longed to "say" or "leave" as "a message"; it could not be guessed 'what he would have felt'. One could not plumb the emotional complex that his unspeaking death presented. This character is not even ambiguously drawn like Janey; the features of his characterization are distinctly different: indirectness of his identification; preservation of his anonymity in spite of his decisive involvement in the tragedy: reiterative stress on his wordless silence that passed into the stillness of death. Such negative features of characterization seem only to be meant to obscure the recognizability of the character's real, distinct individual self: on the broad canvas of characterizations he is reduced to a mere dot of a human presence, so to say. This unmagnified 'dot' of a character seems to have been given a central position on the canvas: it is this stranger that as a "quite young" man brings about a tragic crisis in the married life of the Hammonds. It is this stranger whose unforgettable image will never let them "be alone together again": Janey, a petite wife with "a strong middle-aged husband", can never drop the recollection of the death of a young man in her own arms; Hammond also can never put out of the mind the haunting words of his estranged wife or the transfixed image of his wife with her "young man" in her arms. The inarticulate agony of maddening jealousy will keep churning up his emotions.

The emotional design of the short-story thus seems to be concentric: Hammond's characterization forms the enclosing circle; Janey's, the interior one; the young stranger's, the centre that is common to both. All the elements of the protagonist's characterization diffuse from a central symbolic complex of ironically identical elements; those of Janey's also emerge from this same common origin with stasis of mute agony in obscurity as its functional symbolic meaning. Radiating from the central story element, the obscure story of the young stranger, the symbolic meaning expands to reveal its natural dimensions in the characterizations of "Mr. and Mrs. Hammond".

In Janey's characterization, the stasis of dumb anguish is perceptible in her attitude of self-dramatization: all her self-expression is concealment of her real self, even with "her veil thrown back". She is just the Janey she has always been. The real self is "silent". Her silence after her casual explanation of what 'kept her so long' is obscurely tragic. In Hammond's characterization, his feeling of static agony as a personal tragedy finds its open full expression; nothing is concealed; even the distillation of the tragic experience is unmistakably perceptible. Hammond's responses to the impressions that impinge upon his consciousness are intimately registered for us in plain explicit statements: even his elliptical or broken sentences leave us in no doubt about their only possible meaning in the emotional context. His rational self is not overwhelmed with emotion even when his hauntingly transfixed image of Mrs. Hammond with the young man "in her arms" mocks the denial to him of the same voluntary offer. ("No, he mustn't think of it. Madness lay in thinking of it") Even his sense of failure to resist the relentless grip of the undeniable actual reality is overtly expressed ("No, he wouldn't face it. He couldn't stand it. It was too much to bear!") His expression of all that he thinks and feels is comprehensibly articulate. But the full articulation of Hammond's agony is known only to the reader; it is not known to the other character on the scene. Janey has her own obscurely private secret tragedy: the first chance of a contact with a young man was also the last chance of an experience of actualization of her real self. She has remained lost in her own dark bleak world, "thinking" and "asleep" at the same time. The "change" in Mr. Hammond remains 'unseen'. Janey does not share in his tragic experience of the crisis. The only possible viewer of this change has herself been languishing in obscurity.

The young stranger's agony is obscured by his dumb silence at the moment of death: even with its full articulation Hammond's experience only ironically corresponds to the inarticulate feeling of the dying nameless stranger. Thus all this revealing excessive articulation of the protagonist who seems so much alive stands ironically defined by the obscure intensified emotional complex in the dying heart: it evolves only as a tragedy in obscurity. Hammond's tragedy is the young stranger's tragedy writ large.[19]

Hammond says "something" as "nothing". The cross-cancellation of the denotations of the two words, "something" and "nothing", suggests the irony inherent in his 'excessive articulation': as a tragedy in obscurity all his articulation is only a secretly private expression.

The young man's "excitement, nervousness" seems exteriorized as Hammond's bored impatience. Tenseness at the moment of his death in excitement for union or reunion with somebody on the "land" is manifest as intensity of Hammond's "craving"—before his own psychic death—for communion with one who turns out to be a nobody, a "stranger", when at last they are both on the "dry land". The young man's experience of "nervousness excitement" culminating in feeling of "peace" especially in Janey's arms is analogous with Hammond's restless impatience for peace in palpable nearness of Janey.

What is only vaguely suggested as nascent love for Janey in the proportionately unmagnified characterization of the nameless passenger is palpably dramatized as an all-absorbing, desperately possessive passion for her in the portrayal of the well-known aristocrat Mr. Hammond. The impression that love in the nameless stranger's "heart" was nascent is evoked by Janey's conjectural interpretations of his inarticulate feelings ("'what would he have felt?'," etc. "'The end was quite peaceful'").

The young passenger's mute "message" echoes as Hammond's "strange loud 'hullo' across the water"; the stranger 'didn't say anything'; he spoke "not a word" to sympathetic yet helpless Janey;

Hammond "said something" as "nothing" to the "old" yet formal captain Johnson.

The contrast between the physical features of the central character and the protagonist is only an illusion: the young man "was very ill when he came on board" and all the time Janey was with him he was "too weak even to move a finger"; Hammond is "a strong-looking... man" with "thick gloves"; with his natural fetische for robust health, with his animal impulse to rival the "fine, solid chaps" with their superb "chests", with his boyish vivacity in spite of his middle age: his zest for life does not admit of the thought of "death"; its manifestation is unconscious hunger for sensuous contact with the naked throb of life actualized as a tactual sensation—a contact he has been denied since Janey's departure. But the whole truth about all this palpable actualization of being is defined by the obscure psychic interiorization in cessation of being. The beauty of a flicker is revealed by the gloom in which it dies out.

The central character as a social nobody has his counterpart in the protagonist whose being also is revealed on occasions as that of a 'metaphorically dead' nobody: there are moments when the latter's presence is etherealized.

The very opening scene revealed as Hammond's participation-shot view of the motionless steamliner far away at sea along with "the little crowd on the wharf" contributes suggestions that fit in with our conception of the protagonist as a counterpart of the central character: here too the essence of the character as an intensely animate nobody doomed to a 'metaphorical death "from the very beginning" is appropriately conveyed: the means is etherealization of his figure as he stands "in the front of the crowd": the vision is there, but the viewer is not there; the tensely impatient "little crowd" as a whole seems to be the externalized representation of the tense thoughts and memories crowding in upon Mr. Hammond; the motionless steamliner images forth the tragic stasis of his agony of a life doomed "from the very beginning". Later, when he makes "a bee-line to Janey" and comes in actual palpable contact with her physical presence, he is suddenly out of the picture: it is not that he clasps Janey in his arms; the conscious agent of the act is absent all of a sudden: "he strode up the gangway on to the deck in a bee-line to Janey, and Janey was clasped in his arms": the syntactical twist of the statement in the passive voice seems to have been necessitated by the sense of relapse into inert passivity. Again, while he tensely awaits the return of his Janey who has just left to "say goodbye to the doctor", 'out comes the watch' and 'he stares at nothing': he sits transfixed, thingş happening to him, automatically and in a blank temporal void, as it were: omission of the conjunction, 'but' or 'and', between the two narrative statements ("Out came the watch; he stared at nothing") helps to dispel the idea of transition or succession as a sign of life; inversion in "out came a watch" is used to reinforce the effect of automaticity of the happening; the eyes 'staring at nothing' seem to indicate consciousness that is all blank; there is a psychic void. Still again, when Janey asks "'Do I look ill'"? Hammond 'does not see her': "he only felt that she was looking at him". We feel tempted to ask, 'If Hammond does not see her, what is it that he is looking at the moment? He does not look down to see if she really looks ill. His naked eyes are open, but his visual consciousness is lost: he is again 'staring at nothing': he has only a feeling 'that she is looking at him'. What he "feels" at the moment is all that his being at the moment is. Hammond's presence seems etherealized when he is all feeling, all sensation, all thought. We have this moment when he asks Janey to kiss him. He himself does not make advances to her; he remains passive, waiting for the kiss; his eyes closed, he only feels and feels: "it seemed a tiny pause—... long enough ... to suffer torture": his perception of Janey's kiss is only tactual: the kiss is the same familiar airy kiss. We see him open his eyes, but we have not seen him close them. (He opens his eyes, ironically, at a moment when he unconsciously plunges into a conversation about what precipitates a decisive crisis in their life together.) Thus a drowsy haze seems to encompass all, all that Hammond has been thinking and feeling since he proposed to "get down to things" and came to the moot point: "'Tell me you're really glad to be back, Janey'". Even the speech, in the present emotional context, sounds simultaneously interrogative, imperative and optative.

The process of occasional etherealization culminates significantly: the culmination reveals in a flash the whole real image of the protagonist doomed to a tragically 'permanent situation'. Hammond is imaged as a ghost of his selfhood, arrested in the hell of a static world, left all alone, howling in agony, prayerfully. The great big bed seems to be mocking at his "craving" for a life "alone together". "His coat flung across [the bed] like some headless man images forth 'the deader quick'.[20] The image of a fatalistically resigned soul mumbling his bedtime prayer in a prone position is aptly descriptive of Hammond as he is now: a recluse in his own family with his soul compressed into a single agony of prayer—a prayer without an 'Amen!'. With prayerful resignation Hammond is "flung across" the foot of an altar—the altar of the value of whole togetherness. He stands transfixed, immobilized, arrested, left all by himself, while his wife is inanely, restlessly, outlandishly itinerant. The room in the hotel provided the change of a life-time and the chance has been blasted. The one more chance in the future, their journey together in a reserved compartment, will now be only a ghost of a chance. In the room that now looks "huge, immense", Hammond's tall strong-looking figure seems to have dwindled to a diminutive nonentity.

The protagonist's 'articulation' is 'excessive' but the past history of his 'psychology' remains obscure in spite of his occasional generalization from experiences in the past: "She was just the same. Not a day changed. Just as he'd always known her".... "And she took it all—just as usual. Absolutely composed. Just her little self—just Janey all over": the elliptical, parenthetical or adverbial phrasing of generalizations operating as flashbacks does connote his occasional stabbing realization of what perplexingly and agonizingly still persists—his old, old image of Janey that has undergone no sea-change. The phrasing is also significantly ambiguous—"From the very first moment—": the dash marking the break of the introductory adverbial clause is operative as a tell-tale punctuation mark: the ellipsis with the dash as the mark of a break forms an independent verbal unit ambiguously implying two decisive moments of union in Hammond's life: the moment when Janey uniting with him for the second time "emerged" with "her cool little voice"; and also, perhaps, the moment when Janey had come into his life and he had slipped the ring on her finger. The effect is cumulative; the reader has the feeling that Janey has all along been a stranger, "just as she always had been", queer, half-familiar, remote. But even during such brief haulting pauses in his thought-process the protagonist is not allowed to be caught by a recollection: no visual, auditory, oral, tactual or olfactory image is made to pop into his consciousness. The reason is simple: he is not in the mood to unravel tangled recollections; he has stopped wrestling with the phantoms of the past; perhaps he cannot have the memory quicken dull aches to stinging torture again. It is the culmination of his experiences that has to be dramatized.

Intent concentration on the culminant moment not only helps to obscure the past history of the protagonist's 'psychology': it also serves to accentuate the tragic sense of correspondence between the obscurity of his own traumatic experiences and the secrecy of the emotional background of the inner drama infinitely intensified within the young stranger's stopping heart. Again, it is because of this intense concentration on the crucial moment in the husband's life that the reader's feeling of the tragedy is deepened: the 'dramatic effect' compels speculation about the traumatic experiences in Hammond's married life and the reader's aesthetic experience is richer. Had Janey mistaken his overmastering impulse for gross animal passion on every occasion of their sexual contact? Was there an image in her unconscious of a "young" substitute for her middle-aged husband, which alienated him from her ("you look younger") and then sent her abroad "on a visit to the eldest daughter, married last year" to see a dream in her glimpses of the young couple, her daughter and her young son-in-law? Did Hammond convulse and writhe and simply waste his soul in a mute tearless agony of frustration in a kind of love that was a value to him? Had Janey with her unfulfilled dreams of the exquisite feeling of a tender love been forced to remain withdrawn into a hard shell of egocentric wifehood? Was it her interiority complex that made her seem apathetic, spiritless, cold, dead to all feelings of pity, remorse, or sympathy? Is it all this that he has "forgiven" now? Has he come to see that Janey had been incapable of responding to his kind of passion only as he himself had been unable to understand her philosophy of married love? Does he mean he has "forgiven" all in the spirit of forgetting, not only what Janey has done to him but also what he himself has done to her?

The hallowed mystery of the emotional complex intensified at the moment of the young man's death corresponds to the moral profundity of a whole passion manifest at the moment of intense actualization of Hammond's being.

Hammond's "craving" is dramatized as restless impatience for the uninterrupted realization here and now of a whole togetherness as a value in his married life. His vision itself reflects "this pang like hunger": the dinner-table image in the description opening the short-story represents Hammond's own dreamy vision of his "hunger" fully appeased—a hunger in which there will be no leftovers from the meal, a "hunger" in which "there wasn't any of her to escape". This appetite is only a concentrated passion that transcends the flesh and seeks oneness with what as a deep-souled secret feeling actualizes the real being of the partner: Hammond's passion is concentrated on the real, total self of Janey. The "dark" of the deepening "dusk" that he waves aside is a complex image of all that is likely to desecrate the sanctity of her existence. The image expands to evoke the consistent sense of Hammond's moral awareness of "the dusk" as a "stain": he is morally conscious of his animal, sensual impulse as a "stain" on the beauty of his rarefied passion for one whose sanctity is inviolable only as "his _his" possession: but, ironically, the "stain" lingers as a haunting stain: the image of the young man dying in Janey's arms remains unforgettable, transfixed. Hammond seems ceremoniously deferential when he renames his "Janey" as "Mrs. Hammond" in the same breath ("There she was. There was Janey. There was Mrs. Hammond, yes, yes, yes"). The cumulative effect of gradual crescendo climaxed by the steady emphatic repetition of the affirmative particle, "yes", is consistent with the composite effect of Hammond's characterization. For this characterization is a narrative rendering of a process of integral realization ironically climaxed by a downcast though far-seeing vision of a whole togetherness barren of all reciprocity. The deductive nature of the train of thought which culminates in his imagined picture of himself ("standing over her, watching her little hand fold round the cup") reinforces the impression of his responsibly solicitous, loving care of his wife which he is sure she will reciprocate when he is back home with her. The way the train of thought moves through his mind overriding all unpleasant associations ("It would be just like her not to ...") shows that even in his imagination his attentiveness to his wife's needs is breathlessly rapt, ungrudgingly deferential. His adoration of her features is fetischistic, but it is not abnormal, neurotic, or morbid. All sensuousness is rarefied: "the gentle pressure of her hand was so calming that he put his over hers to hold it there": "her cool little voice" is "the only voice in the world for him". Idiomatically natural occurrence of possessive adjectives as pronouns, "his", "hers" ("he put his over hers"), obviates repetition of the preceding noun, "hands": there is pleasing absence of picturesque verbs ('he cupped his over hers to enfold/clasp/grip/clutch it there') and singularly apt adjectives ('the silky/velvety pressure of her hand was so pacifying/tranquillizing/soothing'). This facilitates achievement of a consistent and expedient effect: tenderness of tactual feeling as a rarefied sensuous experience. Hammond's adoration of what is "the only voice in the world for him" is ecstatic, quiet, solemn. The hand and the voice are the concentrated symbols of all that is most beautiful and elegant and feminine in her personality. Everything about her is "precious"; she is "something ... too precious". Hammond's adoration of the features is exquisitely soulful: it persists even at moments of his paralysingly shocking experience: Janey's hand seems "gentle" even while its gesture re-enacts only the moment when "the young stranger breathed his life away at the end". ("And Hammond saw her lift her gentle hand"); her voice remains the same "small voice" even when her innocent statement about "the end" of the young man's life seems to show she does not know how "the end" she herself has hastened is not "peaceful"; her voice, again, is 'mocking', "airy"; still it remains "precious" for him as "her ... little voice". Her feelings or thoughts are an open book at least when she laughs at him, and he feels she is nearer to him, not "just the same", not "just as he had always known her". However, he cannot allow his curiosity or "craving" to be overwhelmed by his exquisite susceptibility to her sardonic amusement at his follies and foibles. He must "know for certain that she is as glad as he is"; he must have "the truth ... at all coats"; he must be assured she is "really glad to be back". He, therefore, instantly dismisses all his thoughts and feelings evoked by Janey's quizzical comments and prepares to look in the teeth of the facts. Urgency of assurance that Janey is "really" glad is vital. The moment is tense; it is critical and decisive.

As this passion concentrates, it resents all gap, all distance, all interval. He 'rivals his children': he resents their letters as they "rustle in her blouse'; he feels "he could have chucked them into the fire": he wants "to blot out everybody, everything". His "pang-like hunger" does not let him risk getting up to have the darkness which he is sure will enable them to be in nearest approximation to each other's real private self; what is more desirable than this darkness is the imploring hold on the "precious" possession perched on his knees here and now: the future even with its greater advantages of darkness is not so important as the present with its one single tangible advantage of a hold already gained: Hammond feels a bird in the hand is worth two in the bush. At the moment, they are in perfect seclusion; their isolation from the world around is inviolable. The room in the hotel has provided the chance of a life-time and

Hammond wonders if "this craving—this pang like hunger" would "always" be there; they will have one more chance in the first-class carriage reserved for them alone; but that opportunity in the future will not be so propitious: they will "leave the morning after" and their journey by day would mean wasted opportunity; they will not have the "darkness" that they can have here and now; they will not have this "great bed" either. The present opportunity here and now is promising; it is decisive; it is heaven-sent. The best and most comfortable room in the hotel has been reserved for the night. The first opportunity for reunion in isolation was afforded by the privacy of the cab when they had "the red-and-yellow striped blanket" thrown "round them both". That first opportunity was skimpily meagre. The second opportunity has presented itself: it is a reality here and now. The third and final opportunity for such reunion will present itself when they will be travelling "back to Salisbury in a first-class carriage—reserved" for "Mr. and Mrs. Hammond" alone. That one more opportunity will, however, be the last, and the future is uncertain. This second opportunity is superlative; it is abundant, promising, decisive; it must not be wasted. Time is fleeting fast. Hammond is clinging to the moment of "craving". His possessive passion is intensified by his deep emotional awareness of the value of 'here and now' as intense actuality of life. Hammond is holding her body close to his own, but this possessive hold is not only physical: it is in this body that her real self is 'ensconced'; this whole of Janey is a "precious" possession: he must take care that 'there isn't any of her to escape'. The "glasses" would undoubtedly have been a help: they would have helped to magnify and distinguish the image of Janey's "little self" as a specifically distinct individual entity. This eagerness to experience the vicarious thrill of closer proximity to the distinctly palpable individual existence of "his" Janey betokens sensuous love. But this sensuous love is perhaps only an earlier manifestation of Hammond's "craving" to know Janey well enough and thus to feel she is "so much a part of himself that there wasn't any of her to escape". It is not a momentary passion for the comforting glimpse of his wife who has been in Europe for the last ten months"; it is an unconscious expression of a deep-souled "craving" for the integral realization of a value in his married life. Even when Janey 'lies on his breast' and he needs no "glasses", he keeps desperately looking for a means of having a magnified image of her real self that seems 'so remote' from him ("Hammond never knew for dead certain that she was as glad as he was. How could he know? · Would he ever know?"). He seeks such fulfilment of his "craving" as may negate all spatial, temporal, physical and psychic remoteness of his "precious" possession. Janey is "precious" therefore the whole of the present as a reality here and now is precious. It is this tenseness of the tenacity of his hold on the "precious" present that defines the intense actuality of life; the intense reality of the 'precious" present has 'blotted out' the past and deepened its obscurity.

We note a rhythmical pattern of identical climaxes meant to register the heightening tempo in the dramatization of the protagonist's "craving" for an integral realization through closest intimacy: what seems to be an unnecessary repetition of an urgent, eager inquiry stands justified as the rendering of a penultimate climax in the process; the climax defines the extent to which the character's emotional intensity has grown by this time. The subordinate pattern registering the climaxes in the evolving process of craving to know the truth for an integral realization is conspicuous enough to arrest our critical attention. What makes it conspicuous in the emotional design is the increasing intensity in the emotional content. This intensity is heightened in two ways: (1) manifestation of curiosity is made to vary in accordance with the degree of emotional intensity; (2) there is depiction of a mood of frustration and perplexity immediately after each climax. (The emotional tempo is heightened but the protagonist stands transfixed in static agony, mystified, perplexed, and finally, dumbfounded.)

(1) Hammond has already sought Janey's own reply at the first apportune moment of privacy in the cab. His sentence ("'Glad to be home again, dearie?'") has been naturally interrogative and elliptical: he has spoken impromptu. The manifestation of his curiosity is naturally rendered as a point-blank inquiry: the opportunity for an intimate conversation, though propitious, has not been ample.

But the next time when he 'gets down to things' and is ready to look things in the face, we have the expression of the same feeling with a difference: an additional word that comes natural is "really". The sentence, naturally again, is framed as an emphatic statement and not as an offhand question. Choice of the type of sentence is necessitated by the sense of a penultimate climax of eager curiosity as an emotional complex: the sentence sounds imperative, interrogative and optative, all at the same time.

The culminant climax occurs when Hammond makes the last desperate effort in a more earthy way to have a palpable experience of the extent to which Janey is sincere, and passionately breathes his last sentence: "'you kiss me Janey'". Here we have a sentence which is only imperative and optative and not interrogative: the kiss is the last resort; the climax is reached. Time in the perfect privacy of the room is running its course; he is not in the mood to venture hypotheses; he must "get down to things" himself and resort to an earthy means—here and now; reliance on the revealing powers of the earthy resort obviates further interrogation.

(2) Depiction of the mood immediately after the first climax is rather an objective rendering of Hammond's perception of Janey's response: "she smiled; she didn't even bother to answer, but gently drew her hand away as they came to the brighter streets:. The mood of frustration or perplexity induced by the 'gentle' way in which Janey seems to have repelled his advances is not dwelt upon, but it is effectively communicated to the reader already overwhelmed by the accumulative effect of questions confounding Hammond's mind: how is it that she has been "keeping something from him?" Why did she make the remark—"'Bachelor life agrees with you'"? How is it that he still has the usual "feeling he was holding something that never was quite his-his"?

The second climax too is immediately followed by the rendering of the protagonist's mood of despair and bewilderment, but this time the rendering is an intimate registration of some ultimate question with regard to the "craving" itself: "How could he know? Would he ever know? Would he always have this craving—this pang like hunger, etc.?" The questions Hammond is confronted with when he has 'got down to things' are barren of comforting answers. Even if Janey 'tells' him she is "really" glad or is "as glad as he", he has no means of assuring himself of the veracity or candour of her statement ("How could he know?"). This is going to be tragically true of his "craving" in the future, too ("would he ever know?"). The realm of

> the possible is tragically barren; that of the real is already so. The protagonist's mood of dejection and incomprehension is symptomatic of his static agony.

Then we have the rendering of the protagonist's own final realization of the futility of further recourse to any other means of comprehending "the truth". Naturally, he feels "suddenly, horribly tired". The last means of wringing it out of Janey has failed: her lips have only "touched" his own, "kissing them as she always kissed them". She is still "just the same ... just as he had always known her". Hammonds finds himself in the same state that he has been in: he finally comes to feel this state to be a 'permanent situation'. Janey's lips have touched his, "firmly" yet "lightly"; she has kissed the "lips" ("them") and not 'him": all mutuality is between lips and lips only. The adverbial parenthesis is, significantly, not worded thus: 'before she kissed him, firmly, lightly—kissing him as she always kissed him'. The complex syntax adequately registers nervousness characteristic of the experience at the decisive, critical moment.

The subsequent query that he goes on to make after this tragic moment when the life of his life has ebbed away naturally seems much too casual, listless, idle; however it is not without a faint echo of the dying voice of longing for Janey's empathy: "'If you knew', he said, opening his eyes, 'what it's been like-waiting today', etc." Ironically, it is after this moment that Hammond suffers the shock of a life-time: he receives the shock when he goes on to make a customary inquiry ("what kept you so long?"); he is subjected to it when, metaphorically, he is already half-dead. This tragic irony excites our pity.

What elevates this psychic complex of a 'whole' passion to the glory of moral serenity is the character's "craving" for an integral realization of togetherness as a value. It is perhaps this moral synthetic vision of his life as a 'whole' life complete with his alter ego that is manifest earlier as a unifying all-embracing vision. While Hammond is on the wharf his thoughts, speeches and gestures evoke impressions of genial sociability, warm fellow-feeling, extensive empathy, and impulsive generosity.

We also record an impression of his sensitized awareness of reciprocity "across the water" between "the voices on shore and the voices on board" as the two worlds come nearer and nearer to each other. What is, quite consistently, made to pop into his view of the scene is the visual image of "the crew" lowering "the rails for the gangways" or of "the wharf hands" bringing "the heavy gangways along at a sweeping run". All this is characteristic of his unifying synthetic, whole vision. "standing in the front of the crowd" the character seems, as we have seen, to be an etherealized means of intertransmission of greeting "voices". The other element complementary to the protagonist's characterization is the impression of his instinctive responsiveness to characteristic manifestations of life-principle, e.g. living movement, pulsating sound, exuberant health, harmonious consummation, etc. Quite naturally, he "hated to hear of death". The two features of the character—a unifying, synthetic whole vision and instinctive responsiveness to manifestations of life-principle—combine to point to the essentially moral nature of his passion.

The protagonist's image stands out in high relief in the emotional design which is devised to achieve the effect of estrangement or individual loneliness consequent upon obscurity of private agony as a secret tragedy, unshared, silent, dark.

The young stranger's longing or Hammond's "craving" or "pang like hunger" objectifies the intense actualization of being that is perceptible just before life ebbs away. In the story of either character, it is only the culmination of the experiences that is dramatized; the experiences themselves are not rendered. Obscurity of the past in either characterization is deepened by the powerfully distracting effect of life's intense actuality manifest as passionate impatience to achieve whole togetherness.

The quality of 'dramatic effect' thus achieved lingers in the reader's memory with poetic dimensions. The poetic meaning seems inclusive of a serene truth-vision: all that seems fully articulate is only obscurely inarticulate; all circle is only its centre magnified; all life is life in death; 'all is still'.

The 'dramatic effect' in *Daughters of the Late Colonel*, too, involves transmission of the very intensity intrinsic in the conceived content: the total emotional experience is tragic in its manifestation as a transient flicker of 'will to live' in the enveloping gloom of dark hopelessness; the ways of transmitting the intensity of the emotional experience in all its immediacy are imperceptibly functional on the structural-textural level of a plain narrative; the dimensions of the tragic essence are subtly revealed to an empathetically critical reader: they seem to have been deepened by a story element made up of absurd trivialities and by the austerity of the narrative style.

The 'dramatic effect' here exemplifies the modern tendency in fictional art to present such 'subjective selection' of materials' as reflects 'an objective standard of values'.[21]

The tragically static situation in the "lives" of the sisters is rendered in concentration intense and imaginative enough to yield a telling design on both the structural and the emotional level.[22] The structural design is exemplified by the way the short-story begins and ends; it is discernible also in the form of a sketch: the form assumes not only a shape that is tell-tale but also a title that is attuned to the 'atmosphere'.

The sense of tragic stasis that characterizes the transitional phase in the sisters' "lives" is communicated through formation of a dominant parallelism: both the opening and concluding sections reflect an identical process of psychic flux terminating in the void of loss of consciousness; the opening section begins when the sisters are fully awake and ends as they drop off; there is progression from a state of wakefulness to that of sleep. Similarly, "two mornings later", they are more fully awake to the problems they have to cope with—to the reality of not only the present but also the past, to the thrill of freedom from the bondage of what was only an illusion of life, to a sense of futility in the void of Now...?, and to the sunny moment of be-ing through choice from the realm of "the future"; but this full wakefulness finally fades into what is but wakeful sleep, amnesia, which is symptomatic of psychic stasis. This parallelism naturally converges on an image evoking the sense of a moment when all succession as a feature of reality stands transfixed ("a big cloud where the sun had been").

The swift tragic transitions registered in the concluding section seem parallel to the natural transition in the opening section. These transitions also parallel the sisters' occasional lapses into contemporaneity with father—into the past as the present; the lapses show how the process is also independent of or isolated from time: to sink into actual sleep or wakeful sleep is to be psychically existent neither in the past nor in the present nor in the future. The sisters not only sink into sleep; they also seem to be reposing in filmy-eyed hypnotic sleep.

This over-all impression of sleepiness of the characters walking as somnambulists through "a dark tunnel" is by no means altogether inconsistent with a view of the specific ending of the first section composed as a prologue to depiction of a nightmare. The subsequent sections form a scenic whole with a fragmentary sequence characteristic of a nightmarish dream. This nightmare ends when they are awake "two mornings later". The ending of the opening section features a scene in which we find the sisters preparing for sleep. This ending quite congruously shades off into the beginning of the scenic whole composed almost as phantasmagoria of nightmarish images. The sisters sink into sleep and the phantoms born of the gloomy recency of a strangely tragic event in their isolated lonely world start swimming, as it were, in the obscure depths of their psyche. But the phantoms are not blurred: although the phantasmal scenes are chaotic, they are realistically detailed. The effect to be achieved is that of a nightmarish past that is as real as the present; the sisters live in a present that is still all past. The scenic whole mirrors the evolution of the sisters' "minds". It reflects the night life of their "minds", the life that comes into being in the psychic depths of a sleep; this life is a life in both the past and the present and thus its flux is static. What unifies the total structural framework devised by way of an aesthetic rendering of the sisters' psychic stasis is the recurrence of one effect—the effect of lapse into wakeful sleep in which all psychic flux is static. Occasional reversion in the temporal flux in their "lives" is symptomatic of the stasis that plagues their "minds".

The archetypal frame of a square or rectangle formed through choice of an even number of sections is also significant. All flux within this structural frame seems static: the whole transitional phase is conceived as tense moment at once tingling and frozen. The short-story has, naturally, the desired effect of a sketch.

The choice of a matter-of-fact title in preference to an oblique one is perhaps determined by the same imaginative vision of a stark reality—utter colourlessness, absolute sameness, dark hopelessness, of the sisters' "lives".

The emotional design that the story element assumes is also as neatly patterned as the structural one is.

One significant pattern distinctly conspicuous in the emotional design is formed through registration of one characteristic feature of the sisters' "lives"—their tendency to procrastinate.

Chronologically, when there is postponement for the first time, Jug is talking about her father's burial: we perceive here a sense of pity for and also a sense of fear of the father-image now haunting their "lives": the image is that of a father who was "helpless at the moment" of his burial: it is also the image of a father of an unforgiving nature. Jug's justification of the retention of the father's physical presence is to be discerned in her mixed feeling of pity and love for the father who even as a living corpse was at least the residue of 'reason for their living';[23] this feeling seems to be mingled with her sense of guilt and fear, for the sisters are uncomfortably conscious of the fact that they have buried one who was 'the cause of their suffering'[24] as a stern unforgiving father.

The second time when Jug speaks more explicitly of a postponement she is in bed, engaged in an idle drowsy gossip. Postponement this time is motivated by the speaker's stoic attitude: she is 'incapable of real feeling' for father; the hearer has already started drowning her feeling of inner suffering in compassion for the suffering will of other beings, the porter and the mice. Jug dismisses Con's proposal with the flat stroke of a postponement and laughs to scorn her sister's solicitude for the mice 'scurrying' for "crumbs" when "there aren't any". 'Incapable of real feeling' for father, she is solicitous about their own isolation as the only means now of freedom from all social conventions and formalities: alleviation of inner suffering sought through temporary identification with the suffering will of other beings is fallacious; will to live their own free, real "lives" together is the only value now. Jug is wakefully stoic.

The third time, "two mornings later", they are in the father's room and Con proposes to postpone 'settling about father's things'. Here postponement is consequent upon their intense sensitiveness to what is an unnerving experience; the situation is that of their first trespass on the grim privacy of a stern father's posthumous presence. When father was alive the daughters spent their "lives" "keeping out of his way"; trespass was out of the question. The trespass on this next Saturday has been a postponed one: the sisters have brought themselves to come into the room on the last day "during the week". On the "list of things to be" it is, naturally, not even precisely placed in the numerical order natural to a list. Still the sisters feel: 'If it were done, when 'tis done, then 'twer well, It were done quickly' (*Macbeth*). The rendering of the situation intimately registers the tension of the sisters' "minds". The conflicting thoughts involved in their desperate decision, 'If it were done, when it's done' and 't wer well, It were done quickly', are indistinguishable; they keep eddying at the back of their "minds" as a vaguely complex iota of an idea. It is this frozen emotional complex that is externalized later as the sisters have the tactual feel of the snowflakes in the room with its "door" "holding itself tight shut", or with a door without "any handle at all". Postponement here is sympatomatic of their psychic intertia.

Lastly there is an express determination not to postpone what they have been deferring since father's death—dismissal of Kate. Dramatization of this moment terminates this specific pattern transmitting the tragic sense of the sisters' psychic stasis. Their determination not to postpone what they have already been deferring is tragically overwhelmed by the sudden awareness of their existence with the father palpably present with his "thumping stick" and "strange loud bellow". The sisters become their normal regimented selves. Their last effort to burst their hard shells through bold resolution to assert themselves and thus be their real selves is fulfilled by the automatic reassertion of their normal regimented selves. But the very next moment the nightmare ends; the daughters 'remember': never will they hear the "strange bellow" or "the thumping of the stick". Their psychic evolution remains arrested.

The process of the postponements as unmistakable symptoms of the sisters' static psyche culminates in their relapse into the dismal normality of the regimented life ("'Run Clon, said Josephine. 'Run quickly. There's sixpence on the ...'"): it ends where it all began. This helps to create an illusion of psychic evolution.

The pattern formed is significantly rhythmical. The first situation is identical with the third: in both we have a pronounced sense of fear as the motivation of postponement; there is transition, too, from the first to the third: terror of the haunting voice "roaring" disapproval of their "gimcrack excursion" nurtures Josephine's guilt complex; this becomes the feeling of a chill breath of fright when the sisters intrude upon the haunted privacy of one whose voice remained throughout a "strange" voice, unfamiliar, alienating, forbidding. In the first situation the feeling of terror as a guilt complex is not unmingled with a feeling of pity for the "helpless" body lowered into the grave; this whole emotional complex deepens in the third: it all becomes an agony conceivable as an 'If-it-were-done ... it-were-done-quickly' feeling. There is succession manifest only as transfixation. Postponement is characteristic of such a psychic vertigo. The second situation is also rhythmically parallel to the fourth: in both there is intensity of a longing for assertion of selfhood: here too we have a sense of transition: in the second Jug postpones the decision in a mood of insistence on existence in isolation from society outside their world or from the world of the suffering will of others; in the fourth she expressly resolves not to postpone another major decision only in a mood of self-assertion for the experience of their individual existence as a distinctly felt reality. Transition is perceptible in the intenseness of her assertion of selfhood independent not only of others' entities but also of its own entity which has hitherto been only a regimented unit of existence devoid of its essential spirit of freedom. But this deepened intenseness too is lost in the still deeper intenseness of the actuality of existence as her normal regimented self. The moment Jug begins to declare her determination not to "postpone it this time" as they have to have the feel of the moment of freedom and resurrection of real existence, she becomes contemporaneous with father, telling Con to be 'quick' about "sixpence" for "the monkey ... in the street below". Real selfhood is possessed by the inertia of normal self: the pre-natal moment of be-ing is lost in the dark temporal void barren of all inklings of the past, the present, and the future: there is 'a big cloud where the sun has been': Jug's first spontaneous response to the sound in the street below on this seventh day after father's death is an occurrence at a point of time that is all parts of time at the same time. The nature of the whole psychic process is defined by this inner pattern of imperceptible transitions.

The total effect of the situations in which postponements occur is enriched through consistent evolution of an image of dark, narrow confinement. The first time Jug speaks of a postponement obligatory upon them as daughters, she is seated in a tight-buttoned cab with "all its blackness". The second time when she sleeps on a question, she is in bed "frowning fiercely at the dark", "staring across the dark at Constantia". Lazily drowsy, the sisters lie in bed, confined to a dark room, often lost in "silence" ruffled only by "a little rustle, a scurry, a hop"; the only other world in closest vicinity to their own lonely world is that of the mice: suffering of will in that world too is as much obscurely tragic as it is in their own. The third time when Con defers "settling about father's things", they feel confined to a chilly cold room with a door that is holding itself tight shut and is without a handle; or, they feel they are in a room with only walls all around but without any door at all. The fourth and last time when Jug voices a resolute decision not to postpone the decision they have not been bold enough to enforce, they seem to be bursting with the tension of a poise for liberation from their regimented normal selves. But the very next moment they find themselves in the rigid confinement governed by the loud bellow and the thumping stick.

The dramatic point of the narrative where a dash marks a break in Jug's firm, decisive voice ("'If we postpone it this time'") captures the climactic moment in the psychic process of their will to be their bold, free, 'real selves'.

There is registration of the other characteristic features of the two isotates as they stand at once hopelessly condemned to a tragic togetherness and hopefully poised for reciprocity between their individual 'real selves'. This registration too creates a neat rhythmical pattern. The pattern is perceptible in the dramatizations of essentially identical moments when the sisters' individual thought-processes seem convergent and divergent at the same time.[25]

There are six situations dramatizing this tense tragic experience; they are significantly identical story elements: their evolution through the emotional design seems to have been meant to dramatize the gradual intensification of the sisters' unconscious instinctive longing for experience of individual selfhood and reciprocal psychic orientation, which alone can give meaning now to their "lives together".[26]

(i) !... At Eastbourne a mysterious man at their boarding-house had put a note on the jug of hot water.... But by the time Connie had found it the steam had made the writing too faint to read.

This was, chronologically, the sisters' first major traumatic experience of isolated, lonely togetherness. At this stage their togetherness was barren of all possibilities of consummation of individual selfhood through *affaire du coeur*. Their togetherness here was also without intense actuality of an individual experience of the tragedy: if the letter had been addressed to the one, the other would have experienced emotional frustration of her own amorous hopes and she would have felt the stab of realization very deeply; her experience would then have been intensely individual and her own existence in an isolated world of lonely togetherness would at least for a moment have had intense actuality. But unequal intensity of the sisters' individual experiences would then have weakened the tragic effect of their story; it would rather have robbed the tragedy of its very essence: their common experience at the moment was presumably as intensely tragic as their individual experience would have been. Their togetherness was synonymous with individual loneliness; they suffered as one individual. Thus even their togetherness was not without intense actuality of experience. But this intense reality had deeper tragic dimensions: there was a blankly barren rhetorical question in their "lives": to which of the two had the note been addressed? They were not only equally tragic; they were also obscurely tragic. What deepens the tragic effect of this recorded moment is the vagueness about the image of the man who put the note on the Jug: he was "a mysterious man at their boarding-house. Anonymity of this man or indistinguishability of his identity left no scope for their imagination of his image. Their identically tragic selves made them live a life of individual loneliness; what completed the sense of blank barrenness was the utter impossibility of consummation of individual selfhood through marital conjugality or even reciprocal sympathy.

(ii) Josephine's black man was tiny; he scurried along glistening like an ant. But there was something blind and tireless about Constantia's tall, thin fellow, which made him, she decided, a very unpleasant person indeed.... On the verandah, dressed all in white and wearing a cork helmet, stood Benny.

Jug's image of the native runner as an ant scurrying along makes us share her view of the remoteness of her own world with her sister's from that of Benny with Hilda, the unknown sister-in-law: the fully visualized image of the native is reduced to a "tiny" size by the vast expanse that separates her own world of tense togetherness from the world of an easy-going family.

Con's image of the runner becomes subjective, too. The human form of the figure is retained in this subjective image, but the emotional awareness of a sad truth about the link is distinctly individual: there is "something blind and tireless about Con's tall, thin fellow". What makes him "very unpleasant" is absence in him of any trait of individuality that is free and living.

Con's unconscious association of 'unpleasantness' with the image of the black runner is psychologically characteristic of her subconscious intense awareness of the dull tedium that stagnates their "lives": their togetherness is spatialized in a void by the remoteness of the intensely alive world of their own flesh and blood living abroad; it is not only spatially isolated, it is also temporally cut off: the link between the two worlds is by no means a living means of intimately private and sympathetically personal contact; the clock will have stopped by the time it reaches that world: it would then be impossible to say when, on which date, at which specific hour of light or darkness the clock stopped. The image is coloured by the sentimental vision of the tragic sisters. After a brief spell of individual psychic freedom through subjective imagination, the sisters sink back into the void of their "lives" of absolute sameness. The grim reality of the tragic indistinguishability of their individual existence thus defines the general drama of pain.

(iii) 'It would have been such a point, having him', said Josephine.

'And he would have enjoyed it so', said Constantia, not thinking what she was saying.

That Josephine means 'Cyril' by "him" and that Constantia's "he" means 'Benny' and not 'Cyrill' is clear from the context. The narrator's explications of the fact about Con's reply clinches this impression. Earlier, Con has expressed her apprehension and then plunged into a gulf of silence. She emerges at this point of the narrative with the image of Benny naturally still there at the back of her 'mind'. Josephine has made no reply to Con's apprehensive statement and has 'flown off on one of her tangents' with thoughts of Cyril thronging her mind. Bursting out in dreamy ejaculation she has broken her silence here. Con has been unaware of this transition in Josephine's thought-process: still lost in a void she makes only the sound of a voice that sounds still and hollow. This time it is Con that echoes Jug's voice. The process is reversed later, significantly, when both the sisters sink into the oblivion of their 'real selves'. Jug that echoes her sister's faint voice at the later moment 'dies' slowly and a little later than Con: she is the one who has never perhaps been so "sleepy" as her sister who has rather been walking as a somnabulist through this world of walls and walls; Con's "and" ("'And he would have enjoyed it so'") and Josephine's "too" ("'I've forgotten too'") in the respective situations intone contrasted feelings in their individual echoing voices; but the ring in both is hollow: Con's "And" only seems to complement Jug's dreamy statement which is indicative of her creative imagination of wholeness in terms of consanguineous togetherness; the idea of a complement is a fallacy. Jug's "too" also is a complement that is characteristic of only an absolute sameness of a tragic experience of alienation even from "real self". Pertinence of the complement here is ironically tragic.

Josephine thinks of a possibility in the past ("'It would have been such a point, having him'"): her desperate choice even from a future in the past remains unrecognized: individuality of being poised for a wholeness remains uncomplemented. The illusion of a wholesome existence is evoked, but it is disappointed by what sounds in the context like the dull thud of a flat, thoughtless, vague statement. Con's reply is *a* reply; it is not *the* reply. Her absent-minded and ironically contrary reply darkens the whole sunny moment of bid for wholeness. Con does not know what she is saying, but the reader can gather from the context that she is thinking and that she is also fully conscious of what she herself means; her reply is natural to her own thought-process; it is wrong only in relation to the expression of a different thought-process. There is emotional affinity, but of their cross-cancelling concepts of the image the sisters are absolutely unaware. We can see they are "strangers" to each other: they themselves are blissfully ignorant of this one tragic fact about their togetherness at least at the earlier stage of their awakening "two mornings later". A wholesome complex of the images of the individual entities of all the four consanguineously related living members of the Colonel's family is involved in the process of the sisters' "creative" imaginations; but barrenness of reciprocity between the sisters individually creating a whole microcosm for their togetherness reduces the complex to a meaningless and, paradoxically, a negative whole.

The situation here bears almost an exact similitude to the one in which the sisters were not in a position to make out to which of the two the note had been addressed. The relation between the man and either of the two sisters was as obscure as the relation between the sisters themselves is. During their first traumatic experience their "minds" registered no reaction, individual or common. The man was as "mysterious" as their common image of the chosen recipient of the parcel has been just now; both the man and the recipient of the parcel stand misunderstood by the sisters. The link with their image of the complement for wholeness is lost in dark obscurity: the Eastbourne lover was to remain unrecognizable, indistinguishable, unimaginable; individual entities of those who are their own flesh and blood remain lost to them because of the unrevised mutual misunderstanding between them. Similarly, the relation between the sisters themselves is barren of reciprocity. All the links thus intercross, but all are lost. Their togetherness in the two situations has been, respectively, obscurely tragic and fallaciously complemented.[27]

(iv) But at that moment in the street below a barrel-organ struck up. Josephine and Constantia sprang to their feet together.

"Run, Con", said Josephine, "Run quickly. There's sixpence on the . . ." Then they remembered.

Intensification of the mood seems to have occasioned denseness of the narrative texture. The style is ambiguous enough to seem to have captured the conflicting dimensions of the total emotional complex involved. What seems to have called for ambiguity is the complexity characterizing the sisters' experience of the moment. Dramatization of this transistional moment when the sisters 'spring to their feet together' is not without dimensions. The immediate impression is that of reassertion of the presentness of the past as an intensely real reality. The sinister influence of the stern, ruthlessly dominant personality of the cantankerous Colonel as their father has overwhelmed their 'real selves' to such an extent that they still sometimes become the Jug and the Con looking after their father and keeping out of his way: tutored and confirmed habit occasionally takes possession of their indivual selves despite all intensification of their longing for the feel of the intense reality of freedom as the experience of real existence: "a big cloud" of possibly a life-long servitude comes suddenly where "the sun" of intensely actualized real life in freedom should have been and stays there as the only reality. This tragic succession has been recurrent throughout the "week". (We have seen how the past comes to be as real as or more real than the present when even Jug who censures Con for being "sleepy" suddenly begins to relive her yesterdays, dreamily oblivious of the context of her parley with Con in the present.)

Dramatization of the climactic moment is objective enough to admit of what complements the whole tragic truth about the moment. The sisters 'spring to their feet together' not only habitually but also instinctively: what motivates their sudden 'spring' is also their unconscious 'will to live': they cannot but live the residue of life; they cannot help being with one who was 'a reason for their living'. They are tragically unaware of the fact that their sudden spring is but a manifestation of their instinctive 'will to live', to exist, to be. The illusion of life in the past naturally seems more real than the reality of life in the present.

The ambiguity of the style appropriate to the depiction of this tensely dramatic moment of transition in the sisters' psychic evolution dissolves to show how their 'remembrance' ("Then they remembered") is an awakening to the whole tragic reality of the present.[28]

A significant syntactical rhythm created through variation in placing of a dimensional word, "never", in the passage registering what they "remembered", helps to intone the sisters' common feeling not only of freedom from the bondage of the past but also of a loss of a life that was undoubtedly an illusion but never a void. The normal syntactical structure of the two narrative statements ("They would never have to stop the organ-grinder again" ... "The organ—grinder might play there all day and the stick would not thump") significantly encompasses the other two which are marked off by inversion ("Never again would she and Constantia be told", etc. ... "Never would sound that loud, strange bellow", etc.): this evidences the intrinsicality of an emotional complex of conflicting feelings: the rhythmical pattern registers their simultaneity: the tone is mournful as well as dreamy; it is pitiful and also exciting; it is anguished and tranquil at the same time. The total effect seems to be a means of evoking the complex mood of the moment. The first statement ("They would never have to stop," etc.) has a normal syntactical pattern; that is, it is without reversal of the normal verbal order usually resorted to for the sake of emphasis; the last statement has an unemotional "and" ("and the stick would not thump") chosen in preference to an emotional 'but' as a connective between the two plain principal clauses: these two statements harmonize to intone the sisters' feeling of the whole tragic truth about this transitional moment. The sisters feel it is a pity that father's stick would not "thump" any longer to deny what their lonely selves have been pining for. The other two statements with their inversion beat into our minds the sense of conclusive finality in either case.

The tune which the barrel-organ plays also echoes the same throbbing rhythm of the feelings which are irreconcilably conflicting and all equally intensified.

The barrel-organ 'plays' a tune which the sisters interpret in a mood induced by the last word in their thought-process ("thump"). Quite naturally this monosyllabic word is stressed in either of the two possible rhythmical patterns: iambic-pyrrhic-monometric-iambic ("It ne/ver will/thump/a-gain"); and iambic-anapaestic-iambic ("It ne/ver will thump/a-gain"). The other words which register concomitant accentuation, naturally under the emotional stress, are the disyllabic "never" and "a-gain". Thus all the three important words in either of the possible patterns are accented—"never ... thump ... again". All the other syllables in the metrical patterns are unaccented. Even "will" is unstressed; it receives no stress in the sisters' interpretation of the rhythm. The reason is obvious: the natural accent on the dominant word "never" muffles the very force inherent in the sense of certitude that the meaning of "will" involves. The natural accent on the monosyllabic "week" in the predominantly iambic rhythmical pattern ("a week/ since fa/ther di-ed") is due to the centrality of the temporal fact in the speech; the sisters feel that a period as long as "a week" has elapsed and that father as 'the reason for their living' is temporally much too remote—that his consoling presence in the present is now a reality as only an eternally irretrievable reality of the past; they also have the feeling that for "a whole week" they have been in a state of gradual liberation from servitude to life-negating bondage and that they should have realized this encouraging fact earlier. The end of the illusion is simultaneously experienced as a loss of the residue of life and the beginning of the realm of the possible. Con's full and precise statement about the lapse of time since father's death is the expression of only an inarticulate feeling natural to her innocent awareness of the realm of the possible; she is awake, her speech here is of a piece with her immediately next utterance ("'Don't you think perhaps—?'").

The loud, strange bellow had also been 'a voice shriller than all the music' every time their response to it had involved a subconscious feeling of a peremptory denial of musicality as a positive value in life. The voice inside the isolated household was "a loud, strange bellow"; the sound from the outside exciting world had been impressed upon their "minds" as a monkey's "noise". There was no music to break through the ennui of the hush hanging heavily between a familiar "loud bellow" that was "strange" and a monkey's "noise" that belonged "somewhere else". Since then they have been living in a drearily still world alienated even from once-in-the-blue-moon throb of music that evinces the unflagging vivacity of the world outside. Their longing or thirst for "bubbling notes" is characteristic of their "lives" in a deathly still world.

If the indoor hush puts them in mind of their liberation from servitude, if the silence that now fills the house is the recurrence of the voice of God saying, Let there be light, if the deathly stillness drives them to catch at the "bubbling

> notes" as the palpable manifestation of an abiding value in the living world outside, it is also the ultimately tangible manifestation of a barren void: the sisters' intense awareness of this indoor hush as a more real reality is part of their sober realization of the void of the "Now—?" What occupies the sisters' "minds" is 'the sound of the voice that is still', the thump of the stick that is nowhere. The hush is more palpable than the organ-grinder's music; the music will remain drowned in the hush. Sensitiveness to cessation of the voice or the sound as the source of all motivation is rather a full realization of the meaning of the moment, which they have experienced as a tragically static moment; the moment stands still because of the sisters' intense sensitiveness to loss of the residue of life. The cross-cancellation of implications that the full meaning of the moment involves seems to be a means of defining the nature of the void that their "now-?" is.

The emotional complex that this moment of emotional affinity involves is ambiguously illuminated by the sisters' 'strange' Mona Lisa 'smile'.

Externalization of this whole complex of the sisters' feeling is perhaps effected through registration of the changing hues of the sunlight; the shades reflect, as it were, the whole process of the deepening feeling.

In spite of this complex emotional affinity the sisters' natural tendency to be individually and thus more really existent is markedly persistent. Con, a 'regular' dreamer, is awakened to the sober objective reality of the lapse of time; Jug, who was been wide awake to reality, 'forgets to be practical and sensible'. Con 'looks different'; Jug too is no longer what she has been. But later, in their simultaneous sober realization of the tragic truth about their "now", Con's vision is romantic again and Jug's is more really "practical". Con feels as she thinks, Jug thinks of things as they have been and as they are "now". Con is poetic: Jug is prosaic. Both are sober in their own individual ways. They simultaneously orientate themselves to their tragic "now-?"—the "now" that is all rhetorical question, hollow and barren. But their ways of orientation vary as distinctively individual responses to their images of the sparrows, etc., Con is first subjective and then mystic as she 'lifts her big, cold hands as if to catch the notes', and then her hands fallen again, 'walks over to her favourite Buddha': finally she is romantically sober as she thinks of her "Now" dreamily as a poet. The sunlight of realization has "deepened"; it will soon 'shine golden' as the flicker of being. Jug's realization is soberly romantic; her vision of the entire past life is at once objective and subjective; it is mere awareness as intense awareness; it is stoically calm: it involves a deeply tragic emotional complex. The interregnum between the moment when "the sun is out" and the moment when this 'thieving sun touches Josephine gently' is darkly sunny. The sunlight playing over the articles in the drawing-room reveals a whole sad story behind them and awakens memories not as mental images but as vague facts distilled from traumatic experiences: there is no dramatization of the past that the vision is made to cover; there is no representation of the past in audio-visual terms; the past is no longer as real as the present; it is there in the present, but it is without immediacy. The sunlight thieves in to reveal the calm depths of Jug's psyche. The chirping of sparrows that 'sound young' renders Jug unable to keep from the revealing light the darkest tragic depths of their life-time experience as "strangers" to all others and to each other. The rhetorical question ("Ah, what was it crying, so weak and forlorn?") with its answer plainly stated in the sequential paragraph registers a tonal transition in the narrative statement of the tragic reality in their "lives". Jug's subjective response to the chirping of 'young sparrows as only a "queer little crying noise ... inside her" calms down to an objective awareness of the real meaning of the "weak and forlorn" cry. Her earlier vision of the sunlight as the welcome reality in the dark cold unreal world is simultaneously objective and subjective: she 'watches' it but not without imagination; she perceives the whole process of its penetration and revelation and interprets it with an "as though". But her imaginative perception of the process of revelation very soon deepens into sober awareness of the spirit of Time operating as a negative force of obliteration.

The emotional fluctuations in Jug's pensive awareness of all that has resolved into a blank rhetorical question, "But now? But now?", are contrary to the sustained intensity of Con's romantic vision of 'all that has led to' what as a "Now?" is only a question and nothing but a question. Their sober visions of the same tragic reality ("But now?" ... "Now?") are distinctly individual in their processes.

The coming out of the sun really matters at the moment when

they are in dire need of the closest link with the world of life outside. The sunlight and the fountain of notes are concomitant, but the very moment of the sun's coming out is the recurrence of the moment when God said, Let there be light, and there was light. It is the light of Light. 'It really matters'. This realization of the value of life-source is of more practical importance than the awakened consciousness of the value of "a whole week since father died". Con awakens to the reality of time; Jug feels the reality of Life; Con turns romantic again, her hands responsively lifted to catch-nay, as if to catch—the bubbling notes of the drenching melody.

(v) (a) and that was all. The rest had been looking after father and at the same time keeping out of father's way. But now? But now?

(b) What did it mean? What was it she was always wanting? What did it all lead to? Now? Now?

The tragic "Now—?" as a hollow rhetorical question is common to the sisters' "lives". Both the sisters are simultaneously aware of the bleak tomorrows that their "Now?" is. Their realization of the tragic truth is the culmination of their experience of a life that was not a reality but an illusion of a reality. The void of the "Now?" as Jug's vision comprehends it is defined not only by what denudation of the residue of life has left. Even if mother had lived, they would have been denied the thrill of 'life' or 'adventure'; diversions there were, but they were too incidental and casual, too few and far between, too formal and impersonal to let life be anything more than a humdrum existence: ("and they had moved three times and had their yearly holiday and … and there'd been changes of servants, of course.") their "lives" would have been barren of all possibilities of consummation of their individual selfhood through marital companionship, for there had been nobody for them to marry. From the very beginning their life had been blighted by insidious regimentation. The cantankerous Colonel's 'quarrel with his Anglo-Indian friends' denied them the opportunity of contact with "a single man except clergymen", and deprived them even of the knowledge of ways to "meet men": "Even if they'd met them, how could they have got to know men well enough to be more than strangers?" This envisioned eventuality, too, was foredoomed by the sisters' helpless ignorance of the ways of 'meeting men': cynical denial of the knowledge of the ways had incapacitated them for intimacy with "men". The possibility of "having adventures, being followed, and so on" was ruled out by the hard fact that "nobody had ever followed Constantia and her"; even the solitary exception was an anonymous "mysterious man" and the "note" he had put on "the jug of hot water" understandably "outside their bedroom door", had a writing so "faint to read" that "they couldn't even make out to which of them it was addressed". The illusion evoked by this last possibility of sexual or emotional fulfilment through male partnership was also disappointed. "That was all", with its conclusive finality rings out the whole phase of possibilities, all simultaneously dissipated by the concomitant tragic factors; "the rest" that was left of their life was a drab existence, a schizophrenic existence, a fractional existence. The noun phrase, "the rest", is significantly elliptical: the omission of complement perhaps corresponds to the sense of the extinction of real existence during their father's life-time. Now that even that father is dead and the very ground for the "rest" is consequentially eliminated, what remains is but an existence in the void of "But now?" Jug's "But now?" naturally echoes as Con's "Now?".

The void of the "Now?" as Con comes to experience it is defined by the negativity of a culmination of her experience. Hers has been an experience divorced from awareness of what as an innermost longing helps to define or actualize one's individual self;—it has been an experience without simultaneous consciousness of what helps to endow individual selfhood with a distinct reality intense enough to remain unaffected by an illusion as the reality: it has been an experience of an illusion as the reality itself. This vague experience of life has its culmination in what negates itself as a culmination. Negativity of culmination in its turn is defined by the negative nature of the inner voice articulate as rhetorical questions: here we have an evolution of austere rhetorical questions voiced in vacant curiosity, each question evolving from a question that is already darkened; the end of such evolution is, naturally, inconclusively vague. The nature of the inner voice also admits of ambiguity of tone; "what did it all lead to?" means, was it this 'now?' that all this had led to?—was it this 'now?' as nothing but a statically darkened question that all this privately secret search had come to?—all this search for what actualises real self? "Now?" has also the effect of a hollow echo; it sounds like a voice intoned after a pause: "what did it all lead to?" climaxes the evolution of all the rhetorical questions as hollow echoes; and then the innermost voice ("Now?") echoes from the tragic depths where Con's identity stands merged with that of her sister in simultaneous awareness of the void defined by "now?". It is the inconclusive vagueness of the culmination that is conclusively final. "Now-?" as the last question, the only question, the whole question is a new question. This moot question is central to the sisters' concept of their existence together: it is vague enough to make us aware of the uncertain nature of the state they are in. The ambiguity of the tone that the fading echoes of the inner voice admit of serves to give us an idea of the nature of the feeling: the characters are much too obscure for our emotional participation. This deepens the tragic effect. The vague dimensions of the emotional complex here merge into what seems only a void of a feeling. "Now?" is a compound question echoing in this void. The monosyllabic question is starkly austere. Con has come to the heart of her rhetorical questions; she is now prosaic; her questions seem to be only ideas at the back of her mind, bare and empty. The questions are all rhetorical but there is no rhetoric. We feel the void through the words on the page. Con's deepening realization of the void is registered in the interior monologue by means of a pattern of transitions from poetical effusion to factual statement and from empty speculation to a compound question: Con grows more and more prosaic till she comes to see the sober truth: correspondingly her inner voice grows fainter and fainter and its fading echoes sound like the hollow monosyllabic echoes of blank emptiness.

The sisters' deep-souled feelings of the void of their

"Now?" are kindred but even this intense emotional affinity is characterized by distinct individuality of experiences. Their individual interior monologues are simultaneous. They do not occur in chronological order. They do not mingle as one common interior monologue, either. Juxtaposition of the two interior monologues centred upon an idea, "Now?", reveals the concurrence of sober thought-processes with the distinct features of the sisters' individuality intact even at the climactic moment of intense emotional affinity. In Jug's interior monologue there is transition from matter-of-fact statement to an emotional question about what she cannot define; in Con's, the transition is from poetical effusion to factual statement. Jug is logically analytical. Con is fancifully poetical. Still Jug is not without poetical awareness of an undefined longing nor is Con without impersonal consciousness of the hard facts in her personal life even as a poet of passions and longings and near-mystic trance. Jug is not egocentric but she is not without a knowledge that is shared. Jug perceives the thieving sun-light as the last and only palpable link with the world outside or as the unfailing source of life; Con reads meanings into the Buddha smile and her innermost secret self is lost in a world beyond what she poetically feels is a "tunnel". Jug thinks of impossibilities emergent from impossibilities; Con muses over possibilities blighted by impossibilities. Jug is prosaic and then also poetical; Con is poetical and then also prosaic.

The juxtaposition of the interior monologues also forms part of a rhythmical pattern designed to beat into our hearts a feeling of an intensified psychic process tending towards wholeness through reciprocity: the sisters' feelings at this moment of awakening are worked up to the intensity of an unconsciously desperate longing for reciprocal orientation of their secret selves in the interest of whole togetherness.

There is a pattern that emerges from emotional transitions in their simultaneous experience of an essentially kindred feeling; it is imperceptibly criss-crossed by a contrasted design for their combined appearance in reverse order. Reversal of this order is rhythmically alternate.

This is significant: it helps to create an impression of psychic intercrossings between the sisters' secret selves. This contrasted design is perceptible at all the three swiftly successive points of transition in the process. Con appears first, Jug follows, at all these points of the climactic part of the narrative reflecting the whole process of reciprocal orientation as only a tragic process of transitions from awakening to be-ing to amnesia. The contrasted order of the characters' appearance together at these dramatic turning-point of the process is perhaps meant to register the tragic paradox of a common realization that deepens only to remain vague.

(vi) 'Don't you think perhaps'—she began. But Josephine interrupted her. 'I was Wondering if now—' she murmured. They stopped; they waited for each other.

This climactic moment when for the first and last time the sisters feel the thrill of be-ing in nearest approximation to their real selves is also the moment when they stand poised for reciprocity that alone can effect whole togetherness. Their feelings of the sunny moment are intensely kindred: their elliptical utterances are impassioned enough to give us the feel of the undefined yet intense thrill they experience individually yet simultaneously; ellipsis is due to the indefinability and intensity of the thrill. The experience embodied derives its intensity from various contextual elements: tragic failure to articulate the individually secret longing; simultaneity of the thought-processes at the sunny moment; brevity of the moment of nearness to the core of existence actualized through individual experience of freedom; obscurity of a feeling experienced for the first time in life; tension of poise for reciprocity as the only means to the only end now. The effect of contrast is occasioned by the ironically parallel design rendering the last major dramatic crisis. The characters come on to the page in the same order: Con speaks first about the loss of her memory; Jug speaks next, her voice only an echo: but what this usual order is made to register this last time is an ironically tragic culmination of the whole psychic process: loss of memory blots out whatever they have at the back of their "minds": their words, "perhaps" and "now", are significantly terminal in their elliptical utterances: the residue of the inarticulate is rendered all the more vague by the denotation of the words. What is already inarticulate or undefined is conclusively obscured by their sudden loss of the memory of it: intensity of this moment of choice from the realm of "the future", of indefinably palpable reality of existence in freedom is effectively dramatized: the sisters' feeling of this nearness is made to seem intensely individual; they cannot but 'wait for each other' when each has "stopped" short; it is the distinct individuality of feeling in her partner that makes each so eager to share it. The narrator's explanation ("But Josephine interrupted her", "They stopped") is necessitated by the sense of distinctness inherent in the affinity of experience: in each speech here the dash is already there to mark a break and suggest abrupt interruption or sudden loss of words; it obviates the need of the narrator's explanatory statement. But the dash is not enough. Experience of their existence actualized for the first and last time is, naturally, intensely individual. This pronounced feature of the climactic moment has to be brought out in the narrator's statements registering transitions on a deeper psychic level in the simultaneous experience of the thrill ("But Josephine interrupted her", "They stopped"). We do not have the 'But' in the speech ('But I was wondering if now—'); we have it in the narrator's registration of the character's experience intensified as a distinctly individual feeling. "They stopped", captures a moment tingling with the tension of a poise for reciprocity that alone can help to shake off the sterile curse of their togetherness devold as it is of intense individuality. The reciprocal pronoun, "each other", registers the inevitable climax of a process of reciprocal orientation on the still deeper level of individual entity itself: unconsciously they have started reaching out towards "each other; the way "each" bursts out into a dreamy ejaculation reveals her unconscious awareness of the individual entity of the "other" as a complement of her own entity in a togetherness condemned to a tragic state of indistinguishability of individuality. Con wishes to say something "frightfully important" about "the future" of their "lives" together; she seeks her partner's consent or acquiescence when she 'begins': "'Don't you think perhaps-?'": the descending intonation muffled by what seems to be an overwhelming experience of the thrill of real existence in freedom is eloquent enough to convey a sense of wistful expectancy. Jug interrupts her with an irrepressible 'murmur' "'I was wondering if now—'": Jug means: 'I was asking myself if now': her sentence also sounds like a question. It is natural that each elliptical utterance here has the ring of a question: the ring is due to the sisters' sense of eagerness or 'wonder' born of their agony of failure to define their experience of the thrill at the sunny moment when Con has just spoken of "Saturday" and Jug has referred to 'the coming out of the sun'—at a moment when they have awakened from a long nightmarish "sleep": both the verbal order and the intonation here are those of an eager question; but there is no question mark even after the dash; the elliptical sentence then sounds like the statement of some proposal for "the future" of their "lives". Jug only seems to be withdrawn into the privacy of an individual feeling. What she 'murmurs' about is only her life with her sister's in the "now" which as the temporal reality is at once a barren void and a fruitful womb. Con, the regular sleepwalker, is fully awakened; she is consciously aware of the need of her partner's acquiescence or approval; the tone of the voice is ardently eager. Jug, who has 'forgotten to be practical and sensible', is naturally dreamy here: she is unconsciously aware of some question that is common to both herself and her partner in the "now"; the 'murmur' she breathes is drowsy. This interchange of individual characteristics is natural to the process of psychic intercrossing.

The sunny moment when the lively utterances are voiced seems to be appropriately timeless. Con is going to say something about "the future"; what she says is in that present tense also points to the future; but the vague implication of the terminal word "perhaps", blurs these features of the tense. Jug has been asking herself some questions since her welcome of "the sun" or since she "murmured", or she has been "wondering" for "a whole

> week since father died"; all her inner questioning has been a process spanning a period that ends in the "now" as the future of a past ("'I was wondering if now'"): this "now" with its full meaning as both a barren void and a pregnant womb makes the vaguely elliptical utterance all the more ambiguous. The sequence of tense evolves through the two utterances to register on its deeper level a progression from the present to the future and then from the past to the present; the two concurrent processes in reverse transfix the image of the moment and infuse it with a spirit of dynamism that characterizes tension in poise for reciprocity: "The sisters stopped; they waited for each other". The meaning is: 'the sisters stopped short, waiting for each other'. There is no chronological sequence; the moment is a suspended moment; the wordless silence is eloquent: there is an unvoiced question in each 'mind'. The sisters are wonderingly curious. The timeless moment is quietly tense. It is the natal moment of 'be-ing' as a means to an end. The end is whole togetherness.

It is this subdued tone of a question that we find amplified in the very next passage which is only a quick succession of questions—a succession that is, again, only an illusion of succession. It is also the illusion of consummation of reciprocity. The contrapuntally designed pattern of questions in the narrative terminates here. The point of termination captures the intensified emotional complex that the penultimate climactic moment involves: the intensified psychic process is only a giddy whirligig of "minds" in the void of "Now—?"; the eddying concurrence of intense feelings of a perpetual need in the "Now" is tragically interminable. The most important questions in their lives "now" linger as questions at once intense and hollow.

Miss Mansfield's subsequent attempt at intensification of the 'dramatic effect' in *Life of Ma Parker* was a surprising failure: again tears were not pearls but only tears. This lapse only raises eyebrows when two facts are indisputable: many of Miss Mansfield's previous achievements had been discreetly restrained masterpieces; there was a model too to borrow from, a short-story by Chekhov: *Lament*.[29] One wonders if Miss Mansfield was still in the phase of success by a fluke. We can see what slackens the intensity of the 'dramatic effect' in the short-story.

The breathless rhetorical questions and their conclusively disconsolate answer come together to define the situation Ma Parker is meant to seem to be in, for 'her plight is not only isolation, but utter inability to relieve her pain by any means'.[30] What constitutes the essential tragic element of the character is her hopeless longing for a good "cry" in absolute loneliness: the longing is intensified by a loss which seems to have conclusively defined the meaning of the whole of her "life", a life in which she has been suffering unmerited 'disasters'. What she laments over is not the absence of a sympathizer in her world but the utter impossibility of a place in it "where she could hide and keep herself to herself and ... have her cry out—at last": she 'stands', transfixed, "looking up and down" in vain: 'there is nowhere'. The very place where she stands transfixed seems to have dwindled into a "nowhere": If there is a place, it is "a stranger's house": she cannot 'hide herself' here and 'keep herself to herself'; she stands conclusively confronted with what looms large on her mental horizon now as the grim reality of mockingly callous providential irresponsiveness to her agonized questions ("The icy wind blew out her apron into a balloon"). All her questions, ultimate as well as immediate, are barren. Her suffering could be assuaged not by compassion but by her own comforting answers to her agonized questions: the one sympathizer in her life, the literary gentleman (in spite of his 'empathetic'[31] vocation) has been talking like Job's Comforters. What really renders her situation tragic is the resolution of all her unanswerable questions into one question with a negatively conclusive or conclusively negative answer ("There was nowhere").

Whether 'Miss Mansfield goes Chekhov one better'[32] is a question that is out of the question. The situation is different from and not 'worse than the one Chekhov portrayed'[33] in *Lament*. The meaning emergent from the verbal complex conjuring up Iona's situation is essentially different from the one that the specific compositional build-up of Ma Parker's life-story is meant to yield. The meaning of Iona's story is defined by the irony inherent in a pitiful fulfilment of his longing for sympathy: the fulfilment amounts only to tragically static interiorization of his sorrowful consciousness in absolute isolation of hopeless loneliness: the irony is stressed by the reiterative sense of affinity between "Iona and his little horse". The meaning of Ma Parker's life-story is not tinged with irony: there is no ironical fulfilment of her longing for a place "where she could keep herself to herself and ... have her cry out". To say that 'the situation is worse than the one Chekhov portrayed' is to say that the sight of a cow dotingly licking its calf of stuffed straw is the less pitiful than that of a cow that cannot account for the absolute absence of its fondling. The situations are essentially different and equally pitiful. But it is Chekhov who goes Miss Mansfield one better. His rendering of Iona's situation in intent concentration is more firmly controlled. Like Miss Mansfield's rendering of Ma Parker's situation, even the master story-teller's rendering at times lapses into flatly prosaic exposition of the character's 'psychology': Chekhov seems to have forgotten that the details he has previously noted have all been telling enough. However, it remains for the most part of it an 'objective and neutral presentation'.[34] Chekhov's control is centralized; Miss Mansfield has not yet achieved her guru's spontaneous art of concentration. Intensity of concentration in Miss Mansfield's short-story at times seems waning because of: (a) occasional shifts of point of view; (b) needless precis of flashbacks; (c) irrelevance of details within the restricted scope; and (d) moments of relief in the character's agonized life.

(a) *Occasional shifts of Point of View*: Miss Mansfield fails to resist the temptation to resort to use of the other character's point of view. The intensity of 'dramatic effect's is considerably weakened when we are made to see how Ma Parker "looked": "'Poor old bird! She did look dashed'". The sympathizer's appropriation of the reader's response ("Poor old bird!") tends to suspend the latter's liberty of emotional participation. With the emphatic auxiliary ("did") Miss Mansfield goes farther and fares worse. A similar shift of viewpoint is perceptible again when Ma Parker appears to the gentleman to be unsure and unconvinced ("she didn't look so sure", "she didn't look so convinced"): here, too, repetition of the word "looked" only betrays the story-teller's languid, indiscreet, absolute carelessness as to the limitations of the focus of narration she has chosen to handle: she switches over to an extraneous point of view in her eagerness to reveal the pathetic aspects of the situation. The cannon of 'concealment' is grossly violated when this sympathizer is made to speak "aloud, helping himself to the marmalade". If "aloud" serves to expose the sympathizer's emotional insincerity, it also makes the scene seem theatrical. Of course later the element of pathos is intensified by the expressly implicit sense of absolute absence of sympathy: "under his apparent carelessness" the sympathizer has been only "vigilant as a woman" and not compassionate and commiserative as a woman; the mood in which he walks off ("very well pleased with himself", "convinced, in fact") finally clinches this impression of his vacant, insouciant callousness. But the element of pathos is deepened not without disrupting the consistency of the narrative viewpoint. The gentleman's moods could have been reflected in a direct speech with a suggestive concomitant gesture. Consistency of the point of view in Chekhov's *Lament* is never sacrificed for the sake of revelation of the pathetic element from the other characters' individual angles of vision. Iona's sorrowful consciousness remains privately and obscurely interiorized. What induces consistency is concentration on this obscure privateness of Iona's personal tragedy: the point of view remains strictly restricted to the protagonist's restlessly sleepless consciousness.

(b) *Needless precis of flashbacks:* Intensity of concentration in Miss Mansfield's short-story wanes not because the structural composition encompasses flashbacks but because it contains unnecessary recaptitulation of these flashbacks.[35] The emotional experience embodied in Chekhov's short-story has been conceived as a culmination of feelings; the experience even in its initial stage is intense enough: what transmits this intensity in its immediacy is the use of the present tense throughout the narrative.

(c) *Irrelevance of details within the restricted scope:* Of course the narrator's suppression of details in his description of "the state of that kitchen" is quite in keeping with the nature of the genre chosen ("It would take a whole book to describe the state of the kitchen"). But we cannot see how the sudden reference to the gentleman's "system" relates to the grim, despairing pathos that affects the central character whose story the short-story is meant to be. Again, this central character herself has some fantastic visions which seem to be out of keeping with the nature of the mood by which she is meant to be governed.[36]

(d) *Moments of relief in the character's agonized life*: The hopeless

> fixed gloom that is intended to seem to have settled on the character is found dispelled on two occasions,[37] and the preconceived effect of unrelieved gloom is disturbed.
>
> There is no such moment of relief in the 'atmosphere' which Chekhov's short-story evokes: even when Iona twists his mouth into a smile, and with an effort says hoarsely: "'My son, barin, died this week'", or when he "grins" ("'He, he, ... what gay young gentlemen!'"), his 'smile' or 'grin' or 'laugh' seems to reflect only obscure depths of his agonized consciousness: the moment is only seemingly sunny: what is illumined is only a darkly obscure emotional complex. Iona is conscious of the cruel irony he cannot bring himself to endure; at the same time he is aware of the contrast between the gaiety of the young gentlemen and his own misery: perhaps Iona is only dramatizing himself against the circumstance: his "smile' is simulated, self-pitying, cynical.

However, both the story-tellers exercise originality in rendering the static situations obliquely.

What Miss Mansfield depicts is a situation in a static void. This void is defined by what in the present is the one conclusively negative or negatively conclusive compound answer to all her immediate and ultimate questions ("There was nowhere"). The questions have been timelessly rhetorical in the world of the human soul; the one answer in Ma Parker's life is inclusive of the mocking echo which is all that her life now can evoke ("nothing"). She is neither in the past nor in the present as she asks, "'whose boy are you?'". At the moment she is also meant to seem mindlessly vacillating between what she will continue to tend or what will continue to smoulder like her own agonizing questions and what promises no outdoor diversion or affords no view of the vast world outside where she may find the seclusion she is now looking for ("straightening up from the stove and going over to the smudgy window").[38] The void is spatial ("there was nowhere") and temporal (as she is neither in the present nor in the past). It is absolutely sterile ("she'd got nothing"). This void is not only without; it is also within: it is revealed when her interiorized sorrowful consciousness is vacant, empty, blank.

The situation in Chekhov's short-story is made to seem ironically static. The impression is created in two ways: through sustained identification of the central character with his dumb companion;

and through intermittent recurrence of the snow image. The sustained identification of the privately articulate character with the dumb animal helps to convey the irony inherent in equivalency of articulation to dumbness; the intermittent recurrence of the snow image serves to accentuate the extended implication of sympathetic reciprocity as an illusion frozen in obscurely remote isolation from the world. Sympathetic reciprocity is not an impossibility in a world where communication is invariably consummate,[39] 'destination' is always reached,[40] and no articulation is a mere "snuffle". Miss Mansfield's images of "icy wind" and "rain" do not seem to have altered their conventional nature; Chekhov's snow image is an integral part of the emotional design of his short-story; the conventional image has become a poetic image.

The 'dramatic effect' achieved in the next short-story, *Ideal Family*, is the result of intense concentration on the irony characterizing a psychological process which evolves as sustained mutual intensification of conflicting emotions.

The picture showing old Mr. Neave sunk into the "broad lap of his chair" reveals the emotional complex that his intense awareness of an irony involves: the irony lies in the contrariety of the 'reputation' of his family as "an ideal family" and the 'vulgar actuality'[41] of his own position as a nonentity; his identity is relegated to the limbo of a life-in-death; it is isolated from the "young life' around it, the life that does not seem to be 'life, death included'. The people who extol the family as an "ideal" one are crassly ignorant of the 'vulgar' reality: the man who has been the prop of his "family", the man whose tenaciously persevering industriousness has been the source of all "young life" in the "family" is now only "a little withered ancient man", a ghost of his own self, a nobody, a cypher, ungratefully and forlornly "forgotten", already sunk into "the broad lap" of what is now only a coffin on this side of the grave. This 'vulgar actuality is known to him alone: his recognition of the ironical situation that this 'vulgar actuality' has created is privately tragic.

The technique of the short-story helps to discover the emotional complex that is involved in the character's intensely sensitized, privately tragic awareness of the secret irony. The emotional complex seems to have readily lent itself to aesthetic rendering in the form of a short-story. Intensity of the character's experience on "that evening for the first time in his life" calls for intense concentration. The character's susceptibility to impressions of Life either as a ceaseless flux or as an untamably impetuous overflow of youthful energy ("young life") seems to be due only to his morbid obsession: he is obsessed with an image of himself as "a little withered ancient man" already "climbing up endless flights of stairs" or as a 'little old spider ... slipping past the dining room', this obsession intensifies his susceptibility, and his susceptibility evokes the obsession. The psychological process evolving through constant mutual intensification of the two contrary emotions is, naturally, concentrated and complex. Intent concentration alone could facilitate transmission of the intensity characterizing the character's experience. Since the experience is privately tragic, the character's consciousness is reflected in the short-story as interiorized consciousness. Interiorization of the character's consciousness is due to the conception of the character as an old man who because of his nearness to his end is all thought, all feeling, all susceptibility: he even speaks little. The one narrative statement in the concluding passage of the short-story ("old Mr. Neave, forgotten, sank into the broad lap of his chair, and, dozing, heard them as though he dreamed") captures his characteristic posture and reveals the 'dissolution' that has already set in. It is this essential element of the character that seems to have determined the choice of the specific point of view, the third-person point of view. Old Mr. Neave is almost at death's door: he has to seem dissolving, disintegrating. The third-person point of view helps to distance the character, to place him where he belongs, on further and further removes from us. This preconceived desired effect of his characterization seems to have been heightened also by the metaphorical implication of the appropriate temporal setting; "evening".

Our consideration of Miss Mansfield's achievement of the 'dramatic effect' as the most essential technical quality may remain partial if it does not include evaluation of a later short-story *Marriage a la Mode*. Although composed much later than her serene pictures of truth as Beauty (*Garden Party*, *At the Bay*, etc.), it illustrates the extent to which she had come to master the art of intensifying the quality of 'dramatic effect'. Intensification of this technical quality is effected through juxtaposition of the individual worlds of two polarized characters: the 'effect' is naturalized by the flux of events in chronological succession. All revolves round a moment at once decisive and uncertain; the situation dramatized seems to be defined by its intrinsic paradox of dichotomized conjugality involving possibility of reciprocal inclination. Let us take two sentences which seem to stand out as statements central to the narrative design:

> They walked together silently. William felt there was nothing to say now.

The last word of the passage, "now", seems to define rather the very moment that is central to the drama: the nature of the moment which the short-story as a whole is meant to explore is at once decisive and uncertain. What has made William feel "there is nothing to say now" is a deep emotional shock he has failed to absorb: he has been intensely shocked to notice the unabated persistence of Isabel's inconsiderate blithe insouciance and her hopelessly pretentious insincerity; the impression is created by her contradictory utterances: "what a weight!" "I want to, really". She has felt the suitcase is overweight; but she has been too insouciant to pause to think or ask why it is overweight. She has felt the "'weight'" without loss of composure, without embarrassment, without a wince: instead she has given "a little awkward laugh". Her word, "really", has evinced only arrant insincerity. All that she has done and said just now has been transparently insincere. She is still the same woman that she has been since she visited "Moira's party". William is convinced of the unmistakability of the impression: she is irretrievably astray, incorrigibly insouciant, hopelessly insincere. His recognition of hopelessness has shocked him into speechless disillusion.

His impression is strengthened by her immediately subsequent utterances that he dumbly hears. It is clinched by her "little hurried kiss" just before the taxi whisks him away. Thus the moment is decisive.

But this same moment seems uncertain too. His suitcase is of course overweight; but he does not seem to be leaving bag and baggage: he cannot forsake his children; she would not _ perhaps never-cease to be his "darling, precious Isabel". The insufferable persistence of the "dull gnawing" will survive. Even his possessive passion for Isabel seems to have been much too sober and generous, tender and exquisite, idealistic and poetic, to let him resign himself to a life without that "exquisite freshness of Isabel", without his "little kiddies".

But even this meaning of the moment is cancelled out by the contrary meaning simultaneously implicit in the context. The full meaning that the moment is intended to embody is implicit in the simultaneous cross-cancellation of possibility and impossibility of his return to the "rosebush" as "that little boy" that he "still" is. This moment of parting in the full emotional context is made to seem at once decisive and inconclusive. Isabel fails later to resist the temptation to accompany her friends "going for a bathe"; severe compunction harrows her grimly even while she decides to go with them, even while she persuades herself to postpone writing to William. The impression is conveyed by the staccato rhythm of her rapid and broken private utterance: "I will go with them, and write to William later. Some other time. Later. Not now. But I shall certainly write". Her resolve is conveyed naturally by sentences that are fully articulate ("'I will go with them, and write to William later.... But I shall certainly write'"); the metrical pattern is predominantly iambic. Her qualms are registered by the elliptical sentences ("Some other time. Later. Not now."); the rhythm here is trochaic and spondaic, transitions in the rhythm communicate the implicit sense of vacillation.

The nature of the moment, which is at once crucial and inconclusive, helps to define the nature of the crisis which the short-story seeks to reflect: the married life of the husband and his wife is in the touch-and-go phase. It is only a picture of this phase that is focused upon. This touch-and-go phase is strenuous enough to call for intent concentration. The sense of this tenseness lies in the simultaneous cross-cancellation of possibility and impossibility. It is this tenseness that determines the choice of the specific way of rendering the crisis. The specific way is intense concentration. The cross-cancellation of possibility and impossibility of their reunion yields the poetic meaning that the narrative piece is meant to embody. The form that the meaning assumes is characterized by a criss-cross design in which the structural form is set off against the textural build-up; the structural form helps to reflect the divergence which the individual lives of the married couple have been flowing in since "Moira's party"; the textural build-up serves to register the sense of the characters' mutual inclination towards reunion.

The sense of divergence is conveyed through juxtaposition of divergently individual points of view of the two characters involved. This divergence of points of view is sharpened by the opposition between the characters' individual temperaments that have been clashing since "Moira's party". William's life seems to have been lonely: it has been a life of either consciousness interiorized or of emotions externalized. He has been quickly susceptible to ironies in his life now distressingly stressed by his wife's demeanour and utterances. Isabel has been too insouciant to be aware of the ironies implicit in her own utterances. William has remained transfixed, isolated, lonely-a husband reduced to a nonentity, a small fry, a 'has-been': he stands alone, a stranger in his own house. Isabel has been travelling on the social merry-go-round, "laughing in her own way". The party "rescued" her from William and made her "new", leaving the partner alone in his own dream world of values abidingly new. He is left alone with his passion which is unrequited and worried yet pitying and generous, possessive and sensuous yet poetic and idealistic, intense and overmastering yet tender and exquisite. He is all alone with his hypersensitivity to all incongruity and ugliness and corruption; his concept of married life as an Eden of Innocence has faded. He has been dreaming of an Eden in which he will again be "that little boy", etc.—an Eden in which "new" means fresh and innocent and not fashionable and modish, an Eden in which "sleep' is natural as that of his "poor little kiddies with whom he is unconsciously identified and not a "discovery" as it is in the world presided over by the Moira-spirit.

The sense of the characters' inclination towards each other is conveyed, texturally, through the tonal modulation of their individual introspective expressions: the tone of the husband's interior monologues is eager and conciliatory, dreamy and wistful, enamoured and caressing; his feelings are expressed demurely, nostalgically, yearningly: the syntactical rhythm they are attuned to is settled throughout; the tonal pitch of the wife's introspective expressions is heightened and sharp; her innermost questions are at once rhetorical and elliptical; her unvoiced utterances are rapid and broken and half-articulate; the tone of her interior monologue is thus faltering, regretful, anguished. All this evinces her own inclination.

A major portion of Miss Mansfield's literary output during this phase demonstrated her creative capacity; that is, what these short-stories reveal is her capacity for aesthetic rendering of the tragic beauty intrinsic in the manifestation of the 'life of life' as intense actualization of be-ing just before physical or psychic death. The grim reality must have been discovered or perceived as a tragic beauty, as a richly poetic intense lyrical truth, as an objective reality, which is not without its serene beauty—— be-ing in spite of all non-being that keeps defining it.

Miss Mansfield's capacity for aesthetic rendering, for correspondingly non-moral, imaginative dramatization, of a profoundly lyrical a-moral truth naturally developed as her faculty for realizing the a-moral nature of the objective reality as an awe-inspiring serene Truth, Eternal Innocence. The realization of all consciousness or all Experience as a psychic evolution in an eternally initial or nascent state had dawned earlier during the composition of her first song of Innocence, *Prelude*. What sobered her vision of the poetic beauty of incomplete meaning was her assiduous exercise in self-abeyance and her attainment of the capacity for adequate registration of the flicker of be-ing. It was, perhaps, this tragic beauty of the futile flicker of be-ing that was revealed during the subsequent phase. It was now manifest as the serene a-moral beauty of 'Life's diversity. death induded (*Garden Party*), of "all" Life as a "still" spatial—temporal phenomenon (*At the Bay*) of Innocence of Truth as a light that is eternally nascent, inviolably ultimate, and only poetically conceivable (*Doll's House*) of all consciousness as Eternal Innocence (*The Fly*). The two cognate attributes of her creative process, capacity for 'suspension of self-intrusiveness'[42] and ability to manage an aesthetic rendering of the echoes of the Book of Job, facilitated her achievement of a potent technique: her technique was now facile enough to make the 'subjective selection of materials reflect an objective standard of values'. The creative process thus seemed to involve the evolution of an aesthetic urge oriented to spiritual self-purification. The artist was tensely poised for a plunge into a sea of ecstasy at once anguished and bedazzled, awed and aesthetic.

NOTES AND REFERENCES

1. William Walsh, *A Manifold Voice*, p. 162.
2. *Ibid*., pp. 171-72.
3. Martin Stelinmann and Gerald Willen, *Literature for Writing* (typed Copy).
4. *Journal*, p. 81.
5. Quoted by Saralyn Daly, *Katherine Mansfield*, p. 112.
6. Saralyn Daly, *op. cit.*, p. 83.
7. Cf. '... The moral implication is negligible: the centre of interest is the wife's feeling, first of ecstatic happiness, and then at the moment of revelation. We are given neither comment nor suggestion of any moral issue of good and evil, and within the setting this is quite right. The story is limited to this sudden change of feeling, and the moral and social remifications are outside of the terms of reference'. T.S. Eliot, *After Strange Gods*. pp. 35-36.
   Comments—The passages analysed in course of the critical evaluation of the short-story support Beachcroft's criticism of Eliot's remarks: 'The moral meaning of *Bliss*, the parable, 'says Beachcroft, is completely at one with the

story itself.... The images bring out all the implications.... When [Miss Mansfield] is at her best her own agitated quest is absorbed into her art'—T.O. Beachcroft, *The Modest Art*.

8. Cf. 'To a far greater extent than Joyce, Miss Mansfield draws skilfully on the device of characterizing minor action.... The characters (in *Dubliners*) chiefly sit or walk and talk, so that any particularity of action stands out with high significance: Lenchan's skipping gait as he keeps alongside Corley's burly frame in *Two Gallants*; Mr. Alleyne's habit of shooting his fragile hairless head up over that pile of papers on his desk in *Counterparts*.... Although Miss Mansfield's characters are more constantly in motion that Joyce's—they never move about aimlessly.... Harry Young in Bliss rattles and slams his ways about the house in bouncing male exuberance.... Even the constant day-dreams in which Miss Mansfield's characters indulge are made dynamic by such characterizing details'. Sylvia Derkman, *Katherine Mansfield: A Critical Study*, pp. 173-74.

Comments—The comparative view of the two authors' individual capacity for exploitation of 'the device of characterizing minor action' betrays a complacent attitude of reliance upon first impressions unrevised by closer textual study of the verbal complex. Joyce too seems to have been 'skilful' to the same extent. The comparative view seems also to be a myopic vision of 'particularity of action' which 'stands out with high significance': Joyce's 'characters chiefly sit or walk and talk' and 'Miss Mansfield's ... are constantly in motion. A critical vision imaginatively discovering significant minor action cannot possibly allow itself to be prejudiced by such considerations; again, the choice of examples illustrating the author's individual use of the device of characterizing minor action is unmistakably indicative of the critic's unaccountable indifference to consideration of the details as contributory compositional elements; details are directly or obliquely oriented to the totality of the structure peculiar to each individual short-story: particularly Harry Young's action reveals his character, not the character that he is as a 'figure in the carpet'. (The present study of Bertha's gestures is, however, an attempt to illustrate Miss Berkman's intelligent and illuminating conclusion: 'Even the constant daydreams ... are made dynamic by ... characterizing details'.) The emphasis placed in *Two Gallants* on Lenehen's minor action ('Looking') helps to elicit the effect of a character nonchalantly attentive to the moral horrors all around him: thus we are made to feel that his capital sin is sloth, which is symptomatic of the paralysis that has deadened the Dubliners' sensibility. In *counterparts* even an apparently trivial element (the way the narrator refers to the central character) is fraught with 'high significance': Farrington is referred to simply as "the man": the cumulative effect is that of a dull routine of Farrington's existence: of the reduction of his distinctively recognizable individuality to an anonymous nonentity: Farrington as a character seems to have been meant to give the impression of a replaceable cog in a mechanical, soulless operation. When in the office scenes we learn Farrington's name through its use by Mr. Alleyne, we are not aware of the irony of his recognition as a distinctive individual by the very force that is responsible for his de-humanization.

'Characterizing details' in both the authors function as symbolical motifs within the living form of their masterpieces and invariably *remain* unobtrusive; it is these carefully developed motifs which give their short-stories unity of effect.

9. The short-story has been included also in 'an anthology of stories that presents many variations on the theme of Leshbian love./*Lesbian Love in Literature* ed. Stella Fox.
10. Cf. Miss Berkman's remarks on Bates's criticism of Miss Mansfield's style: 'The points Mr. Bates neglects are that the appropriateness of... tone to the subject-matter of a story must be considered and that the adoption of the same tone by the author in the expository or inter connective material as in the interior monologue may not actually be a flaw... Joyce in his passages of interior monologue displays his usual acute sensitivity of ear in adapting the idiom he employs to the nature of his subject. To Eveline, uncertain, driven to confront a critical issue, he gives a very simple mode of expression, as befits a young sophisticated girl;... to the romantic lad in *Araby*, the most poetic imagery in the book. Then, by a deft transition he resumes his ground outside the character and the prose becomes again wholly impersonal... Miss Mansfield ... sustains throughout a story one persisting note.... Instead of transmitting thought or feeling through a formalised literary medium, she casts the whole narrative into the informal tone she employs for the expression of interior consciousness',—Sylvia Berkman, *op. cit.*, pp. 178-79.

   Comments—Perhaps what is truer in the case of *Bliss* is this: the 'one persisting note' is due to the intensity intrinsic in the climactic nature of the protagonist's experience at the moment of a crisis involving a moral conflict between values of Nature and Culture: it is, perhaps this intensity of the experience which accounts for this 'one persisting note'; the very story element vibrates with a sense of drama that is climactic from the start; the increasing tempo of prose rhythm precludes perceptibility of the rapid connections made between interior and exterior view: the passage analysed previously shows how the rapid connections are imperceptible. What is desirable is subordination to the total tonal effect. Thus in *Eveline,* Joyce not only gives to his protagonist 'a very simple mode of expression, as befits a young sophisticated girl' but also emphasizes the basic tension of the story in carefully chosen diction: Eveline's shallow life is reflected in her shallow feelings: stasis of her emotions is due to the paralysis that benumbs the Dubliners: she is incapable of making love: she can think of herself and her situation only by means of a series of tawdry cliches: her association with Frank is over-dramatized; it is defined as an 'affair'; Frank is simply a 'lover'; her own state is defined in pulp-literature terms ("unspeakably" weary); her reassertion of her choice to leave betrays a falsity ("As she mused, the pitiful vision of her mother's life laid its spell on the very quick of her being"); moreover, the first section of the short-story is characterized by 'a general flatness both of vacabulary and of sentence structure' ("And yet during all those years she had never found out the name of the priest whose yellowing photograph hung on the wall above the broken harmonium beside the coloured print of the promises made to blessed Margaret and Mary Alcoque"); the diction of this static early part of the short-story is sharply contrasted against the almost frenzied conclusion of the last struggle; the protagonist's words too are eloquent enough to reveal the very meaning of her story—her subconscious or unconscious awareness of the paralysis that has crept upon Dublin: "Few people passed" seems to mean: 'few people pass out of the Dublin paralysis; no one in this city is going anywhere; everybody here is simply 'circulating' (like Gabriel in *The Dead*). Perhaps she would never see again those familiar objects from which she had never dreamed of being divided'; her imagination has never taken her beyond her native city; she seems to be only unconsciously aware of the unreality of her projected flight with Frank. The diction lends a subliminal reinforcement to the theme of the short-story. Similarly in *Araby*, it is not simply that 'the most poetic imagery' is given to 'the romantic lad': there is replacement of the experience itself by a specific verbal arrangement which is unalterable; "the high cold empty gloomy rooms" exemplifies omission of punctuation which is calculated and 'a combination and order of adjectives which help to describe a total impression': the word "high" suggests that the boy looking up at the house is small; the boy perceives the "cold" and associates it with the "rooms" themselves: the order registers the boy's further realization that the "rooms" are "cold" because they are "empty": the final emotive adjective, "gloomy", describes their total impression. But the words in his interior monologue are at times Joyce's words: ("I could interpret these signs"; "gazing up into the darkness I saw myself as a creature driven and derided by vanity".)

11. Eileen Baldeshwiler concisely yet comprehensively explains the creative process involved in Miss Mansfield's handling of detail: "profound experience will leave common things intensified and illumined, but with a tragic, secret knowledge always presented by indirection"—"Katherine Mansfield's Theory of Fiction" *Studies in Short Fiction*, Vol. VI, Summer 1970, p. 432.
12. For example (i) "'Now how am I going to prove that I do?"; (ii) "'Will you be warm enough?" "Sure?"; (iii) "I am" (as an answer to "you're very absurd, sometimes'") "you don't mind being left??"; (iv) "Rot!" etc—*Collected Stories of Katherine Mansfield*, (i) p. 131, (ii) p. 134, (iii) p. 136, (iv) p. 143.
13. For example (i) "They are the first to leave the dining-room. She rises, gathering her shawl. He takes a chair and sits on the balcony (ii) He hears her stirring", etc. *Ibid.*, (i) p. 141, (ii) p. 143.
14. Cf. "In *Miss Brill* I choose not only the length of every sentence, but even the sound of every sentence. I choose the rise and fall of every paragraph to fit her ... it seems to me there mustn't be one single word out of place, or one word that could be taken out"—*Letters*, pp. 360-61.

    Cf. 'The focus placed on Miss Brill is even more concentrated than Joyce's focus on Maria (in *Clay*), for Miss Brill, a solitary figure throughout the story, is revealed wholly by means of the interior monologue in association with external scene'.—Sylvia Berkman, *op. cit.*, p. 162.

    Comments—The way the short-story is made to end shows Miss Mansfield has not yet mastered the art of revealing a character 'by means of the interior monologue in association with external scene': the impression of Miss Mansfield's immaturity in this respect is confirmed also by Miss Brill's subjective interpretation of the 'external scene': Miss Brill herself emphasizes the meaning of each trivial happening; the very instrument of implication, the running stream of feeling, here gives rise to the obvious. As a matter of fact, it is the focus placed on Maria in *Clay* that seems more concentrated: the details are more objectively registered: the missing plumcake makes us feel that Maria can go all queer in masculine company: She loses her plumcake as she would lose her virtue if any man wanted her to lose it; she loses the second verse much as she lost her plumcake; thought of a man sets her all aflutter; her song reveals her instinctive, 'scarcely conscious rejection of world's judgement of herself' (A. Glasheen) her body itself is as diminutive as her emotional life. But Joyce also fails to resist the temptation to sentimentalize the ending of his short-story: we scarcely need Donnelley's tears to indicate the ironic contrast.

15. Saralyn Daly, *op. cit.*, p. 90.
16. Sylvia Berkman, *op. cit.*
17. "The reader but not Miss Brill sees the similarity to her fur-piece . . . she creeps off home and conclusively recognizes her true kinship: "She went into the little dark room—her room like a cupboard."—Saralyn Daly, *op. cit.*, p. 90.
18. Peter Thorpe, "Teaching Miss Brill", *College English* 1961-62.
19. Cf. 'Unlike the leisurely development of *The Dead*, Miss Mansfield's presentation is sharply condensed'.—Sylvia Berkman, *op. cit.*, p. 165.
    Comments—'The leisurely development of *The Dead'* is due perhaps to elaborateness of the 'structure' and the technique meant to discover the broad theme implicit in the title: the short-story seeks to dramatize gradual extinction of Gabriel's personality: his self destroyed, his identity gone, he finally becomes one with all the living and the dead. What Joyce has chosen to explore is Gabriel's insensitivity to the inner lives of the people among whom he moves. The episodes which precede the last scene of revelation are carefully built up: we are made to realize that he lacks the warmth which would have encouraged a growing intimacy with his wife: finally he awakens to the fact that he is one of the dead living among the dead. However, the episodes, which carry progressively very serious implications take place not in isolation but within the framework of the party. This party with its gaiety, its hospitality, seems to symbolize the inner warmth with which life is enveloped; the snow, the expanded metaphor, alludes to the cold exterior with which Gabriel is gloomily shrouded. The 'dramatic effect' which distinguishes Miss Mansfield's 'presentation' is due to the climactic nature of the moment of crisis in her protagonist's life. The technique here is meant to discover the theme of agonizing estrangement implicit in the title: all the three characters are strangers to one another: the ironical identification of the protagonist with the nameless young man is central to the emotional design that the story element assumes.
    Miss Mansfield concentrates on what Joyce concludes with ('The special theme of Gabriel's relationship to his wife resides within the broad theme implicit in the title', Berkman admits.)
20. The phrase is taken from the concluding statement of a critical note on Miss Mansfield's short-story *The Daughters of the Later Colonel*: "The quick are deader than the dead"—Martin Stoinmann and Gerald Willaen, *op. cit.* (Typed Copy).
21. Saralyn Daly, *op. cit.*, p. 113.
22. The implication of the statement is perhaps not inconsistent with that of a comprehensive explanation of Miss Mansfield's fundamental concept of 'structure' (peculiar to the *genre* which 'came natural' to her): "what the problem

of structure finally comes down to for Katherine Mansfield is determining how much can be omitted without robbing the characters of their 'situation'" Eilen Baldeshwiler, *op. cit.*, p. 431.

23. Arthur Nelson, "Katherine Mansfield: Artist in Miniature" *Art of Modern Fiction* ed. West and Stallman, p. 156.
24. *Ibid.*
25. It was perhaps Miss Mansfield's critical vision of such complexity in her composition that made her write these words: "I have written a huge long story of a rather new kind, it's the outcome of the *Prelude* method—it just unfolds and opens—But I hope it's an advance of *Prelude*, In fact, I know it's that because the technique is stronger"—*Letters*, p. 359.
26. The statements substantiate Miss Mansfield's theory of fiction: that if form can be described structurally, it can also be seen as organic: "If a novel is to have a central idea we imagine that central idea as a lusty growing stem ... the author chose with infinite deliberation the very air in which that tree shall be nourished ... he is profoundly aware that its coming to perfection depends upon the strength with which the central idea supports its beautiful accumulations."—*Novels and Novelists*, p. 227.
27. Cf. 'In this story the focus centres on the two spinster sisters, Constantia and Josephine, in a series of scenes which shows them in relationship to various members of their narrow word, but in a more complicated pattern than Joyce employs in *The Dead*'—Sylvia Berkman, *op. cit.*, p. 169.

    Comments—What seems to be a comparatively less 'complicated pattern' in Joyce's short-story is just a different means of defining the tragic stasis. It is a means specified by the nature of that stasis which palls the milieu at large: the 'narrow world' of the protagonist is a dramatized representation of the milieu that the concentrated creative vision of the moralist in the artist of 'epiphany' naturally covers. Dramatization of the protagonist's relationship to the various members of his own narrow world assumes a pattern that is perhaps equally complicated; this pattern forms only a different design on the fictional canvas which is also more inclusive or comprehensive than the one chosen for the magnified portraiture of the two isotates dwindled to an iota of being: the sisters here stand in relationship not only to 'various members of their own world' but also to themselves in their togetherness and their private individual selves in inviolable isolation from each other. Characterization of Gabriel is subordinated to the broad theme implicit in the title of the short-story; portraiture of the two isotates is subordinated to the restricted implication of their piteous togetherness hopelessly doomed as it is by insidious regimentation of their individual selves, 'real selves'. The design formed by the patterns in Joyce's short-story registers the gradual attrition of the protagonist's personality in the world of "The Dead"; the design emergent from the patterns distinguishing Miss Mansfield's dramatization of the isotates' intrinsically barren relationship images forth a concept of togetherness as the residue of an iota of lonely existence. Gabriel finally becomes one with "all the living and the dead"; the "daughters" as two isotates isolated from all and even from each other dwindle to an iota of be-ing. What complicates the individual patterns formed in course of dramatization of the gradual extinction of the characters' individual personality in the void manifest as life-in-death is the density of the verbal texture occasioned by the intensity of the epiphany. Examples of a few compositional elements in the verbal complex of Joyce's short-story may be sufficient to help us to envisage the far-reaching extent to which the 'complicated pattern' of demonstration of the protagonist's relationship is intricate enough to evolve. Irony of increasing power helps to occasion a structural rhythm perceptible in alternation of elation and depression, culminating in a finale indicative of correlation between the protagonist's psychic extinction and the milieu's barren stagnation. Reversal of the weaning of the symbolically expanding contral image of the "snow" co-operates with this structural rhythm to establish the theme implicit in the title. The irony of increasing power effects the structural rhythm of rising and falling and rising again only to fall: it is discernible in the psychological dramatization of the central human element embodied as an ego-centric character: waves of anxiety overwhelm moments of self-assurance as the protagonist's experience of discomfort every time is compensated for by a minor victory. Inherence of the seed of self-destruction corresponds to intrinsicality of suggestions of death in the weave of the narrative texture which is intercrossed by a more conspicuous pattern of references to the deceased, the moribund, and the living dead. The rift in marital lute is consistent with lack of genuine appreciation of music. Even religion as a traditional value is at a dead-end; possibilities of further procreation are precluded in a family in which 'the masculine line has run out' leaving only women and a child that is female.

28. The textual analysis that follows may help us to see what Miss Mansfield really meant when she complained that the prose of fiction produced by her contemporaries was 'still an almost undiscovered medium': "We live in an age of experiment... when writers are seeking after new forms in which to express something more subtle, more complex 'nearer' the truth; when a few of them feel that perhaps after all prose is an almost undiscovered medium and that there are extraordinary, thrilling possibilities ..." *Novels and Novelists*, p. 92.
29. Saralyn Daly, *op. cit.*, p. 91/Saralyn Daly has referred to the English version entitled *Misery*/.
30. *Ibid.*
31. *Ibid.*
32. *Ibid.*
33. *Ibid.*
34. Cleanth Brooks, *Understanding Fiction*, p. 207. Chekhov's rendering of his protagonist's situation is, surprisingly, only seemingly 'objective and neutral': the critical reader of his short-story fails to see the reason why some plain narrative statements have been included in the structural framework (e.g. "But the crowds hurry by without noticing him or his trouble. Yet it is such an immense, illimitable grief. Should his heart break and the grief pour out, it would flow over the whole earth, so it seems, and yet no one sees it. It has managed to conceal itself in such an insignificant shell that no one can see it even by day and with a light", *op. cit.*, pp. 205-6): when the reader goes over the short-story for the second time he finds the preceding dramatized portions telling enough (e.g. "'you do not know how to drive. Keep to the right!' calls the officer angrily ... a coachman from a private carriage swears at him; a passer-by who has run across the road and rubbed his shoulder against the horse's

nose looks at him furiously as he sweeps the snow from his sleeve. Iona shifts about on his seat as if he were on needless, moves his elbows as if he were trying to keep his equilibrium and gapes about like someone suffocating, who does not understand why and wherefore he is there" *op. cit.*, pp. 203-04).

35. For example "If she could only cry now, cry for a long time, over everything beginning with her first lace and the cruel cook", etc._ *Collected Stories of Katherine Mansfield*, p. 308

36. For example "and Ma Parker never knew for certain whether she saw or whether she fancied she saw a great fan of white dust come out of her poor dear husband's lips ..." etc.—*Ibid.*, p. 305.

37. For example "And the cook was a cruel woman. She used to snatch away her letters from home before she'd read them, and throw them in the range because they made her dreamy.... And the beedles! ... Here Ma always gave a little laugh ...."
"'You'd find his lungs chock-a-block with white powder' ... She fancied she saw a great fan of white dust", etc.—*Ibid.*, pp. 304-05.

38. Cf. ('To a far greater extent than Joyce ... Miss Mansfield draws skilfully on the device of characterizing minor action .../Joyce's/characters chiefly sit or walk and talk, so that any particularity of action stands out withhigh significance.—Lenehen's skipping gait as he keeps alongside Corely's burly frame in *Two Gallants*; Mr. Alleyne's habit of shooting his fragile, hairless head up over the pile of papers on his desk in *Counterparts*. Although Miss Mansfield's characters are more constantly in motion that Joyce's, they never move about aimlessly ... Ma Parker, reviewing the miseries of her life, seeks to escape remembrance through the physical activity of clearing the literary gentleman's dirty flat. Even the constant daydreams kin which Miss Mansfield's characters indulge are made dynamic by such characterizing details'.—Sylvia Berkman. *op. cit.*, pp. 173-74.
Comments—Miss Berkman's remarks again exemplify only partial consideration of 'the device of characterizing details': she has seen 'the device' as a compositional element which may be significant enough even in isolation from what it must seem subordinated to. Within the restricted scope of the specific fictional *genre* any 'particular it of action' cannot but be directly or obliquely relevant or subordinate to the meaning meant to be emergent from the total verbal complex. 'The device of characterizing minor action' as utilized by Joyce and Miss Mansfield is illustrated with examples which do not seem to reveal the 'high significance' as a part of the total meaning. The examples reveal the character of the characters, not the characters themselves, woven into the fabric of the verbal complex as they stand within the aesthetic framework. Perhaps Miss Berkman is aware of the significance; only she has not explained it. 'Lenehen's skipping gait' and 'Corley's burly frame' may have been seen as significant characterizing details—the 'skipping gait' as an index of the aimlessness of Lenehen's life in the streets; the 'burly frame' as the true embodiment of a perverted code of gallantry. The head that keeps shooting up over the pile of papers" is the head of a bossy bully who is all "pile of papers" minus a human heart. Joyce's characters may have seemed to be chiefly sitting or walking and talking because of the paralysis that deadens the Dubliners. Ma Parker's 'physical activity' may have been viewed as the only means of

'escape' which she has of course been seeking. But one feels that Miss Berkman's presentation of examples does not evince critical consideration of their relevance. The place names along Lenehen's route in *Two Gallants* contribute a sense of local reality; they also emphasise his lack of direction: his circular movement around the city parallels that of the warm summer air of the opening sentence; it suggests hopeless acceptance; the gold coin itself functions as a fitting climax to the related motifs of Ireland's political, economic and spiritual degradation. In *Counterparts* "the man" steering "his great body along" is just an automation erect upon two legs bearing the semblance of a human being: he seems to be moving in the dull round of workaday existence. Ma Parker as a tragic character lost in a spatial-temporal void significantly stands transfixed between the smouldering even and the closed window, between the consuming agony of the present and dark hopelessness of the future.

39. For example "'I don't understand what you lie for, . . . you lie like a brute'" "God strike me, it's the truth".—"Lament", *Understanding Fiction*, p. 205.
40. For example "'Thank God, we have at last reached our destination', and Iona watches them disappear through the dark entrance".—*Ibid.*
41. William Walsh, *op. cit.*, p. 172.
42. *Ibid.*, p. 162.

5. Technique as Discovery
(ii) Achieved Content

Miss Mansfield's last four short-stories registered a sudden transition in her philosophy of life. Her dazed recognition of the grim reality manifest as futile intensity of 'will to live' in the face of death as a negative force was now a calm vision of the loftier Reality: it was a vision of Truth itself which by virtue of its all-inclusive, a-moral nature is awe-inspiringly beautiful. It was perhaps this serene beauty intrinsic in the eternal innocence of Truth that she conceived as 'the light that childhood throws on life'.[1] Even 'the people'[2] portrayed as characters in the short-stories of the penultimate phase were only innocent children, so to say: with all their ripened sagacious maturity they only stood dazed before manifestations of some grim incomprehensible reality. 'Childhood' was defined also by their strange despairing innocence: it threw light on life, illuminating it as the manifestation of desperate 'will to live', to be, to feel the individuality of one's entity: life was revealed only as the evolution of the irresistible urge to contend with the futility of intense actualization of one's being in the Gorgonian shadow of Death. Even the eternal Innocence of Truth was seen as an awe-inspiring beauty, the light thrown on life of childhood revealed life's ineffable beauty ("Isn't life?"—*The Garden Party*), its epic stillness ("All was still"—*At the Bay*), its eternal nascence ("'I seen the little lamp'"—*The Doll's House*), its intrinsic a-morality ("he could not remember"—*The Fly*). The light thrown on life was now diffused as fingers of light catching a landscape of Life made all foggy by Time. This tranquillization of the secret agony of perplexed despair was due perhaps to intensification of Miss Mansfield's distinctive creative process which was now governed by an ambition at once spiritual and aesthetic.[3]

The last four short-stories make us see how Miss Mansfield's longing for spiritual purification through aesthetic achievement or vice versa was fulfilled to a solemn extent.

The four short-stories exemplify simultaneous intensification and naturalization of the 'dramatic effect'. What has facilitated this achievement in the two short-stories about Consciousness and Time (*At the Bay, The Fly*) is perhaps the author's imaginative exploitation of reciprocity between the individual potentialities of the two cognate attributes of the creative concentrated vision; the one attribute is choice of the appropriate point of view; the other is choice of the expedient time scheme. The two attributes in course of their reciprocal enrichment of their individual potentialities produce a style characterized by a narrative quality intensified as a dramatic quality: the style is colourless enough to make the author's 'subjective selection of materials' reflect 'an objective standard of values'.[4] Reciprocity between the potentialities of the two attributes is exemplified by etherealization of the point-of-view character or by diffusion of the omniscient narrator's point of view within the restricted scope of a significant time scheme. The technique thus helps to elicit the effect of a tranced vision of the loftier Reality, which reveals its eternal Innocence as serene Beauty only when seen in perspective.[5] The time scheme is conceived on a symbolic level for the effectual exposition of the very nature of Time as an all-encompassing static Reality or as a cosmic force relegating all consciousness to the limbo of its womb which consumes all, including itself. This necessitates diffusion of the Point of View either through etherealization of the view-point character or as multi-personal focus of narration.

Evolution of this whole creative process naturally involved ardent persistence in the 'attitude of personal detachment'[6] and in exquisite refinement of creative sensibility. In her achievement of a technique potent enough to capture the beauty intrinsic in the ultimate tangible manifestation of transcendent reality, Miss Mansfield attained the spiritual 'purity' she had along been striving for. Her composition of these last few Songs of Innocence perhaps involved the whole of her being. She was rather levitating without being airy.

Of the four short-stories that Miss Mansfield composed in course of achieving her *beau ideal*—'purity' of her sensibility through mastery of her art—the first was *Garden Party*. This short-story finds its consummation in successful communication of her exalted attitude of a 'joyous acceptance'.[7] of 'life's diversity, death included'.[8] The concentrated vision has drawn upon the potentiality of its cognate attribute, choice of Point of View—for adequate revelation of the nature of "life" as a reality that is only poetically conceivable: it yields a characterization appropriately through etherealization of the point-of-view character; the character called into being cannot but be of "artistic" and 'entranced sensibility';[9] she has been conceived as a means of poetic understanding of the "beautiful" truth that transcends all barriers.

Perhaps the point of the short-story is the sense of puzzled wonder that the elliptical question echoed as "'Isn't it, darling?'" poetically registers: "'Isn't it, darling?'" is a rhetorical question eternally elliptical and enigmatic. The blank ("'—?'") that is bare and colourless is indicative of the indefinability or inconceivability of the nature of "life"; the echo ("'Isn't it?'") seems to have been meant to linger or to create an effect of unfading reverberation. The blank is suggestive also of an imaginative experience that is indefinably poetic—an experience of "life" which, with its diversity blended into unity, is truth with a capital T or Truth that is Beauty. The rhetorical question is enigmatic as a question which can echo only in a poetic feeling too deep for words. The echoing question thus poetically articulates a dark yet entranced realization.[10]

It is this moment of realization which Miss Mansfield's imaginative concentration explores; the central character is awakened to a transcendental truth that blends diversity of life into unity and makes it seem "simply marvellous" and beautiful. The essential feature of the character is an emotional inquisitive awareness of 'human solidarity';[11] this solidarity is part of the truth that transcends all social and conventional barriers. The character's awareness of this transcendental truth is a deeper yet innocent sense of what is the nearest palpable reality to the impalpable.

The moment of awakening begins with the protagonist's inquisitive awareness of a truth that transcends all barriers and ends with a mute poetic feeling of Truth as Beauty. What awakens the protagonist's sensibility to this palpable manifestation of transcendental truth is a poetic fancy that sees 'a world in a grain of sand and a heaven in a flower' but which fails to give 'a local habitation and a name' to the beauty that it discovers and thus remains mystified in its ecstasy. The point lies in the poetry behind the blank. Laura's empathy or her sympathetic vision of the young man's blissful "dream" in worldlessness of eternity is the culmination of (a) a deep-reaching imaginative experience refined and enriched by inquisitive and at times sensuous awareness; (b) an instinctive and infallible experience of the truth that transcends all barriers; (c) a profound yet naively innocent awareness of the ultimately tangible manifestation of the transcendent reality.

(a) *A deep-reaching imaginative experience refined and enriched by inquisitive and at times sensuous awareness*: Laura's loud thinking echoes a "remote ... peaceful" voice: "I am content". This anthropomorphic concept of a state of consciousness beyond death has its counterpart in Laura's emotional image of "what the band would sound like to that poor woman" just across the road, an image which reflects her imaginative awareness of 'human solidarity' as a truth transcending all barriers: she reads the "smile" of one of the workmen; she forgets "all about the karakas in her wondering at him caring for things like that": she goes deep into the feeling of another workman: "what was he thinking?"; even within her own 'class' of "bright birds—... in the Sheridans' garden for this one afternoon" she is a good 'mixer', passionately friendly: "Ah, what happiness it is to be with people who are all happy, to press hands, press cheeks, smile into eyes." Laura is a flower of love.[12]

Her imaginative vision of the young man's other-wordly bliss or his beatitude is the sublimation of her affinity with the karaka trees and the canna lilies from the world of Nature—an affinity which she has experienced imaginatively and sensuously: "They were like trees you imagined growing on a desert island, proud, solitary, lifting their leaves and fruits to the sun in a kind of silent splendour". Laura's dream-like perception of the trees in her garden reveals dimensions of her total poetic sensibility characterized as it is by inviolability of her pristine isolation from the Sheridan family that is only theatrically dreamy and apathetically worldly: "the green bushes bowed down as though they had been visited by archangels"; "She crouched down as if to warm herself at that blaze of lilies; she felt they were in her fingers, on her lips, growing in her breast". The young man seems to Laura to be "far from all ... things": he seems to be "given up to his dream", his "sleeping face" eloquent enough to articulate the ecstasy of "this-is-just-as-it-should-be". This near-mystic rapport with the poetic truth behind the still "face" is only the apotheosis of Laura's imaginative awareness of poetry behind the commonplace: "Darling little spots. Especially the one on the inkpot lid. It was quite warm. A warm little silver star. She could have kissed it". Laura's vicarious experience of the total visual blindness in death ("his eyes were closed; they were blind under the closed eyelids") is but the exaltation of her instinctive capacity for perception through senses synchronized by intense sensitiveness: She sees what she hears: "The house was alive with ... running voices", there sounded the rustle of Sadie's print skirt on the stairs.

(b) *An instinctive and infallible experience of the truth that transcends all barriers:* The experience is intensified by compassion and 'inner debate'.[13] The rhetorical question in the interior monologue ("what did garden-parties and baskets and lace—frocks matter to him?") is, obviously, of the type in which the questioner gives the answer too ("He was far from all those things"). This form of rhetorical question gives us the feel of the calm serenity into which Laura's realization of the transcendental truth has been exalted: the stylistic device resorted to is of course that of a striking substitute for a statement of contrary effect, but the pitch is toned down by the simple answer that immediately follows and by the Biblical sequence of 'and's' in the question itself. At the same time the particular form of the rhetorical question parallels Laura's perceptions of the transcendental truth: her perceptions throughout reveal an outlook characterized by simultaneity of curiosity and conviction, interrogation and assertion, a question and its answer. (The rhetorical question is elliptical only when the outlook is exalted into the trance of a poetic feeling of Truth as Beauty). *Godber*'s man asks, "'know those little cottages just below here, miss?'" Laura thinks aloud: "Know them? Of course she knew them," "Why couldn't she have workmen for friends rather than the silly boys she danced with ...? She would get on much better with men like these." The syntactical structure of all the rhetorical questions in this form later sheds all its adjectival and adverbial clauses when the 'inner debate' has purged Laura's instinctive and infallible experience thoroughly and the moment of pristine awareness of the whole truth is reached: "what did garden-parties and baskets and lace-frocks matter to him? He was far from all those things": the simple repetition of 'and's' reminiscent of Biblical syntax and the open vowelled expansiveness combine to reinforce the effect of a calm realization of the transcendental Truth as Beauty.

(c) *A profound yet naively innocent awareness of the ultimate tangible manifestation of the transcendental reality:* Laura's sensitive awareness of 'human solidarity' is but an innocent sense of the impalpable reality that manifests itself in human relations: "There lay a young man, fast asleep—sleeping so soundly, so deeply, that he was far, far away from them both. Oh, so remote, so peaceful. He was dreaming. Never wake him up again". What seems to be 'sound sleep' here is the palpable aspect of the impalpable reality—the ultimate tangible manifestation of the worldless, spaceless, timeless reality beyond all sensory perception. Laura's perception here is gradually penetrative: "there lay a young man": visual sensation deepens: everyday familiar expressions, "fast asleep", etc., are qualified by adverbials in an order suggestive of gradually penetrating interpretation of the sensation: "soundly ... deeply ... far, far away"; and lastly, the wording of a mystic feeling ("oh, so remote, so peaceful") is changed into a poetic definition of the feeling ("dreaming") in terms of familiar experience ("Never wake him up"): all perceptual experience, which covers a whole gamut of feelings, recedes the moment the mystic realization ("Oh, so remote, so peaceful") dawns upon the character and returns to its initial stage of pure sensation: "His head was sunk in the pillow, his eyelids were close". Laura's penetrative perception is inquisitively incisive: it delves deep into the palpable reality and then becomes a feeling of what is impalpable. The concluding words of the mute monologue capture the calm serenity into which Laura's perception of the palpable reality ("sleep" or "dream") has been finally exalted. This extra-sensory perception of the young man's 'happiness' parallels her dream-like imagination of "happiness" in human company: "Ah, what happiness it is to be with people who all are happy, to press hands, press cheeks, smile into eyes".

Laura is only unconsciously or innocently aware of the timeless music that the 'marvel' now in beatitude seems to be enjoying. 'The sweet music of human speech' that this "solitary soul" "on a desert island" has been dying for is nobler than the music that her practical, theatrical sister Jose makes as she bangs on the piano making it sound "more desperate than ever". Laura has an ear for the undying music that the inarticulate universal language of "friendliness" is: she is instinctively responsive to the sing-song call of one of the workmen, and not only to the call but also to "the chock-chock of wooden hammers". The very thought of "the friendliness of it" sends her into a compassionate, ecstatic, speechless trance ("the-the-"). The sing-song call harmonized with "the chock-chock" is the palpable aspect of the impalpable reality that is only emotionally conceivable ("The friendliness of it"). It is this deeper music of "friendliness" that seems to have become the ultimate music of worldlessness. Laura's awareness of the audible music is not unmingled with her feeling of the soul-awakening deathless music of the poetry of life.

Laura's characterization seems to have been consummated

through creation of an identical character, Laurie. With his echo, "Isn't it, darling?" Laurie, we feel, can have only such a name as echoes Laura's: his is a name homonymous throughout but synonymous in the end. Establishment of Laura's synonymity with this character in the last sentence is necessitated by not only the sense that the poetic realization is shared but also the meaning that the question only echoes as an eternal rhetorical question. The two near-identical characters are complementary. The fact is substantiated not only by the mutuality of fondness ("'I do love parties' ... 'Rather'") or even concurrence of opinions ("'Isn't life—? ... 'Isn't it, darling'"); it is demonstrated also, on the textural-structural level, by the significantly common phrase "warm voice". Laurie's "warm voice" is "boyish" when life brims in Laura and it is "loving", when she stands purged by sober melancholy; it complements her breathless 'gasp' of vivacity as well as her deep wordless moan of profound sorrow: "Laura shook her head. She was crying"; and then, naturally immediately after Laura's articulation of her vision ("It was simply marvellous"), it mingles with her voice: it becomes an echo of it ("Isn't it, darling?"). The homonymous name becomes a synonymous one; Laura's intonation of her sense of puzzled wonder ("Isn't life—?") has its natural echo or its poetic vibration in the "warm voice" of the only "matey" that she has in her own life.

Laura, "the artistic one", is appropriately conceived as a character of 'entranced sensibility'. Her characterization is done in three ways: (a) through occasional etherealization of her physical appearance; (b) through simultaneous exposure of her contrary features; and (c) through consistent evolution of evocative imagery.

(a) Etherealization of Laura's physical appearance is resorted to at two significant points in the narrative. The two points mark important stages in the evolution of the character. In the opening scene etheralization is effected in two ways: first through representation of the character's vision alone; then through omission of the reporting verb or the principal clause in the narration of the character's speech. In the first case we hear the inner voice of the character; in the second, we hear the real voice in snatches of conversation. But in neither case is the character immediately identifiable. We hear two voices of the same speaker; and this sense dawns on us as we read on.

The opening paragraph is the description of Nature in the garden and beyond. As we read on we come to see which of the names can be linked with the window-view. Thus the window-view turns out to be a mental snapshot of the garden: the sensibility of the viewer is revealed to us.—"The sky without a cloud" reflects a sensibility that is "pristine"; the sensibility is passionless and calm ("windless"): it is loving and compassionate ("warm"): it is innocent and susceptible ("sky without a cloud"). This sensibility is not without imagination ("the blue veiled with a haze of light gold"). We also feel that the viewer is in the springtime of life ("as it is sometimes in early summer"). The viewer notes two objects—"the dark flat rosettes", and "the green bushes ... visited by archangels". They pop into view as meaningfully contrasted objects: they are contrary enough to image forth the opposed values in the world of the viewer. "The dark flat rosettes" grossly betray their ornamentation of artifice: they correspond to all that is theatrical and false in the Sheridan part of the viewer's world. "The green bushes ... visited by archangels" present a remote contrast: they reflect the viewer's 'moral selfhood:[14]

But the vision of contrast is synthetic: "And after all the weather was ideal". The synthetic vision is characteristic of the viewer's "artistic" self. This artistic self emerges as an image that embodies a unifying principle.[15] The very opening sentence reveals what the 'moral selfhood' of the viewer consists in. Deep within the viewer's self there is a moral conviction: there is an awareness of unity in diversity; there is an attitude of 'acceptance'; there is a serene realization. The inner voice of the viewer here is the voice of this real self. It is this voice that lingers as an echo: "'Isn't life—?' (Isn't it, darling—?)". "And after all" as the opening phrase is significant: it comes to mean "in spite of all".[16] In the light of the total impression of the character the picture is transparently recognizable as a vision characteristic of a whole self, an "artistic" self. The sensibility of this "artistic one" is distinguished; her consciousness of 'life' with its 'diversity' is exalted into a calm—a calm which is the culmination of all inquisitiveness. "And after all" strikes the keynote of the drama.

The character is all vision. It is significant that a story about such a character begins with the rendering of a vision. The window view is a peep-hole view of a whole self, an "artistic" self, a being that is all poetic vision. Representation of the vision alone is artistic. The point of view is unidentified: the description reads like an account given by the all-knowing narrator. Only a vision is there because it is as a vision that the character evolves.

Identification of the vision is done obliquely. All links with the telling name ("the artistic one") are tenuous. The name is not used in indirect narration; it is used in the speech of a character that is not what "the artistic one" is. We can see that all this is a way of widening the gap between the vision and the viewer to the fullest possible extent. Starkly objective dramatization helps to dissolve the link. This dramatization involves omission of the reporting verb or the introductory principal clause in the narration of the character's own speech ("Where do you want to marquee put, mother?") Thus we are aware of only a shimmering image. It is this shimmering image that functions as the image of "entranced sensibility".

Substitution of the vision for the viewer at this important point in the narrative is a considered device. There are two reasons for recourse to this device: first, the 'atmosphere' is that of a drama ringing with a question; the very first speech of the character is worded as a question, pure and simple: "'Where do you want the marquee put, mother?'"—it is the inner voice of an inquisitive self; it is the voice of a character that is all curiosity. Secondly, the 'atmosphere' here is parallel to the one that is created again when the second part of the story about the character begins there too we hear only questions after questions, all voiced again in curiosity: "'what's the matter? What's happened?' ... 'Where? How? When?'"

The same way of drawing the character can be noted at the two dramatic points in the narrative. At both the points we have the core of the character—a being that is all curiosity. There is consistent omission of reporting verbs or principal clauses in the narration of the speeches. There is no 'said Laura' or 'said she'; there is nothing that might help one to see one's way clear to the right source. In the opening scene it is not clear which of the Sheridan girls at the breakfast table puts the question about "the marquee". The mid-story parallel too keeps us in the dark about the questioner: we are not told which of the two Sheridan girls is putting questions after questions about "a man killed".

The character evolves as she goes deeper into "life". There is movement from the one question about "the marquee" to the other questions about "a man killed": the sense of progression from the earlier question to the later ones is also a sense of movement from life without any thought of death to life on the point of only questions and questions about death. The movement involves a process of spiritual refinement. Whatever is gross in an already etherealized presence grows subtler. In the opening scene the character's vision is all sensory experience; her question about "the marquee" too is much too worldly. In the mid-story scene the character is face to face with the last truth about life; this truth is quaint: the end of life can come like a bolt from the blue. The character freezes into what is only 'how—?' only 'when—?', only 'where—?' Here it is only the questions that give 'a local habitation and a name' to the character.

The second half of the story has a dramatic beginning. The character gets an eye-opener. The answers to the questions reveal the hard core of reality: a death is a reality; the core of this reality is not without the irony of unreasonable suddenness. It is this irony that makes death a blind force, an a-moral principle. Death through "accident" too is in the natural order of things. This paradox is a tragic irony. There is "diversity in life" also because of this irony. Death is 'included' in its fuller sense. Faced with this naked core of reality, the character drops her identity and emerges as her real self. The impression is naturally that of a shimmering image.

Laura's questions after the news follow in quick succession; they are uneasy; they voice a sympathetic human concern. This sympathetic concern is a human element in the character. Emotionally charged monosyllabic articulation of the concern gives us the feel of the 'quick'. This quick seems to throb through the blanks for 'said Laura', etc,. We can see that there is 'said the cook' but that there is no 'said Laura', no 'said she', not even once. The character with the milk of human kindness comes to life. The voice here is that of the character's inner moral selfhood; it is no longer Sheridan; it is not "copied". It is what it is, what it is meant to image forth is a character reduced to her innocent selfhood.

Apart from the rhythmical pattern of questions we have the recurrent motif of 'stammer'. Here we find still another deeper level on which the character evolves. The stammer, as we shall see, is heard whenever it is a moment of poetic trance: the character stops short: the articulate fades into the inarticulate. There is a poetic feeling: it is mute because it is much too deep for articulation. The last moment is that of a mute poetic realization of truth that 'life' with its 'diversity' is, 'death included'. The character is made up of not only what she says but also of what she fails to say.

Semi-etherealization of the character's physical appearance is another means of drawing the character. The opening scene ends with a narrative statement; "Away Laura flew, still holding her piece of bread-and-butter". The inversion ("Away") and the image evoked by the verb ("flow") succinctly convey the essence of the character. The essence is her romantic sensibility: the moral selfhood of the character, the 'friend' in the character, the un-Sheridan daughter in the character, is romantic. "The artistic one", we can see, is a romantic lover of Music. She breaks away from a world reverberating with bombastic theatricality that is without sweet music of "friendliness". She flutters away from a world resounding with "Pom-ta-ta-ta-ta-a" which ring out life itself, life that is music of "diversity, death included".

There is another significant point in the narrative where semi-etherealization of the character's figure is noticeable. The aspect of the character revealed at this point in the human drama is cheery: Laura is under the spell of the gay occasion, 'the garden party': "Away she skimmed, over the lawn, up the path, up the steps, across the verandah, and into the porch". The inversion ("Away") this time is meant to make us see Laura's prance. The tripping movement of clauses is accentuated by rapid succession of prepositions ("Over the lawn, up the path, up the steps, across the verandah, and into the porch"): we see Laura as she frisks and flounces all the way up. But the figure is a blur. This blur is characteristic of the shimmering image of 'entranced sensibility'.

There is similar succession of prepositions in a later narrative statement about a sober Laura: "(And this time she didn't wait for Em's sister.) She found her way out of the door, down the path, past all those dark people". The movement of clauses is accentuated again by prepositions. But the emotional context here is serene. Laura has just had a glimpse of the "picture" of truth as Beauty. This context affects the movement of the clauses: it slows it down. The effect is tonally enriched by the open-vowelled expansiveness of "out of", "down", "past all those dark people". The "way" now is "a way out" of a "dark" world, "down" the "broad road" between two worlds, "past all those dark people".[17] The moment is that of a realization, a discovery, a sense of puzzled wonder. Laura here is not escaping; she is emerging. The movement is slow; the mood is serene. But the figure is again a blur.

This character of "entranced sensibility" is conjured up also through tonal variation. The two narrative statements about Laura's gait have almost similar syntactical patterns—in both we have clauses accentuated by prepositions in rhythmical succession.

There is similarity, but we are aware of the tonal variation too. The clauses in "over the lawn, up the path", etc. reflect a gay aspect of the character: what lends a tripping movement to the clauses is the gay context with its corresponding sound-effect of short-vowels: "up", "across", "into". In the second statement the clauses ("out of the door, down the path, past all those dark people") register the movement of a sober Laura; their movement is slowed down by the onomatopoeic succession of long vowels and the calm mood of the moment is captured.

The difference between the individual effects of similar patterns is sharpened by the way the two sentences begin. The first begins with an inversion ("Away she skimmed"); the second has the simple subject-plus-verb-plus-object-plus-adverbial-complement pattern ("she found her way out of the door"...). The inversion captures the spirit of freedom in the character. This spirit is characteristic of her romantic sensibility. The spirit itself is captured here: the character moves freely between the two worlds—the world of "friendliness" and "the chock-chock of hammers" on the one hand, and the world of the "telephone" and the "piano" on the other: the world of values, and the world that is all falsity. There is an inviolably isolated, private world of joyful freedom between the two worlds. The simple subject-plus-verb-plus-object-plus-adverbial-complement pattern conjures up a sober presence: the gay character has been sobered by the complementary vision of the whole truth about life. Choice of the normal verbal pattern for the rendering of a sober mood comes natural.

(b) Simultaneous exposure of the character's contrary features helps to image forth the complexity inherent in the process of her awakening. The character's gestures and mannerisms and thoughts are usually contrary: all point to opposed sets of values—the one set is inherited from the ethos of the Sheridan household; the other is inherent in her own imaginative, virtuous outlook on life.

The inversion ("Away") and the picturesque verb ("flew") in the sentence, "Away Laura flew, still holding her piece of bread-and-butter", conjure up an image of a free bird in flight. They convey the relevant sense of sudden freedom and burst of gaiety. But this impression is immediately cancelled out: the subsequent adverbial clause ("still holding her piece" etc.) carries a contrary implication. The flight of freedom is burdened with a thing that will make the character 'blush' and 'try' to "look severe and even a little bit shortsighted". The character stands transfixed when she feels the simultaneous conivery sets of values, so to say, all at the same time: "Laura wished now that she was not holding that piece of bread-and-butter, but there was nowhere to put it and she couldn't possibly throw it away". She feels the pull of the world she has just come into, the world of the marquee men; at the same time there is the pull of the Sheridan ethos which she cannot bring herself to resist. The "piece of bread-and-butter" contends with the outflow of emotional effusion ("Laura wished now that she was not holding that piece"); but it has so much of Sheridan flavour in it that she finds it difficult to part with it. When there is a transition from 'affectation' to 'shame', it reveals only the re-assertion of the character's moral conviction: "'Good morning', she said, copying her mother's voice". We are aware of this transition as we hear her melting voice: guttural articulation ("'Good morning'"), which has the ring of Sheridan theatricality, melts into liquid articulation ("'Oh-er-have-you-come?'"), which as a stammering rhetorical question echoes the speaker's inner voice. The 'little girl' in Laura becomes a Mrs. Sheridan; and then, startled at the sound of the voice she has 'copied', regains her real, natural self. The blurred impression that the transition creates is characterized by contrariety. There is triple exposure: Laura, "her mother" in her, and the little innocent girl that she is—all are revealed in a single flash. The "little girl" in Laura stammers thrice: she stammers for the first time when the warmth of nearness to the throb of "friendliness" sends her into a blissful trance; she stammers for the second time when she hears the sweet music of "friendliness" ("The friendliness of it, the-the-"); she stammers lastly when she is face to face with the whole truth that "life" is with its 'diversity, death included' ("Isn't life—?"). This last stammer is the elliptical articulation of a poetic feeling that finds its natural expression as a rhetorical question. The recurrent stammer thus grows more and more inarticulate: the first is full but vacant ("Oh-er-have you come? Is it about the marquee?"); the second is emotionally choked ("the friendliness of it, the-the-") the last is awed and ecstatic ("Isn't life—?"). We can see how the character evolves in poetic trance. Again, in the speech, "'How very nice workmen were ! And what a beautiful morning! She mustn't mention the morning. She must be business-like. The marquee", the first two exclamatory sentences have significantly similar verbal patterns. Laura is characteristically aware of the deeper affinity between the "workmen" and Nature ("a beautiful morning"). The conjunction ("And") is a telling conjunction: the movement from the one sentence to the other is breathless; the tone is dreamy. Laura's awareness of the deeper relationship is entranced. But this awareness is innocent, too: she does not know the "workmen" and the "beautiful morning" are so close; she only feels they are naturally together. Then we note a tonal shift. There is a transition from heartfelt ejaculation ("How very nice workmen were ! And what a beautiful morning !) to what sounds tutored and strained ("She mustn't mention the morning. She must be business-like. The marquee."). The previous impression is dissipated by the tone, the structure, the meaning of the statements that follow: the voice is constrained; the structure grows tighter; the suggestion is that of inhibition of impulse. Vocalization of the 'inner debate' is the more realistic for this tonal variation. The variation this time is in reverse order. The change here is not from a copied "Good morning" to a little girl's stammer, from 'affectation' to 'shame', from hollow formality to innocent artlessness. This time the movement is directed back towards the Sheridan set of values: "she mustn't mention the morning. She must be businesslike". The fluctuations in reverse order rather prismatically refract the same image of the character that is nothing if not all "inner debate". The piece of bread-and-butter is an unwelcome obstruction between Laura and the workmen ("And she pointed to the lily-lawn with the hand that didn't hold the bread-and-butter"): it is a token of the Sheridan ethos. The lily-lawn is a world as natural as that of "friendliness". The bread-and-butter is naturally kept aloof: the Sheridan ethos is not allowed to foul the world of values, the world of friendliness, naturalness, artlessness. The way the character is postured helps to show how the world of values here remains inviolably isolated. Here too the character does not know how she is acting: her action is instinctive, characteristic; she is innocently unaware of her 'moral selfhood'. (This 'moral selfhood' is realized when the character comes out of 'the dark world' with the whole vision of a poet.) The tell-tale gesture is a narrative statement; it is not simply a detail. The character is already on the path of that realization. Here we have the character's image on two levels: the one is the tonal level; the other is the visual. On the tonal level her speech ("How very nice workmen were ~! ... she must be business-like. The marquee.") is suggestive of her sudden withdrawal into the hard shell of her Sheridan self. But on the visual level ("And she pointed to the lily-lawn", etc.) her appearance reveals her unconscious or subconscious awareness of a great world of values—the world of Nature and common man united by bonds of naturalness and artlessness. Synchronization of the images on the tonal and visual levels helps to enliven the impressionistic effect of "inner debate".

(c) Consistent evolution of evocative imagery appropriately characterizes the latter half of the total structure. The images recur and come to form rhythmical patterns. This effects the evolution of the character. There are only two images: the one is "picture"; the other is "hat".

"Picture" is a key-word in all the three passages in which it occurs. But the meaning of this key-word varies, for the moods of the three passages are contrasted. The design of characterization thus effected is naturally criss-crossed.

In the passage in which Mrs. Sheridan gives Laura her own hat and holds up her hand-mirror for her we find depiction of a moment that is paradoxically complex. Laura is uneasily haunted by the reality of the tragedy; so she turns aside from the unreality of all gaiety. The "hat" has come to betoken social superiority of her household; it is associated with a joyous occasion. Laura has realized the falsity of it all. She turns aside from the "picture" that she "herself" may "look" with this hat "popped on". This "picture" she feels is but a reflection of something false, unreal, and wrong, too. With her moral self withdrawn, Laura turns aside. She has popped the hat on anyhow. But she cannot bring herself to look at herself. Her gestures are contrary again, and again we have a glimpses of the deeper self as the moral force at work. Laura cannot look into the "hand-mirror" and see if she really 'looks a picture'; she cannot see what she looks like, that 'hat' popped on; of course the hat is "made for" her; but the way Mrs. Sheridan stresses the point ("The hat is yours. It's made for you. It's much too young for me.") is enough to make us see that the hat is not without a link with Mrs. Sheidan. The reflection of Laura with this hat popped on ("a picture") is just an image in a mirror; it is an image in the mind of Mrs. Sheridan. It is unreal, untrue. To "look such a picture" is to be unreal, to look into the glass only to see what Mrs. Sheridan has seen ("I've never seen you look such a picture") is to look at the unreal reflection of another unreal reflection. The whole complex of meanings the key-word carries creates on the page an 'atmosphere' of unreality.

The rendering of the moment registers a significant transition—

a transition from dismissal of gaiety as unreality to recognition of tragedy as reality. This transition reveals a glimpse of Laura's inner moral self.—"But" ("'But', she began"), in this first "picture" passage, seems to be simply a word that marks the point of transition.

In the passage in which Laura has another glimpse of the poor woman and the little children and the body being carried into the house, her sympathy for the bereaved family seems to have been irrepressibly effusive; now it is fanciful ("it all seemed blurred, unreal like a picture of the newspaper."). What has hitherto kept her emotionally perturbed is dismissed with a shrug: "but it all seemed blurred, unreal, like a picture in the newspaper. I'll remember it again after the party's over, she decided". Her sympathy is subordinate to a "plan". The incident seems to be just a chance occurrence, just "a picture in the newspaper". A picture in a newspaper is usually "blurred": it can be only vaguely recollected later; a newspaper is fated to lie crumpled: such tragic events are soon forgotten. A picture in a newspaper is "unreal": it is rendered untrue by the passage of time; what it shows was there as a reality, but it is no longer there, and a question comes to be truer than what only seems to have been a fact: was it ever there? The key-word "picture" here reveals another dimension of unreality. This dimension is not that of false values as illusion but that of all reality as illusion. The "picture" itself is never a reality.

Laura's vision includes the images of "that poor woman, those little children and the body being carried into the house". It is a brief vision of the whole bereaved family, the dead body included. The repetitive pattern of demonstrative pronoun plus adjective ("that poor, those little") helps us to gauge the depth of Laura's compassion, too. But all these images are dismissed: that poor woman, those little children are shut off from sympathy for a period of time; they all become a passing fancy. This ironic reversal helps to enliven the design for "inner debate".

The transition this time is from dismissal of tragedy as unreality to recognition of gaiety as reality. Laura turns aside now from "a picture" that she can "remember again after the party's over": she cannot give priority to this "picture" in her "plan". If remembered later, this "unreal, blurred ... picture" will become a vaguer blur. But Laura at the moment is too gay to mind: she is again Sheridan enough to live, move and have her being in a world without thoughts of death and 'dark world',—"But" ("But it all seemed unreal") is again the word that significantly registers the point of transition.

The word "picture" recurs lastly in the depiction of the moment when Laura is shown the dead body. Here too we have the rendering of still another moment that is complex paradoxically. Laura is "afraid"; this is natural. But it is only her own feeling that the woman in the room voices. Laura shares the woman's vision of the dead young man. In her interior monologue before this "picture" she feels it is "wonderful, beautiful", the dead man is a "marvel". The "picture" this time is not flashily artificial like the image of gaiety (the hat). It is not evanescently unreal, either, like "a picture in the newspaper" fated to lie crumpled and ignored. The "picture" the woman uncovers is the picture of a tell-tale reality: its beauty lies in its being only what it is and never anything else.

Here in this last "picture" passage we have a transition from a sense of fear to a sense of beauty, from a sense of pity to a sense of awe, from a sense of reality to a sense of revelation.—There is no "But" in this "picture" passage, because there is no sense of "but" in sense of beauty, in sense of awe, in sense of revelation. There is of course a sense of "but" in turning from unreality to reality or from reality to unreality. But there is no sense of "but" when "All is well. This is just as it should be". All sense of "but" has become here a sense of revelation.

We can see that this simple word "But" stands out in the two previous passages. In both it marks the point of transition. The transitions are mutually in reverse order. The process is characteristic of "inner debate". The word is naturally absent in the last "picture" passage. The moment is that of nearness to the last truth about life—the truth that is "wonderful, beautiful". It is the moment of a calm and there is no 'but' at such a moment.—'But' is one of the most prosaic of words. Still the pattern it forms in the "picture" passages has a functional significance: the "picture" passages are designed to dramatize the "inner debate" and the culmination of it. The way the word works makes us see how our author's art is an art which does not show through the design.

The other recurrent image-pattern evolves from the key-word "hat". The hat image within the range of its recurrence takes on a symbolic value: it represents "the whole social milieu of the Sheridan class: leisure, consumption, caste distinction'.[18] There are ten references to "hat". The pattern formed is so neatly designed: in the chronological order, each pair of references stands sharply contrasted with the previous one: each corresponds to a stage in the process of Laura's awakening. Her characterization filters in through the design of a specific image-pattern: the pattern is marked by a consistent evolution of cross-cancelling impressions.

The first two references to the hat ("In the hall her father and Laurie were brushing their hats"; "Mother says you're to wear that sweet hat you had on last Sunday") are details meant to acquire a symbolic value: at this earliest stage of her awareness of the hat she is blissfully ignorant of its dark meaning for her; she does not know as yet that it is going to be to her what the piece of bread and butter has been—an unwelcome thing between herself and the world of values. The "hat" is an emblem of Sheridan values. Laura's first awareness of it is innocently objective. It is appropriate that the reference to the "hat" here is preceded by a self-evident image of a gay Laura ("Away she skimmed, etc.). The hat is made to pop into view: it is meant to accumulate a symbolic value. The next time the hat-image occurs in Laura's own monologue ("Mother says you're to wear that sweet hat", etc.). Here Laura only reports her mother's speech: the narration is indirect. The italicized word, "sweet", does make us see that her awareness is not objective: her own stress on the word seems to let out the secret of a subjective feelings. But the word is underlined because at the moment the character is too innocent and gay to see what it is that is being passed through her. It is underlined not because she is as much aware of sweetness about the hat as her mother is. She is under the spell of the occasion; she is not yet under the spell of the hat. But in either reading of the underlined word one fact is plain: the spell has started working. The mother's dreamy gay voice 'floats down the stairs'. It is the voice of the soul of the Sheridan household: It is this soul that presides over its life. Laura here is a medium through which the soul's corrupting voice is being transmitted.

Then we have the next two references to the hat. The first is made when Laura finds her mother "trying on a new hat"; the second, when her mother describes her as "a picture" and Laura turns aside. On both these occasions Laura is poignantly aware of the grim reality of a tragedy "outside the front gate": she just catches sight of the hat as she gets sight of the "dressing-table" and her mother's "knees" and her hand-mirror". The moment is not that of a spell. It is the moment of dismissal of all gaiety as unreality.

We can see how the first pair is contrasted in mood with the second: the first shows Laura as a gay girl brimming over with high spirits; the second presents Laura in a different "colour" ("'What's given you such a colour?' and Mrs. Sheridan turned round").

In the third pair we have the first reference when Laura is "quite by chance" bewitched by a "charming girl in the mirror, in her black hat trimmed with gold daisies", etc.; we have the second when Laurie goggles his eyes at her "absolutely topping hat". The pair reveals Laura narcissistically in love with her image with the hat popped on.

In the fourth pair, the first shows Mrs. Sheridan admiring Laura's looks with the "becoming hat"; then there are guests chanting a chorus of praise as Laura moves about, the hat pooped on. This fourth pair presents Laura as a "glowing" girl completely under the spell of the hat by this time.

When we have the last pair, first we have Laura wishing "if only it was another hat"; then we see her "tossing her velvet-ribbon over her shoulder". This last pair unveils her real self—the deeper moral self. Laura stands here with her "pristine sensibilities" or her "moral selfhood" resuscitated: she is ashamed, repentant, apologetic-down on her knees before the "picture" of a serene truth, her voice soft as the glow of altar candles: "Forgive my hat".

Diffusion of the focus of narration in the next short-story as the multipersonal point of view is occasioned by Miss Mansfield's dreamy concentration on a day in all life "*At the Bay*". This life with all its categories of existence is seen against the appropriate background of the sea, the ultimate tangible manifestation of eternal innocence. The creative process seems to have evolved as a tranced spiritual vision: the comprehensive yet dreamily lyrical vision of the epic 'stillness' of all life "*At the Bay*" has necessitated exploitation of the potentiality of the omniscient view-point. The exploitation has been conducted to the extent of accommodation of a ubiquitous viewpoint incessantly registering the flux of life in obscure isolation. The time scheme imperceptibly reveals the interminable cyclic pattern of temporal succession evolving as the illusive manifestation of time, the inconceivably non-existent, impalpably "still" eternal reality. This reciprocity between the potentialities of point of view and time scheme thus occasions embodiment of a poetic philosophy: all Experience, all Consciousness, all life is eternal Innocence.

It is, perhaps, in the last suspended sentence("All was still") that we have the point of the lyrical short-story. We can see that the enormous verbal complex that precedes this last narrative statement begins with an elliptical sentence ("Very early morning") and ends with a hypothetical one ("Then the cloud sailed away, and the sound of the sea was a vague murmur, as though it walked out of a dark dream"). Every word in this complex tends towards this last short and simple sentence ("All was still"). The effect-collecting pause after the penultimate sentence and the impact of finality which the last sentence registers with its calm drawling tone, its utter colourlessness, and its comparative short-ness, make use feel that this concluding narrative statement stands isolated in the total verbal texture. "All" refers to the atmosphere in the last episode which ends with the silence subsequent to a question that has remained unanswered ("Nobody answered him"); the word also alludes to the entire atmosphere of the world created on the page in the twelve sections: it has its immediate relevance to the silence that falls when the last puzzling question in the short-story goes unanswered; through this relevance to the silence of answerlessness the word relates to the barrenness of the questions the world in the twelve sections seems to be ringing with.

"All was still" provides the peep-hole view of the nature of the world contemplated in the twelve sections: the twelve sections are all 'stills' from life. There is of course a sense of progression when the same character re-appears, but the sense of progression terminates either in a sense of barren interrogation or in that of a situation that involves an unanswerable question. These stills are stills also because "All was still". All life here stands "still" in a frozen moment not only because its flow comes to a standstill at the point of its culmination but also because all its flow in time is only an illusion of movement: the temporal process that creates this illusion of progression is characterized by a cyclic recurrence which is eternally interminable; and consciousness that develops with the passage of time remains innocent throughout because all its questions remain unanswered, barren, agonized. This whole process has been captured as a frozen moment: it has been seen as one. The short-story reads like a sketch because what it seeks to image forth is tragically static and barren and dark. The crisis the short-story seeks to render is not the one that reveals a truth about human nature. Here life itself is revealed as an eternal crisis: the whole process of it is a dark mystery. It flows on with its questions unreasonably answerless: the oldest of the characters is appropriately made to say: "Life is like that": 'Life-is-like-that'-ness is eternally unquestionable, its temporal pattern interminably cyclic, and its flow only an illusion of progression. The intended effect is that of a dark mystery that barren stagnation of all 'Life' is. An enormous verbal complex evolves in the space between the opening sentence and the penultimate statement. The opening sentence of the short-story is elliptical: it is thus indicative of the nature of time that is eternally nascent. The penultimate sentence is hypothetical; it is worded in a tense that is ambiguous. The "dream" itself is vaguely timeless: it denotes something which one seems to see or experience during sleep; thus it points to the present: It is also the externalization of an internal process generated by individual experiences: in this sense it relates to the past; it implies, again; a mental picture or pictures of the future: with this implication it seems to be linked up with the future, too. Thus "dream" points to the present, the past and the future, all at the same time. All these temporal dimensions of the "dream" (merged into a vague complex) stand darkened by obscurity. The vague temporal complex is poetically expressive of the timeless mystery that is inviolably obscure even in its manifestation as the sea. The impersonal comment implicit in the concluding sentence thus relates to the termination of the flow of not only life but also time in which life flows: the natural chronological order indicated by 'the faint temporal connexion from section to section[19] also terminates in this dark void of stillness': both Life and Time in which life flows terminate in a dark void; and the tragedy lies in the cyclic continuity of the process as a dark mystery.

Use of the present tense in the last section is also consistent with the specific unity of time aimed for. The transition in the sequence of tense is perhaps necessitated by the desired effect of proximity of all Life with the still point of time that stills "All". Immediacy of the "still" nature of Time is chilling. The moment that this last "still" captures is the secret moment of exposure of a lonely self to the extrinsic complex of existential categories[20]; the exposure is a means of reciprocity of relation between the two: it facilitates the expansion that a soul characteristically seeks for the sake of its consummation: the fulfillment consists in perfection of the process of reciprocity between the lonely self and the extrinsic complex and simultaneous retention of the inviolability of the isolated self as an individual psyche. This whole complex process is secretly yet palpably revealed at this moment of still silence when the interiorized consciousness involves an uncommon experience of tantalizing proximity with the world that environs it. The tense used for such a moment is naturally the eternal present tense.

The transition in the tense-scheme in the last twelfth section has its parallel in the variation of the sequence of tense distinctly discernible in the central sixth section of the narrative build-up—the centre-spread "still" that depicts a moment with its dimensions of the past, the present and the future.

Linda 'dreaming the morning away' recalls the picturesque past with her father at "their Tasmanian home" and hopes for the happy future when her dream of "escape" will come true; but she remains static in the present, hopeless, agonized, and lonely, with all her ideas and thoughts and feelings about her life in the family and about life and death in the world, darkened by overwhelming perplexity. The stasis is poetically imaged through etherealization of her figure in the concluding paragraph of the section where we have a headless, faceless, mindless Linda lost in a timeless moment; and, significantly, this image of stasis is shown through the eyes of the "toothless" baby, still in the stage of pure sensation, the first stage of all consciousness. The image of Experience-as-all-perplexity corresponds to the image of pure innocence. Experience and Innocence become one fused complex. What the simple two-dimensional frame of the picture here reveals or, more appropriately is meant to reveal, is the vague image of Linda's breasts which her "toothless" baby is too innocent to name and identify; the vague image is coupled with the sharply outlined image of the baby making "a tremendous effort" as he lies between the two breasts: the two breasts, significantly all blur here, seem, in the present context, to be symbolic of the reciprocal overlapping of expanding psyche and self-revealing non-human entity: the process of reciprocal orientation is perhaps "the mysterious passage' between the diverse 'categories of existence'.[21] The symbol is significantly viewed through the baby's eyes: it seems to have been meant to correspond to the image of Innocence. This correspondence helps to convey the intended meaning: all psychic evolution is eternally nascent. Linda's face is out of the frame of the quiz close-up: her facial expressions are out of the focus: we cannot read her mind; thus we are made to see the relevant implication—her individual psyche is lost in the timeless moment that is the past, the present and the future, all at the same time. Again, first we have an intimate depiction of Linda's interiorized consciousness concentrated as it is on momentous questions in life: then we share the "toothless" baby's objective vision of what is definable only as "something". This transition too parallels all psychic transition from Experience to Innocence in Time in which all transition is but an illusion. The process of Beryl's own orientation as an individual psyche retains the inviolability of her isolated self. This process too is captured at a timeless moment. The consistent sequence of the present tense is natural to the moment.

At the approximate center of the carefully patterned framework and 'near in time to the story's high noon[22] we have a simple homely scene dramatized as a dialogue between Kezia and the grandmother. The revelation in the full daylight at noon here is sharply contrasted against—and at the same time in perfect harmony with—the mystery concealed in the dark of the "still" midnight imaged in the last section. The revelation is that of a vast range of human consciousness extending from innocence inquisitive enough to articulate the first and last question about life to experience mature enough to accept the unquestionability of the fact that: "Life is like that". This revelation of human consciousness as consciousness ranging from innocence to experience is in contrast with the mystery of all consciousness as eternal Innocence; it is in harmony with the mystery on a deeper level: the process of all inquiry, all 'acceptance', all dismissal terminates in a void of oblivion; all psyche is only Innocence writ large. The revelation in the full day-light is thus equivalent to the mystery of the still dark moment. Innocence here excels all experience when it evinces serious curiosity about the most fundamental aspect of life; and Experience becomes one with this Innocence as the two lie "in each other's arms". This reciprocal overlapping of the two extreme phases of human consciousness is characteristic of the incessant ebb and flow of psyche: this concept of the total psyche is reflected in the fundamental image of the sea which is the ultimate terrestrial reality nearest to the inconceivably non-existent reality: Time; the sea is the dominant image because disorder is its order and this disorder as order is the basic principle of not only Life but also Time.

We can see how the characters who people the human world live, move and have their beings in the present which defines the temporal truth about all Consciousness as eternal Innocence. Dimensions of the present vary with the characters. Stanley lives in the bustling present and thus stands nearest to the apparent aspect of time as defined by the clock. Jonathan keeps struggling throughout as he feels he is being sucked down by the quicksand of routine existence as a smothering curse of recurrent Mondays. The members with their hedonistic philosophy of life or seize-the-day attitude to life live in the present that is isolated from the past and the future. Alice confronted with a life of "freedom" in the complacent present feels "awkward" and her mind flies "back to her own kitching"; she wants "to be back in it again", a life in the present drives back another life into the present. Mrs. Stubbs as the embodiment of 'a heavy corporeal element'[23] stands between a remorseless past and a blessed future and is smugly complacent in her "glad widowhood". Grandma with her calm acceptance of the unquestionability of the fact that "life is like that" lives in the realistic present. The two isotates, Linda and Burnell, with all their psychic adventures beyond the present, remain hopelessly transfixed in the tragically sterile present. The children living in the eternal present stand in sharp contrast with all the adults whose lives seem to be restricted to the superficial dimension of the immediate present: it is only the children that live in 'shadows of eternity'; it is only in their life that we glimpse the 'bright shoots of everlastingness'; it is because of them that the short-story becomes a song of Innocence. This accounts for the temporal isolation of one whole section devoted exclusively to the portrayal of the world of the children: the portrayal is purged of any allusion to any aspect of time. This world of children is the nearest human world to the cosmic; it is the last 'door of perception' in human life. The image of innocence is the image of Timelessness.

We find this world of human consciousness in the foreground. Even this fully developed consciousness is only perplexed awareness of an a-moral truth—"life is like that". The supramundane vision of the whole psychic complex reveals this uppermost stratum of consciousness as consciousness that is all perplexity: the paradox deepens the tragic effect of the story of the human characters. However, the dominance of this stratum of consciousness is not to be allowed to restrict the critical approach to the psychological implications of the human situations alone.[24]

The subject of the short-story is life with all its categories of existence and degree and variety of consciousness: the drama in the human world in spite of its manifest dominance is subordinated to it. Dramatization of the human element has to admit of no development on the level either of characterization or of plot; the characters are meant to seem as symbolically typical as the day. The fundamental image, the sea, reflects not only the whole psychic complex of reciprocally overlapping features of consciousness but also the impalpable reality of Time with its eternal ebb and flow as a boundless ocean of nothingness. To orientate the human element to this implicity dominant image of the sea is to perceive a rich poetic meaning. This meaning eludes the critical vision restricted to or distracted by the familiar aspect of life.[25] The contrast between the finite and the infinite is thus an illusion. The song of innocence reads like an Epic of Innocence. The short-story is a creative integral realization of this compendious complex as a reality evolving in self-negating Time and thus manifesting itself only as an Image of Eternal Innocence. The narrative piece seems to have been composed in an inspired moment of a lyrical vision of this epic Innocence.[26]

Human consciousness as all Innocence is represented in the opening scene by what seems to be an archetypal image of the nameless shephered, "an upright old man" with his sheep. This "grave, fine-looking old man", the first human figure to appear on the scene, prefigures the total human psyche that constitutes the human element in the short-story; the range of human psyche presented within the framework of the narrative piece extends from the pure innocence of the "toothless" baby that cannot even identify or name the soft "pink" 'thing' to the mature wisdom of the grandmother whose accumulated experience has ripened into an attitude of calm acceptance of the last fact about life—"life is like that". The shephered as a mute and anonymous figure and with the archetypal aura about him protypifies the speechless and unnamed baby with his "perfect beam"; as a "grave, fine-looking old man" with his "wet beard" he prefigures the grandmother, "the old woman" who is the oldest of all the characters that people the human world. In between these two extreme limits of human consciousness we have the gradations of individual human psyche: what substantiates the impression of unaccountable mystery about his figure is his itinerant image, his ageless anonymity, his mute wordlessness. This mystery corresponds to the riddle that all human experience as eternal innocence is. His vaguely cast shadow is perhaps the total image of the human psyche that the human world at the bay presents. The shepherd is a human figure in closest approximation to the vastest spatial non-human reality, the sea, which reflects the whole psychic complex as a manifestation of eternal Innocence: he is like the children on the beach, who, temporally, stand in inviolable isolation. We find this poetic image appropriately silhoueted against a "morning" which seems timeless and universal: the "morning", indicated elliptically, is perhaps the image of the day when God saw darkness on the face of the earth and said, let there be light, and there was light; or the image of the human psyche eternally shining in its angel 'infancy'. With his anonymity so universal as to maintain the inviolable isolation of his traditional image as part of timeless nature, with his wordlessness eloquent enough to echo the ringing human voices of souls floating in Time, with his uncertainty as an itinerant figure moving between his unknown home and his unguessable goal, the shepherd lingers in our memory as a hallowed symbol of the total human psyche.

The lowest degree of consciousness is registered by means of the appropriately scanty characterization of the "toothless" baby. His pure sensory awareness is the index of Innocence that all human psyche ultimately is. Linda's developed consciousness is mature enough to explore mysteries of existence; she is adult enough to seek orientation of her individual psyche as an inviolably isolated lonely self. In its moments of intense concentration her consciousness seems to have read the mind of the baby. But Linda's extrasensory vision is interpreted by the omniscient narrator who seems to have been conceived as a character in closest proximity with the ultimate Psyche; the interpretation cannot be dismissed simply as Linda's own. There is some paradoxical co-relation between Innocence as Omnicience and human psyche as all innocence. The answer that Linda hears mentally is just a plain statement of the fact that the ultimate Psyche is not without awareness of all that goes on in human psyche as only incessant interrogation: the answer to Linda's moot question is not a revelation of the secret that the question seeks to probe; it is just an acknowledgement of the question, not a key to the question. Reciprocity between Innocence as omniscience and human psyche as all innocence is obliquely dramatized. The "toothless" baby's vision exemplifying the lowest degree of human psyche comes to take on a symbolical significance. This imaginative exploration of the first category of human consciousness enriches the author's aesthetic vision of the whole psychic complex awe-inspiringly transfixed in Time as eternalized innocence: the 'continual changing of positions',[27] the reciprocal overlapping of features of consciousness, is viewed only as an incessant process of ebb and flow in the ocean of the great Nothingness, Time. The shepherd, the baby, the sea, are significantly mute characters; they keep inaudibly humming an eternal chorus of Innocence.

The next higher degree in the scale of innocence is marked through depiction of Lottie's consciousness. The little toddler is a sweet blossom of humanity, fresh from God's own home: she is a flower with all its sweetest petals still folded, all dewy, printless yet homely. Thus she stands in between the speechless baby with a smile that is a "perfect beam" and her sister Isabel who can even teach her grandmother to suck eggs, so to say, and thus is still only a charmingly innocent child. Lottie is the only human link between the angel that "knows all about that" and the naturally real child whose precociousness as naïve innocence is perhaps all human psyche in its nascent state. She is purity and simplicity and sweetness of innocence incarnate. She is the archangel of the Eden of the Eternal Now.

This delightful impression seeps in gradually: it is sustained by a characterization that illustrates inviolability of an angelic soul isolated from the human world not only psychically but also temporally and spatially.—Psychically, she likes to be "left to go in her own way": she doesn't "follow at all". She is 'a donkey that keeps forgetting it is a donkey'; she is still too innocent to accept the hypothesis or rules in a game ("I don't not want to play") she is blissfully ignorant even of the difference between play and real life; to her they are one and the same. The sense of the inviolable isolation of her individual psyche is maintained through consistent revelation of her real self as a soul much too naked for assumption of "forms" (which the other children "jump off" when they are frightened out of their senses by the face at the window): she does not know what she is to "be" ("what'll I be?'") and waits for the other children" to decide for her"; when she learns what she has to say she asks solemnly, "when do I have to say it?" and later she not only forgets what she is ("I've forgotten what I'm") but also says what is contrary to expectation (she forgets the "much easier" dog's "Bow-wow" and says "Hee-How" at last). Isolated from her own worldly world of make-believe and assumptions, she is, naturally, "a silly". She "makes a floating island", nay, she is one. "she is always making a fuss"; misfit in her world of hypotheses and imagined order, she is still nearer to the world that is beyond all make-believe, all hypotheses, all order. It is this archangel that is the first to observe the foul intrusion of what is "true" and "real" and extraneous to the sacrosanct integrity of the Eden of the Eternal Now: it is she who gives "such a piercing scream that all ... jump off the forms".

Temporally, too, she is "a floating island" in the boundless ocean of the great Nothingness, Time. Her real self is defined by her own utterances: " 'what'll I be?' ... I've forgotten what I'm". She has long since been playing the game of beasts, but she has not has been able to see how one's self during a game is different from the self in life before or after the game. Here is a soul cut loose from the control of terrestrial temporality: her sense of time is sense of timelessness: all chronological order in her individual world is "a fuss". She is nearer to the Beyond where Time is always what it is not, an eternal fuss. She does not see what she will be; she does not know when to say what she has been told to say; she forgets what she is when she has to say what she has been taught to say; and she says at last what she has just been told to say but what none thought she would say. She forgets what she is; she forgets even what she has just been told to be; but she recalls suddenly what she has long since been forgetting again and again. Her simple logic is the logic of the mystic. She can only imagine the eternal simultaneity of all points of time ("But then everybody will see it the same time as me").

Spatially, this "floating island" of a soul exists in or moves through several spatial dimensions. While trying to get over the stile by herself she stands "half in the paddock still and half in the tussock grass"; she looks "down at Kezia as if from a mountain height"; and she finds "there's nothing to sit down". She is, again, one without a sense of spatial direction ("Then you had to put one leg over. But which leg? She never could decide"): she stands transfixed, her gestures implying coincidence or simultaneity of mobility and immobility. As the nearest human self to the transcendental Being, she seems, appropriately, to be isolated from yet ubiquitous in all spatial reality ("as if she expected to be wafted out to sea") or to be withdrawn into inviolable interiority ("she scrambled to her feet with a face of horror and flew up the beach again"). Against the background of the vast measureless expanse of the sea Isabel's "twelve strokes" and Kezia's "eight" seem algebraic rather than arithmetical figures of spatial measurement; Lottie's "own way ... to sit down at the edge of the water ... to make vague motions ... as if she expected to be wafted out to sea" is indicative of the Alpha and Omega of all space as extension or locus of the finite body: she is significantly "a silly", a cipher among figures.

Isabel's precociousness by no means detracts from her naturalness and integrity as a sweet innocent child. She comes next in the ascending order of degrees of consciousness in its prime phase. The image emergent from the dramatized exemplification of this category is that of a character that protypifies the older maturing characters. With her precociousness the character embodies innocence as experience as the older characters represent all experience as all innocence. Her "cock-a-doodle-do" heralds a whole phase of Experience in the human world. But what endears this egg-out-to-teach-the-chicken sort of kid to the critical reader is the verisimilitude of her portrayal—a portrayal that is instinct with a comprehensive poetic truth. She is as sweet as Lottie, no more no less. Both are equally fresh human blossoms of the childrens' Eden of the Eternal Now: Isabel is hand-planted; Lottie is air-sown. Kezia with her kindly innocence, her sense of values, her sedate curiosity, and her imaginative vision is a grandmother in frock. She does seem to be in advance of her age, but her portrayal, too, like Isabel's, delights the reader as a characterization that conforms to life-like realism and evokes an impression of a truer child.

Pip and Rags, the two children from the Trout family, are meant as characters to add a new dimension to the complex of Innocence formed by the Burnell children; their inclusion in the microcosm seems to have been necessitated by the sense of an additional means of apotheosis of the children's world: the apotheosis has been achieved through spatial expansion of their world and simultaneous creation of an effect of homely intimacy with an image of the Infinite. Spatial expansion of the world of the children's game is effected through the evolution of a star image. "The lovely green thing" found on the open beach is "as big as a star"; the "little starfish inside" Rag's hanky as an open secret imparted in a closed room is by no means remotely reminiscent of what it resembles or of where it belongs. The total complex of associations functions as an image in evolution, and the line of demarcation marking spatial contrast between the open space (the beach, the sky with its 'star', or the sea with its "starfish") and the closed room (where the secret folds of the hanky conceal what Rags proposes to "try and tame") is blurred: the innermost recesses of the privacy of the child who proposes to "tame" the starfish cast the magic spell of a more than-natural world. This objectification of a close link between the innermost recesses of privacy with an inviolate secret treasured up in it and the transcendental space with its dimensions covering the home of the star and the world of the starfish, beyond the room, beyond the beach, is a means of revelation: it helps to reveal the secret correspondence between the children's game with its sacrosanct value of 'tensionless order'[28] and the Infinite that is never without order and is itself a timeless tensionless a-moral play.

The effect of this star-in-the-pocket homeliness is naturalized and deepened by the intimate rendering of a moment when a similar treasured secret is shared by only two of the children who are also the only two children that have temperamental affinity with each other. This is a moment when inviolable isolation of an individual innocent self in intimate proximity with an inviolably sacrosanct secret is also preserved. Lottie and Rags are magnetically drawn towards each other _Lottie as the lambkin that is "left behind" waiting for her sisters to help her over the stile or strays out of the herd as "a silly", and Rags as the "sheep" or the little lamb that trots behind and seems to wait to be carried. Their first meeting is as much suggestive of the intrinsic innocence of the one (Lottie) as their last meeting is of that of the other (Rags): the only two identical characters that come to share a strictly between-you-and-me secret stand inviolably isolated by virtue of their extreme innocence and mindless simplicity transparently manifest and their open yet unrevealed secrecy tacitly enjoined. Rags, the "sheep", is a quietly inconspicuous child character. Through his casual appearance only twice even in "stills" exclusively devoted to children this tiny tot is reduced to non-entity. His characterization is composed of bold strokes and the strokes are by no means absent-mindedly dabbed on the canvas. They are telling enough to image froth a sheep of a child that is primordially symbolical like the shepherd. As a sheep of a child the character forms part of an image-complex that leads us back to the point where we have the tangible manifestation of the ultimate psyche as eternal innocence; the sea, which is understandably represented as the abode of innocence (it echoes the bleating of the lamb).

It is in the characterization of the two boys from the Trout family that the creative integral realization of the complex of innocence formed by the Burnell children finds its consummation: the two boys are the human images of the shepherd's sheep-dog, Wag, that rounds up the "flock of sheep" and heads it "for the steeper, narrower rocky pass that led out of crescent Bay and towards Daylight cove". Pip orders the girls about without a police whistle "both on the beach and in the room, and the game has order without tension; Rags forbids

Lottie to undo the knotted hanky and the secret he simultaneously reveals and likes to remain concealed is an open secret which is obviously tensionless. This tensionless order or open secret corresponds to the tensionless order or open secret that the Infinite is as an a-moral play. There is correspondence between the revelation of a secret open to "All" on the beach and then open to only two, and the revelation of the great secret that "life is life that". This correspondence between the children's world and the Infinite is established through the characterization of the two boys. Their characterization is a means of expansion of the world of the children into a timeless and spaceless Eden of Innocence; it is at the same time a means of concentration of innocent vision on the image of the infinite, which is revealed later in the innermost recesses of a child's privacy as a specimen of contrariety; simultaneous vision of something "as big as a star" is later a concentrated view of something that is neither a star nor a fish and still is both rolled into one. This simultaneous process of expansion and concentration that the characterization of the two children involves helps to bring the world of the children into close proximity or intimate communion with the image of the Infinite. Apothesis of the world necessitates this evolution of the image-complex of a child walking the earth with a star in his pocket: Pip and Rags metaphorically head the "flock of sheep" for a "steeper, narrower rocky pass"—out of the bay, "towards Daylight cove"; the "narrower"pass with its denotation of gradual concentration and the "cove" with its suggestion of an enclosure help to define the nature of the process of revelation Pip and Rags are meant to make. The two boys round up the whole flock and the bleatings are answered by ghostly flocks and herds from under the sea whose ebb and flow is a timeless song of innocence.

Experience as a complex in its totality stands contrasted against the complex of Innocence. We find their dimensions enriched by a variety that corresponds to the concept of contrariety, not simply to that of oddity of human nature:[29] all oddity here is but a manifestation of Contrariety as Beauty of the Infinite. Thus the complex of Experience functions within the range of the concept of disorder with or without tension: the choice of the range of disorder as a concept is determined by the very nature of what Experience as contrasted against Innocence is. Recourse to concomitant exploration of the concept of disorder is necessitated by the inherence of contrariety in the complex of Experience; it is required also by the sense of Beauty inherent in contrariety in the total complex of human psyche—the great beauty of Innocence embracing all Experience.

To say that order and disorder is the major theme of the short-story[30] is to put the cart before the horse: 'order' and 'disorder' are concepts explored as the expedient means of dramatizing in true perspective the two broad aspects of human psche, Innocence and Experience: they are the means of objectifying the beauty of diversity discovered as the whole truth about Life: the concepts do not constitute the theme itself because then they do not seem to encompass the third complex manifest as non-human phenomena. This third complex by virtue of its comparatively closer proximity with the Deaf and Dumb Infinite is too subtle a gradation of Life to reveal its lines of demarcation between order and disorder. This complex is a whole with not only the sea as both a reflection and an echo but also a drop of the sea suspended from the tip of a leaf since a point of time lost in the dark of the midnight. The omniscient narrator's supramundane vision does not miss the dark secrets beyond the approach of human psyche. The forces of order and disorder are of course incessantly active in obscure regions but as concepts for the total complex of psyche they seem to have been explored in true perspective, that is, up to the point of communicability of the shade of distinction.

Exploration of the concept of disorder, to revert to our point, helps to set off the beauty of integrity that characterizes the Eden of the Eternal Now. On the structural level of the composition the complex of Experience seems to overwhelm its counterpart within the framework. But even with its enlarged proportion it seems to be subordinated to the minor complex of Innocence. The concept of disorder within which the complex of Experience functions shades off into its counterpart, the order concept, as a point where "all" is "still", thereby revealing the whole process of contrariety as Beauty of Eternal Innocence. The concept of disorder is, however, comprehensive enough to encompass the whole communicable process of contrariety: the complex of Experience functioning within this concept is naturally without a central point positive enough to facilitate orientation of each character in the adult world; but it is not without its outermost fringe: with its function as an overlapping extreme the fringe does represent a positive limit of the complex. The inner structural composition of the complex presents a paradox; the encircling fringe is there, but the central point is nowhere: characters in the adult world are all isolated "floating" selves moving from nowhere to nowhere: even the character defining the outermost fringe, through her calm resignation and cool acceptance of life as it is, seems to be nowhere since her statement, "Life is like that", is intrinsically a rhetorical question (why is it all as it is?), it is a question eternally barren of a positive answer: what distinguishes this oldest character in the adult world is her perceptible proximity with Innocence: the grandmother looping and weaving the thread is knitting all experience, so to say, into wisdom, all questions into an answer, all diversity into unity; she drops the knitting, she swings back in the rocker to tickle Kezia and be tickled by her; she becomes a child, tickling and laughing and then forgetting all, all experience. This moment of oblivion as the moment of close proximity with Innocence is the temporal point where Experience and Innocence shade off into "each other".

All disorder as the perplexing truth about the world of experience is set off against order as the comprehensive name for the integrity, naturalness, and synthesis that characterize the world of innocence. The final emergence of innocence as the sole dominant complex encompassing all psyche exemplifies the positive consummation of all disorder in order.

It is, perhaps, in this sense that 'a haunting light' is thrown on the 'Kingdom of childhood' from different quarters at once. But there is one fact that merits reconsideration. The number of 'quarters' from which 'a haunting light' is thrown on the kingdom is not so restricted as to be only 'three'. A whole complex of Experience with its varied and shadowy images of individual psyche is there to cast its own 'haunting light on the kingdom' and in the process reveal itself as part of the total psyche that is an eternal all-inclusive kingdom of Innocence: what the 'haunting light' comes to reveal is a 'kingdom' that embraces all life. The revelation is reciprocal, and this reciprocity of revelation of Experience as Innocence and innocence itself as all Experience is by no means at variance with the obvious implication of unilateral projection of the 'light'. The kingdom illumined by the 'haunting light' eclipses or subordinates all that is a means of revealing it, for it is the concept of Innocence embodied as the 'Kingdom of Childhood' that constitutes what is central to the total philosophical context. The whole world of experience is eternally subordinated to the one and only one kingdom, the kingdom of Eden.

Mrs. Kember representing an extreme degree of adult experience is the absolute antithesis of the Lamb in the Eden of the Eternal Now: our mystified impression of this 'creature' impels us to voice the mystic question: "Did he who made the Lamb make thee?' Isolated as she stands in her own world, Mrs. Kember is "a horrible caricature" of individual psyche: hers is a monstrously worldly self, paradoxically cut loose from the immediate world which environs her. She stands segregated even in her own house: ("she didn't care two pence about her house": and "would call in her indifferent, tired voice, 'you might heave me a handkerchief if I've got one'.) She is a wife estranged from her husband: ("he ignored his wife just as she ignored him"; and the husband is "at least ten years younger than she".) As a social being, too, she seems tobe alienated from the society at the Bay: her dress, her mannerisms, her social behaviour are all incongruous with the social manners of the colony: they all give bad name to her. She is, naturally, the choice morsel of juicy gossip. She is dissociated from the world of Nature despite all her genuine and characteristic impulse to expose her whole self to the warm, throbbing body of Nature. Her characterization is appropriately restricted to the limited frame of a single 'still': this highlights the one attribute of the character: her monstrously and outlandishly egotistical nature: she is the snail under the leaf in our author's universe;[31] a self isolated from her environs, with a philosophy of life perversely rationalized and impulsively practiced for sheer fleshly sensual thrill. Mrs. Kember is a freak of psyche, and as such represents a monstrous existence that is an incongruity in the world of Life. Evolution of the animal imagery[32] resorted to in the composition of her picture finds its consummation in the savagely outrageous utterance she is made to voice: "'I will not eat you'" and the absolute antithesis of the Lamb (Rags or Lottie) is revealed. With her open privacy bordering on lack of a sense of shame or remorse or on cynical rationalization of a "fast" life as a natural life, Mrs. Kember is poles apart from the children with their open secret which expands their world into an Eden on earth. She is outlandishly alien to her own world of adult people: to some of these adults an obscure secret is open as a profound revelation. She is an inscrutable mystery desecrated through self-exposure. She is an evil force unleashed in the world of disillusioned characters seeking escape or resigned to a life of calm acceptance or still eager enough to explore experience. She has her counterpart in Mrs. Stubbs, a character that stands at the furthest distance from all the other adult characters. Both are smitten with the sterile curse of childlessness, the curse that bodes ill for any world of Life. She has a lean and hungry look; she thinks too much; such women are dangerous. She is a great observer: she looks quite through the deeds and words of others; she loves no plays as Jonathan does. She is an unsexed woman: she is not what she is. She stands sharply contrasted against Beryl, the lone figure of innocence in the adults' world of Experience, the only explorer of the dark realm of the possible. She is the embodiment of Experience that corrupts innocence. She is a Tiger in the world of the Lamb.

Mrs. Stubbs's characterization as part of the complex of Experience is specific as an appropriate rendering of a quaint manifestation of the spirit of disorder. The quaintness of the manifestation consists in the comicality that results from tensionlessness in disorder. This comicality, set off by the conceivably implicit dramatic irony of utter ignorance of tensionlessness, is perceptible on two levels; on the physical level, the topsy-turvydom that characterizes Mrs. Stubbs's world as a world natural to her is a perennial source of pure humour; on the psychic level, the absurdity of a philosophy of life practised as "glad widowhood" and accepted as the best philosophy is intrinsically comical but not divorced from its own moral considerations: on either level, the perceptible manifestation of disorder is characterized by tensionlessness. Of the facts that the order taken for granted is but an illusion of order and that this disorder is tensionless, the comic character is utterly ignorant. The dimension of comicality is enlarged by this dramatic irony. Comicality on this physical level is inherent in the absurdity of the setting in general and of a situation or two in particular. The very shop, identified as a human head and distinguished as Mr. Stubbs's is an image of disorder. We can trace the evolution of this image complex: the "long string of bathing dresses" and the "extraordinarily mixed ... sand-shoes" as the ghostly tokens of their wearers are all mixed up; the windows are arranged as "precarious pyramids" and are thus faintly suggestive of fantastic topsy-turvydom, spatial (colossal monuments insecurely perched) as well as temporal (anachronism inconceivably grotesque); the "notice" for HANSOME GOLE BROOCH ... ON OR NEAR BEACH", which has been there "from time immemorial", has its suggestion of mock-eternity reinforcing the previous one of spatial or temporal anomaly; it has also its apparent oddity of malspiced orthographical composition that betrays Mrs. Stubbs's tensionless lapses into gross misspelling. Besides, Mrs. Stubbs's own photograph embodies the oddity of a spatial and temporal overlapping ("miraculously skirting the carpet-border, there was a dashing waterfall"; "on her right stood a Grecian pillar," etc.). Her Primus stove, which she pumps up as tensionlessly as she pumps up her philosophy of "glad widowhood" and "freedom" images forth an intrinsic feature of disorder—absurdly abrupt transition: Alice's expression of her feeling of beauty, "sweetly pretty", is cut in sharply contrary half when the "roaring Primus Stove" 'fizzles out': this awkwardly abrupt transition from the shouting above roaring to the frightening silence oddly resonant with the hollow ring of "pretty" dramatizes a situation simultaneously ridiculous and frightening. Comicality inherent in the fantastic oddity in the setting and the situation arouses risibility. But even on this plainest level of the narrative, humour seems to have been toned down: the commonplace enunciated with an air of profundity subtilizes the humour. Comicality on the psychic level is perceptible in the philosophy of life that Mrs. Stubbs reposes in. Inherence of comicality in her rationalization of what is inconsistent with not only 'good sense' but also the greater values of consummate womanhood stimulates a consideration that is essentially moral. But the kindly contemplation of incongruity on the level of values and the artistic expression thereof enrich the critical experience of moral consideration. Mrs. Stubbs's choice of a life of "glad widowhood" is rendered more vicious by the conceivably concomitant attitude of a complacence in a life of childlessness. This inference is substantiated by Mrs. Stubbs's utter unawareness of a world that is an Eden on earth; it is justified also by the successfully communicated essential signification of her individual 'shibboleth", "freedom". Mrs. Stubbs's individual concept of freedom naturally involves a sense of relief for good from the botheration of child-bearing: communication of this concept is effected obliquely through complete silence about this particular aspect of her womanhood even as "glad widowhood". Mrs. Kember, the only identical character with a quaint concept of freedom, is called "childless"; her estrangement from her husband and the lesbian passion she secretly exhibits[33] point to the impossibility of consummation of her womanhood in this respect in the natural order of things. Utter silence about this aspect of womanhood in her characterization, too, forms a tenuous parallelism within the contextual range covered by the complex of Experience. The parallelism helps to intensify the sense of a 'sterile curse' that is complementary to the concept of evil the two identical characters are meant to represent in the world of Experience. The curse is, appropriately, unobjectified.

The odyssey of the innocent self adventuring on the heavy sea of Experience is in itself an epic tale of moral difficulty in steering clear of the Scylla of Mrs. Kember's shocking hedonism and the Charybdis of Mrs. Stubbs's sinister cynicism, both equally minatory evil forces of disorder, the one with tension, the other tensionless. In the world of Experience they are foils of all psychic orientation.

Mrs. Stubbs without her husband and without any 'child' in her life stands as "a horrible caricature" of Linda who is not without her husband and children and is still almost a grass widow and an insouciant mother: the 'glad widow' is a "horrible caricature" of a tragic isotate who is essentially human with her consciousness characterized by the spirit of inquiry. Comicality as horror or horror as comicality is the height of disorder without tension as in Mrs. Stubbs's case or of disorder with tension as in Mrs. Kember's. Both these characters are portrayed as 'horrible caricatures' of human psyche.

Jonathan, the only tragic character in the world of Experience, is portrayed in one 'still' with Stanley and in another with Linda. His total portraiture reflects the image of an innocent self caught in the vicious coils of a rigid order. His portrayal appropriately juxtaposed in a 'still' with Stanley's dramatizes the stasis that is the whole truth about his tragic self. The tragic character is in anguish of stasis as she stands transfixed—between rigid routine order assumed by Stanley and the spontaneous ebb and flow natural to the sea, between order with tension, and disorder-as-order without tension, between an iota of human consciousness interiorized by immediate interests of life in the bustling present and a vast abundance of timelessly undulating ebb and flow reflecting all psyche as eternal Innocence. This tragic self of the character is revealed later in another equally appropriate juxtaposition of his portrayal with that of Linda's, the tragic isotate with the sharp edge of her suffering smoothed by her philosophy of 'acceptance'. The full import of the functional role of this character filters in through the total design of his characterization sketched on two levels, the one consistently symbolical, the other elaborately explicit: his eagerly inquisitive human consciousness is exposed to manifestations of psyche egocentrically insensitive or unfathomably mysterious on the first level and compassionately sympathetic yet perplexingly disappointing on the other. The stasis is doomed to cheerless gloom. It is this perplexed, agonized, disintegrated self that desecrates the Eden with all its beauty of order without tension. Lottie's blissful 'stasis' characterized by simultaneity of psychic expansion ("wafted out to the sea") and interiorization ("up the beach again") has its "horrible caricature" in Jonathan's tragic stasis. Kezia chooses "to be" what Jonathan in his anguish longs to cease to be; but as a "bee" Kezia gives "a shudder" when the face of this "somebody" is seen pressed against the window. Stasis of confinement is blissful in the Eden inside the room. But it is tragic in the wordly world of the poor uncle; the "bee" in the room has been blissfully ignorant of its confinement since it assumed the "form"; it is only at the moment of what seems to be premonition of some dreaded intrusion that sudden realization dawns on the "bee". The "bee" of the Eden cannot see the justifiability of slamming a door on the "garden undiscovered, unexplored" . The "bee" beating its wings in the void of Experience is all the time looking for an exit to "escape" through the adventure here is possible only after the "escape"; the adventure as a venture into the interior of the "undiscovered, unexplored" colourful possibilities (a garden), a venture inspired by undying curiosity characteristic of intense will to seek psychic orientation, has not yet begun. Kezia is an adventurer; Jonathan is a dreamer of adventure. Jonathan's characterization forms part of Kezia's. We can see that it is for this dear "uncle Jonathan" that the door opens; it is the inquisitive child in him that unobtrusively mingles with the tumbling crowd on its way "back home". The "pale face" with its "black eyes" and "black beard" is for the children "true" and "real" and not "just for the game", but it is only "a horrible caricature" of his real self restlessly moving about as an inquisitive child in the universe of Experience. Pressed against the window, the "pale face", the "black eyes" and the "black beard, only reflect a psyche tortured and twisted by impotent agony: they are indexes of all the tragic features of his psyche—the stoic attitude of self-dramatization which he has candidly assumed with an unabashed theatricality about it; the "dramatic intensity" that "makes the meanest hymn put on an unholy splendour"; his impatience for an answer to "the maddening mysterious question"; his poignant awareness of lack of "stamina" and "a guiding principle"; his painfully interiorized consciousness of furniture and stationery within the confines of his office as things more real than the scene and the setting. Naturally there is "a look like hunger in his black eyes".

Stanley's characterization. is a means of dramatizing a significant feature of the world of Experience— elemental egoism that is an oddly outlandish evil in a living microcosm compounded of overlapping features of consciousness. This evil force of the character's interiority complex is fittingly operative within the concept of a wrong kind of order with tension. Structural juxtaposition of his portrayal with that of Jonathan against the setting of the sea compounds a suggestive scene. This scene is transparently symbolic of incapacity on the part of their individual selves for psychic orientation: interiorization of consciousness results in isolation of psychic entity. Stanley's later portrait as a member of his family or as Linda's husband sustains the import which this symbolically designed initial portrayal succinctly conveys. The meaning of this individual characterization evolving within the preconceived concept of wrong kind of order in tension is fully realized in its contrast with the characterization of some of the angels of the Eden—the characterizations which evolve through the concept of right kind of order without tension. The three vignettes composed for the individual characterization of Stanley stand sharply contrasted against almost identical 'episodes' interposed for glimpses of the Eden. A rough sketch of the whole process of this complex of characterizations marked by contrast is conveniently traceable. Stanley strikes out to see and as quickly swims in again, and as he 'rushes up the beach', he feels "cheated"; Lottie who also likes "to be left to go in her own way" sits down "at the edge of the water to make vague motions as if she expected to be wafted out to sea"; when "a bigger wave than usual, an old whiskery one" comes lolloping along she flies "up the beach again". The situations are almost identical; Stanley's interiorization is symbolized by his gesture; Lottie's retreat into inviolably sacrosanct interiority of her innocent self is enacted by her recoil from the "old whiskery one". The second vignette dramatizing Stanley's single-day pre-office hours in the family reveals his habitual insistence on observance of the rigidity of a code to which he has subjected his entire family: Pip ordering the "beasts" about in the room or telling all on the beach to "look the same way" commands them only with his hypotheses for the game. The control exercised by the rule-and-measure mathematical Stanley is an attribute of the character conceived as a manifestation of the concept of wrong kind of order. His control wrecks the family; Pip's command integrates his world and helps to elevate it to the glory of proximity with the Infinite. The third vignette that juxtaposes the character with his life-long partner, Linda, first creates an impression of a change of heart in him but concludes with a speech or two both articulate and inarticulate: the inarticulate though "true" remains unspoken "for some reason": while the articulate with its ironical suggestion of interiorization ("'Lets' go in'") is casually substituted for it. Kezia and grandmother during their mid-day hour of the fundamental question and answer seem to be psychically engrossed in one common topic, death in life, but they laugh it all away with a 'Never'—a 'Never' that is the name for all oblivion, a 'Never' that is the whole truth about "all" that eternally stands "still". Functioning within its own concept of order of a wrong kind, Stanley's characterization in this last vignette, naturally, registers 'tension'. Stanley's feelings and thoughts are introverted; he 'goes in' at the last moment even after all that forgiving gesture. We see how evil lurks in 'intimacy which divides.'[34] Kezia and grandmother's union, a significant narrative element operative within its appropriate concept, right order without tension, exemplifies remoteness that unites. Union is an ultimate value: it suggests ultimate order without tension. Stanley resents the "maddening intrusion" of the dreamer wasting his soul in romantic agony; the children in the room loathe the "pale face, black eyes, black beard pressed against the window" unanimously identifying it as the image of "somebody" oddly outlandish. Stanley hopes to have the whole of the place so vast as the sea solely for himself: even if he were willing to submit to the ebb and flow of the sea, he would have liked to be left all by himself. Resigned to such self-centred isolation, Stanley resents all denial of his privacy., His egotism is grotesquely monstrous in the human microcosm that comes into being only through reciprocal psychic orientation.[35]

The third complex, the complex of lower existential categories, seems to be in immediate proximity with what represents the ultimate psyche. The creative vision of the omniscient narrator rolling from earth to heaven and from heaven to earth discovers in depths of this complex the inarticulate mute self-expression of the ultimate psyche. There is an image that seems central to the whole complex of the flora and fauna 'At the Bay'; "The manuka tree, bent by the southerly wind, was like a bird on one leg stretching out a wing". The image evoked is that of a bird preening its wings for a skyward flight; the implication of the image involves the sense of fusion of psychic features, of conflation of existential categories. The image is suggestive of the infusion of the spirit of freedom in the tree itself in which the free bird sits: it alludes to the spirit of freedom poised for orientation to the extra-terrestrial and horizonless space. This eternal spirit of freedom which the tree rooted to the earth embodies is an aspect of Life that evolves as the tangible manifestation of the infinite; it is an essential feature of innocence that is tensionless, calm and inviolable. The image is also expressive of the oneness of the two distinct categories of flora and fauna "At the Bay". The total image complex is a fused whole. This fusion of existential categories exemplifies the ceaseless process of overlapping psychic features. The process reveals itself only to a supramundane creative vision.

The specific concept within which this third complex functions or evolves is the concept of order of a right kind, that is, order without tension. It is a concept built up for the adequate expression of the sense of all contrariety as far-linked harmony manifest as fusion of psychic features and existential categories. It is perhaps this concept that necessitates 'use of liquid lapsing movement with presentation of exact actuality'.[36] This third complex ranges from the life of lower animals to the life-spirit evolving in the world of objects concealed in obscurity: the objects are imperceptible even to the omniscient narrator with all his supramundane perceptive vision which keeps rolling from earth to heaven and back. It is by virtue of its operation within this concept of right-order-minus-all-tension as 'the ideal natural order'[37] that this category of zoological existence helps to facilitate 'a return of the mind to tranquillity'[38]: it shows how there is 'responsible order among the feckless'[39], it reveals the spirit of freedom with which it is poised for oneness with the Infinite Life. Lottie's re-appearance is of course meant "to recall the images and feeling of the opening, to effect a return of the mind to that tranquility". But this is doubtful in the context of what seems to be only a temporarily peaceful resolution of the conjugal conflict between Stanley and Linda: theirs is "an intimacy which divides"; their reconciliation is not without 'tension' which still persists. Tensionlessness is the functional element of contrast. It characterizes the concept of order or disorder within which this whole complex of non-human categories evolves. Thus it is a means of intensifying the parallel functional element of tension: this zoological world like the room of the "bee" and the "donkey" and the "rooster" is a realm of Innocence: it is meant to illumine and also be illumined by the world of Experience. Integrity in the non-human world as manifest in suffusion of the physical form with the spirit of the ultimate Psyche or in the palpable self-expression of the Psyche itself is a value the world of Experience is denied. Integrity is the ultimate order or harmony without tension.

The whole zoological complex is a coherent whole. The principle of 'responsible order among the feckless' is the principle of 'a natural ideal order'; it is quite consistent with the ultimate order which is without tension; the ideal order is natural; the attribute of integrity is central to the concept of Innocence. The dog controlling the herd symbolizes this principle of natural order as the integrity of all 'responsible order among the feckless, of natural order as the manifestation of the ultimate self-ordering Being. Wag is the Pip on the same sea beach of the Eden, nearer to the Paradise of the Eternal Now. Both seem to exist in the blissful isolation from all temporality. Portrayal of Wag furnishes a deeper dimension of the concept of innocence. The spirit of freedom poised for oneness with the infinite Life is symbolized first by the goldfinch that "flew over the shepherd's head and, perching on the tiptop of a spray, ... turned to the sun ruffling its small breast feathers"; it is symbolized later by "the manuka tree" which "bent by the southerly winds, was like a bird on one leg stretching out a wing". Evolution of the symbol seems to have been meant to represent the process of gradual fusion of existential categories. The first stage of the evolution is characterized by a poise for freedom through intimacy with the source of all worldly life: the bird that has turned off to the sun is nearer to the palpable heart-throb of Nature than Mrs. Kember; in this sense it stands in contrast to the other characters too that are only groping in the dark even when the sun is full on them. The second then emerges as the culmination of the whole process: there is suffusion of the form with the spirit or the form itself is the spirit embodied. Integrity of form as all spirit or of spirit itself as the form is, again, the essential characteristic of the non-human existential category; it is the fundamental attribute of eternal innocence. The spirit of freedom embodied as the goldfinch at sunrise seems to be poised for escape to the eternal realm of Life through exposure to the source of all Life; as the manuka tree at the sunless hour of midnight, the spirit is eager to be one with the Life-spirit beyond. Evolution of the symbol is antithetically parallel to the evolution of the image-complex of the bee that we find in the human characterization of a soul beating his wings in the void in vain. The bee of the Eden (Kezia) humming a honeyed song of innocence in blissful unawareness of any confinement is nearer to or has affinity with the goldfinch or the manuka tree. What symbolizes the spirit of freedom is a means of discovery of the ultimate issue, Innocence.

Miss Mansfield's creative integral realization of the profound sense of far-linked harmony discovered in all this contrariety seems to have found its consummation in her assimilation of the compositional elements too.

There is a poignant contrast between the ceaseless evolution of Life as an a-moral force and the development of human consciousness with its irresistible spirit of inquiry and final desperate resignation to a life of acceptance. Interminability of Life's flow is suggested by the drama of "something happening" constantly in unobserved privacy of physical phenomena: the sense of ceaselessness of the flux is communicated also through a design suggestive of timeless recurrence of a diurnal pattern. Insouciance on the part of this timelessly operative life-force in the non-human physical world intensifies the agony of all barren interrogation and desperate resignation in the human world.

But the two interminable processes are, simultaneously, reciprocal. This reciprocity reveals a profoundly a-moral truth: the moment of gaiety in the human world corresponds to the timelessness of gaiety that reigns supreme as eternal innocence in the world of the flora and fauna. The free flow of feeling in the natural order without tension is timelessly concurrent with the flux of life evolving in similar tensionless order. Dramatization of the free flow of feeling is therefore unobtrusively subsequent to a quiet liquid rendering of the incessantly operative force in the non-human world of physical forms: "now a stone on the bottom moved, rocked.... And now there sounded the fainted 'plop'. Who made that sound?... And how strong, how damp the sea-weed smelt in the hot sun...."

The ceaseless flux in the realm of flora and fauna "at the bay" is exposed in all its naturalness to the comprehensive creative vision of the omniscient narrator. The exposure involves revelation of "a watching, listening" human presence. This presence is not only a ubiquitous being gratuitously presiding over all physical phenomena hidden or isolated from the human world. It is also the deathless soul of the omniscient narrator timelessly "watching and listening" to and for "something" even in the obscurest nook of Nature. A 'human presence' is always there to stand proxy to the narrator. Beauty of contrariety, of natural order, of "something happening" in obscurity never goes unnoticed: it has its consummation, so to say, in the "watching and listening" of a timeless poet to whom Nature whispers in her hours of undisturbed privacy—in her sequestered world conjured up by the shrill of insects shrieking out their sex life.

Physical forms of life impinge upon the creative consciousness of the narrator also as expressive symbols of the human characters.[40] Neither human psyche nor physical matter possesses the attribute of the profoundly secret realization: the human psyche does not know it is being symbolized by the physical forms; the physical forms cannot realize that they symbolize human psyche. Still the process of what fuses the two into one specific whole goes on. This symbolization evinces consummation of a secret process—the mysterious passage between fine gradations of existence.

Exquisite refinement of Miss Mansfield's sensibility is exemplified by the way the content is achieved in her next short-story, *Doll's House:* the omniscient narrator's point of view has been conceived as a means of preserving the inviolability of the sacrosanct truth that shines as the Light of Innocence. The light that is timelessly nascent in obscurity is correlated to the creative light within: the creative light is perhaps the artist's dawning realization that Truth with the beauty of its inviolable Innocence calls for a vision distancing it as a loftier Reality. While identifying her own emniscient author's point of view with the fictional eye drinking in, from a discreet distance, the sublime poetic beauty of "the little lamp", Miss Mansfield seems to have tasted enlightenment at once aesthetic and spiritual.

The short-story presents a truth-vision: the pure being of the child dwells in the realm of light, a realm where no 'Line is drawn' anywhere; the child is on the side of the angels; the realm is inviolably sacrosanct. Intense actuality of this pure being of the child is manifest in 'the rapt intensity' of his 'self-forgetting attitude'[41] to the toy as his personal reality.

Of all the children in this world on the page, the two are the most innocent: the one is Kezia, the youngest child of the Burnells, the other is Else, Kezia's alter ego in the Kelvey family. Both the children belong to the realm of light. The thing that gives rise to their individual attitudes is the same. Their attitudes to this thing are also identical: both are in a 'trance of contemplation'[42] before the toy lamp; to both of them this thing is "the best thing" in the doll's house; they are both enamoured of this one thing. When Kezia saw the toy house for the first time, what she "liked more than anything, what she liked frightfully, was the lamp". She has been in a trance since she saw it. There are only a few occasions when this character is conspicuous in the emotional design of the narrative, and on each occasion she seems consciously or subconsciously aware of this one image: it stands out in her memory of the toy house. Else does not know this. She has heard Kezia's talk about the lamp as the best thing in the toy house; but she does not know Kezia has taken it to her heart. She herself gets too little time to see the whole of the doll's house. Kezia too while showing the inside of the toy house to her does not begin with the lamp ("'There's the drawing-room and the dining-room, and that's the—'"): it is only after she has conveyed an over-all impression ("'the drawing-room and the dining room'") that she comes to the point of drawing Our Else's attention to "the best thing" she herself has privately discovered in the toy house; although her account is breathlessly concise and we can see that she is feverishly eager to speak of 'what she has liked frightfully', the revelation is delayed. But the very next moment when she is about to speak of "the best thing", there is a sudden splintering interruption and the name of "the best thing" remains untold. Else runs away without stopping to ask Kezia which thing she meant to show next: she remains ignorant of Kezia's next word. But what she too has "liked more than any thing" inside the toy house despite a momentary glimpse of the world there, is the same "little lamp"; she speaks of it with "a rare smile": the only image that lingers in her memory is that of the lamp. When she says she has "seen the little lamp" she does not simply mean she has seen what she once heard Kezia pointing out as "the best thing" in the toy house; when she recalls the image she is glowing with "a rare smile". The lamp is as much her own discovery as "the best thing" in the toy house as it is Kezia's. For both of them "the little lamp" is the most delightful thing there: it 'sums up all the perfections'[43] of the doll's house; it is a thing of beauty, a thing of beauty that is a joy for ever. Kezia's vision of this beauty is just Our Else's vision writ large. Else seems to have had an integral realization in a flash, deep deep in her innocent soul: she has been thrilled to the depths of her being and her experience is skin to Kezia's. Significantly her experience of the beauty of the image as a private reality remains concealed in the hallowed obscurity of 'the lonely reaches of the inarticulate':[44] Kezia's vision of this thing of beauty is analytical, discriminating comprehensive; Our Else's is synthetic, concentrated, integral. This difference in degree of the 'rapt intensity of their self-forgetting attitude' to the toy lamp is due to gradation of their individual consciousness as paragons of innocence. But we can see how Kezia's trance grows in intensity till it becomes a 'trance of contemplation' which Else shares just before Mrs. Beryl's shattering interruption: Kezia's first vision of this thing of beauty is full, comparative, deep-seeing; next time when she puts her elder sister in mind of "the best thing" she speaks only a few words about it and remains silent: nobody seems to have paid heed to them; lastly she is about to direct Our Else's attention to it when Mrs. Beryl's sharply forbidding voice splits her speech and the name of this thing of beauty remains unrevealed. The process seems to register her deepening trance. Our Else's blissful recollection shows she has had an instantaneous integral vision of beauty inherent in the image. What Kezia 'liked frightfully' had its beauty in its potentiality as a light for the world in the house. It was this nascency of light in "the little lamp" that the youngest Burnell child instinctively responded to. Her response involved unconscious awareness of a feeling of some secret affinity with the tiny lamp of nascent light.

What in the language outside the world of the child is only unpoetically describable as an exquisite handiwork on a miniature scale is to the child a reality of its own world: with its 'diminished size'[45] the child's toy is 'a model of the way it would like existence to be':[46] the child is lost in this more real world of its private reality; it escapes limitations of human-size scale; it becomes the pure being that it is. This becoming is liberating: it begins to exist truly becauses it is free to be itself in the more real atmosphere of its private reality.

With this primary conditon of real existence in the more real world fulfilled, the innocent self of the child Kezia instinctively yet unconsciously responds to what as nascency of light is secretly correlated to the purity of her being as a perfectly innocent child ("The lamp was perfect"). With its timelessly nascent light the lamp 'lives eternally': it lives in the realm of the possible; its existence is defined by its creative freedom in which it keeps becoming what it potentially is. It stands out of the crowd of things inside the toy house: it is the only "perfect thing in the doll's house; it is "the best thing" there. Nascency of light corresponds to nascancy of consciousness that is perfect innocence. "The father and mother dolls and their two little children were really too big for the doll's house. They didn't look as though they really belonged". naturally, parents are oddly outlandish in the world of children. With their 'souls drunk with too much stay', with their mature consciousness and consequential loss of innocence, they are incongruous in the world of innocence. "The two little children asleep upstairs" are unaware of the light that is the soul of the doll's house: they are very much like the children who are allowed two at a time to peep into the world inside the toy house: not one pair is like the conspicuous set of two on the side of the angels, Kezia and Our Else, or Lil and Our Else; none of the pairs, individually or even mutually, has experienced the thrill of discovering what images forth perfect innocence as a nascent consciousness, the beauty of childhood; none else has "seen the little lamp" which corresponds to the real selfhood of a child; none inside "the ring" has talked about the tiny lamp; none has paid heed to the talk about it. The pair inside the toy house has its counterpart in the pair inside "the ring"; both pairs are "asleep".

What seems to be telepathic communication between the two children who have "seen the little lamp" is part of a triangular process of secret transmission of light that is nascent: the light passes from the smiling lamp to Kezia and then from Kezia to Our Else: the lamp smiling as a nascent light glows finally as Our Else's "rare smile". The smile of the nascent light points to becoming of the lamp in the realm of the possible: this becoming is manifest in a meaning that the lamp takes on for Kezia: it evokes the sense of creative freedom in the realm of the possible, or real existence ("I live here". The lamp was real"). The "rare smile" of the child with her nascent consciousness or perfect innocence is an index of intense actuality of her pure being in her own realm of creative freedom: the realm is that of personal reality in which the child really lives as she experiences in creative freedom the ecstasy of imaginative fulfilment; this actualization of being is perceptible in the 'rapt intensity of her self-forgetting attitude'; to the toy. The lamp 'becomes' "real". The child is back to her own realm. The moment the short-story captures is a moment when both "live" in the world where they belong. The light is perhaps 'the true light which lighteth every man that cometh into the world. All the three—Kezia, Our Else, and the lamp shine in 'Angel-infancy' in an Eden of Innocence.

Just before Our Else is seen 'nudging up close to her sister', these two Kelvey sisters have been found "dreamily" looking "over the hay paddocks, past the creek, to the group of wattles where Logan's cows stood waiting to be miked". The rapt intensity of their self-forgetting attitude to what they have just felt to be a thing of beauty as a joy for ever naturally makes their eyes only roll over the objective phenomena: their "dreamy look is almost an unseeing look": it's a far-away look. Even natural lines of demarcation between one natural phenomenon and another are all blurred because of the dreaminess of the look at this moment of 'rapt intensity'; the continuous vision seems to be a whole vision of a microcosm in which man, Nature and animals are all of a piece: it is a vision which reveals itself only to the innermost, angelic soul of a perfectly innocent child. The impression is reinforced by the effect of purity of Our Else's vision: she has 'forgotten the cross lady' she does not recollect the image of the lamp covetously (She does not covet her neighbour's wealth); the wandering look of the children is naturally directed to what as a nascent phenomenon in the objective world ("cows stood waiting to be milked") corresponds to their own being in a realm of the possible, the realm in which 'life' shines in its Angel Infancy; the narrator, too, finds the entire inside of the toy house revealed to him in a flash; from a high vantage point overlooking all the 'rooms'; the narrator naturally looks through the eyes of the angel, hovering above the Eden and beholds all the rooms simultaneously: "The whole house front swung back, and there you were, gazing at one and the same moment into the drawing-room and the dining-room, the kitchen and two bedrooms." Freed from limitations that are real to the groundlings, the mystic experiences all in a flash. The soul of the child is that of a mystic: it is the soul of one who has escaped all limitations of human-size scale. "That is the way for a house to open: why don't all houses open like that?... perhaps it is the way God opens houses at the dead of night when he is taking a quiet turn with an angel...." We can see where the child's logic belongs.

There is no line drawn between the Kelveys themselves in spite of difference in degree of their innocent consciousness. Lil, the elder, seems of course, a shade mellower than Else: with her unquestioning acceptance of "her subordinate station"; and the consequential proneness to resign to humiliating shame, she seems to have cut her eys-teeth; Else has acquired no attitude at all: she does not even know what it feels like to blush. She can only 'stop chewing and look'. She does not know what's what. She is helplessly innocent. Lil 'burns with shame': Else is simply "dazed". Lil is fearfully and doubtfully hesitant; Else is openly inquisitive. Lil 'breathes loudly'; Else is "still as stone". Lil can give "a silly shame-faced smile" Else can only stare. Lil shakes her head harder; Else only 'twitches her skirt'. Lil goes 'huddling alone like her mother', Else 'goes through life holding on to Lil'. Gradation of their innocent consciousness seems to be just a means to an end: the end is exploration of the concept of nascent consciousness within the hallowed range of perfect innocence. Difference in degree of their innocent consciousness obliterated by diverse elements in the composition—persistence of the image of their close huddled togetherness; restriction of the range of their consciousness to the limits of intrinsic innocence; recourse to use of a consistent pattern of animal imagery as a means of defining the instinctive intuitive nature of their understanding of each other. Lil and Else live, move and have their beings inside their own ring, and this ring admits of no line of demarcation. Gradation of the Kelveys' nascent consciousness as innocence has its subtlety enlightened by the contrasted gradation of innocent consciousness inside the ring presided over by Isabel: Else does not even know there are 'powers that go with being eldest'; with Lil "marching in front"; Else can only 'hold on behind'.

There is no line drawn between the Kelveys and Kezia, either. "The big white gates of the courtyard" do seem to draw a line between the Burnells and the Kelveys, the "two at a time" and the "two little dots". But Kezia, swinging in and out on the gates, is only 'hovering at the edge' of her own world, the point where the Kelveys "hovered". The concept of nascent consciousness within the hallowed range of perfect innocence is enriched by the inclusion of this uninfected character of kindred nature. Kezia belongs to the hallowed "ring" of the Kelveys: she is a Burnell child with a Kelvey soul. Her companion in her own family is Lottie; it is with this character that Kezia stands bracketed. The Kelveys have their counterpart in this pair of angels. Lottie is older than Kezia, 'the youngest Burnell child', as Lil is older than Else, the toddler that "holds on behind". Correspondingly, Lottie is a character parallel to Lil: she is less childlike than Kezia is; Lil is less innocent than Else; but she is passive with her unquestioning acceptance of the Burnell doctrine as Lil is passive with her resigned acceptance of her "subordinate station". Lottie is less pure than Kezia because she is slightly infected with the ethos of her Burnell family. This slight infection seems to be the reason for her exclusion from the charmed circle of the three 'hovering' angels of this paradise of innocence: what saves Kezia from the infection is her potentiality for a free choice which is liberation from servitude: she stands out of the crowd on her Burnell side of the "line"; her creative freedom in 'the rapt intensity of her self-forgetting attitude' to the lamp actualizes her pure being as a child. Even though she is bracketed with Lottie twice by the narrator, her selfhood with its potentiality for creative freedom remains in inviolable isolation. She speaks of "the best thing" that Isabel has forgotten only when the latter has "finished". Expression of her real self through a speech which only evinces continuity of her blissful trance is not allowed to mingle with Isabel's indirectly reported speech which smacks of 'the wine of too much stay' in the Burnell world: Isabel's "voice" is so "very proud": it has a smack of attitud-inizing; weighed in the balance it is found wanting: it does not manifest the purity of self-forgetting attitude that characterizes Kezia's neat interposition, "'you've forgotten the lamp, Isabel'". What the "voice" 'goes on telling' 'makes a great sensation': the proud voice, the great sensation, all betray utter absence of the 'rapt intensity', of the original purity of a private experience of joy. The way Isabel's speech and the collective response of her audience are rendered intensifies our awareness of this absence. The word "real", which Isabel must have used in her direct speech, is not the word with a toddler's meaning of it, Kezia's meaning of it ("The lamp was real"): Isabel uses this word again when she reports on the lamp herself: "'you couldn't tell it from a real one'". She speaks as an adult, not as a perfectly innocent child. She knows what's what: she is conscious of distinction between reality and representation of reality; she has not remained unmarked by the clumsy fingers of life; her deliberate mispronunciation of the word "tiny" as "teeny" betrays her incapacity now of appreciation of the value that 'diminished size' has in an innocent child's own microcosm. To a child the reality created by a tiny toy is more real, more natural: a toy is a dream and a reality rolled into one.

This contrasted element makes us aware of the rapt intensity of Kezia's sustained ecstatic trance in creative freedom and thus of the inviolable nature of her pure being: typographical isolation of Kezia's reported speech in the narrative design helps to spotlight the true image of the character that is in a crowd and still out of the crowd.

"The big white gate" seems to open on to a realm where the Kelveys belong. The image of the Kelveys as 'two little dots is perhaps meant to represent the core of their innocence made indefinable by their silence: each 'little dot' is an unamplified story of tragic piteous innocence; their story is an unsung song of innocence. Kezia's sustained vision of the gradually enlarging "dots" is, then, a vision of their natural psychic orientation: the vision is characteristic of a mood of passive resignation to whatever expands itself "towards her" as a complement to her own self which is split by an incisive question: "'But why not?'" She has not joined her constant companion, Lottie, who has gone "upstairs to change her pinafores: she has "thieved out" of a world where she has not been able to see why the Kelveys have been treated so cruelly. Throughout this episode during "the dinner hour under the pine trees", Kezia also seems to have been standing aloof, "outside the ring", 'by herself', "staring", "listening". She has had only one thing on her mind: "At last everybody had seen it except them". Then she has witnessed the orgy of the children's "merciless satisfaction in playing with their victims". She is dazed. It is in this mood that she has had this vision of the Kelveys as two dots. The innocent selves of the Kelveys reveal themselves in the realm where they 'belong'. The shadows of the Kelveys seem to represent their innocent selves, their naked souls, which exist in secret communion with the neglected, common roadside flowers ("beside them walked their shadows, very long, stretching right across the road with their heads in the huttercups"): the Kelveys themselves are in the flower of their days; they are April innocent. The whole situation is symbolic of the natural need of innocent, naked souls for reciprocal orientation ("The Kelveys came near"). This need for reciprocity of psychic expansion in the free, rarefied, calm realm where 'nobody is about' obliterates all lines of demarcation: "Kezia clambered back on the gate; she had made up her mind; she swung out". Kezia's gestures define her need—her individual need for psychic expansion. We have found Kezia herself brushing "through the thick buttercups at the road edge"; but there her pure innocent self seems tainted, though only temporarily, by its association with Lottie's indoctrinated self. It is the this taint that is manifest in her nervous gestures as she 'steps off the gate'. But the purity of her being saves her, for she 'hesitates' ("then she hesitated') and clambers back on the gate and swings out: "She had made up her mind": the need of the pure being for orientation was pressing; the moment too was opportune: "nobody was about". Kezia brushing through the thick buttercups herself and then beholding the Kelveys' shadows rolling over the buttercups belongs to the world of these modest, air-sown wayside flowers, the world of the lowly and lonely, meek and mute, almost orphaned and outcast children. This world is an Eden of intrinsic Innocence. So it is only as a hovering angel of intrinsic innocence that Kezia poses the question, "'But why not?'" She has proposed to "ask the Kelveys just once" not out of pity for them. She has not yet known pity: she is still too innocent to have pity. Pity presupposes consciousness of hierarchy. Kezia does not seem to have this consciousness. She is blissfully ignorant of the reason why the Kelveys cannot be asked in just once; when Lil says, "Your ma told our ma you wasn't to speak to us". Kezia doesn't know what to reply. Mrs. Beryl thinks, Kezia 'knows quite well why not', but Kezia does not know why not; she still exists in a naked state of nescience. She is curious; she is not rebellious.

Kezia is not proud of the toy house as a Burnell possession; Lil 'doesn't seem to mind the question at all'; Else has "forgotten the cross lady" and recalls the image only as a thing of beauty. There is no line drawn anywhere in the realm of the angelic trio. All the three children, Kezia, Lil and Else, are of innocence all compact.

We can see how this truth-vision lends itself to literary treatment most readily in the form of the short-story.

The toy house which precipitates the crisis, 'stands at the centre of the composition'.[47] It gives rise to different attitudes in the world about it. These attitudes constitute the story element in the short-story. The one attitude that survives helps to set forth the theme: It is the real child's "self-forgetting attitude" to "the best thing" in the toy house. The narrator sees the toy house through the eyes of only the Burnell children, Isabel, Lottie, and Kezia. The girls at school who are allowed 'just to stand quietly in the courtyard while Isabel points out the beauties'. see the toy house as the Burnell children have seen it. (The toy house is not seen through the eyes of the "Little Kelveys". The two who have always been "outside"; they have only "hovered at the edge" and "listened"; they have hardly been able to notice its 'thick bright colours, sharp definition and bold actuality.[48] No sooner do they come near enough to have a look than they are "startled" by the thundering orders of the "the cross lady") The

Burnell children have an accepted privilege: the toy house is their possession. They are absorbed by attachment to it. Its sensuous appeal ('thick bright colours', etc) is naturally tantalizing; Isabel is proud of it too; of all these children she stands in nearest approximation to it. Their schoolmates listen to its description given in a proud voice; each detail makes a great sensation. Even the dinner hour is given up to talking about it. The little girls talk and talk and talk about it significantly between mouthfuls of "their thick mutton sandwiches and big slabs of Johnny cake spread with butter" they feast their eyes upon their doll's house. The toy house has its sensuous tantalizing appeal. It becomes the rage. But Kezia has a pure vision: she has seen the soul of the doll's house—the little lamp with its nascent light as a thing of beauty. She has been in a trance since her first glimpse of it. The sense of the trance has been communicated obliquely-through etherealization of the character. Isabel points out only the "beauties"; she has not seen the beauty inherent in the little lamp. Her jocular mispronunciation of the word for it betrays her blindness to it. Her dictatorial insistence on rigid observance of formality in what as child's play is a source of pure joy precludes the possibility of any intense individual experience of the thrill of a discovery.

The doll's house, especially with its 'thick bright colours'; makes a solid emphatic impact also as the central image of the short-story. Meaning associated with the particular 'colours' cover the whole range of the psychological implications that the drama involves. Each of these 'colours' is expressive of two opposed meanings simultaneously implicit. There is only one 'colour', "white", which has one single meaning. Each of the 'colours' other than the 'white' is mentioned thrice; the "white" occurs only once. "Yellow" ("bright yellow", "yellow varnish", "painted yellow") is nearest the light; it carries with it the nature of brightness and has a serene character; it signifies love and concord. But this same colour is extremely liable to contamination; it is disagreeable if sullied. It is connected with the idea of sin; it is a colour of envy, of jealousy; it represents discord and all the evils in its train. The two associations define the nature of the attitude that responses of the children inside the "ring" manifest: they are innocent children parochially indoctrinated. "Green", the spectrum neighbour of "yellow", is the symbol of life, soul's regeneration, wisdom. It also signifies, by opposition, madness, jealousy, moral degradation. Both the associations are respectively consistent with the meanings implicit in characterizations of Kezia and Else on the one hand and those of Mrs. Beryl and Willie Brent on the other (or even those of the little girls who exult in the cruel success they have achieved and who fight jealously "to put their arms around Isabel—to beam flatteringly, to be her special friend", etc.). "Red" is a colour that excites and stimulates. It is associated with warmth, sunlight, love, shame. This same colour is suggestive of revolt. We also know that a predilection for this red colour is very marked among the hysterical. The ideas associated with the colour can also be found in the characterizations of characters involved in the drama: Kezia stands distinguished by virtue of her warmth of love; Else goes "red" all over again and again. Kezia's question is simply a spontaneous expression of her curiosity; but it revolutionizes the whole Burnell ethos. The opposed meaning is implicit also in the children's 'fascination' that 'becomes hysterical excitement'.[49] "White", the colour of snow and swan's feathers, is representative of purity, freshness, neutrality, peace. All these ideas are summed up in the characterization of the most innocent of all the characters, Else, the only character with a pure vision. Appropriately, she "wore a long white dress, rather like a nightgown". The colour is mentioned only once; this is consistent with the singularity of the character that has had a pure vision. (The vision illuminates her face with "a rare smile" 'as one lamp lights another nor grows less'.) The other three colours are named repetitively because as tokens of two opposites simultaneously they cover a wide range of emotional complex characterized by contrariety.

Imaginative concentration naturally charges details with indirectly or directly relevant connotations; the truth-vision (inviolability of pure innocence with its intrinsic potentiality of a pure vision of beauty) as a revelation in a flash calls for concentration on a crisis and all that is 'a local habitation and a name' is charged with meanings. This concentration on the crisis which embodies the truth-vision is complemented by a point of view that is expedient: the point of view is that of a narrator who sees the situation as a whole. The choice of this specific point of view is determined by the indispensability of recourse to a conventional method of story-telling. Rendering of this type of crisis in intent concentration cannot admit of reversal of the chronological order of events; only a smooth-flowing narrative can accommodate successive revelations of the inviolability of pure innocence: all the revelations are obviously meant to culminate as a serene revelation of what has been inviolate as the intrinsic potentiality of pure innocence—a pure vision of beauty.

Before we consider the other factors that account for the choice of the specific point of view as the only possible choice, let us see how pure innocence is made to seem to have remained inviolate in the vicious coils cumulatively formed as a result of indoctrination of innocent consciousness: the coils seem to have been represented by "the ring" immediately round the toy house and also by the larger, threateningly all-encompassing ring round this whole Eden of Innocence. At the centre of the design conceived as a complex of inharmoniously overlapping 'ring' representing the major shades of consciousness, we find "two little dots" as an image of nascent consciosness, perfect innocence: "the two little dots" seem to form the common centre of what stands secretly hallowed as 'a charmed circle' expanding the obscurity ("nobody was there") towards another 'charmed circle' on the Burnell side of the "gates": the Kelveys bear a charmed life as Kezia does. The sense of the inviolability of the Kelveys' 'charmed circle' is conveyed through a characterization of them that is not without perspective: the picture is not without what we call the art of conveying distance or sense of third dimension. Apart from the conspicuous means of suggesting the inviolability of their isolation (through their portrayal as social outcasts) there are two appropriately inconspicuous methods of ensconcing them in the inviolable sanctum of lonely isolation.

The Kelveys remain voluntarily withdrawn into their own ring of silent loneliness in isolation, the ring in which they stand huddled up throughout the drama. Appropriately, the very first time they are referred to, their identity is only vaguely suggested: the first introduction defines their identity in terms of a unit of arithmetic ("the two" ... "the two"); this helps to obscure their substantial identity; at the same time it seems to have specified their distinctive essence as only "two little dots" in the design of disagreeably overlapping rings representing degrees of consciousness. Repetition of the identifying phrase, "the two", makes us see their human image recede further into obscurity: only two subtle strokes and the compound image of the essential features of the twin characters is sketched: they are "always" so withdrawn, so introverted, so uncommunicative. Their identity is substantiated only after a vague introduction: the process parallels the one which shows them first as "two little dots" and reveals them only gradually as "the Kelvy sisters". "The two" are so withdrawn also because one of them is piteously helpless and the other has to 'mother' her. But they seem to have become one when they 'squeeze through the white gate'. Piling up of participial phrases in the description of their flight across the big courtyard makes these "two", who are already introverted, seem still more interiorized; "Burning with shame, shrinking together, Lil huddling along like her mother, Our Else dazed, somehow they crossed the big courtyard and squeezed through the white gate". They "shrink together" perhaps to become "the two little dots" again, to return to their elemental essence, to be what they are in their own realm of real existence.

Synonymous expressions of this sense of their withdrawal into absolute isolation recur throughout the narrative: this helps to sustain the desired effect of the inviolability of their isolation. They 'move away' as 'there is nothing more for them to hear'. They stand outside the ring, only "listening". The implicit sense of their speechlessness during their stay "outside the ring" contributes to the same intended effect of the inviolability of their isolation. The narrator is scrupulously careful not to desecrate the sanctity of 'the lonely reaches of the inarticulate': he refrains from venturing into the depths of Else's habitual silence. The only expressions of the twin characters are facial: Lil only gives "a shame-faced smile" which is always "silly"; Else only 'looks' and 'stares' and 'stops chewing'; but all such expression is only a negation of expression. Lil's "shame-faced smile" is of course an index of her emotion; it does betray her resigned acceptance of her "subordinate station"; it also makes us mark the degree of her consciousness that seems a shade superior; but it is a "silly", stupid, idiotic "smile". It betokens only naïve innocence. Else's 'look' or 'stare' is too blank. It is rather innocence itself manifest as a 'look' or a 'stare'. Else looks a picture of innocence. We are aware of inconceivable or obscure depths beyond their dumb silence, their individual 'smile' and 'look': the smile is not the teacher's "special smile"; nor is the 'look' a tutored look ("white Lottie and Kezia looked pleased"). What they betoken is at once absolutely easy to construe and manifestly impossible to conceive. Their gestures are their words; they 'never fail to understand each other'.

The narrator's jocular exposition of their family background also subserves the same end—expression of the narrator's own compassionate attitude dominated by a complex of attitudes: twice during his brief exposition of their background the narrator seems only to have adopted an ironical tone.

The irony implicit in the narrator's elliptical remark, "Very nice company for other people's children!" involves an understandingly compassionate attitude: even as "the daughters" of a lowly woman and a condemned lawbreaker they have remained 'uninfected', uncorrupted, unblemished; they do not even know that their origin is ignoble; they do not know ignominy from respectability; their association with "other people's children" is an utter impossibility; they are born to live alone even in the world of "children"; their absolute loneliness is at once pitiful and hallowed.

The narrator's awareness of the laughable incongruity characterizing their droll dressing is not unmingled with a sober sense of a positive value that seems inherent in it. Diversity of the "bits" they are "dressed in" seems to have universalized the identity of the two children; the "'bits'" Lil is "dressed in" have origins which are odd ("tablecloth", "curtain"); Else who is already "strange" looks stranger: "dressed in" what is probably "a grown-up woman's blouse" and wearing "little boy's boots", she is at once a grown-up woman, a boy and a child already "strange". The incongruity of their dressing had a fundamental quality of naturalness that marks all specimens of disorder: the children are not aware of the oddity. Absolute artlessness is the origin of what the narrator admires: the narrator experiences 'delight in disorder', so to say. In spite of all Burnell-Logan-Lecky 'bits' on their person, they are themselves; in spite of all incongruity in the dressing, they have beauty of innocence; in spite of all their distinct conspicuity, they remain obscurely inconspicuous; in spite of all, "the little lamp" of innocence burns inextinguishably, incessantly, eternally.[50]

The real child, "Our Else", as the central character of the short-story and the "real" lamp as the central image in the total emotional design seem to be conspicuously correlative. It is the exalted conspicuity of correlation between the central character and the central image which defines the meaning of the short-story.

The name chosen for this central character, "Our Else", is peculiar to the nature of the role she is meant to play: The compound devised as the name for this central character precisely defines the peculiar spirit of the character that distinguishes her from any other character within the framework of the short-story: she is a 'real' child in a world of children not so real. She is real: she cannot but be "Else". Literally, the part of the compound name, ("Else") has the denotative meaning of 'otherness': the word is familiar only as an adverb following an indefinite or interrogative pronoun: the range of its denotation is restricted: it means: 'besides, in addition' (e.g. anyone else, who else—?), 'instead' (e.g. what else—?), 'otherwise, if not' (e.g. run, else you'll), 'in or to some other place' (e.g. elsewhere). This sense of otherness is the essence of the character: the child stands "outside the ring"; she is not even forgivingly forgetful ("But now she had forgotten the cross lady"). What makes the child real is concisely revealed in the glow of "her rare smile": she experiences pure pleasure in her sweet recollection of the moment of ecstasy: the recollection is not melancholy: she does not sigh for the toy house with its "little lamp"; what flashes upon her inward eye is a thing of beauty which is a joy for ever; experience of 'the bliss of solitude' is naturally inarticulate. Else is still lost in the dream world created by the toy lamp as her personal reality. Actualization of "the little lamp" at nightfall, automaticity of the creation of a night in the world of the family within the toy house whenever the door is snapped to, sleepiness of the lamp throughout the night dimly revealing a reality in unnoticed seclusion: all this is unquestionable to her young mind: this unquestionability is the source of the child's ecstasy, her single brief utterance ("'I seen the little lamp'") is a lyrical expression of this ecstasy. Her broken English not only naturalizes her characterization as an outcast child; it also corresponds to the raw crude element of 'integrity' that distinguishes her as a real child. This hearty utterance of the child that "scarcely ever spoke" is spontaneous yet calm: the child is in a trance at the moment, "dreaming" with her eyes open. It is the entranced child that 'shines in its Angel infancy'. Else is a picture of serene childhood. With her potentiality for experience of pure pleasure she is distinctively real. The "smile" betokens intense actualization of her being as the universal child.

The image of this child who is "real by virtue of her otherness seems to have been universalized through use of the possessive adjective, "our", as part of the name coined for the character: The child that feels pure joy in entranced intimacy with its plaything belongs to a classless society, a universal society, a divine society of cherubic children: "Our" is the narrator's word: the narrator's moral vision of the whole situation has discovered Else as the only hallowed image of angel infancy in the Eden of innocence called into being by the toy house. The image is too sacred to be allowed to seem to be the inhabitant of a world other than the one where she belongs, the realm of universality.

Perhaps it was *The Fly* which embodied Miss Mansfield's ideal of spiritual purgation through aesthetic creation or vice versa. She succeeds in evoking in the short-story not only 'an atmosphere of sheer and terrible fatalism'[51] but also a microcosm which evolves as an awe-inspiring manifestation of Truth. The success betokens sobriety of her poetic philosophy. The omniscient narrator objectively watching the unfoldment of the grim drama sensitively registers the gradual attrition of the protagonist's being: the evolution of the process facilitates simultaneous revelation of the nature of Time that is all-consuming as well as self-consuming. The time scheme accommodates intermittent flashbacks revealing gradual consumption of the point-of-view character in the womb of Time, which keeps absorbing his consciousness continuously and incomprehensibly. The omniscient author's point of view intermittently merges with the protagonist's. This occasional mergence functions as a means of registering the protagonist's experience of his incomprehensibly tragic helplessness as a victim: Time keeps consuming his consciousness till he is totally identified with the victimizer; but ironically, he is, at the same time, synonymous with the victim. The creative vision of this grim reality is also a vision of the a-moral Beauty intrinsic in the cosmic concept of Time. To achieve a masterpiece which 'wrings the heart without the least concession to sentiment'[52] is to have succeeded in making the 'subjective selection of materials' reflect 'an objective standard of values'. The success of the creative process is due to complete 'abeyance of self'. The truth-vision conceived is grim, but the creative vision is tranced, serene, profound. The moment of crisis which this short-story seeks to render in imaginative concentration is the moment of a tragic realization in the life of the protagonist, the boss. The moment presents itself as a situation in which the protagonist is found struggling with Time: during this struggle he is tragically unaware that Time is slowly and steadily consuming his own psyche in course of its evolution. The range covered in concentration is that of a moment typical enough to illustrate the truth-vision at the back of the author's mind—gradual atrophy of psyche as a natural result of its involvement in the evolution of an a-moral force that feeds on self-destruction.[53]

What makes the rendering of the moment of this tragic experience seem aesthetic is the appropriate choice of a concentric design of characterizations which through its presentation in right perspective helps to 'reflect an objective standard of values'.

The truth-vision seems to relate to the concept of the Great Time which consumes all psyche, leaving it only "puzzled", dazed, blank, reducing it to an iota of consciousness, equating even human consciousness with a fly's consciousness, establishing all consciousness as an eternally innocent consciousness. Metaphorically, consciousness caught in the web of Time strains at it in vain: all its questions resolve into the ultimate interrogation: 'what is it that we are a part of that we do not see?' The web of Time only lures the questioning spirit of Consciousness to its extinction. All souls are pitted against the callous force of Time: of this force they are either only half-aware or innocently ignorant.

Thus all the characters in the short-story seem to move in a cyclic progression: they live, move and have their beings as parts of a whole, 'an incomprehensible ... pattern which feeds on self-destruction'. The fly is killed by the boss: despite all its "courage and "the right spirit" as its heightened instinctive awareness, it is too innocent a soul to see the 'wanton boy'. The boss that kills the fly is being killed slowly and slowly by some boss of all bosses (Time: in spite of all his detached consciousness of a self gone dead within him ("he wasn't feeling as he wanted to feel") and of his assumed, bolstered self-assurance, he keeps wondering what it is that has drained his life of its only meaning, of its inexhaustible potentiality ("feeling as he wanted to feel"); groping for its identity he casually identifies that life-negating force too: "Time, he had declared then, he had told everybody", etc.: the iterative syntactical pattern here, "he had declared ... he had told ...," with that loud word, "declared", reinforces the desired effect of his over-consciousness and his own "courage". But the pity is he doesn't suspect the identity. Woodifield has already been 'killed' and reduced to a mere semblance of a human being, a piping "old" fellow and a peering "baby" rolled into one; he is past feeling, lost to all sense of the incompatibility of his son's grave with the "nice broad paths about it", to all sense of incongruity of an irrelevant digression. Macey 'dodging in and out of his cubby-hole like a dog that expects to be taken for a run', is a faceless man minus all sense of his individuality or freedom: the killing force in his life has been the boss, whose own consciousness is changed from a "feeling of wretchedness" to comatose amnesia by a force he cannot specify. The boss's eclipsing domination renders Macey faceless; later the boss himself with all his "fat body" and "heavy steps" becomes an apparition walking through the walls.

The one characterization that is central to the design of all characterizations is that of the fly. The choice of the title seems to have been determined by the symbolical dimensionality of this central character. The posthumous apparition of the fly towering over the human world spotlighted within the framework of the narrative composition is a poetic image of the tragic truth about all human psyche. What happens to the innocent consciousness of the fly is a profound tragic truth in life: what keeps its consciousness in the dark is an unanswerable mystery that intensifies the tragedy intrinsic in life. The image evoked by the title and the only picture emergent from the drama in the human world yield implications which resolve into a tragic sense of identification of the fly with the protagonist, the boss. What intensifies this tragic sense of their identification is the irony of their synonymity on the ultimate level of anonymity in spite of the violent physical contrast that they present on their elemental biological level: the one stands in diminutive perspective beside the other. Consciousness in the fly is innocent awareness with a sense of wonder; consciousness in the boss is an experience of a whole life-time with a sense of mystery. The fly does not and cannot see the boss; the boss does see Time but he stands "for a long moment staring at nothing" and finally even fails to "remember" anything. His profound consciousness turns out to be innocent consciousness. His psyche is only a fly's psyche writ large.

In the opening scene where he sits talking with Woodifield, the boss is out of his "grave", jubilant and joking, animated for a moment by the idea of what can bring them both back alive: this manifestation of 'will to live', of will to 'cling to life's fast pleasures', is a part of the story element which helps to intensify the pathos inherent in the truth about the boss; as an element of dramatic irony, its full meaning involves the sense of the boss's ignorance of the tragic fact that his own utterance stresses: the boss himself has been 'out in the cold', in his "grave"; in spite of his attempt to shut himself up in the lonely room, he will remain "in the cold" of a life which is but an illusion of life: The "old friend" he has been speaking to is himself the image of a soul already mangled by omnivorous Time: Time has already consumed much of his life: he is "five years older"; he has also experienced the first fatal blow of Time ("stroke"); an "old man" and a baby rolled into one, he is a freak of Time; he has now become an instrument of Time, dropping a "blot" of news on the boss whose eyelids "quiver" like the wings of the fly he will be killing; the boss is overwhelmed by the blot: jolted out of repose he has desperately sought in the "beautiful stuff", he is shocked into shuddering speechless disillusion. But he does not know that Time robes all psyche of the least awareness of the irony.

The protagonist's vision has already become blank: his voice has already become the voice of a ghostly self ("'Quite right, quite right! cried the boss, though what was quite right he hadn't the least idea'"); his vision has already become a 'stare at nothing'. This faceless, headless, lifeless ghostly nobody recrosses "the bright carpet". "The door shut": the reflexive verb and the sound-effect achieved through close juxtaposition of hard dentals resolve into an oblique way of expressing a sense of sudden absence of the agent of all activities: 'the door shuts'; we do not see him shut it: he moves in the room like an 'invisible man'. Even "the fat body" with its "firm, heavy steps" is an ephemeral apparition. The figure is faceless: the 'participation shot' makes us feel that there is a downward look of downcast eyes. A sense of self-mockery, of an ironical awareness, a realization of futility on the part of the protagonist looking with unseeing eyes ('staring at nothing') and no longer "proud of his room", is obliquely conveyed: the means is an objective, panning participation shot. To the boss hitherto glorying in material prosperity, "the bright red carpet" is only "bright" and no longer "red" too: all that remains is its specious 'brightness' which is painfully mocking. The protagonist's etherealization at this moment of a crisis seems to evince only a further success that Time has achieved in course of its evolution as a destructive and self-destructive process. The situation is ironically paradoxical: a fat body with firm heavy steps is only an ephemeral apparition, a nobody, living a ghost of a life, a life which is now 'but a walking shadow only 'a tale told by an idiot, signifying nothing'.[54]

The interior monologue begins and ends with significant concomitant gestures ("the boss covered his face with his hands"; "The boss took his hands from his face"). We have the interior monologue in between the images of these two concomitant gestures. The darkness conceivably consequent upon the first gesture ("covered his face with his hands") blots out the world of "the bright carpet" and "the spring chair" and shuts him in his petty world with its only meaning of life. Since the remark about "the boy's grave", the boss's self has been dwindling, waning, atrophying, receding further and further into its innermost recesses, losing its consciousness ("made no reply"; "what was quite right he hadn't the least idea"). 'The door shuts' indicating further interiorization. The first gesture ("covered his face with his hands") is symbolic of the last door that shuts. The second gesture ("took his hands from his face") reveals a "puzzled" face. What has perplexed the boss is a change—a change not only in the boy's "photograph" but also in his self; for the change is coincidentally degenerative ('the expression was unnatural. It was old, even stern-looking. The boy had never looked like that"; and ... "Something seemed to be wrong with him. He wasn't feeling as he wanted to feel"). The implications resolve themselves into a tragic connotation: the boss is no longer his natural conscious self. It is this unnatural, "cold", "stern" self that is imaged in the subsequent fly-episode. There, in the fly-episode, even the self that is conscious of the unnatural self ("Something seemed to be wrong with him. He wasn't feeling as he wanted to feel") is absent: there we have only the unnatural self, demented, possessed, dehumanized.[55] The boss that 'picks the fly out of the inkpot' and the boss that 'has an idea', the boss that 'feels a rush of relief' and the boss that 'decides that this time should be the last', the boss that looks and the boss that speaks, the boss that acts and the boss that thinks, are one and the same. The moment that the fly-episode is meant to dramatize is a tense moment of curious identification of the two characters, the boss and the fly, on the ultimate level of anonymity ("'you artful little b—'"). What intensifies the tragic pathos palpitating at the moment is the dramatic irony of the boss's ignorance of the success which the unidentified force has already achieved by asserting itself as an ultimate truth through establishment of synonymity of all psyche on the level of indistinguishable anonymity.

This gradual concentric interiorization of thoughts, feelings and impulses is symptomatic of the protagonist's spiritual atrophy as the manifestation of the eternal principle established by the Great Time—ultimate fusion of all categories of psychic experiences as Eternal Innocence. The boss's consciousness ranges from an essentially human emotion (a wish for a solitary moment to weep) to a bewildered awareness of a strangely unfamiliar experience ('the feel of not to feel any more'),[56] from a whole souled determination (or confidence that he is also the 'boss' of his wish to weep) to a stupefying or stunning experience of the loss of determination ("He wasn't feeling as he wanted to feel"). This whole evolution of consciousness is made static at the mere touch of cold Time that the protagonist finds himself confronted with: Time looms large even on his interiorized mental horizon. Naturally the thought-process evolves through ideas that gather in agonized concentration: "his boy was an only son. Ever since his birth the boss had worked at building up this business for him: it had no other meaning if it was not for the boy. Life itself had come to have no other meaning". The movement of every sentence is different, but the cumulative effect is that of gradual concentration of vision. A full-stop after "this business for him" would have been too long a pause to give the effect of synonymity of "this business" with "the boy". The process terminates in a deduction: "Life itself had come to have no other meaning". This deduction pinpoints the specificity of the character conceived as a mean, selfish father, a 'regular' businessman. Choice of the type of personality is appropriate. The protagonist's consciousness had to seem limited: it is of a type that has never expanded beyond the limits of "this business for him" which has given meaning to his life. Thus his consciousness has remained restricted to the only meaning of his life for him. The only meaning of his life was: "this business for him"; his son gave meaning to "this business"; "this business for him" gave meaning to his life; the son who gave meaning to his business and thus gave meaning to his life is dead; therefore, "this business for him" has lost its meaning; and this life that has been all business has lost its only meaning. The major portion of this monologue is devoted from this point onwards to the revelation of this specificity of the character who seems to have been conceived as only a human fly for a Wanton Boy. The boss's consciousness centres round the image of his son as he probes in the darkness of the shell he has just shut himself in or withdrawn into. The narrator's voice is still: the boss is all alone; his consciousness has receded into its innermost recesses; it is just an iota of consciousness, a consciousness skin to the fly's. The boss is helplessly aware of the nature of Time: "But all that was over and done with as though it never had been ... Six years ago ... Now quickly time passed! It might have happened yesterday". Confronted with the nature of Time he stands "puzzled". Enmeshed in the web of Time even his reviving consciousness is now a bewildered consciousness of a strangely mysterious experience ("Something seemed to be wrong with him. He wasn't feeling as he wanted to feel".), an experience which involves a deeply perplexed awareness of a greater loss than the loss of his son—the loss of grief. His tragedy lies in denial to him of grief of loss over grief, of 'the feel', just for a lonely moment, of grief over loss of grief. The boss's feeling of the strange experience is akin to that of the fly that finds the impending setbacks incomprehensibly mysterious.

The far more highly developed consciousness in point of which the boss is superior to the fly is as insignificant as a fly's iota of consciousness. All consciousness is a fly's consciousness eternally enmeshed as it is in the web of Time. The boss's human consciousness limited to the only meaning of his life is a wordly, and in ultimate analysis, a biological consciousness; it is just an iota of consciousness—a fly's consciousness. It cannot comprehend the nature of Time and accept it as a Truth that is Beauty: it cannot see what does not let him feel as he wants to feel, and why he cannot feel as he wants to feel, and how it is that he cannot feel at all; the fly's consciousness, in the same way, cannot comprehend what is happening; it cannot see what or who it is, or can be, and why it cannot bring itself to outlive the blot and live as it wants to live, and how it is that it cannot "stir". The boss is "puzzled"; the fly is "stunned".

In the depiction of the moment when the boss notices that a fly has fallen into his inkpot, the past participle tense in the noun clause ("that a fly had fallen") registers what we may call a mysterious moment of Time-veiled transition in the process of gradual interiorization of the protagonist's consciousness: the boss sits starting into the "broad inkpot" at his own projected image and his experience of the emotional affinity is intensified; the moment is that of psychic oneness with the consciousness that the image represents as a synonymous and anonymous soul. There is correspondence between the fly "trying feebly but desperately to clamber out again" and the boss desperately straining at the web that enmeshes him as a dazed soul. There is a transition in the process of his psychic interiorization or of concentration of his consciousness into what we may call elemental consciousness: we notice this transition in the lapse of the protagonist's tragic consciousness of his psychic atrophy into blank unawareness of his existential synonymity with the anonymous soul inside the inkpot. The way the transition is registered is telling enough to define the nature of Time that encompasses and consumes all consciousness. The precise word which defines this nature is the ambiguous "again" ("clamber out again"). The fly had already fallen: the boss did not see it fall; he noticed it just when it was coming out; how did the word occur to him? If the word indicates the fly's simple biologically instinctive wish to remain out as before, it is just an example of fluently loose redundance, for the phrasal verb, "clamber out", is enough. But even as an example of redundance the word takes on functional significance as even its common or usual denotation obscures the moment with ambiguity. The word implies the fly's second or third attempt, and this implication only complicates the question. How could the boss be sure of any repetition of the attempt? Perhaps the interval between the fall of the fly and the boss's notice of it is meant to be a passing peep-hole view into the womb of Time which both unfolds and enfolds all that we perceive or interpret as succession. A soul's consciousness of all repetition of its attempts and even of its attainment of the end is callously consumed by Time which leaves all consciousness dazed as a fly's consciousness: futility of all concentrating intensifying consciousness is tragically inevitable.

The episode makes us see that the fly and the boss at the moment are one and the same—the fly "trying feebly but desperately to clamber out again" and the boss trying in vain to live life without that pang of loss of the only meaning and thus without that agony of the loss of grief—to live life even for a moment through use of the "beautiful stuff"—and then 'again' making a desperate effort to be lonely enough to feel the grief over the loss of grief. In spite of their physical contrast, both seem synonymous on their elemental level of insignificant and indistinguishable anonymity. The fly that is killed is the boss himself ("'you artful little b-'"): by "b" perhaps the boss means 'boss'. Thus the boss is the fly and also Time itself; the tragic irony inherent in this conflation of concepts is appropriately dramatized through a rendering that is starkly objective: the boss's subjective vision of the fly ("artful little b-", "a plucky little devil", etc.) exemplifies only his intense subconscious awareness of his identification or synonymity with the insignificantly tiny dot of life inside the "broad inkpot". The boss's murmurous utterances define the state of his own being; dramatizing himself against circumstances, he has been "artful" himself; trying to "clamber out" of the "broad inkpot" of his dark lonely world, struggling for a gasp of relief under unaccountably repetitive blows of an unidentified force causing loss of grief over the loss of grief, the boss is "a plucky little devil" himself. The tragic irony implicit in the dramatized situation is deepened by the obvious sense of the boss's unawareness of his identification with the great destructive and self-destructive force itself that has been operating through him. The boss reduced to the psychic level of the fly is no longer his earlier self that has been "puzzled" by the nature of Time ("But all that was over and done with as though it never had been", "six years age, six years .... How quickly time passed

! It might have happened yesterday"). He is no longer conscious of Time as an objective or subjective reality ("How quickly time passed !"); now deeper inside the all-encompassing womb or "broad inkpot" of the vast, transparent yet dark reality of Time, he is passively conscious of only a manifestation of its real nature ("this time, the task began from the beginning"): he is too near the spirit of Time to see the whole of it as an objective reality distanced from himself: he can see only one thing: he is only "trying again"; he will 'try again' and again to feel the grief over the loss of grief; every time this struggle has been begun "from the beginning", and all his struggle in the future will be a struggle "from the beginnng".[57]

The story of the tragedy is a story which cannot end with the death of the fly. The tragedy still persists, and after such a harrowing experience it is all the more dismal as the boss is again the hoss with the double life, again resorting to "the way to tackle things", with the 'Never-say-die' attitude as the only means to the end—experience of life with a meaning. He can now repose only in the attitude of self-dramatization; he gets a definite fright at the thought of the experience he has had in his desperate search for loneliness in which he wishes he could weep, feel as he wanted to feel, and grieve over the loss of grief at least, if not over the loss of the only meaning of his life: he is "positively frightened" at the idea of what he actually feels when he wants to feel the greater loss of grief, the idea of what he becomes and comes to do when he wishes to be sane and cool and his real self again: the "grinding feeling of wretchedness" sets in now when he has come to see all that his wish to flinch from a double life means. The bell he presses for Macey helps to ring out all that has happened, all that he has seen and felt and done; but at the same time it rings in a double life which is all question without an answer, a life without its only meaning, a life in death—but at least a life with his meaning of it now. The "fresh blotting-paper must soak up the "dark patch" that still oozes round the image of his synonymity with "the artful little b –" blotted divertingly on his consciousness: this "fresh blotting paper" will mean a fresh revival of the double life which has now his own meaning of it ("we cling to our last pleasures"), the meaning which involves the sense of an eternally unanswerable rhetorical question. "Look sharp" is an echo which mocks its origin to prove that it is original and is thus an echo of a voice characteristic of a double life. The voice is bemocked by its echo which asserts itself as the real voice, a voice strained and delirious because of all that his bossy self has come to see during the exercise of its power even beyond its limits: he became the boss of his wish to weep and could not make himself even feel; he tried to boss "Time" about too ("Time, he had declared", etc.); but it only puzzled him and diverted him with a tiny dot of life which revealed itself as the manifestation of a profound tragic truth about all psyche. The "Financial Times" is an image with an ironically paradoxical implication: life with its only meaning and Time that consumes all life with all its meanings seem tragically mismatched in course of their evolution. The damn-care gesture ("flipped the Financial Times") is manifestly characteristic of the double life. The gesture this time is an index of a deliberate conscious effort on the part of the boss to assure himself of his security in his "snug" life with its bell for an "old dog" and all that "beautiful stuff" and "bright-red carpet"—to make himself understand that his life as a boss (with its "drop of something" which can bring him back alive) has enough power to drown all drops that kill slowly and slowly. The fly on the tip of the blade has to be seen clearly as a thing which is so many things at the same time. The characteristic features of the boss's "snug" life—the bell for Macey, the stern 'Look-sharp-about-it' orders, the flipping of the paper-knife—are all clustered for the flashing audio-visual montage effect of an agonized double life: they are all illumined by what is just the last brief flicker of consciousness; the very next moment the flicker goes out and there is a dark void of utter oblivion ("feel to wondering what it was he had been thinking about before, ... For the life of him he could not remember."). Time consumes all consciousness: all consciousness of Time is gathered back into the self-negating flux of Time.[58]

Miss Mansfield's vision of Time consuming all Consciousness and reducing it to its elemental state as Eternal Ignorance or Innocence is a serene vision. The meaning of *The Fly* seems to have been pre-echoed by the Book of Job.

Technique as 'achieved content' was perhaps perfectly exemplified by these four masterpieces in which 'the truthful full life'[59] was portrayed, appropriately 'with a sense of mystery, a radiance, an afterglow,[60]: life's crisis was rendered in each in intense concentration: the subjective vision was only dreamily concentrated on the dead face. (The Garden Party), the undulating sea (At the Bay), the little lamp (Doll's House), the tiny fly (Fly), each having been discovered as the nearest physical thing to the metaphysical: each image was only delicately touched on and the loftier Reality was adequately defined.[61] Each short-story was emotion crystallized into thought and fixed in form.[62] The a-moral nature of the loftier Reality had to be preserved; so the artist never 'slanted' the content: so to say. The creative process now had its well-springs in the purged, enlightened, joyous spirit: it was with the 'vision of Love and Innocence' that the creative skill was now combined; the 'joyous acceptance of life'[63] was also admiration of the beautiful or of the awe-inspiring sublime Beauty.

Miss Mansfield's art was now reverent imitation of God; it was a shadow of divine perfection. Her work was now a delight in God's work, not her own. God was now breathing His life into her soul, although, ironically, only to snuff out her life—and that just when she was qualified to say, Let there be a short-story, and there was a short-story.

NOTES AND REFERENCES

1. Antony Alpers, *Katherine Mansfield*, pp. 319-20.
2. "Ah, the people—the people we loved there—of them, too, I want to write. Another 'debt of Love'".—*Journal*, p. 94.
3. "Sometimes ... the emphasis is on a sort of rebirth; ... it is to be completely occupied (to the exclusion of all other feeling) by 'an intense longing to serve my subject as well as I can'; or it is to be made 'crystal clear' for the divine light to shine through; or it is 'to be simple as one would be simple before God'... She expressed it in many different ways: some artistic, some unmistakably religious: but they all have essentially the same meaning. And they all belong to that rare province of human experience where art and religion are veritably one".—J.M. Murry, Katherine Mansfield and other Literary Portraits, p. 85.
4. Saralyn Daly, *Katherine Mansfield*, pp. 112-113.
5. "Delicate perception is not enough: one must find the exact way in which to convey the delicate perception".—*Letters*, p. 312.
6. William Walsh, *A Mansfield Voice*, p. 162.
7. J.M. Murry, *op. cit.*, p. 88.
8. "That is what I tried to convey in The Garden Party. The diversity of life and how we try to fit in everything, Death included"—*Letters*, p. 454.
9. Don W. Kleine, "'The Garden Party: A portrait of the Artist", *Criticism*, V, p. 362.
10. Cf. Miss Berkman's general observations on the narrative methods of Chekhov and Miss Mansfield as they reveal 'the characteristic attitude of each writer towards his material':—'neither one is greatly interested in event as event, or even in the primary emotion inhering in an event .../Chekhov's concern is never with action in itself but with the emotional repercussions of action on the characters involved ... Thus in *Enemies* the death of Kirilov's son and the elopement of Aboguin's wife are employed secondarily, to give rise to the theme

that suffering does not always unite men but can produce hostility and bitterness. Miss Mansfield [too]... usually presents her material not for the overt meaning of the happening but to make a tangential point, slanting the elements of the central situation to extract an oblique theme ... *The Garden Party* juxtaposes social gaiety and sudden death to revel the bewildering shock a young girl suffers at the knowledge that in life such incongruities can co-exist'.—Sylvia Berkman, *Katherine Mansfield: A Critical Study*, pp. 154-55. *Comments*—The 'general observations' explain the 'narrative method' of the individual authors only casually and prosaically. What, as a matter of fact, characterizes their 'narrative method' is a wholeness of communication which is consummated in the evocation of a vague feeling of a truth (psychological or poetic): the easily paraphrasable meanings ('suffering does not always unite men but can produce hostility and bitterness', 'the bewildering shock a young girl suffers at the knowledge that in life such incongruities can co-exist') are restricted to the story element which is only a means to an end; even what seems to be the point made out clearly and unambiguously, in the concluding paragraphs of *Enemies*, is only a part of the 'narrative': the passage reflects the 'psychology' of the character; is does not state 'the theme' itself. The meaning emergent from the total verbal complex is perhaps more deeply psychological—to forget all grief and suffering and experience bitterness is as much human as it is to experience grief and suffering and forget all human considerations. But the reader is made to feel this psychological truth as a subtle truth about human nature. Similarly, in *The Garden Party*, the full meaning is not simply a 'bewildering shock' but an emotional complex involving an intense awareness of a transcendental Truth that is Beauty, of Beauty that is intrinsic in 'life's diversity, death included'.

11. Don W. Kleine, *op. cit.*, p. 363.
12. "(The Latin name means laurel, of course)" Fred C. Robinson Mansfield's 'Garden Party', Explicator 24 (1966). Item 66.
13. Don W. Kleine, *op. cit.*, p. 363.
14. *Ibid.*, p. 364.
15. The view is inspired by Mr. Kleine's critical vision of the 'sense' that the short-story conveys: "Miss Mansfield's statement ('The diversity of life and how we try to fit in everything, Death included') Letters. seems ... a little misleading. Is it her story's primary effect to convey a sense of 'the diversity of life'? Does she really show how 'we try to fit in everything'? Rather, if one would be accurate, the story conveys Laura's realization of life's diversity; it shows how she finally fits in everything."—Don W. Kleine. *op. cit.*, p. 360.
16. "Beauty Triumphs over ugliness 'in spite of all' ... in spite of all, the sleeping face of the dead man in *The Garden Party* murmurs that all is well." J.N.Murry, *op. cit.*, p. 93.
    "Beautiful Life: In spite of everything one cannot but praise Life".—Letters, p. 367.
17. Note—It will not, however, be wrong to say that the movement of clauses in this second statement also is rapid: Laura is not a bit in the mood for a moment's stay in this "dark" world of "dark people" ("she didn't wait for Em's sister"). But even this reading of the narrative statement does not conflict with the inference that the character has undergone a change. In a recitation of the

short-story, say, for an LP record, the statement may sound rapid, too. The reader on the mike may quite reasonably feel that Laura at the moment cannot but find her "way out of door"—that she has only one feeling here: the sooner she gets away from the dark world of this truth about life, the better: she cannot bring herself to stand the shock of this truth. But neither meaning of the narrative statement detracts from the rich poetic ambiguity of Laura's elliptical ejaculation ("Isn't Life—?").

18. Warren S. Walker "The unresolved conflict 'Garden Party'" *Modern Fiction Studies*, Winter 1957-58, Vol. III, No. 4 (Typed copy).
19. William Walsh, *op. cit.*, p. 176.
20. Miss Mansfield rehearses the process by which category of existence supports and shades into the next". *Ibid.*, p. 181.
21. "Katherine Mansfield had an exquisitely sure sense of the fine gradations of existence and the passage between them. *Ibid.*, p. 180.
22. Saralyn Daly, *op. cit.*, p. 94.
23. William Walsh, *op. cit.*, p. 182.
24. Cf. '... In [Chekhov] we find an indispensable element which is strong in his writing and weak in hers: the sense of a country, a place, the sense of the unseen characters, the anonymous people, what we may call "the others" from which the people of his stories are taken. Miss Mansfield's *At the Bay* is one of the minor masterpieces of our language,—but who are these people, who are their neighbours, what is the world they belong to? ... Too self-sufficiently, they drop out of the sky and fill the little canvas. There is no silent character in the background. True, there is the mystery of life and death, suggested by the grandmother's memories of her dead son. But in a story like Chekhov's *The Steppe* there is something else besides the mystery of life and death: Russia, the condition of Russia, is the silent character, always haunting us. "—V.S. Pritchett, *The New Statesman and Nation*, 3 February, 1946, p. 87.
    Comments—Miss Mansfield's short-story with its New Zealand words and usages does evoke the local scene ("the bush-covered hills" "paddocks", etc.): it is not without 'the sense of a country, a place'. The 'people' and 'their neighbours' are the colonists. With their varying degrees of consciousness and orientation of their individual psyches, they form only one of the categories of existence; this category completes the image of Life at the bay as an interminable flux in Time: 'the world they belong to' is a whole microcosm of which they form only part and which evolves in Time as Life that is only a palpable manifestation of the ultimate truth—Eternal Innocence. The meaning of the short-story is not restricted to the psychological implications of the drama in the human world of the colonists. The whole microcosm evolving in Time is reflected in the sea. This 'sea' is the background. With its distinctively characteristic feature of disorder without tension, this sea reflects the dominant feature of the whole microcosm: all disorder with tension or without tension is eternally natural order: it is Eternal Innocence. Even the human consciousness of 'the mystery of life and death' is only a part of Life that evolves in Time as Experience and fades into the eternal state of Innocence as the ultimate truth about all that seems to evolve. In Chekhov's short-story, 'the silent character' is the image of Nature herself: it is a means of objectification and familiarization of the spirit of Nature.

'*The Steppe* is presented passionately, with great intensity, as though it were imperiously demanding that it should be understood and given 'general idea', identified with the free flight of steppe birds and liberated from the heartless power of the savage kites hovering over it—the dry prosaic and soulless masters, the Varlamovs—and that it be given a singer ... Nature wishes to be humanized, so that it should no longer appear as a green monster, and its beautiful tranquility should not be the peace of the graveyard.... Both man and nature want to be worthy of each other, each suffers from the contradiction between beauty and ugliness, from senseless primordial forces and cruelty' (Vladimir Yormilov, A.P. Chekhov: 1860-1960 p. 139).

To embody this theme Chekhov has lavishly used homely comparisions ("It was as though someone had struck a match across the sky" ... "There was the sound of someone far away walking over an iron roof") vividly conveying the impression made by lightning and thunder on his small hero; Chekhov also ascribes human emotions and attitudes to animals and plants, thereby showing the link between man and nature lower on the biological scale: "The grass, half-dead and already doomed, was trying to persuade someone piteously and earnestly, that it was not to blame and that it had been unjustly scorched by the sun. it was asserting its passionate desire for life, saying that it was still young, and would have been beautiful but for the heat and drought".

Man and Nature in Miss Mansfield's short-story form part of the Truth that Time leaves defined as Eternal Innocence.

25. Cf.'... Several ... moments could be linked together to form [an] extended picture, to give the sense of great scope. And this is precisely what Chekhov and Katherine Mansfield have done ... [In *The Steppe*]we experience with the boy the now sensations ... For nearly everything along the journey comes to us as part of the boy's impressions ... Occasionally Chekov himself interprets *The Steppe*, but this pushing the boy out of the immediate foreground of the story, this shift from character to author and back again, is skilfully done.... In Katherine Mansfield's story, *At the Bay*, the curtain is lifted, not on several moments in one person's consciousness but on one or two moments in the consciousness of several people, so that the ensemble of a whol family emerges'—Dorothy Brewster & Angus Burrell, *Modern Fiction*, pp. 365-68.

Comments: What necessitates the choice of an expanded scale in the two short stories is the nature of the themes the individual authors have sought to dramatize: in *The Steppe* it is, perhaps, the fusion of the spirit of man with that of Nature or impregnation of his youthful spirit with the mystery and beauty and terror of Nature; in *At the Bay*, it is the flux of all Life in Time as only an epic manifestation of the ultimate Truth, Eternal Innocence. In Miss Mansfield's short-story there is variation of the method 'of pushing the centre-of-consciousness character' out of the immediate foreground of the story, of shifting from the character to the narrator: it is perceptible in subordination of the multi-personal point of view to an omniscient narrator's point of view simultaneously operative in both the human and the non-human world: the objective is registration of the flux of all Life at the bay, revealed as it stands between the morning and the midnight. Since the essential story element is not restricted to the drama in the human world alone, the ensemble that emerges is not simply that of a family but of a whole microcosm evolving in the womb of Time that keeps all evolution in a state of eternal nascency.

26. The short-story illustrates one of Miss Mansfield's theories of fiction: "Emotion is essential to a work of art; it is that which makes a work of art a unity. Without emotion writing is dead; it becomes a record instead of a revelation, for the sense of revelation comes from that emotional reaction which the artist felt and was impelled to communicate". *Novels and Novelists*, p. 236.
27. Saralyn Dely, *op. cit.*, p. 93.
28. *Ibid.*, p. 95.
29. 'Williams Walsh, *op. cit.*, p. 182.
30. Cf. "[The story pursues] the consideration of order begun in Prelude".—Saralyn Dely. *op. cit.*, p. 92.
31. J.M. Murry, *op. cit.*, p. 92.
("This vileness, this snail on the underside of the lead"—*Letters*, p. 230).
32. For example "The sat hunched up ... her arms round her knees ... And she gave her strange neighing laugh ... swam away quickly, quickly, like a rat".—*Collected Stories of Katherine Mansfield*, pp. 217-20.
33. For example "'Mercy on us, ... what a little beauty you are! '... she touched Beryl's waist. ... 'Why be shy? I shan't eat you ... 'Really, it's a sin for you to wear clothes, my dear'"—*Ibid.*, p. 219.
34. William Walsh, *op. cit.*, p. 178.
35. The foregoing analyses of the human characters illustrate the distinctive feature of Miss Mansfield's concept of characterization: "However deep the knowledge a writer has of his characters, however finely he may convey that knowledge to us, it is only when he passes beyond it, when he begins to break new ground, to discover for himself, to experiment, that we are enthralled." *Novels and Novelists*, p. 114.
36. 'William Walsh, *op. cit.*, p. 117.
37. Saralyn Daly, *op. cit.*, p. 99.
38. *Ibid.*
39. *Ibid.*
40. William Walsh, *op. cit.*, p. 181.
41. *Ibid.*, p. 167.
42. *Ibid.*, p. 168.
43. *Ibid.*
44. Sylvia Berkman, *op. cit.*
45. Walsh William, *op. cit.*
46. *Ibid.*
47. *Ibid.*
48. *Ibid.*
49. *Ibid.*, p. 166.
50. 'In spite of all'—the phrase mysterious and simple as life—contains the secret of herself and her art.... Beauty triumphs over ugliness 'in spite of all'. In spite of all, the little lamp glows gently and eternally in The Doll's House"—J.M. Murry, *op. cit.*, p. 93.
51. Quoted by John Cournos, "Introduction", *A World of Great Stories*, p. 8.
52. *Ibid.*
53. *The Fly* has perhaps never been seen as a short-story, cf. "Granted the difference of genres, exactly the same critical procedure is in order for realistic fiction as

for a poem ... some ... critics of *The Fly* have gone astray by ignoring the story's technical limitations, and various abstract 'themes' have been read into it, like 'time', 'cruelty' and 'life'"—F.W. Bateson and B. Shahevitch, "Katherine Mansfield's Fly: A Critical Exercise":
Essays in Criticism, Vol. XII, No. 1 (January 1962), pp. 44-45.
Comments: It is rather surprising that neither in the controversy which the collaborators' "critical exercise" precipitated nor in the "exercise" itself do we find the most vital consideration involved. The 'story has not been seen as a narrative piece which aims at an aesthetic rendering of a life's crisis in imaginative concentration; that is, it has not been seen as a short-story. The collaborators themselves 'have gone astray by ignoring' the basic fact that a "story's technical limitations" are never exclusive of the conditions which its peculiar nature as a distinctive genre creates the critics commenting on the collaborators have not examined the aspects of 'the story' in relationship to its peculiar nature as a specific literary 'genre'. "The critical procedure" is of course "exactly the same", but it should never be divorced from consideration of the peculiarities which distinguish the one "genre" from the other: because it is this consideration which facilitates or ensures recognition of the way the implicit meaning stands intrinsically modified or specified. The "procedure" which is practised in ignorance of reciprocity between the subject matter and the technique only sidetracks the critic from his apposite purpose: it deprives him of the opportunity of penetration to the core of the truth embodied.
The analysis that is presented is an attempt to cut through the controversy unleashed by the collaborating critics (*Essays in Criticism*, Vol. XII, No. 3, July 1962).

54. The way the characterization of the protagonist is effected makes us see how Miss Mansfield practised what she demanded of her contemporary novelists. Commenting on the art of characterization in a novel by Wm. Gerhardi Miss Mansfield advised the author 'not to tell the reader what he is to feel about the characters portrayed'.: "your begin to tell us what we must feel about them ... that's not necessary. One feels they are being 'shown off', rather than seen". *Letters*, p. 477

55. Cf. 'what could be more unpromising than to interpret moods that terminate in such acts as the crushing of a cockroach or the torturing of fly? Both chekhov and Katherine Mansfield have used such moments [in *Small Fry* and *The Fly*] to probe below the surface, with the idea of stirring the devils that lie waiting there.... Both stories reveal the spiritual aridity of these men whom we have seen in moments of casual cruelty. But they reveal something more deeply profound and universal: the lower depths filled with devilish impulses and desires, hatreds, frustrated affections that lie just beneath the surface of socialized consciousness. It is a terrible business: this stirring of these impulses from their quiescent state to a condition of active frenzy. Chekhov's *Enemies* shows you something of the monsters which lie just below the surface'.—Dorothy Brewster and Angus Burrel. *Modern Fiction*, pp. 362-64.
Comments—Perhaps Chekhov and Miss Mansfield use 'such moments of casual cruelty' or of 'active fenzy' not 'with the idea of stirring the devils that lie waiting below the surface' but with the idea of registering their protagonists' tragic realization: the protagonists have realized the unalterability of the plight

or the piteousness of the predicament that they find themselves implacably condemned to: what we really find the two authors 'stirring' is an emotional complex compounded of an intensifying feeling of self-pity and an overwhelming sense of impotence and helplessness. The difference lies only in the nature of the protagonists' individual realization of the tragic truth: the nature of the 'realization' that Chekhov registers in *Small Fry* is meant to remain restricted to the naturally psychological implications which the drama of emotional development 'from a quiescent state to a condition of active frenzy' involves: the nature of the boss's realization in Miss Mansfield's short-story, *The Fly*, seems to have transcended the limits of psychological realism which usually remains restricted to the psychological implications of the human element dramatized and analysed: the boss's realization is the realization of a transcendental truth about all consciousness, human or non-human, as only a fly's consciousness: the realization is dramatized as his dazed recognition of the interminability of a circumrotatory process: this process equates a 'boss' with a fly, establishing their ultimate synonymity as eternally anonymous beings rolled into one in the womb of Time. Nevyrazimov's realization is realistically psychological; the boss's is intensely philosophical. Nevyrazimov, the petty clerk, first identifies the cockroach with himself and pities it; later he identifies it with his boss and destroys it. The boss in *The Fly* identifies the fly with himself and pities it and tortures it to death, but he does it all with a cynical attitude of self-dramatization, and attitude born of his unconscious recognition of his affinity also with Time itself. Nevyrazimov contemplates several methods of escape-flight and rejects them all; then he also thinks of winning promotion by drafting a secret report libeling his office colleagues; in the boss's case, what we find disclosed is not a 'process a elimination' but a process of gradual interiorization and attrition of his psyche: this process culminates in a blank mental state of dazed amnesia, by extended implication, in vacant unawareness of the gradual consumption of his consciousness by Time. The moment of climax in Nevyrazimov's realization of his predicament comes when, driven to complete impasse by an overwhelming sense of impotence, he thinks of the addressee of the letter and feels his anguish reach a breaking point. The process of gradual interiorization of the boss's psyche concentrically gravitates towards what is only an iota of consciousness, a mental state much too blank for recollection or even awareness of the intensification of his fatalistic realization: his consciousness at the climatic moment of his experience is a fly's consciousness.

Again, even in *Enemies*, it is not the 'devilish impulses' that Chekhov stirs from their quiescent state; it is perhaps simply the essentially human feelings which he reveals; what he discovers 'below the surface; is not a monster but a man for whom it is as much natural to forget all suffering and experience bitterness as it is to discard all human considerations in the dark hours of suffering. The boss that seems to be torturing the fly to death is neither a monster nor a man: he is a being who is psychically dead, with all his consciousness already consumed by Time: his total self finally starts operating as the force of Time itself. Kirilov's 'active frenzy' is characterized by fragility of an evanescent emotional complex; the boss's is divorced from even his impersonal consciousness of it. If, however Kirilov is a monster, it is simply because he resolves to remain a monster even in the remote future when much time will have passed and his sorrow also will have been relieved but this intensified emotion is evanescent and thus characteristically human. If the boss is a monster he does not even know that he is a monster; but his intensified emotion is all dazed, blank, vacant consciousness that defines the ultimate truth about all consciousness, human or non-human. Kirilov is a man: the boss is a symbol.

56. Paulette Michel-Michot, "Katherine Mansfield's '*The Fly*': An Attempt to capture the Boss", Studies in Short Fiction, XI 1 Winter 1974 [Typed copy].
57. Cf. "The third and final drop marks out the difference between them [the boss and the fly]. The fly dies—dies from too much grief. So the Boss who in the beginning seemed to be a fly, is not a fly after all".-Robert Wooster Stallman, "Katherine Mansfield's 'Fly'" Explicator III Item. 49
    "In The Fly the central symbolism is confused. Obviously the boss stands for a superior controlling power—God, destiny: or fate—which in capricious and impersonal cruelty tortures the little creature. At the same time the boss is presented as one who has himself received the blows of the superior power through the death of his only son ... Thus the functional role which the boss plays in the story does not fuse with the symbolic role. "Sylvie Berkman, *op. cit.*, p. 195.
58. Cf. "His [the boss's] final amnesia is desperately self-protective, and it brings his experience to a sympathetically drawn and poignant close".-John V. Hagopian, "Capturing Katherine Mansfield's 'Fly'": Modern Fiction Studies, IX, p. 388.
59. Quoted by Saralyn Daly, *op. cit.*, p. 112.
60. *Journal*, p. 94.
61. The four short-stories exemplifying 'achieved content' evidence the "feeling of inevitability that there is in a great work of art", pointing to a life beyond the life we know: "I don't believe in the limitations of man; I believe in the heights'. I can't help it; I'm forced to. It seems to me that very feeling of inevitability that there is in a great work of art-is a proof—a profession of faith on the part of the artist that this life is not all."—*Letters*, p. 459.
62. 'You must feel before you can think; you must think before you can express yourself. It is not enough to feel and write; or to think and write. True expression is the outcome of them both, yet a third thing and separate'.—*Novels and Novelists*, pp. 196-97.
63. J.M. Murry, *op. cit.*, pp. 84-85.

6. Conclusion

While reviewing the development of technique in the short-stories of Miss Mansfield, we discover two phases which seem to be subtly varying: in the earlier phase, 'the gift that had produced '*Tiredness of Rosabel*'[1] was spectacularly recovered in the composition of *Prelude*; in the later, this 'gift' was intensively developed: potentialities peculiar to the genre, which had already been recognized in *Prelude*, were painstakingly exploited in the subsequent narrative pieces: Miss Mansfield delved into their exploitation indirectly through experimentation with semi-dramatic forms and directly through continuous creative endeavour to achieve the quality of 'dramatic effect'; the potentialities were all solemnly realized in the last few masterpieces of 'achieved content'. (*Garden Party*, *At the Bay*, *Doll's House*, *The Fly*).

The 'gift' was the genius singularly characteristic of a short-story writer: the genius, we know, produces a narrative piece which invariably aims at an aesthetic rendering of life's crisis in intense imaginative concentration: the purpose, perhaps indisputably, is communication of a truth-vision that is truer than the one that life presents.

In *Prelude* this 'gift' was impressively recovered in the sense that the quality of 'dramatic effect' was achieved as an exquisitely refined narrative quality: the 'crisis' passing as a subtle transitional phase of 'possibilities'[2] was viewed in appropriately protracted dreamy concentration: there was an exquisite adaptation of the narrative style to the poetically beautiful incomplete meaning intrinsic in the nascency of a new life in the new house; a 'story' was 'told with a sense of mystery, a radiance, an afterglow'.[3] The nature of the rendering was now expressively aesthetic. Materials selected were telling enough to communicate the author's calm vision of the "mystery, richness and goodness" of Life as a poetic truth. This obviated the omniscient author's recourse to 'summation', which had marred the artistic beauty of the first precocious achievement produced by the 'gift' (*Tiredness of Rosabel*).

The creative process involved in the composition of *Prelude* drew upon potentialities already exploited; perhaps by this time the process had matured in course of the author's unconsciously growing realization of her failures as a short-story writer.[4] The potentialities utilized in the earlier short-stories were all coherently developed in *Prelude*.

Miss Mansfield had been resorting to externalization of a character's emotional experience since her first precocious achievement (*Tiredness of Rosabel*). This recourse to externalization betokened her intuitive recognition of the potentiality of the creatively concentrated vision that singleness of crisis naturally demands: the device of externalization of emotional experience was now employed as a means of revealing the complexity of the central character (Linda in *Prelude*); it was now potent enough to help to define what the complexity of the character was subordinated to, that is, it could now reflect the wholeness of the microcosm evolving as the manifestation of a value—'coherence of ... attitudes'.[5] Externalization of character's emotional experience was now a kind of elaborate symbolization conspicuously and advantageously central to a design of characterizations appropriately concentric. Intensification of the emotional content had been effected, through use of devices both plagiarized and invented, in her re-composition of a poignant short-story by Chekhov as a new short-story with a new meaning (*Child who-was-Tired*). This attempt at intensification had been her first conscious exercise in achievement of the requisite quality of 'dramatic effect'. In *Prelude* intensification of the emotional element was achieved through registration of the tenseness in a low key; the tenseness was intrinsic in the very moment of the characters' individual choice from the realm of the possible or the future. The devices utilized in *The Child Who-Was-Tired* were now smoothly automatic and consummately effectual. The fundamental image was exalted as an 'objective correlative'.[6] Creation of the 'atmosphere' was effected through exquisite registration of moments in the nascency of a new life revealing 'possibilities of development and contrast'[7]; it was achieved through dreamy concentration on the evolution of the microcosm. 'Unity of time' was subordinated to poetic purpose—discovery of the lyrical beauty characterizing the incomplete meaning of the characters' individual choice from the realm of the future. 'Rhythmical patterns' now inconspicuously rendered the intermittent manifestations of the psychological situation central to the story element: the manifestations that implied dichotomized conjugality or 'arrest of development'.[8]

Her early exercise in composition of anecdotes by way of learning the art of compactness contributed to her spontaneous achievement now of narrative structure at once compact and loose enough to assist naturalization of the 'dramatic effect'. Even the severe intensity of a strongly emotional experience that strained a protagonist at the tense moment of a decisive crisis (*Birthday*) was now made to seem low, and thus it was considerably heightened: the most complex character in *Prelude* (Linda) was made to make her choice from the realm not of the future but of the timeless presentness of 'the secret life of things'. A state of pathetic uncertainty (*Swing of Pendulum*) was now an equivocal situation defined simultaneously by the arrest of the characters' development and by the 'possibilities of development'. A narrative style exquisitely adapted to the significantly gradual revelation of the essence of the character having in freedom the feel of the real existence of her individual self (*How Pearl Button was Kidnapped*) was elaborately refined: the refinement was now elaborate enough to be appropriate to the poetic characterization of a complex character arrested by her conflicting impulses and poised at the same time for escape into the secret world of things. 'Combination of interior monologue and impersonal narration'[9] which had assisted evocation of the full image of the character as a mother (*Millie*) was also welded on an elaborate scale; for there was an attempt now at the recreation of a whole microcosm manifest as a vague complex of psychically interiorized individuals, all seen only as beings of the moment just at the moment of being. Registration of the shades and nuances of situations and in-between emotions which had necessitated expansion of the narrative scale (*Something Childish but very Natural*, *Indiscreet Journey*, *Little Governess*) was now exquisitely sensitive: the freedom given to the subject and the multi-dimensionality created by the multi-personal point of view were now controlled by an 'attitude of personal detachment'[10] manifest as a tranced dreamy vision: in spite of the consequential expansion of the narrative scale there was continuous concentration only on shadowy subtleties: the beauty discovered was lyrical: the poetically incomplete meaning of 'possibilities'.

Miss Mansfield's failures in course of her endeavour to achieve mastery of the technical essence of the specific genre, were all ameliorated during her composition of this first song of innocence (*Prelude*). Broadly, the failures that precluded her recognition of the real form were due to several negative factors. The most obvious factor was the vagueness of her conception, or her misconception of the nature of the subject or the theme peculiar to the short-story as a specific literary genre. Irresistibility of her temptation to view a situation from angles extrinsic to the point of view chosen, or fallibility of the very choice of the focus of narration, also invalidated her attempts at the requisite intensification of the preconceived effect. The one unquestioned factor was her lack of understanding of the prime need: an objective aesthetic rendering of the subject within the purview of the concentrated vision.

Her exercise in re-composition of a masterpiece by Chekhov (*Child who-was-Tired*) had posed a challenge to her 'gift'; so while turning out some of the subsequent short-stories Miss Mansfield had been inclined to search for the story element in the course of the very composition of the narrative pieces; some of the pieces were, therefore, only glimpses of the flux of life (*Germans at Meat, Frau Fischer, Indiscreet Journey*). *Prelude* captured the lyrical nature of the meaning implicit in life's flux as a poetically incomplete sense. The meaning discovered in the natural flux of life had sometimes been significant too, but the meaning had involved no sense of change or crisis and the narrative composition had leaned towards the genre of the reportage (*Indiscreet Journey*). In *Prelude* the meaning was deeply significant because it involved the requisite sense of a crisis (a family moves house and this reveals a poetic truth defined by the coherence of the members' individual attitudes to this transitional phase in their life). Before she composed *Prelude* Miss Mansfield had not realized that an ending suggesting an unresolved conflict would be more in keeping with the peculiar nature of the genre which characteristically dramatizes only situations too brief to yield a complete meaning (*At Lehmann Frau Brechenmacher Attends a Wedding*). This element of unresolved conflict as the essential ingredient of the story in a short-story had often been comprehended, too, in many of the narrative pieces that had preceded *Prelude* (*Birthday, Swing of Pendulum, Blaze, Ole Underwood*). But it was only in *Prelude* that this element was utilized strictly in accordance with the true nature of the short-story: the unresolved conflict of individual attitude revealed only 'possibilities of development and contrast', (of course as lyrical manifestations of a value in life, the value of 'coherence', of "mystery, richness and goodness"). The conception of the meaning meant to emerge from the verbal build-up had on occasions been manifestly confused (*Blaze, Ole Underwood*); the meaning in *Prelude* was not confused in spite of a multitude of complex and nebulous characters; the meaning was now consistent and coherent even as an incomplete meaning. The potentiality of the point of view as an effectual means of preserving the nature of the emotional content had not been thoroughly comprehended before *Prelude* was composed. Even when a situation was telling enough, Miss Mansfield unnecessarily included the first-person narrator as an additional character within the framework of her narrative composition (*Frua Fischer, Bains Turcs*): she came to see the validity of objective dramatization only during her composition of *Prelude*. She had not been able to see that the shift of viewpoint within the narrative framework initially specified by the choice of the protagonist's single viewpoint only adversely affected the intensity of the intended effect (*Birthday, Swing of Pendulum*). The creative process involved in the composition of *Prelude* evolved through 'vision of Love and Innocence'[11] which implied in 'attitude of personal detachment'. This 'abeyance of self' delivered her from temptations and awakened her sensibility to the need for preservation of the adequate degree of intensity. The potentiality of the multi-personal point of view, which had been wasted because of its unnecessary use as a means of obscuring a pathetic character (*New Dresses*), was imaginatively exploited in *Prelude*: here it helped to achieve a greater objective: registration of the evolution of a whole microcosm as a complex of half-defined beings of the moment. Failure to recollect a recent emotional experience in tranquillity had occasioned only a lapse into melodrama (*Wind Blows*); 'discipline of remembrance'[12] and the control of 'the gift of empathy' by the 'attitude of personal detachment' now helped a personal private experience to take on a deep universal significance. The tendency to 'sympathetic summation',[13] which she had gradually learnt to stifle, was finally counterbalanced by her proclivity towards choice of objective dramatization of the ending: the omniscient author's 'summation', which had blemished the beauty of her first precocious achievement (*Tiredness of Rosabel*) was later the protagonist's generalization from her experience (*Frau Brechenmacher Attends a Wedding*) or compassionate judgement voiced by the central character sympathetically softened by her conclusive realization of the whole truth about a terror in her life (*Little Girl*). The author's recollection of the haunting father-image had grown 'aesthetic' by degrees.[14] It was only in *Prelude* that the conception of the father-image (*Mr. Stanley*) was consummated as realization of a 'character'. The narrative structure that had been loose (*Violet*)[15] was tightened through choice of telling episodes and their arrangement in significant order. Conscious contrivance, exemplified by creation of a character meant to function as a means of revelation (*Woman at Store*), was discarded: as a result of the freedom given to the subject by the attitude of 'personal detachment', there was now 'a remarkable absence of manipulation'.[16]

During this early phase of her literary career Miss Mansfield only kept striving for recognition of the real form of the short-story or for recovery of her 'gift'. This is evident from the intermittence and precociousness of her achievements: what corroborates this impression is unmistakably her tendency to 'revert to superficialities,[17] surprisingly even after an achievement which with its noticeable merit of 'depth of perception,[18] must have given her aesthetic satisfaction of having recovered the 'gift' (*Birthday*, *Swing of Pendulum*, *How Pearl Button was Kidnapped*, *Bains Turcs*, *Millie*).

During the later phase she composed masterpieces of greater 'depth' and keener 'perception'. Even her tentative experimentation with point of view was gainful. Her craving for thorough recognition of the form and for coherent development of its potentialities only intuitively utilized so far was intensified. What stirred up this craving was her consciousness of her recent recovery of the 'gift' or her constant awareness of the first momentous crisis in her life which had occurred as the dawning realization of a sacred 'debt of love'.[19] This explains why she felt constrained to embark on painstaking experimentation with point of view even when she had achieved fairly comprehensive understanding in *Prelude* of the most essential feature of the short-story as a modern genre: in *Prelude* she had already achieved refinement of style as 'special prose,[20] through intensification of the narrative quality as a dramatic quality for adequate registration of moments caught just on the wing. The craving intensified by the psychological crisis in her life, which had overwhelmed her with a sense of 'debt of love', naturally counteracted and offset the earlier tendency to 'revert to superficialities'.

Recovery in *Prelude* of the gift that had produced *Tiredness of Rosabel* was paralleled by realization in *Garden Party* and subsequent masterpieces, of the 'vision' that had materialized as a song of 'Love and Innocence'. But the process of this realization was distinctively characterized by intensification of an ambition at once spiritual and aesthetic: there was a creative aesthetic urge to recognize the real 'form' through achievement of 'purity of vision' or an inner spiritual urge to achieve 'purity of vision' through recognition of the real 'form'; the one urge was cognate with the other. The poetically picturesque beauty of the 'real living simple truthful full life,[21] as the Beauty of Truth was prismatically refracted through a beatific vision which was simultaneously aesthetic. The process had been assisted by the earlier achievement of the quality of 'dramatic effect'. But this antecedent state was still that of myopic vision of Truth: to Miss Mansfield Truth was still only a grim reality. The stage was not yet that of a whole vision of 'life's diversity, death included',[22] a vision characterized by a calm attitude of 'joyous acceptance of Life'.[23] Perception of the tragic beauty intrinsic in the grim reality was aesthetic no doubt, but it had yet to evolve through a whole vision of 'Life's diversity, death included'. The distressing obsession with the concept of Death as a grim metaphysical reality had yet to develop into a poetic philosophy of life—Life as a manifestation of Truth which with its intrinsical Beauty of Eternal Innocence is an absolute value. The phrase 'spiritual-aesthetic ambition' had yet to be a portmanteau word, so to say.

The short-stories subsequent to *Prelude* registered the gradual intensification of this focalized ambition: in course of her endeavour to 'recognize the form' the ambition had been only aesthetic;[24] after *Prelude*, which had been born of her 'vision of Love and Innocence', it was also spiritual.[25] The diligence with which she delved into exclusive exploitation of the potentialities of point of view as a means of achieving self-abeyance and refinement of the narrative style was conscientious enough to betoken this ambition.

What indirectly yet inordinately intensified the ambition was also occurrence of a momentous psychological crisis in her life: the crisis which gripped her while she was still engaged in experimentation with Point of View was the growing realization of the imminence of her death: it was momentous because it involved a crucial transition in her attitude to 'life': her obsession with the idea of her own death was intensified as half-bewildered consciousness of the very concept of death as a grim metaphysical reality. Intensification of the obsession awakened her to a tragic reality revealed as futility of intense actualization of being prior to extinction of life. This tragic reality was perceived as a profound lyrical truth.

Her aesthetic perception of the tragic reality was quite characteristic of a mellowing philosophy of life which had been evolving through transitions: from satirical visions of appearance masquerading as reality (IN A GERMAN PENSION sketches a clearly Chekov) to compassionate attitude to the vulnerability of human nature (*Woman at Store, Bains Turcs*): to a calm vision of High Morality manifest as savage motherhood (*Millie*); to an ecstatic awareness of the inviolability of the sacrosanct value that life remains even 'in Time of Breaking of Nations' (*Indiscreet Journey*); to a serene realization of 'the richness, mystery and goodness' of life (*Prelude*).

The author's obsession with this theme, the tragic reality manifest as futility of intense actualization of being, was, perhaps, the natural culmination of her intermittent realization of a truth about individual life. Hitherto the truth had been manifesting itself as intense 'will to live' or as an experience of freedom that is an experience of existence itself, or as any emotional complex that the moment of choice from the realm of the possible or the future involves; this truth was a subject which Miss Mansfield had been exploring aesthetically before she found the whole of it resolved into the concept of a complex formed by 'beings of moment' in relation to one another just at an intense moment of being (*Prelude*). She had already attained the 'vision' of 'Love and Innocence'; she had had an aesthetic realization of the lyrical beauty intrinsic in the moment of being; it was quite natural again for her aesthetic sensibility to perceive or discover beauty in the tragic futility of intense actualization of one's being just before one's real or spiritual death.

The aesthetic expression of the pessimistic philosophy of life naturally evinced a developed sense of exquisite adaptation of a tight 'form' to the rigid truth perceived: the technique, both studied and original, helped to discover, enrich and retain the intrinsic nature of the grim truth: the expression of the philosophy was impersonally emotional and reticently poetic. The nature of the story element naturally called for a fictional 'form' intimate enough to register the immediacy of the tension that exhausts the character at the moment of crisis and exquisite enough to express this pessimistic philosophy of life in a subdued lone.

Refinement of the narrative style had been achieved through experimentation with what assists the requisite preservation of 'the attitude of personal detachment'. It was perfectly exemplified by the dramatic quality in majority of the short-stories finished as masterpieces of 'dramatic effect': Miss Mansfield had undertaken the experimentation with the focus of narration with a view to making her words on the page roll like billiard balls.

This earlier achievement of the quality of 'dramatic effect' ensured preservation of intensity or instantaneity of effect even in straightforward narration of events. Unaccountability of the tragic circumstance in which one feels constrained to contend with the futility of intense actualization of one's being in the face of death was a recently discovered truth-vision which had left her uncomfortably dazed. It was her achievement of the quality of 'dramatic effect' that had helped her to maintain the reticent silence consequent upon her dazed recognition of the grim reality. Now her silence was tearless and solemn, spell-bound and rapturous, awed and reverent: this silence was constrained by her calm vision of the 'objective standard of values,[26] of 'life's diversity, death included' (*The Garden Party*), of the Epic 'stillness' of all flux of consciousness as Eternal Innocence (*At the Bay*). Intensification of the narrative quality as a dramatic quality could now help her to preserve this profound silence. The quality of telling 'dramatic effect' imparted to the narrative by the adjustment of unity of Time to the focus of narration had helped to heighten the intensity of the tragedy of stasis. In two of her last short-stories, *At the Bay* and *The Fly*, unity of time had to subserve a philosophical purpose—achievement of the 'effect' of stasis on a cosmic scale; the anthropopsychic concept of Time was now a mystical concept: "all" seemed to evolve through it as something "still" ("All was still" *At the Bay*), all human consciousness seemed to be eternally equated with non-human consciousness, with a fly's consciousness (*The Fly*). The rendering of the moment of crisis was 'dramatic' enough to transmit to the reader the tenseness of the moment in all its immediacy; the moment captured was that of intense actualization of the protagonist's being prior to extinction of her or his individual 'self' (*Bliss*, *The Stranger*, *Ideal Family*). Imaginative discipline capacitated the author to achieve perfection in is appropriately subtle characterization of the protagonist emotionally involved in the evolution of a transcendental reality (*The Garden Party*, *The Fly*). The multi-personal point of view had been employed with a view to preserving the inviolability of lyrical beauty manifest in fragility of an evanescent emotion of nascent love (*Feuille d' Album*). Exploitation of this specific focus of narration was gainful again. It facilitated objective depiction of the awe-inspiring beauty intrinsic in the epic '*stillness*' of the flux of all life "*At the Bay*".

We can now see how all that she had achieved in her first real modern short-story as a lyric 'in special prose' was developed in the short-stories she composed during her last phase. An exquisitely refined narrative quality already recognized in *Prelude* as one of the intrinsic potentialities of the specific technique—which has to be dramatic and narrative at the same time—was now exploited all the more imaginatively. The dreamy tranced vision that had defined the nature of the omniscient author's point of view in *Prelude* was now a serenely comprehensive view of life, assuming angles adequately appropriate to the oblique manifestations of the truth-vision: the delicate refinement of the narrative quality sustaining the impression of a dreamy tranced vision had been achieved in *Prelude* as a result of the dawning 'vision of Love and Innocence'. The vision of Love had already necessitated control of 'the gift of empathy' by the 'attitude of personal detachment'. Now, when she came to compose her last few short-stories, that dawning 'vision of Love and Innocence' naturally ripened into an enlightened attitude: it was now an attitude of 'joyous acceptance of Life', life as a manifestation of Truth instinct with serene poetic Beauty: there was acceptance of 'Life's diversity, death included' (*The Garden Party*), of all flux of Life in Time as an illusion of a flux (*At the Bay*), of Truth as a light that shines as the inviolably sacred beauty of Innocence (*The Doll's House*), of all human and non-human consciousness as eternal Innocence in the womb of Time (*The Fly*).

Thus, the omniscient author's tranced vision of lyrical beauty intrinsic in the poetically incomplete meaning of 'possibilities of development and contrast' (*Prelude*) naturally became an "artistic" character's synthetic vision—a vision intrinsically characteristic of an 'entranced sensibility'[27] (*The Garden Party*). The crisis sensed in the nascency of the new life seemed to consist in the dawning of 'possibilities'; it had revealed itself as the lyrical beauty of life's flux; the crisis rendered in *At the Bay* was the manifestation of the interminability of a temporal pattern evolving to reveal only the eternally static nature of the evolution of all experience, all consciousness, all life. Characterizations of the children in *Prelude* had presented them as curious adventurers living intensely, endowed with 'a vitality unqualified by the bias of a priori';[28] the children in *At the Bay*, a short-story about the interminability of the temporal pattern involving the evolution of all life as only an illusion of evolution, were conceived as angels of the Eternal Now; in *The Doll's House* the image of inviolably sacrosanct innocence was pictured on the exalted level of mystical symbolization as a timelessly nascent light that shines beyond all barriers, in absolute isolation of a world of its own. The time scheme in *Prelude* had been used to provide only a brief glimpse of the nascency of a new life in the new house. This time scheme too was now made to operate symbolically: now it was instrumental in revealing the nature and function of Time itself (*At the Bay*, *The Fly*).

It is this calm vision of Life as a manifestation of Truth hallowed by a serene Beauty that distinguishes Miss Mansfield's poetic philosophy from the aesthetic thesis that 'the more subjective women writers'[29] seem to propound. The 'women writers are: V. Woolf, Elizabeth Bowen, Katherine Anne Porter, and Eudora Welty. Of course these 'cultivators of sensibility' have 'moved in kindred lines of development';[30] after the death of Miss Mansfield they all have explored 'the short-story medium with similar needs for expression'. But they only seem to have affinity with Miss Mansfield.

These 'cultivators of sensibility' avoid the extremes of romantic optimism and nihilistic pessimism: they present their quiet negativism of their recognition of the wasteland that is modern life with a subtlety that stops just short of inconclusiveness. Miss Mansfield is distinguished not only by her singular beatific 'vision of Love and Innocence' but also by her achievement of a complex technique of simple story-telling potent enough to make us reflect on life as the manifestation of Truth that is Beauty.[31] The art does not show through the design, and through this design pulsates the very 'real living simple truthful full life' with all its poetic dimensions. It is this achievement which ranks this artist among the great story-tellers of all times.

NOTES AND REFERENCES

1. Antony Alpers, *Katherine Mansfield*, p. 108.
2. "... a nest of relationships which were rich and ancient but also thronging with possibilities of development and contrast". William Walsh, *A Manifold Voice*, p. 160.
3. *Journal*, p. 94.
4. Miss Mansfield's honest and frank confessions in her Letters and Journals evidence her acute consciousness of her 'failure' in course of recognition of the 'form: e.g. "I read what I wrote and I feel: No, this is all once removed: it won't do ... I've got to reconstruct everything". *Letters*, p. 114 (1918: February 14). "Finished An Ideal Family yesterday. It seems to me better than *The Doves*, but

still it's not good enough ... I didn't get the deepest truth out of the idea ... this kind of knowledge is too easy for me ... this looks and smells like a story, but ...I don't want to possess it ..." *Journal*, p. 257 (1921: July 23).

5. William Walsh, *op. cit.*, p. 160
6. Eileen Daldeshwiler, The Lyric Short-story: The sketch of a History", *Studies of Short Fiction*, Vol. 6, No. 4, Summer 1969, p. 448 (Typed copy).
7. William Walsh, *op. cit.*, p. 160.
8. *Ibid.*, p. 158.
9. Sylvia Berkman, *Katherine Mansfield: A Critical Study*, p. 49.
10. William Walsh, *op. cit.*, p. 162.
11. J.M. Murry, *Katherine Mansfield and other Literary Portraits*, p. 84, p. 85.
12. William Walsh, *op. cit.*, p. 156.
13. Saralyn Daly, *Katherine Mansfield*, p. 24.
14. Celeste Turner Wright has traced the evolution of the image in Miss Mansfield's short-stories ("Katherine Mansfield's Father Image". The Image of The Work, ed. B.H. Laehman et al.) but his study is nakedly biographical and not critically literary.
15. Cf. "Perhaps the story could not have been cut by one half page but it could have been split in two"—Saralyn Daly, *op. cit.*, p. 49.
16. William Walsh, *op. cit.*, p. 160.
17. Saralyn Daly, *op. cit.*, p. 31.
18. *Ibid.*, p. 37.
19. *Journal*, p. 94.
20. *Ibid.*
21. Quoted by Saralyn Daly, *op. cit.*, p. 112.
22. "The diversity of life and how we try to fit in everything, Death included". *Letters*, p. 454.
23. J.M. Murry, *op. cit.*, p. 88.
24. A typical statement, "I don't 'just ramble on'. I'm a powerful stickler for form. I feel as fastidious as though I write with acid". *Letters*, p. 4 (1913: Summer).
25. For example, one of the statements characteristic of the later phase of Miss Mansfield's literary career. "The older I grow, the more exquisite I want to be, fine down to my miuutest particulars ... to carry it all through". *Letters*, p. 225 (1919: October 15).
26. Saralyn Daly, *op. cit.*, p. 113.
27. Don M. Kleine, The Garden Party: A Portrait of the Artist: Criticism, V, p. 362.
28. William Walsh, *op. cit.*, p. 161.
29. Saralyn Daly, *op. cit.*, p. 118.
30. *Ibid.*
31. Miss Mansfield's advice to a young contemporary novelist was distinctively characteristic: "Go on writing like that. I mean with that freshness and warmth and suppleness, with that warm emotional tone and not that dreadful glaze of intellectuality which is like a curse upon so many English Writers". *Letters* I, p. 479.

Index of the Short Stories Discussed

[Exclusive of the short-stories only casually mentioned]

Explanation: [v, ii] (226-251) = [Chapter v, Section ii] (pp. 226-251)

Chronology of the Short-Stories Selected

(C = Date of Composition, P = Date of Publication)

Tiredness of Rosabel, The	:	August 24, 1908 (C)
Child-who-was-Tired, The	:	February 24, 1910 (P)
Germans at Meat	:	March 3, 1910 (P)
Baron, The	:	March 10, 1910 (P)
Luft Bad	:	March 24, 1910 (P)
At Lehmann's	:	July 7, 1910 (P)
Frau Brechenmacher Attends a Wedding	:	July 21, 1910 (P)
Sister of the Baroness, The	:	August 4, 1910 (P)
Frau Fischer	:	August 18, 1910 (P)
Birthday, A	:	May 18, 1911 (P)
Modern Soul, The	:	June 22, 1911 (P)
Journey to Bruges, The	:	August 24, 1911 (P)
Truthful Adventure, A	:	September 7, 1911 (P)
Advanced Lady, The	:	(later included in IN A GERMAN PENSION)
Swing of Pendulum, The	:	" "
Blaze, A	:	" "
Woman at the Store, The	:	Spring, 1912 (P)
How Pearl Button was Kidnapped	:	September 1912 (P)
New Dresses	:	October 1912 (P)
Little Girl, The	:	October 1912 (P)
Sunday Lunch	:	October 1912 (P)
Ole Underwood	:	January 1913 (P)
Pension Seguin	:	May 1913 (P)
Violet	:	June 1913 (P)
Bains Turcs	:	July 1913 (P)
Millie	:	Summer 1913 (C)
Something Childish but very Natural	:	December 1913 (C)
Indiscreet Journay, An	:	February 14, 1914 (C)
Little Governess, The	:	March 18, 1915 (C)

Apple Tree, the	:	October 1915 (C)
Wind Blows, The	:	October 18, 1915 (P)
Prelude	:	May 1917 (C)
Two Tuppenny one, Please	:	May 3, 1917 (P)
Late at Night	:	May 10, 1917 (P)
Black Cap, The	:	May 17, 1917 (P)
Pictures	:	May 31, 1917 (C)
Mr. Reginald Peacock's Day	:	June 14, 1917 (P)
Feuille d'Album	:	September 20, 1917 (P)
Dill Pickle, A	:	October 4, 1917 (P)
Je ne Parle pas Francais	:	February 13, 1918 (C)
Sun and Moon	:	February 1918 (C)
Bliss	:	February 18, 1918 (C)
Man without a Temperament, The	:	January 10-11, 1920 (C)
Miss Brill	:	October 26, 1920 (C)
Stranger, The	:	November 3, 1920 (C)
Daughters of the Late Colonel, The	:	November 27, 1920 (C)
Lady's Maid, The	:	December 6, 1920 (C)
Life of Ma Parker, The	:	January-February 26, 1921 (P)
Ideal Family, An	:	July 22, 1921 (C)
Marriage a la Mode	:	December 31, 1921 (P)
Garden Party, The	:	October 13-14, 1921 (C)
At the Bay	:	October 1921 (C)
Doll's House, The	:	October 30, 1921 (C)
Fly, The	:	February 20, 1922 (C)

Bibliography

Note: (Dates and publishers are those of editions to which I have had access).

A. Works of Katherine Mansfield:
  I. Fiction
    Collected stories of Kateherine Mansfield/Constable. London 1968.
  II. Other Writings
    Journal of Katherine Mansfield
    The Letters of Katherine Mansfield. Ed. John Middleton Murry/Alfred A. Knopf. New York 1932.
    Novels and Novelists. Ed. John Middleton Murry/Beacon Press, Boston, 1959.

B. Works Related to Katherine Mansfield:
  I. Studies (Including explications of single short-stories).

Alpers, Antony: *Katherine Mansfield (A Biography)*/Jonathan Cape Ltd. London. 1954.

Anonymous "Katherine Mansfield's Stories" *Times Literary Supplement*, 2 March 1946.

Armstrong, Martin: "The Art of Katherine Mansfield" *Fortsightly Review*. CXIII, pp. 484-490.

Arnold and N. Diakonava: Analytical Reading:

Assad, Thomas J. "Mansfield's 'Fly": Explicator XIV. 1955 Item. 10.

Baldeshwilder, Eileen: "Katherine Mansfield's Theory of Fiction "Studies in Short Fiction" pp. 421-432.

________: "The Lyric Short-story: The sketch of a History" Studies in Short Fiction: Vol. 6, No. 4 Summer 1969, pp. (Typed Copy).

Bates, H.E. The Modern Short-story.

Bateson, F.W. and B. Shahevitch: "Katherine Mansfield's 'Fly': A Critical Exercise": *Essays in Criticism*, Vol. XII, No. 1, January 1962./plus the critics engaged in the controversy that the collaborators' 'Exercise' occasioned in the subsequent numbers of the journal (Vol. XII Nos. 3 & 4)/

Beachcroft: The Modest Art.

Bell, Pauline "Mansfield's 'Fly'" Explicator XIX (1920) Item 20

Berkman, Sylvia: Katherine Mansfield: A Critical Study/New Haven: Yale University Press: 1951/

Boyle, Ted E. "The Death of the Boss: Another Look at Katherine Mansfield's 'Fly'": Modern Fiction Studies 1965. pp. 183-184.

Brewster, Dorothy and Angus Burrel: Modern Fiction. pp. 360-377.

Cowley, Malcom: "Page Dr. Blum" Dial September 1921. pp. 365-367.

Cox, Sydney: "The Fastidiousness of Katherine Mansfield": Sewance Review XXXIX (1931): pp. 158-169.
Daly, Saralyn: Katherine Mansfield:/Twayne Publishers, Inc. New York (1965).
Davis, R.M. "Unity of Garden Party"/Studies in Short Fiction II pp. 61-65.
De Beauvoir, Simone: The Second Sex/A Four Square Book: Lands borough Publications London (1960).
Eliiot, T.S. After Strange Gods:
Gargano, James W. "Mansfield's 'Miss Brill;" Explicator XIX (1960) Item 10.
Greenfield, Stanley B. "Mansfield's 'Fly'": Explicator XVII (1958) Item 2
Hagopian, John V. "Capturing Katherine Mansfield's 'Fly'": Modern Fiction Studies IX pp. 385-390.
Hormasji, Katherine Mansfield:
Hubbell, George Sheton "Katherine Mansfield and Kezia". Sewanee Review: XXXV No.3 (1927): pp. 325-335. (Typed Copy).
Hynes, Sam. "Katherine Mansfield: The Defeat of the Personal": South Atlantic Quarterly, L II (1953) pp. 555-560.
Jacobs, Willis D. "Mansfield's 'Fly': Explicator V (1947) Item 32.
Kleine, Don W.: "'The Garden Party': A Portrait of the Artist": Criticism V.
________: "Katerine Mansfield and the Prisoner of Love Critique Winterspring 1960 pp. 20-33 (Typed Copy).
Michelle-Michot, Paulette: "Katherine Mansfield's 'The Fly': An Attempt to Capture the Boss": Studies in Short Fiction XI 1. Winter 1974.
Murry, John Middleton Murry: Katherine Mansfield and other Literary Portraits London. Constable (1959). Chapter 2.
Nelson, Arthur: "Katherine Mansfield: Artist in Miniature" Yale Literary Magazine CVI.
O' Connor, Lonely Voice pp. 133-134.
Oleson, Clinton W. "The Fly Rescued" College English XXII No.8 (May 1961) pp. 585-586.
Orvis, Mary: The Art of Writing Fiction/Prentice Hall: NY
Pannwitt: Harbara: The Art of Short-Fiction
Pritchetl, V.S. The New Statesman and Nation: 2 February 1946.
Rea, J. "Mansfield's 'The Fly'": Explicator XXIII (1965) Item 68.
Robinson, Fred C. "Mansfield's 'Garden Party'": Explicator XXIV (1966) Item 66.
Ryan, Alvans "The Doll's House": Insight II/Frankfurt: Hirschgraben 1964/ pp. 247-250.
Schneider, Elizabeth: "Katherine Mansfield and Chekhov" Modern Language Notes June 1935. pp. 394-497.
Shanks, Edward: "Katherine Mansfield" London Mercury XVII 19278 (January). pp. 296-293.
Stallman, R.W. "Katherine Mansfield's 'Fly'" Explicator III 1945 Item. 49.
Steinmann, Martin and Gerald Willen: Literature for Writing.
Sutherland, Ronald: "Katherine Mansfield: Plagiarist, Disciple, or Ardent Admirer?" Critique Vol.V No.1 Spring-Summer 1962. pp. 58- 76.
Taylor, D.S. "A Dream—A Wakening": Modern Fiction Studies IV No.4 (1958-59) pp. 361-362.

Thomas, J.D. "Anatomy of a 'Fly'" College English XXII No.8 (May 1961) p. 586.
________: "Symbol and Parallelism in 'Fly'": College English XXII NO.4 January 1961 pp. 256-258.
Thorpe, Peter "Teaching 'Miss Brill'": College English: 1961-62.
Van, Kranendonk, A.G. "Katherine Mansfield" English Story VII April 1930. pp. 49-57.
Vagenknecht, Edward: "Katherine Mansfield": English Journal XVII (1928) pp. 272-284.
Walker, Warren S. "The Unresolved Conflict in 'Garden Party'" Modern Fiction Studies: Winter 1957-58 Vol. III No.4 pp. 354-358.
Walsh, William: A Manifold Voice.
Weiss, Daniel A. "The Garden Party of Prosperins". Modern Fiction Studies IV No.4 (1958-59) pp. 363-364.
Welty, Eudor: "The Reading and Writing of Short-stories" Atlantic CLXXXIII February 1949 pp. 54-58.
West and Stallman: Art of Modern Fiction.
Whitridge, Arnold: "Katherine Mansfield": p. 256.
Wright, Celeste Turner: "Darkness as a Symbol in Katherine Mansfield" Modern Philosophy LI (1954) pp. 204-207.
________: "Katherine Mansfield and the Secret Smile": Literature and Psychology V (1955) pp. 44-48.
________: "Mansfield's 'Bliss'": Explicator VII (1949) Item 48.
________: "Katherine Mansfield's Image": Literature and Psychology X (1960) pp. 80-81.
________: "Katherine Mansfield's Father Image": The Image of the Work, ed. B.H. Lehman et al./University of California Publications: English STudies, II (Berkeley and Los Angeles; University of California Press, 1955). pp. 137-155.
________: "The Genesis of a short-story" Philol. Quarterly. XXXIV pp. 91-96.
Yen, Yuan-shun "Katherine Mansfield's use of Point of View" Dissertation Abstract:/ University of Wisconsin 1967/pp. 647-648.

Index